JELLICOE

John Winton

JELLICOE

LONDON
MICHAEL JOSEPH

First published in Great Britain by Michael Joseph Ltd
44 Bedford Square, London WC1
1981

ISBN 0 7181 1813 8

Typeset by Rowland Phototypesetting Limited
Bury St Edmunds, Suffolk
Printed by Hollen Street Press, Slough
and bound by Hunter and Foulis, Edinburgh.

List of Illustrations

Between pages 160 and 161

List of Maps

Chapter 1

To his family, and to his colleagues in the wardroom, he was always Jack. To the lower deck he was, as one biographer claimed, Hell Fire Jack, Jacky-Oh, Dreadnought Jack or even, (perhaps apocryphally) All-Jelly or Jellymould. To his partners and opponents on Home Counties tennis courts, he was 'Rushabout' Jellicoe. To his Grand Fleet captains he was, as William Fisher commanding *St Vincent* wrote, 'our beloved Commander-in-Chief, the finest character that ever was'. To Lord Fisher he was also 'my beloved Jellicoe'. Even King George V wrote to him as 'my dear J'. 'You are our Idol', ran the telegram from the Tenth Submarine Flotilla, after he had been dismissed as First Sea Lord, 'and one who we would follow to the Death.' But Haig, on the other hand, thought he was 'an old woman'. Lloyd George at one time classed him as one of the 'numbskulls' on the Board of Admiralty.

He liked sardines and detective stories, skating and family tennis parties. He disliked onions, after-dinner speaking, the date of 21 June, and obstreperous young officers who thought they knew better. Although he was only a small man he had an imposing presence, so that everybody noticed when he came into a room. People meeting him for the first time were always surprised by his small stature and his humility, contrasted against his towering professional reputation. He was one of the most intelligent officers ever to join the Royal Navy, but he found it difficult to delegate work and responsibility. He was passionately loyal and devoted to the Service and to his friends, to a point where his loyalty and devotion to some of his friends was sometimes not in the best interests of the Service.

He was a Service celebrity from quite early in his career. The C-in-C, Admiral Tryon, and over three hundred other officers and men perished when the *Victoria* went down in 1893, but Commander Jellicoe was the only survivor mentioned by name in the penny ballads about the tragedy sold in the streets afterwards. After the Boxer Rising other officers were writing to their mothers, 'Of course I know Jellicoe.' During the First World War his name entered the choruses of music-hall songs. His puckish features, large nose, firm chin and the wrinkles at the sides of his eyes appeared on countless postcards and cigarette cards. His unmistakable face was recognizable on children's dolls, Toby jugs and commemorative medallions. Young girls had his portrait in their lockets, back to back with their sweethearts.

John Jellicoe was a true representative of the old Navy, the Victorian Navy of sail and ironclads, yet he was also the Victorian Navy's link with the twentieth century. To him fell the task of leading the Navy's greatest fleet into action after a century's theoretical speculation. He was loved, admired and respected as perhaps no admiral had been since Nelson, but people criticized him in a way they have never done to any other admiral before or since. He was criticized for being too cautious, for not annihilating the enemy's fleet, for not being Nelson. He did his utmost, to the best of his ability, but he had to bear the brunt of a nation's disappointment at a time when the newspapers were powerful enough and prejudiced enough to make that disappointment most clearly heard.

Towards the end of his life, when Jellicoe set down some reminiscences of his family and his boyhood, he said, 'From my earliest days I never thought of any other career than that of the sea.' As he said, this was not surprising because he came from seafaring families on both sides. His father, John Henry Jellicoe, master mariner in the Merchant Service, went to sea at the age of twelve and commanded his own ship at twenty-one. He joined the Royal Mail Steam Packet Company and eventually rose to be a marine superintendent and commodore. His wife, Lucy Henrietta, *née* Keele, had naval connections for several generations. Jellicoe's great-great-grandfather, Philip Patton, was a captain in the Navy and fought at the battle of La Hogue, where his life was saved by a silver tobacco box in his breast pocket which stopped a musket ball. His son, also Philip, fought in nine general actions under Boscawen, Hawke, Pocock, Rodney, Digby and Hyde Parker, became an admiral, and was Second Sea Lord at the time of Trafalgar. Three of Lucy Keele's uncles were naval officers: Henry Keele was a surgeon RN, Charles fought in the Burma War of 1824 and rose to be an admiral, while the youngest, Edward, was killed as a midshipman on board HMS *Java* in the action against USS *Constitution* on 29 December 1812.

John Rushworth Jellicoe was born, the second son, on 5 December 1859 at 1 Cranbury Place, Southampton, a narrow, three-storeyed, rather unimpressive and modest-looking little house which his father had rented. He was to have an extra Christian name, Henry, after his father, but this was dropped when his name was registered. Rushworth had been a family name since his mother's ancestor, Captain John Rushworth RN, who had died in 1780.

The family went to some financial sacrifice to give Jellicoe the basic education for the Navy – in fact at one time his father believed they could not afford it. But his mother was determined, and at six and a half Jellicoe went to a dame school in Southampton run by the two Misses Shapcott, who taught him reading, writing and arithmetic. At eleven he moved to a preparatory school called Field House at Rottingdean, a few miles east of Brighton. Here he was taught classics and mathematics by the two joint owners and headmasters, the brothers Billy and Jimmy Hewitt.

At Field House one of those eerily prophetic happenings took place which sometimes occur in the early lives of those who are to become famous in any particular walk of life. Jellicoe had told the other boys he intended to join the Navy, so one of them composed some doggerel verses about him. The first line of the chorus was, 'I'm John Jellicoe, Commander of the Fleet.'

Certainly Jellicoe was much brighter than the average naval officer, although his mother engaged a village schoolmaster to give him extra coaching in mathematics. Traditionally the Navy has seldom attracted men of exceptional intellect and has had to rely on some member of a seafaring family such as the Jellicoes, who would have joined the Navy in any event, also happening to be intellectually outstanding – which young Jellicoe certainly was. After a time the village schoolmaster told Mrs Jellicoe, 'I don't think you quite realize what a clever son you have. He has just solved a problem in half an hour which took a friend of mine over a week to do. Your boy doesn't need any extra coaching.'

In 1872 Jellicoe was given a nomination for the Navy by Captain Robert Hall, a friend of his father's, who was then Naval Secretary to the Admiralty. Delighted by this, Jellicoe was inspired to write on the fly-leaf of one of his books, 'This book is the property of Admiral Sir John Jellicoe'! His uniform was made and delivered by a naval outfitters, but the cap was bought at a local shop in Ryde, in the Isle of Wight, where the family were living. To young Jack it was clearly not the proper Service pattern – not a 'pusser's cap' – and he refused to wear it. When his mother insisted, he took the cap up to his room and jumped on it until it was unwearable. Wearing a new cap from the naval outfitters, Jellicoe passed into *Britannia* in the summer of 1872. In his term of thirty-nine cadets he was second to a boy called Wingfield.

The *Britannia* young Jellicoe joined was the old training ship, the fifth ship of her name in the Navy, which had been laid down in 1860 as the 131-gun screw line of battleship *Prince of Wales*. Renamed, in 1869 she had replaced an older and smaller *Britannia* which in September 1863 had been brought round from Portland and moored in the River Dart above the town of Dartmouth. Close upstream of her lay the old two-decker accommodation ship *Hindustan*, which had been brought from Devonport in 1864. The two ships were connected stem to stern by a walkway.

All *Britannia*'s masts and rigging had been removed except the foremast, which was still rigged for the cadets to practise on, with a safety net stretched beneath it. The space of the upper deck was almost completely built over with classrooms, model rooms and special accommodation for the ship's officers. The guns had all been removed and the gun-decks were used as dormitories, messrooms, bathrooms and promenades. The long triple tier of empty gun-ports had glass panes framed with wooden sashes.

Two terms of cadets joined every year, and each term spent two years in *Britannia*. Every cadet kept all his belongings in a sea-chest and slept in a hammock, the two junior terms in *Hindustan*, the two senior in *Britannia*. All four terms ate on the four long tables in the large cadets' messroom which was also used as a general assembly space for morning prayers, inspections and evening preparation, and as a mess where the cadets spent their spare time reading, writing letters and ragging about.

It was a spartan regime of hard exercise and fierce discipline. The day began with a swim in a cold salt-water bath and proceeded on its laid down course, the passing hours marked with the ship's bell: prayers, inspection, classes, meals, boat-work, exercise. Food was plain but plentiful: slices of stale bread with a scraping of butter and weak tea for breakfast, beef and beer for dinner, cake and milk in the afternoon, cold meat for supper, roast chicken on Sundays once a month.

The work fell into three broad parts. There was 'study', consisting of mathematics and navigation; 'out of study', which was French and drawing (so arranged by Their Lordships, it was said, that naval officers could accurately sketch headlands and other conspicuous navigational marks as they sailed past them); and seamanship, which comprised sailing lore and signals. Although steam machinery had been in use in the Navy for half a century before Jellicoe joined, engineering was not in the *Britannia* syllabus, nor was any instruction in naval history.

After school the cadets changed into sports gear or flannels for football or cricket, walks and cross-country runs ashore. 'Out of bounds' orchards and game coverts were always strictly defined and there was generally a Royal Marine sergeant waiting to pop up unexpectedly from behind a hedge. A flotilla of four-oared gigs and pair-oared skiffs (known then, and still to this day at Dartmouth, as 'blue boats') was available, and launches and cutters for sailing. Occasionally there were longer sailing trips in the *Ariadne*, although these were discontinued in 1873, or in the *Dapper*, a 300-ton barque-rigged gun-boat dating from the Crimean War.

Discipline and the general ruling of the ship, apart from academic studies, was in the hands of a captain RN, assisted by a commander, three lieutenants, a master at arms, four ship's corporals and half a dozen cadet captains and chief cadet captains chosen from the senior term. The academic staff had no disciplinary powers but a report of slack or inattentive work by a cadet was punished, with no appeal. Punishments were severe. Cadets could be caned with their trousers on or birched with their trousers off. They could also be confined to cells, on a reduced diet of bread and water. Offenders in the third (or worst) class for conduct wore a white stripe on the arm and ate in the cockpit or in a special messroom. They also had extra drill, with bar-bells or heavy Brown Bess muskets. Other punishment regimes involved offenders being shaken earlier in the morning and being kept on their feet after the rest had turned in, often being made to stand at attention facing the main deck bulkhead for an hour at a time (a punishment for the lower deck which was not actually abolished from the fleet until 1912).

A strict hierarchy of seniority ruled in *Britannia*. 'Fagging' – making a junior run errands and perform extra tasks – and any harassing of juniors was officially forbidden, but the cadets had an illicit private system whereby any cadet could 'fag' cadets two terms junior to him. Thus fourth termers could fag first and second termers, while third termers could fag 'news' only. The seniors also exercised other privileges, such as wearing their caps tilted far enough back to show their hair. Cadets had a shilling a week pocket money, cadet captains two shillings, chief cadet captains half a crown. They could bring ten shillings back off leave, but were not allowed to bring food or fruit on board.

A cruel streak is always apparent in naval training, and there was bullying in *Britannia*. There had been several serious cases, which led to an outcry and an investigation under Captain Randolph, just before Jellicoe joined. The most powerful check on abuse at Dartmouth was the Great British Parent. Over the years the training of staff of the Navy, and especially those at Dartmouth, developed a very great respect for the GBP, who was quite capable of writing to *The Times* or of enlisting the local Member to get up and beard the First Lord in Parliament. The GBP was always ready to protest against bullying, unsuitable diet, what it considered excessively harsh discipline, defective hygiene on board, or indeed any point touching the cadets' welfare, even on one occasion going so far as to protest publicly at the choiceness of the epithets directed at their offspring. During Jellicoe's time on board Captain Foley was ordered to carry out an investigation into the salubriousness of *Britannia*'s bilges.

Britannia was an almost completely enclosed world of its own. The cadets led an introspective, insular existence, shut off to outsiders, which the Navy actually maintained at Dartmouth with very little change up to the outbreak of the Second World War. Very little ever

11

happened to disturb the routine. Admiral George Ballard, who joined *Britannia* in 1875, a year after Jellicoe left, recalled that:

> ... the life of a cadet in the *Britannia* was as much unlike the life of a naval officer afloat as the ship herself was unlike a seagoing man-of-war ... Nor was there anything in the harbour or neighbourhood to excite our interest in naval affairs. A boy at Burney's [a school at Gosport] had ships of the Navy before his eyes every day, but Dartmouth was only a minor commercial port, and a cadet in the *Britannia* never saw a seagoing man-of-war at all, except for the few occasions on which one of the small sailing brigs attached to the seamen's training ships at Plymouth or Portsmouth happened to anchor for a day or so near the harbour entrance. This was regarded as quite an interesting occurrence.

In this enclosed world of strict routine and strenuous physical effort Jellicoe spent two years. In his photograph he evidently composed his features into solemn repose, but he also exhibited his share of high spirits and mischief. He worked, played, did extra drill for scrumping apples, and climbed about in the rigging. All second termers had to touch the truck, the round piece of wood on the very top of the foremast, 120 feet above the deck. This could only be done by shinning up the last fifteen feet of bare pole. Jellicoe managed it, but was not such a daredevil as his term-mate Wingfield, who reached the truck and then slid down the rope from it to the flying jib-boom, 150 feet away.

John Jellicoe's only disadvantage was his height. He was four feet six when he joined and only four feet eight and a half when he left. When the First Lord, Mr Ward Hunt, visited *Britannia* and inspected the cadets he stopped in front of Jellicoe. Years later Jellicoe recalled with chagrin the great man's remark, 'What a puny lot of cadets you have here.'

Jellicoe wasted no time or energy in kicking against the system, but accepted the situation as it was. He made up for his lack of height with tremendous application at his studies. Captain Foley once met Mrs Jellicoe in Ryde, when he was having tea with a friend. After Mrs Jellicoe had left, Captain Foley remarked, echoing the village school-master, 'I wonder if Mrs Jellicoe realizes that her son John is one of the cleverest cadets we have ever had.' In the summer of 1874 Jellicoe passed out of *Britannia* top of his term. As his prize for coming first in study, Jellicoe was awarded a silver inkstand. Jellicoe was promoted midshipman on 17 July and went to the port admiral's flagship *Duke of Wellington* at Portsmouth and thence for appointment to his first seagoing ship.

Jellicoe had joined the Navy, always a conservative organization, at a time when in some ways it was at its most reactionary. The Admiralty Board of the day was weak, riddled with faction and intrigue, and vulnerable to personal eccentricities and idiosyncrasies. Naval officers were recruited almost entirely from a self-centred, self-defining, self-perpetuating section of society, as though they were all members of some semi-aristocratic yacht club, electing and re-electing each other, and their sons and nephews, over and over again. Promotion to the quarterdeck from the lower deck was always theoretically possible, but was virtually impossible in practice.

Ironically, and almost paradoxically, it was a time of enormous technological change for the Navy. New ships were built and commissioned, new machinery fitted, and new guns designed and fired. But all the tremendous advances in propulsion machinery, guns, mountings, and armour platings were introduced as though in an intellectual vacuum. Little thought was given to the Navy's strategic employment or its tactical development. It was assumed that the country needed a strong Navy. It was assumed that the country also had a strong Navy. In the long years of Victorian peace the Navy maintained ships in over a dozen stations abroad, but had not fought a fleet action since Trafalgar, nor a ship-to-ship engagement since Navarino in 1827. The Navy badly needed operational experience, but the only active service officers and men could get was ashore, on one of the numerous naval brigades of the nineteenth century (while Jellicoe was at *Britannia* a naval brigade was serving with distinction in the Ashanti War). There was no naval staff. Officers were not concerned with strategy or tactics until they became admirals, when it was assumed that knowledge of these subjects would suddenly appear, fully formed like Minerva from the brow of Jove, on achieving flag rank.

Jellicoe's first ship could not have been more aptly chosen to represent the Navy of the 1870s. She was HMS *Newcastle*, a 4000-ton full-rigged frigate with auxiliary steam power, launched in 1860. She had a complement of some five hundred officers and men, and was commanded by Captain Robert Gordon Douglas RN. *Newcastle* was part of the Flying Squadron, which was commissioned periodically to 'show the flag' at various ports but mainly to give young seamen more intense and continuous 'blue water' sea training than they would normally have had in the fleet. Besides *Newcastle*, the Squadron at that time consisted of four similar wooden frigates – *Narcissus* (flying the flag of Rear-Admiral Randolph), *Topaze*, *Doris* and *Immortalité* – and a modern composite wood-and-iron frigate, HMS *Raleigh*.

Jellicoe joined *Newcastle* on 22 September 1874 at Sheerness. She sailed on 18 October for Portsmouth, where Jellicoe's mother came over from Ryde with a gift of fruit and to say goodbye. From Portsmouth the Squadron went to Plymouth and then to Gibraltar, arriving there in ten days under sail on 6 November. Although *Newcastle* was fitted with a steam engine she generally proceeded everywhere under sail. The whole emphasis of life in the Squadron was on sail drill, which for both officers and men was the one sure path to promotion in the Navy. *Newcastle* had a total of 51 guns, from 68-pounder muzzle-loaders down to machine guns. The guns were normally fired at practice once a quarter, when the quarterly allocation of ammunition was used up. Ranges were not much more than a thousand yards. Gunlayers looked along the barrels of their guns and fired at what they saw, in a way which had not basically changed since Nelson's day.

The Flying Squadron cruise proved to be splendid experience for a young officer, giving him a chance to see the world and learn his trade. From Gibraltar the Squadron went to St Helena, Rio de Janeiro, the Falkland Islands, to Bombay where the Squadron were escort for the Prince of Wales (later King Edward VII) on his visit to India, and on to Japan. Although in later years Jellicoe's only memories of the places he visited were of the food — the sweets of Esmeralda's in Gibraltar, the custard cakes in Madeira — it was a hard and energetic life for him and the other midshipmen. They lived in conditions even more spartan than in *Britannia*. Over a dozen midshipmen messed in a gunroom which was no more than a small, smelly space on the maindeck, keeping their clothes and all their belongings in the passageway outside. Their food was as primitive as their mess — the usual sailor's salt beef one day, salt pork and pea soup the next. Lime juice was issued after a week at sea. The midshipmen each subscribed thirty shillings a week to a gunroom messman who supplied tea, potatoes, tinned meat and vegetables as extras. They could also run up a monthly bill of ten shillings for jam, cocoa, condensed milk and such delicacies as sardines — for which Jellicoe developed a taste he kept all his life. Midshipmen were allowed a wine bill of up to ten shillings a month, with an additional five shillings for those over the age of eighteen.

The midshipmen kept watches at sea and in harbour, learning how to take sights, how to handle parties of men, how to deal with the various events and emergencies of shipboard life. Every forenoon and on occasional afternoons they received instruction in navigation from the naval instructor on board. But watches and boat running took priority over school, which the midshipmen themselves disliked and found every pretext to avoid. With their other duties, the loss of sleep that watchkeeping entailed, and the various commitments and distractions of life in a man-of-war, it was very difficult for any midshipman to concentrate, although Jellicoe had a very good instructor in *Newcastle* called Mr Tims.

Jellicoe himself was always proud to have served in sail. In his opinion, there was nothing quite like it for training hand and body and mind. A midshipman was closer to the ship's company than he would ever be again in his Service career. A good midshipman was invaluable to the commander and to an officer of the watch, to act as their deputies aloft, to maintain discipline and to see that the sails were handled properly. An emergency aloft – a rope stranded or parted, a sudden squall, or sails to be taken in – might occur at any time, and to serve aloft required physical strength, agility and courage, as well as a high degree of teamwork and loyalty.

The penalties for errors were real. Although it was quite possible for a man to fall 120 feet and escape unharmed, a fall usually meant death or at least serious injury. The midshipmen in *Newcastle* normally drilled on the mizzen mast, the smallest of the three, where the sails and gear were commensurately smaller for the boys to handle. Even so, towards the end of the commission one of Jellicoe's fellow midshipmen, Harry Rivers, fell eighty feet and, though he broke the main force of the fall by catching at a rope, he was still seriously injured.

One of the most common emergencies under sail was a man overboard. It happened no less than twenty-four times in *Newcastle*'s two-and-a-half year commission. Only half the men who went overboard were safely recovered. It always required superb seamanship to bring a sailing ship making as much as nine or ten knots up into the wind, lower a boat and back the sails to take the way off. Once in *Newcastle* the evolution went seriously wrong.

The ship was homeward bound, running at eight or nine knots from Hong Kong to Singapore, when the captain of the mizzen-top slipped and fell overboard while heaving in the log line. Wingfield, Jellicoe's daring term-mate, and two able seamen at once went after him. The ship was brought up almost into the wind while the starboard, lee-side boat was lowered. The boat was not fitted with patent disengaging gear so that, for a successful launch, both falls had to be slipped simultaneously by order. The release was bungled, the falls' slipping was mistimed, and two of the crew were left hanging on the ends of the falls, while the boat itself drifted aft where it was in danger of being smashed under the swell of the ship's hull as it rolled to and fro. The ship meanwhile was still going ahead at some five or six knots. Because of the delay the ship had sagged away almost a mile to leeward of the lifebuoy by the time the boat, two men short in its crew, was clear.

Jellicoe had joined those manning the port-side boat, which did have patent disengaging gear, fully expecting it to be called away. The chief engineer came on deck and said he could raise steam in an hour, but the offer was refused. There was a very heavy sea running and Captain Douglas had made up his mind that the risk of losing the boat and its crew, as well as the four men in the water, was too great. So he recalled

15

the boat, although the lifebuoy could be clearly seen, with Wingfield and the other men close to it.

For Jellicoe, perched up in the port lifeboat, it had been an instructive episode. In the haste to save lives, lives had been lost. A longer delay to allow more way off the ship, a little more care in lowering the boat, and the men would probably have been rescued. The Captain had had to make a most difficult decision, balancing the lives of the depleted boat's crew against those four in the water. As it was, feelings ran high in the ship for some time. Four men had been left to drown, whom the ship's company thought should, and could, have been saved. There was an enquiry when the ship got back to Sheerness, at which Mrs Wingfield, the midshipman's mother, was present throughout. It was a painful ordeal for her and for Captain Douglas. But his decision was vindicated and he was completely exonerated.

In later life Jellicoe recalled some of the highlights of the cruise: visiting Napoleon's tomb at St Helena; shooting at Port Stanley; the 'Wideawake Fair' of breeding gulls on Ascension Island; cricket at St Vincent; the ship rolling thirty-five degrees each way in the Roaring Forties; treading grapes at Cape Town; rounders and a tug-of-war at Woosung. At Port Arthur Jellicoe's leave was stopped for a fortnight for some mishap aloft; the midshipman of the top took responsibility for any errors. In harbour he took one of the ship's cutters away on all her trips in all weathers. After a long day's boatwork in very hot sun at Nagasaki, Jellicoe suffered sunstoke and lay for three weeks in a cot in the captain's fore cabin and in his delirium had to be restrained from jumping out and overboard.

During *Newcastle*'s cruise Jellicoe at last began to grow, and actually shot up five inches in 1875. He found it hard to alter his uniform to fit him. At one point he had only one pair of shoes that fitted, and to achieve that he had had to black a pair of white canvas shoes with boot polish.

When *Newcastle* reached home again Jellicoe went on leave, in his own words,

> ... after a most interesting and enjoyable two and a half years' cruise during which I necessarily became much attached to life in a sailing ship. The sight of a squadron of frigates under full sail, and indeed the sight and movement of one's own ship, gave a sense of pleasure I have never experienced in steamships. It is not too much to say that I preferred in those days being at sea to being in harbour, merely as a result of the exhilarating effect of working a ship under sail.

After foreign service leave spent at home in Ryde, Jellicoe joined his next ship on 10 July 1877 at Devonport. She was the 10,000-ton five-masted ironclad *Agincourt*. She and her two sister ships, *Minotaur* and *Northumberland*, were the longest single-screw warships ever built and were the biggest fighting ships afloat for nearly a decade. All three went well under steam, making up to fourteen and a half knots, but were almost impossible to handle under sail, being the slowest and unhandiest to windward of all the Victorian ironclads. *Agincourt* herself was laid down in 1861 at Lairds, Birkenhead, as *Captain*. She was renamed during building and completed in 1868.

Agincourt was laid out on a generous scale. Her upper deck was a vast, uncluttered space, like a parade ground, on which a company of troops could have drilled with ease. Her complement of 800 men all berthed on the main deck, between the guns. This deck too had a majestically clear sweep almost from bow to stern, with no transverse bulkheads to obstruct the view. It was possible to stand at the stern and look, through several messes of men, right forward almost the whole length of the ship to the bows. This arrangement, though bad for damage control, made for healthy messdecks which were much better ventilated than in most ironclads. But it was unpopular with the ship's company, who preferred their living spaces closer and stuffier. They had all the fresh air they needed aloft and in addition their tables and mess gear all had to be cleared away every time battery gun drill was carried out. Ironically the officers, who would not have minded better ventilation, were messed on a lower deck.

The ship had just been refitted, and rearmed with seventeen nine-inch muzzle-loading rifled guns, firing from a broadside battery. She commissioned under Captain Richard Wells as flagship of the Second-in-Command of the Mediterranean Fleet, Admiral Sir John Commerell, who had won a Victoria Cross as a commander in the Sea of Azov during the Crimean War. The c-in-c was Admiral Sir Geoffrey Phipps Hornby, the best seaman and ablest admiral of his day and arguably the finest admiral of the late Victorian era. 'Uncle Geoff' (the nickname was not a term of affection but of guarded wariness) was intensely efficient, hard-working and highly competent, and in-sisted on the strictest letter of the law in everything. His flagship *Alexandra*, like all his ships, was run according to the book in every particular. Trivial offences against regulations, even self-confessed by the culprit, were likely to be punished in the most draconian manner. Curiously, Phipps Hornby had first seen action many years earlier in *Princess Charlotte* at the bombardment of Acre in 1840 — and then never again. His judgment as c-in-c was so accurate, his dispositions so skilfully made, and his precautions so well taken, that he actually prevented the need for his fleet ever to go into action. It could be said that Phipps Hornby prepared so carefully for war that war never came.

When the Russo-Turkish War broke out in 1876 the British Government's policy was, as it had been earlier in the century, to support the Turks against the Russians and if possible to prevent the Russians seizing Constantinople. The Mediterranean Fleet was the most important stabilizing influence in the area, and when the Russians crossed the Danube the fleet was ordered to the eastern end of the Mediterranean, where the ships anchored in Besika Bay, an open roadstead on the coast of Asia Minor, near the ruins of Troy, some ten miles south of the western entrance to the Dardanelles. In the event most of the ships were to stay at Besika Bay for two years.

Agincourt joined the fleet at Besika in August 1877, and Jellicoe was kept busy watchkeeping and boat-running. In such an exposed roadstead the boats occasionally had to survive the risks of bad weather. One evening another midshipman in *Agincourt*, Jellicoe's cousin Charles Rushworth, brought his cutter off from shore under sail and was ranging his boat alongside the ship's gangway when one of his crew fell into the water. Charles Rushworth jumped overboard to rescue him, but there was a heavy sea running and both he and the midshipman were drowned.

From time to time ships left to refit at Malta, to do steam tactics or quarterly gun-firing, but for the most part they stayed at Besika swinging round their anchors, being supplied by colliers and stores ships. Ashore the countryside was bleak, barren and thinly populated. Eventually a small village of corrugated iron or wooden shanties, known as Bumboat Town, with cafés, grog shops and stables, sprang up on shore.

The fleet had to make their own amusements. There was walking, to the ruins of Troy, swimming, fishing with seine nets and afterwards grilling the catch on charcoal fires, and some shooting – partridge, quail, snipe and a few pheasants were available on some of the nearby islands. In November a pack of beagles arrived from England, officers and men followed hounds mostly on foot, but some on an amazing variety of mounts, from the C-in-C himself on his own horse, to donkeys hired from the local Levantines. They hunted hares, on one notable occasion a wild cat, and there were rumours of wild boar.

In December 1877 the city of Plevna fell to the Russians, and the war seemed about to end in a Turkish defeat. On 23 January 1878 the Admiralty telegraphed to Phipps Hornby, who was then at Vourlah Bay, to proceed with his fleet to Constantinople. Phipps Hornby took the precaution of sending the dispatch vessel *Salamis* ahead to Chanak with a letter to the Forts Commandant, informing him that the ships had orders to go through and asking for his acquiescence. But to Phipps Hornby's extreme annoyance another Admiralty telegram cancelling the operation arrived as the ships were nearing the fort. The ships returned to Besika Bay.

Finally on 12 February the C-in-C again received orders to pass through the Dardanelles without formal permission from the authorities, and to anchor his ships in the Sea of Marmora, off Constantinople. The ships were to return fire if fired on, but were not to dally to silence a fort. One of the forts was reputed to have a 50-ton Krupps gun mounted in its embrasure, so this order seemed to the fleet to be somewhat optimistically phrased.

The fleet began to weigh anchor just before dawn on 13 February 1878. It was a bitterly cold morning with a very strong northerly wind blowing as Phipps Hornby's six ironclads – *Alexandra, Agincourt, Achilles, Swiftsure, Sultan* and *Téméraire* – with *Salamis* bringing up the rear, headed for the Dardanelles entrance in line ahead. The clear visibility was soon obscured by a heavy snowstorm which completely blotted out the nearest coastline and the navigational marks leading to the Dardanelles. The ships all had steam sirens but Phipps Hornby had forbidden their use, in case they betrayed the ship's positions to the forts. The passage would therefore have to be made almost blind, each ship feeling her way. Fortunately Phipps Hornby had under him some of the finest captains in the Navy, and he relied on their seamanship to achieve a passage which, but for the urgency of the moment, would have been foolhardy and which he would never have considered for a moment.

How foolhardy was quickly demonstrated when a sudden clearance in the blizzard revealed the frigate *Raleigh* aground on an island down to leeward. *Salamis* was once again instructed to go on ahead and inform the commandant that the ships intended to go through, come what may, and to ask the forts to refrain from firing for humanitarian reasons.

Meanwhile the blizzard had closed down again and made any signalling between ships or any proper station-keeping impossible. Jellicoe was signal midshipman huddled on the bridge in the freezing wind, with his telescope to his eye, as *Agincourt* crept up channel. The forts might open fire at any moment. It was a nervous time for a young man who might soon be having his first experience of action, and Jellicoe's heart was thudding, but as he later wrote to his mother, 'I did not feel at all nervous, I am surprised at you asking such a question of the future Admiral Sir J.R. Jellicoe, K.C.B., &., &.'

At the narrowest part of the channel, guarded by the fort with the 50-ton Krupps gun, Jellicoe saw the flagship *Alexandra* run aground and reported it. Captain Wells could not believe it, but it was so. It transpired that when *Alexandra*'s guns were cleared for action the boats had been turned inboard on their davits and they had upset the magnetic compass. In the thick weather and with the lack of leading marks this had not been noticed on the bridge. So Jellicoe's sharp eyes had correctly summed up the situation.

Sultan was ordered to stand by the flagship, while the other ships felt their way past. *Agincourt* and *Swiftsure* anchored off Gallipoli, while the other four, including the refloated *Alexandra*, went to Prinkipo (Princes Island), ten miles from Constantinople.

The presence of the ironclad squadron in the Sea of Marmora had a powerful deterrent effect on the Russians, who were within easy reach of capturing Constantinople, and effectively saved the city. But this was not realized at the time, and as the Russians were within twelve miles of the Turkish lines at Bulair and likely to attack at any moment, Admiral Commerell had authority to take any steps he thought necessary to protect the Turkish defences.

As there was only one other midshipman, Cecil Burney, in the ship, Jellicoe was kept busy in charge of two steamboats and four cutters, as well as being third signal officer and a dispatch rider, taking letters to the general in the lines, and riding all over the peninsula with orders and letters for the ships anchored in the Gulf of Xeros. 'The Admiral sent for me,' he wrote to his mother on 10 March, 'and asked if I would like to ride over to the Gulf of Xeros with despatches. I said "yes" promptly. He then offered me his horse. The horse was fresh, but I am acquiring skill in horsemanship and managed him all right.'

Later in the year Jellicoe was lent as a watchkeeping officer to HMS *Cruiser*, a sailing sloop attached to the Mediterranean Fleet for training seamen and midshipmen in practical seamanship (she eventually survived to become the very last sailing ship in the Navy). After Jellicoe had been on board for some months *Cruiser* was ordered up to Prinkipo to join the main fleet and Phipps Hornby himself came on board to inspect her. The admiral wanted to see a test of seamanship and told Captain Hext, commanding *Cruiser*, to detail off one midshipman to take charge of unmooring ship, make plain sail, sail round the fleet, return, remoor, furl sails, coil down ropes and report. Hext chose Jellicoe, who, inwardly nervous but with a very clear unflustered voice, began to take charge of the evolution.

Characteristically Phipps Hornby decided to put pressure on young Jellicoe, to see what he was made of. As *Cruiser* headed towards the flagship close-hauled on the starboard tack, Jellicoe opened his mouth to give the orders to go about. But the admiral said no, and Jellicoe had to hold on, while the great sides of the ironclad loomed nearer and nearer. Every yard nearer meant a greater risk of the huge mass of the flagship taking the wind out of *Cruiser*'s sails. In any case *Cruiser* needed time and space to go about, and a collision looked more likely every second. At last Hornby nodded and told Jellicoe to put her about.

Even now, Jellicoe might have hurried his orders, or given them in the wrong sequence, which would have been disastrous. But he took his time and kept his head. The Admiral had been right. There was room enough. *Cruiser* came smoothly and correctly round, and bore away nicely on the port tack. Phipps Hornby and Jellicoe were both pleased by the incident. Phipps Hornby told Jellicoe, 'You have handled the ship under sail in a most skilful manner. I would be pleased to have you on the bridge of my flagship as any one of my lieutenants.' Jellicoe wrote to his mother:

The Admiral complimented me afterwards on the way I did it, which was rather an honour. He also told me that Captain Hext had given a very good report of me and told him that I was a very good officer of the watch. He finished up wishing me a first class in Seamanship. I thought you would like to know this, though it seems rather conceited to talk about it.

Jellicoe might have a chance of good results in seamanship, but he had had very little time for other studies. He had been too hard-worked in *Agincourt* to take and work out the observations of sun, moon and stars which had to be submitted at the same time as his seamanship examination. If it had not been for a kindly instructor who obligingly 'faked' a moon sight for him by writing it out backwards from the solution, he might have failed.

When the war was over, and before the fleet left, the ships all went up to Prinkipo so that the officers could see Constantinople. Jellicoe was busy boat-running, and took Admiral Commerell up to Constantinople in the steam pinnace, a ten-mile trip which took an hour and a quarter. He wrote:

On Thursday I made two trips up, going up for the Swedish Ambassador to bring him down to lunch with the Admiral. I brought his two daughters down with him and nearly fell in love with one of them. They were very nice girls about 17 years old and spoke English perfectly. I took them up again in the evening and by the time we parted we had become quite friends. They asked me to come up and see them, but as we sailed on Saturday there was not time.

This was Jellicoe's first recorded affair of the heart, at the age of nineteen, and like many sailors he found there was no time. However, as the Service saying goes, the first turn of the screw mended all broken hearts, and Jellicoe, always susceptible to women, once said, 'I got engaged in every rank.'

In September Jellicoe took his examination in mathematics and passed in third place out of the 106 midshipmen in the Mediterranean and Channel Fleets. Phipps Hornby was also pleased with the result, knowing that Jellicoe had been in *Cruiser* for four months before the examination and had had no chance to do any school work. He wrote to Hext to say that he was glad that learning seamanship did not interfere with mathematics.

At Malta, on his birthday in December, Jellicoe was examined in seamanship by a board of captains. He got a first-class pass. He obviously did know his subject well but he shrewdly suspected another reason in his favour – 'The mail came in during the exam and the Captains were more interested in their letters.' With good reports from his captain and his C-in-C, and his first-class pass in seamanship, Jellicoe went home to study at the Royal Naval College, Greenwich.

Jellicoe was intelligent enough and strong enough of purpose to overcome the difficulties and disadvantages of the naval system of education for young officers of that period. But there were others, his contemporaries, who would reach flag rank at the same time as Jellicoe and would fill most of the senior appointments in the Navy in the years leading up to, and during, the First World War, who were not so fortunate or so intelligent. Their point of view was well put in an article called, 'On Naval Education' which appeared in *MacMillan's Magazine* in December 1878. It was written by 'A Naval Nobody', and datelined Besika Bay.

A Naval Nobody's theme was that the navy, through a noble and glorious profession, neglected the minds of its young officers most shamefully. Naval officers showed no interest in geology or natural history. 'A man of war visits an unknown country, say New Guinea. And what information do we bring back? Can we describe what the special characteristics of the country are, what the botany, what the geology, what the fauna? Scarcely one scientifically intelligible word: a tree is a tree, a palm a palm, a bird a bird, an insect an insect!' The author complained that naval officers were not taught foreign languages:

How often have I seen two naval officers of different nationalities bowing and grinning to each other idiotically, comprehending each other less than two monkeys would, unable to exchange a word, unable even to rub their naked stomachs by way of something to do with their hands, and as outward signs of mutual amity and peace, as do the New Guinea savages!

Looking back on my service afloat as a 'mid', I can think of no single advantage that I have therein, no advantage whatever which I could not equally have gained by serving that time (or a great part of it) on shore at a college, going to sea occasionally for a sailoring cruise in some small craft in the Channel.

A Naval Nobody not only complained about officers' general education but also about their instruction on professional matters.

I call the whole system of our naval education utterly faulty; not only that education which does not bear directly on our profession, but to that also which does do so. I say that we, the navy's youth, are in some professional matters most deplorably ignorant, and the day will come when we, and England, will wake up to the fact with a start. It sounds impossible, inconceivable, that it is only a privileged few who are allowed to make a *study* of gunnery, practically and theoretically; only a privileged few who are initiated into the mysteries of torpedoes; only a privileged few who are taught thoroughly the all-important knowledge to a sailor of surveying and navigation; not even a privileged few who are taught – with any practical result – that science which has displaced the science of utilising the winds – the science of steam; and yet all this is so!

Chapter 2

Though stating his case somewhat overheatedly, A Naval Nobody was in fact following a long naval tradition, of criticizing the state of the Navy. He was also proving another old Service saying, that naval officers could only write two kinds of articles, both about naval training. There was a great deal of substance in A Naval Nobody's complaints. For instance, there certainly was a Service suspicion of fields of knowledge outside the Navy, a distrust of officers with 'outside interests', above all a mild contempt, not always concealed, for the 'clever' officer. The native British distrust of the man who was 'too clever by half ' was translated in the Navy into the expressed belief that the intellectually bright officer, the man who 'chased x, y and z', the 'three-oner' who got first-class passes in his examinations, must also of necessity be a duffer at seamanship. The 'x-chaser' might know all there was to know about algebra, it was believed, but would be utterly useless on deck in a gale at sea. There was even a song about it. A 'three-oner' was somebody who '. . . shouted when the ship was flat aback, "Let go the starboard alpha cosine theta stunsail tack." '

For the Royal Naval College, Greenwich, where Jellicoe now went, A Naval Nobody also had some hard words: '. . . a *farce* as is the naval college at Greenwich. For that that college is a farce no one who has studied there will deny.' A Naval Nobody complained of the 'discipline fit only for boys and ship-board life. Your "harassing legislation" worries and sickens us. We gladly escape from your misnamed college, letting pass the honours which we might there gain. . . .'

Jellicoe certainly did not let honours pass, nor did he find the discipline irksome. Seamanship, Greenwich studies and gunnery at Portsmouth were the three examinations for promotion to lieutenant, and he made up his mind to be a 'three-oner' if he possibly could. With a seamanship first already behind him, he went on to get firsts at Greenwich and in gunnery. Normally he would have been promoted at once. But that year there happened to be four other sub-lieutenants with three firsts and the Admiralty decided, for some impenetrable reason, to promote the four in order of their seniority as midshipmen. Jellicoe was the most junior and had to wait the longest, being deprived of his earned promotion for another eight months.

In March 1880, as a sub-lieutenant, Jellicoe was appointed signal mate to the ironclad *Alexandra*, flagship of Phipps Hornby's successor as C-in-C Mediterranean, Admiral Sir Beauchamp Seymour. The Admiral was known as the 'Swell of the Ocean', the captain was Lord Walter Kerr, and the officers led a most hectic physical and social life. Jellicoe played cricket and rackets, went to dances and regimental balls and fell in love. 'I went to a large dance at the Club here on Tuesday given by the Xth', he wrote home. 'I was afraid I shouldn't get any partners as I did not know a soul, but I danced all except the square dances, and did not come away until it was all over. I did not get on board till 4 a.m. It was a very jolly dance and I liked it very much but of course as *she* was not there my thoughts were far away the whole time.' Nothing is known of this '*she*'. Clearly, she was Jellicoe's fiancée as a sub-lieutenant.

Sail drill was the watchword in *Alexandra*, and as she was flagship there was a special pressure on her midshipmen and captains of tops. Sail drill was carried out every Monday morning in harbour. In Malta, whenever there were several ironclads in Grand Harbour, crowds used to gather to watch from the ramparts and the top of the Baracca as the ships competed to make sail, shift topsails, strike top-gallant masts and upper yards, all against the clock. The sight was worth watching. It was always an exciting spectacle as the leading hand of the upper yardmen swung himself on to the royal yard as it was swayed up across, stood on it almost to the truck of the mast, and then rode it down, while the parral was passed, clews toggled and sails hoisted, all in a matter of a few seconds. Then all the upper yardmen who were working above the cross trees jumped on to the back stays and ropes and came sliding down to the tops. This also only took a few seconds, after which the mastheads were reported clear and the ship was ready under all plain sail. The time allowed for the whole evolution was one minute thirty seconds. A slip meant a fall of 180 feet to the deck, and as the ship's reputation depended upon her drill the topmen constantly took risks, so that at one time it was customary to make the signal after every fast and furious drill, 'Report number of killed and injured.'

After eight months Jellicoe was promoted lieutenant and came home overland through Italy, visiting Rome, Florence and other places on his way. He contracted dysentery in Florence and for the rest of his journey home he was very ill and in great pain. He went straight to bed when he reached the house in Surbiton where the family was then living, and was laid up for three months during which he went on half-pay — the only period on half-pay in his entire fifty-two years service in the Navy.

Jellicoe had already applied to specialize as a gunnery officer, but he had first to serve at least a year at sea as a watchkeeping lieutenant. On

25

3 February 1881 he was appointed to his old ship *Agincourt*, which was flagship of the Channel Squadron, flying the flag of Vice-Admiral Arthur Hood and commanded by Captain Elibank Murray.

The Channel Squadron, in which once again the whole emphasis was on sail drill, led a leisurely existence, going on quiet cruises at about four knots down the coasts of Portugal and Spain as far as Gibraltar, visiting Vigo, Lisbon and Arosa Bay. After over a year of this somewhat dull and routine existence, in May 1882 the Squadron, now commanded by Vice-Admiral Sir William Dowell, was ordered to Malta. As in Phipps Hornby's time the Mediterranean was the most important strategic naval theatre and once again there was a political upheaval, this time in Egypt. Backed by the Egyptian army and the nationalist party, Arabi Pasha had led a revolt against the Khedive and was now in virtual control of most of Egypt.

Agincourt left Malta on 4 July 1882, with a battalion of the 60th Rifles on board. The ship called at Cyprus to embark General Sir Archibald Alison and his staff, as well as a number of horse-boats, horses and mules. With all the extra men and gear the ship was very crowded, and even *Agincourt*'s massive prairie of an upper deck was almost impassable with horse-boats and assorted stores. Below, the ship's company shifted in the forward messes, where they 'double-banked'. The 60th Rifles had the after messdecks, while their officers shared cabins with the ship's officers.

Meanwhile a crisis had been developing at Alexandria, where the Mediterranean Fleet had already arrived. On 9 July Beauchamp Seymour issued an ultimatum to Arabi Pasha, that the mounting of extra guns in the seashore forts overlooking the harbour must cease. Not surprisingly the ultimatum was ignored. When it expired on the eleventh the guns of the fleet began to bombard the forts. It took most of the day to silence them, and their return fire was disconcertingly good. That evening the first landing parties of sailors and marines went ashore to keep order in the city.

Agincourt had been going to Port Said but was ordered instead to Alexandria, where the 60th Rifles were urgently required to join the garrison of the city against Arabi Pasha's forces outside. *Agincourt* arrived on 13 July, too late for the bombardment, but after a very fast passage for such a comparatively elderly lady.

At first there was a slight hesitation in command, because the army was suffering from an embarrassment of leaders. As Captain Arthur Knyvet Wilson, commanding the torpedo depot ship *Hecla*, said, 'We have seven generals and none of them knows what to do.' But when General Sir Garnet Wolseley arrived he quickly took a firm grip on matters and evolved his famous plan, which was a subtle and well-kept secret, to launch his advance on Arabi's forces not from Alexandria, as everybody thought he would, but from Ismailia, which was nearer Cairo and offered a splendid route for marching, over hard-packed, firm sand.

Because of Wolseley's change of plan *Agincourt* did not actually disembark her troops at Alexandria but went to Port Said. Jellicoe took a party of bluejackets to the battleship *Orion* at Ismailia, where George Willis, Captain Fitzroy's clerk and secretary, remembers him coming on board. 'A very grimy young officer, called "Jellybags" by his friends on board. He was a wiry, well-built young man, inclined to be quiet and thoughtful, but with a dry humour, and was very popular.'

At Ismailia Jellicoe saw his first shots fired in anger. On 20 August 1882 *Orion*'s boats, filled with armed men, were rowed ashore. With memories of the days of the Napoleonic Wars, the oars were muffled by wrapping the men's black silk neckerchiefs round the tholes where the oars passed through the rowlocks. The landing party arrived at about 2 a.m. and after some rifle fire captured the governor's house. The governor and his harem were brought on board *Orion*, where they lived for a time behind screens on the upper deck.

At dawn the guns of *Orion* and of the corvette *Carysfort*, both ships lying in the Suez Canal, opened fire on Arabi troops and a troop-carrying train at Nefiche, a small village two miles south of Ismailia. The range was about 4000 yards, and the targets were actually invisible from deck level. *Carysfort*'s foremast was used as a spotting top, and the guns were aimed on bearings taken from her mast-head. To give *Orion*'s guns extra elevation, to achieve a howitzer-like trajectory, the whole ship was heeled to starboard by transferring ammunition and by emptying the port-side boilers of water.

Meanwhile, to the north of *Orion*, Wolseley's force could be seen arriving; Willis described it: '. . . as far as the eye could reach the ships stretched away into the desert like a long, moving, jointed snake, and on the far off horizon appeared a mirage of masted transports all inverted over a glassy pool.'

A naval brigade landed with the army and a naval officer, Lieutenant Wyatt Rawson, guided the force by the stars on a night march to Tel-el-Kebir. A night march across strange country, to be followed by an engagement with an ensconced enemy soon after daylight, is always fraught with dangers. But the evolution succeeded and on the morning of 13 September Garnet Wolseley's mixed force of cavalry, infantry, Highlanders, Indian troops, blue-jackets and marines conclusively routed Arabi Pasha's army. Rawson was mortally wounded during the battle and died next day, asking his doctor and friends, 'Did I not lead them straight?'

Jellicoe was disappointed not to be chosen for the naval brigade. In fact, after he had been on board *Orion* for three weeks Captain Fitzroy sent him back to Port Said with dispatches for the C-in-C. Fitzroy wanted to conceal that he was communicating with the C-in-C at Port Said because Wolseley's change of plan, to start from Ismailia instead of Alexandria, was still a well-kept secret. At that time Arabi's men still held the west bank of the canal and would certainly see and might even intercept a Service boat. So Jellicoe had to go by night, on one of the native launches taking refugees from Ismailia to Port Said. He himself was disguised as a refugee and had a most unpleasant trip, herded cheek by jowl with a close-packed crowd of evil-smelling and vermin-ous fellow passengers. Jellicoe's company of bluejackets arrived a few days later and he took them ashore to join the other naval parties helping to garrison Port Said. This was Jellicoe's first active service, for which he qualified for two medals, the Egyptian Medal 1882, and the Khedive's Bronze Star.

Jellicoe came home in September 1882 for a nine months' academic course with eight other lieutenants at Greenwich. This was the nearest the Navy allowed its officers to come to a university existence. It was hard intellectual work, but there were many social compensations. Jellicoe worked hard and played hard, as he did all his life. He loved to play games, loved the comradeship of sport and the competition of one against another. He played football and rackets, and was scrum-half for the College rugby XV against opposition of university and first-class club standard. He was a good cricketer, and although he never reached the standard of his elder brother Frederick, who was a Cambridge blue, Jellicoe was devoted to cricket all his life.

Sport counter-balanced his work in the classroom, where he showed his real ability yet again. Stimulated by the intellectual encouragement of lecturers such as the mathematician Professor Carlton Lambert, Jellicoe passed out top of his class with 2,911 marks (2,700 were needed for a first-class pass). As a result he gained an Admiralty prize for first place of £80, a very large sum in those days, equivalent almost to a year's pay for a sub-lieutenant, but subject to income tax, because the clerks at the Admiralty had been too idle ever to contest the matter on behalf of the winners with the Inland Revenue.

From Greenwich Jellicoe went to *Excellent*, the gunnery school at Portsmouth, for the long course to qualify him as a specialist gunnery officer. *Excellent* was then still in the doldrums of conservatism, inefficiency and intellectual sterility. The gunners' house ashore, the 'Excellent House That Jack Built', had been erected in the 1860s, but officers and men still lived in the old hulk *Excellent*, with another old hulk, *Calcutta*, moored just ahead of her, off what was later to be called Whale Island but was then still known as Mud Island.

When Jellicoe joined, men still drilled with antiquated smooth-bore muzzle-loaders such as those used at Trafalgar, loosing guns and beating to quarters as in the old days, the rolling of the ship being simulated by having a hundred men doubling back and forward across the upper deck. Most of the work in the ships was done by scores of 'deadheads', naval and army pensioners dragging out the last years of their lives in the soporific calm of *Excellent*, in a way of life which had been unchanged for years (indeed it was actually called 'The Forty Years Routine'). Mud Island itself was occupied by several thousand rabbits and several hundred convicts who were levelling parts of the island and enlarging others, using spoil from new extensions being made to Portsmouth dockyard.

The Forty Years Routine was about to be swept away, and there were other changes apart from landscaping. A violent stimulus, like a gigantic electric shock, was administered to the whole establishment by the appointment of Captain Jackie Fisher in command of *Excellent* in 1883. He had received a CB for his services as captain of the battleship *Inflexible* in the bombardment of Alexandria and in the later campaign against Arabi Pasha, and after recovering from a severe attack of dysentry in Malta, he joined in April. At once he began to make his presence felt like a typhoon. Fisher wrinkled the deadheads out of their cherished cabooshes and crannies and filled the ship with active service ratings, actively learning gunnery. The smooth-bore muzzle-loaders were landed and replaced by quick-firers. New firing ranges were laid out, and Fisher formed an 'experimental staff' to carry out trials on new guns large and small, to test new gunnery machinery and evaluate developments on new gun-sights.

Jellicoe had passed his gunnery course, again with a first class, to become a fully qualified gunnery officer, and in May 1884 he joined the junior staff of *Excellent*. One of the senior staff officers was Commander Percy Scott, the man who was to do more than anybody else to drag the Navy's gunnery into the twentieth century. Thus the great triumvirate of Fisher, Scott and Jellicoe, who were between them to do so much for the Service, came together for the first time.

It was a very fortunate appointment for Jellicoe, bringing him directly under the eye of Fisher at just the right moment. Like the men under him, Jellicoe worked hard. An account of life at *Excellent* at that time as written by James Woods, who joined the Navy as a boy in 1878 and went to *Excellent* when Jellicoe was on the staff. Woods later wrote several books under the pseudonym of Lionel Yexley.

Instruction began at 9.30 a.m. and went on until 3.45 p.m. with, as Yexley said, 'no red tape' and no distractions. Leave was given until 7 a.m. five nights a week. Men on the course were told by the staff, 'You know nothing. You must start again from scratch.' The motto was 'Attitude is the art of gunnery and whiskers makes the man.' It was all in the greatest contrast to Yexley's previous ship, the rotten-planked, cockroach-infested, threadbare-rigged *London*, store, hospital and guardship for the East Indies Station. Yexley thoroughly enjoyed *Excellent*; he was being taught his trade by men who knew. Yexley was in Jellicoe's class for instruction and was a member of what must have been one of the very earliest 'field gun's crews' who exercised dismantling, transport and reassembling a field piece against the clock.

Early in 1885 the 'Penjdeh Incident' took place, one of those 'panics' which periodically afflicted Victorian England. On 30 March the Russians attacked and seized the village of Penjdeh on the frontier of Afghanistan and, as Great Britain was pledged to support Afghanistan, there existed for a few weeks a real possibility of war with Russia. The Russian Black Sea Fleet was mobilized, and on 25 March the Admiralty began to assemble a fleet under Phipps Hornby who was then C-in-C Portsmouth. Such was the state of the Navy and the disposition of ships around the world that it actually took three months, until June, to assemble the fleet, by which time the crisis, like so many crises, had more or less evaporated. But such was the shortage of men that for a time deserters were offered an amnesty if they gave themselves up and rejoined.

Phipps Hornby flew his flag in the ironclad battleship *Minotaur* and chose Fisher as his flag captain and chief of staff. Fisher for his part chose Jellicoe to serve on his staff (choosing him, incidentally, over the heads of and from a large number of other officers). On 7 June Phipps Hornby hoisted his flag in *Minotaur*, leading a 'Particular Service Squadron', which by that time had no particular service to perform. Phipps Hornby took them to Berehaven in Ireland for a programme of exercises and trials which included the charging of the Berehaven boom by the torpedo ram *Polyphemus*.

Polyphemus was an extraordinary warship, the result of an extended preoccupation of the Victorian Navy with rams, and the original Thunder Child of H.G. Wells' *The War of the Worlds*. She was fitted with a torpedo tube in the extreme tip of her ram, and had other torpedo tubes amidships. She looked like a long metal cigar with a superstructure fitted on top of it, but she acquitted herself well against the boom. Jellicoe was actually on board as she charged and said that, '. . . it looked at one moment as if a 6½-inch hawser would sweep her upper works.' But according to one of her engineer officers, '. . . she just slowed down gradually and by her great momentum then cut clean through the boom.' Phipps Hornby wrote to his wife on 30 June, '. . . ran Polyphemus at it [the boom], trying to stop her with Whitehead torpedoes; but she was well handled, escaped them all, and blew up part of the boom, but hardly made it passable.'

The squadron then went to Blacksod Bay for exercises which, as was to be expected under Phipps Hornby, were unusually warlike and realistic for the Victorian Navy. The capital ships lowered their small, second-class torpedo boats to practise attacks on the fleet. There were mock battles between fleets. Phipps Hornby's ships at one point were discovered and betrayed by what he called a 'dirty little torpedo boat'. This was the first time torpedo attack had been exercised on such a scale against a fleet, and these were the first attempts to evaluate this form of attack. In fact, these were the first fleet exercises with a strategic purpose, and the first experiments in such fleet tactics.

Those summer manoeuvres of 1885 under Phipps Hornby had a forward-looking modern air about them, as though for the first time the Royal Navy really was shaking off its 'wooden walls' mentality and trying new weapons and tactics more in keeping with steam and steel. Once again it was young Jellicoe's great good fortune to be present, to see and hear all that went on. The exercises ended at Portland on 22 July, when Phipps Hornby held a farewell dinner party, and two rockets were fired to show 'operations concluded' with 'many expressions of thanks for lessons given'.

In September 1885 Jellicoe was appointed gunnery officer of the ironclad battleship *Monarch*, an historic vessel, though by then some way past her prime. Laid down at Chatham in June 1866 and completed in June 1869, *Monarch* was the Admiralty's solution to a fierce controversy of the late 1860s concerning turret ships. Captain Cowper Coles, with strong backing from the press and certain influential opinions, had designed the turret ship *Captain*. A committee of officers and constructors under the Chief Constructor, Edward James Lyon, had produced *Monarch*.

Monarch was the first ocean-going warship to fight under steam instead of sail, the first to be built of metal, not timber, and the first to mount her main armament in turrets outside the hull rather than in batteries inside the hull; in short she incorporated all three of the great advances in Victorian warship design, and her proportions of length to beam were preserved in many future battleships until the first World War. Trials soon showed that apart from having only one screw instead of *Captain*'s two, *Monarch* was superior to *Captain* in every respect: she was more economical in coal consumption, her turning circle was smaller, she was faster at every point of sailing, and her freeboard was so much greater that she could fire her guns at sea in weather when *Captain* would have had her gunports shut.

Monarch lay for some years in Alexandria, which led to a most embarrassing experience at the time of the Penjdeh 'scare'. Summoned suddenly to Malta, with the c-in-c flying his flag on board, *Monarch* broke down and drifted off the usual frequented sea lanes. She was missing, with the admiral on board, for some time. An investigation showed that she had swung to her buoy in the warm, shallow and tideless water of Alexandria harbour for so long that her propellor shaft and stern tube had become badly infested by a minute marine growth which had an extremely hard shell. This was not discovered during the periodical turning of the shaft in harbour, but under steady steaming conditions the shaft seized in the stern tube.

However, when Jellicoe joined her *Monarch* had been refitted and recommissioned for service in the Channel Squadron. Jellicoe's own particular responsibility was of course, the guns, and particularly the main armament, the four great guns, the first 12-inch muzzle-loaders with rifled barrels to be fitted in any British warship. They weighed 25 tons each and fired a 600-lb shell to a maximum of 7000 yards. The two drum-shaped turrets, each mounting two guns, were placed amidships. They stood seven foot high above the deck and twenty-six feet across their diameter, with two oval ports cut to admit the gun barrels. They were normally trained by steam engine, but in emergency could be trained by hand. The guns were retracted for loading, and the gun firing would carry the guns back into their loading position, but otherwise the carriages were worked back and forward by hand, using a six-handled winch on the deck below. Alterations of range were made by shifting the gun trunnions in three slots, to elevate or depress the barrels; this, too, was done by hand, assisted by hydraulic jacks.

Because loading, running the carriages in and out, and shifting the barrels for elevation were all done by hand, the gun's crew had to work extremely hard in a very confined space. Only a very well trained and physically fit crew could ever fire both guns at any higher rate than about one double round every two minutes. *Monarch* also had two 9-inch and 12-inch guns mounted under the topgallant fo'c'sle, and a 7-inch gun on the main deck in the stern, mounted so that it could be traversed to fire through three ports cut in the ship's side. She had taken part in the bombardment of Alexandria, firing 125 rounds of 12-inch (which, as it was a hot day, must have been very warm work for the crews), fifty-four 9-inch and twenty-one 7-inch.

Life in the Channel Squadron was very much the same as it had been in *Agincourt*, but there were occasional excitements. *Monarch*'s rival *Captain* had capsized in a gale in the Bay of Biscay in September 1870 (taking Cowper Coles down with her) and one night when the Squadron was under sail in heavy weather off Lisbon *Monarch* must have come very close to the same fate in much the same waters. She rolled twenty-five degrees and shipped tons of water on board, flooding one of the magazines. *Monarch*'s safe angle of heel was officially a little over twenty degrees.

Jellicoe was also cable officer, in charge of working anchors and cables on the fo'c'sle. *Monarch* had a steam patent capstan on the fore maindeck, but after so many years in service her cables and gear were not in the best repair. On one occasion the ship anchored in Gibraltar Bay in the unusual depth of water of forty fathoms (240 feet). Possibly an anchor was let go when the ship still had considerable way on. The great weight of cable dangling from the bows took charge and the sheet anchor cable thundered out to the full extent of the inboard deck clench. Jellicoe was at the capstan brake trying to bring the cable under control when the cable came up bar taut, a link parted, and a heavy compressor block hit Jellicoe on the head. He lay on his back in his cabin, concussed, for two days. If he had not been wearing a cap he would very probably have been killed.

On days when *Monarch*'s guns had their quarterly firings at target practice, the ship's boats were landed because they were likely to be damaged by the blast (for the same reason, the ship's company's 500 hammocks were not stowed in high bulwark hammock nettings, so common in Victorian warships, but on a flying deck above the upper deck). One day, when *Monarch* was rounding the eastern side of Gibraltar on her way to the firing range, a steam ship was sighted aground on rocks to the north. There was a rocket-firing apparatus ashore, but no rope had been passed. A strong south-easterly wind was blowing and the ship was on a lee shore.

There was only one boat on board, the captain's galley, which was hanging out of blast range on the stern davits. It was only a light gig, not at all suitable as a lifeboat, but Jellicoe asked to be allowed to take the galley in with volunteers to try and get the steamer's crew ashore. The captain gave his permission and the galley, with Jellicoe in command and his chief gunner's mate as coxswain, pulled inshore to a point under the lee of the steamship, between the vessel and the shore, and actually under the rope which had by then been fired by the rocket apparatus.

Nobody on board the wrecked vessel seemed to know how to work the breeches buoy. Jellicoe's bowman caught hold of the rope and the galley's crew started to haul themselves along the rope nearer to the ship. Jellicoe called to the men on board to jump into the boat when it came close enough. Unknown to Jellicoe there was a very strong current running along the shore at that point, which began to turn the galley broadside on to the sea. When Jellicoe saw this he told the bowman to let go the rope and the crew tried to row the galley head to sea again. Before they could do it a huge wave broke inboard, caught the galley partially broadside on, capsized her and threw her crew into the sea.

The crew started to swim for the shore. Jellicoe was afraid they would never be able to reach it and hailed them to hang on to the boat. They were all too far off to swim back and only Jellicoe and the chief gunner's mate stuck to the boat, which was floating bottom upwards.

The would-be rescuers now needed rescue themselves. The gig slowly drifted inshore with Jellicoe and his coxswain still clinging to it. The crew of the rocket-firing apparatus threw them lines weighted by sandbags and everybody eventually got on shore safely, although the coxswain never properly recovered his health afterwards, having swallowed quantities of sand when the gig turned on top of him. That evening the wind dropped, the sea died down, and shore boats recovered all the steamer's crew except for one man who was drowned while trying to jump into a boat. Jellicoe and his crew were awarded the Board of Trade Life-saving Medal.

Jellicoe left *Monarch* in the spring of 1886 to join the new battleship *Colossus* which commissioned under Captain Cyprian Bridge at Portsmouth on 13 April. She was the first of her class – the only other one was *Edinburgh* – and was one of what might be called the many interim designs of battleships of the late nineteenth century with which naval designers were gradually feeling their way to the modern concept of the Dreadnought.

Colossus had been laid down in June 1879, and had thus been a very long time in building. She had some novel features: she was the first battleship to be built of steel instead of iron, and the first to have electric lighting throughout and not just in specialized compartments; she also had what was called a 'fully extended water balance chamber', which was supposed to increase her stability as a gun platform in rough water.

For Jellicoe as her Gunnery Officer *Colossus'* chief technical interests was the return to the breech-loading in her main armament. The Admiralty had had a brief flirtation with breech-loading in the 1860s, but had discarded the idea because the guns were actually dangerous: in certain conditions they could be fired when the breech was not properly shut. But navies on the Continent had had breech-loaders for years, and sooner or later the Royal Navy would have to return to them.

Colossus' breech-loaders were 12-inch, weighed forty-three tons, and were mounted in pairs in round turrets. The turrets were in echelon, the port-side turret placed diagonally forward of the starboard turret. The superstructure forward and aft of the turrets was specially narrowed to allow both guns to fire directly ahead and astern. The guns were elevated and depressed hydraulically and were loaded with basically the same procedure as muzzle-loaders, but in reverse, the charge being hydraulically rammed into the breech from below the gun-deck. Five 6-inch breech-loaders with newly designed mountings were placed in the superstructure.

As a rising young gunnery officer Jellicoe had been specially picked to undertake the trials of bringing *Colossus'* new guns and equipment into commission. Trials they certainly were. In May 1886 Jellicoe,

Bridge and Fisher attended the gun-firing trials in *Collingwood*, another battleship similarly armed. Fisher had the deepest misgivings about these Mark II guns, and said he fully expected the muzzle to blow off. His expectations were exactly fulfilled. On 4 May, off the Isle of Wight, one of *Collingwood*'s after 12-inch guns was loaded with a 222-lb charge (as opposed to the full bore charge of 400-lb) and a 720-lb shell filled with water. When the gun fired, the last eight feet of the barrel leading up to the muzzle disintegrated. Fortunately nobody was hurt, although the ship's superstructure nearby was damaged. *Colossus* was forbidden to fire her guns, which were eventually withdrawn for case-hooping which strengthened the last few feet of the barrel at the cost of two tons more in weight. The *Collingwood* gun accident attracted the notice of the press, who by the late 1880s were becoming much more alert to happenings in the Navy. 'We are on the eve of a new panic in regard to the Navy,' said the *Daily News*.

Colossus joined the Channel Fleet at a time when there was still, unbelievably, a lively discussion on whether or not ships should have masts or sails. Many naval officers thought that warships should have full masts and rigging, if only as travelling gymnasia for training men in nerve and muscle. The mastless advocates, which included Jellicoe, replied that a mast always ran the risk of falling or being knocked overboard in battle and fouling the propellors. Besides, it was all useless top hamper. Another (unspoken) objection was that, if masts and rigging were kept, ships would continue to be judged solely on their sail drill and smartness aloft, and not by the accuracy of their shooting and the rapidity of their salvoes.

As a result of this controversy *Colossus* was ordered to convoy the masted ship *Impérieuse* to Gibraltar and back in the summer of 1886. The weather was very rough and Jellicoe observed the effects of different wave intervals on the two ships. In some sea states *Colossus* was rolling seventeen degrees each way and water was washing into her gun-ports, while *Impérieuse* was moving only a bare two degrees. At other times, when *Impérieuse* was rolling as much as twenty-five degrees each way, *Colossus* only rolled five degrees. It all depended on the length of the waves.

The 'balance chamber' was given a full trial and was not a success. It extended the full width of the ship and was half-filled with water, the idea being that the deadweight of inertia of the water would delay the ship rolling until the water, so to speak, 'caught up'. In practice this free surface water actually aggravated the rolling in certain sea conditions. The water sluicing to and fro and smashing against the ship's side each time put a tremendous strain on the plating at those points. As Captain Bridge said, 'After a rather exciting trial in heavy weather in the Bay of Biscay, it was found prudent to give up using it.' The warrant officers, whose mess was just above the balance chamber, were delighted. The sound of the water had kept them awake all night.

When *Colossus* returned to England she was guard ship for Cowes Regatta. Jellicoe landed two guns' crew teams ashore and ran a competition between them which was very popular with the public. This was one of the forerunners of the field gun competition held in later years at the Royal Tournament in the old Agricultural Hall in London. While *Colossus* was at Cowes the Queen asked to see one of the new gun turrets with their hydraulic loading. Part of the turret was dismantled so that the Queen could view the crew and the machinery more easily, but at the last moment she was indisposed and did not come. The Princess of Wales, later Queen Alexandra, came instead and, as they said, '. . . won the hearts of all on board'.

Because of the troubles with the guns *Colossus* spent what Bridge called 'many weary weeks' at Spithead, while modifications and trials were carried out. One cold day, when there was a gale blowing and a very strong tide running, a sailor fell overboard from one of the ship's boats; he was swept quickly away and it seemed probable he would drown. But Jellicoe jumped overboard and swam with what the Bridge called '. . . extraordinary vigour, breasted the waves continuously, and succeeded in reaching the man before the latter sank, and in keeping him afloat until a boat which I had dispatched picked them both up'. The sailor was unconscious when he was brought back on board, but Jellicoe '. . . smilingly received my congratulations and commendation and walked quickly to his cabin to put on dry clothes'. Oddly, Jellicoe received no Royal Humane Society's Medal or any other commendation for the rescue.

When *Colossus*' guns had been modified and strengthened, and approved for firing, she went to the Mediterranean to serve her commission. Normally, her Gunnery Officer would have been expected to go with her. But clearly the naval gods had already placed their thumbprint on Jellicoe's forehead. He was plucked out of the ship and appointed to *Excellent*, where he went in December 1886 as Experimental Officer, a post inaugurated during Fisher's time as captain. Even at this early stage of his career it seemed that Jellicoe was already being groomed for some special destiny.

As Experimental Officer Jellicoe was responsible for planning and supervising the trials and evaluation of new guns, mountings and equipment. He also had command of the gun vessel *Handy*, attached to *Excellent*, in which some of the trials were carried out. It was the perfect job for Jellicoe, who enjoyed the intellectual challenge and it also appealed to the painstaking, meticulous side of his nature. There was the novelty and excitement of new weapons. He attended the gunnery trials of every ship on commissioning and had the chance to go to

36

sea in *Handy* from time to time. The first trials of the new short calibre 13.5-inch gun were carried out in *Handy*. Jellicoe took her to Woolwich to have the gun fitted and then to Shoeburyness range for firing.

Fisher was Director of Ordnance at the Admiralty and was using every means in his power to press the Navy to develop the Elswick 30- and 70-pounder guns. During trials the weight of the projectiles was increased to 45 and 90 lb and the guns became known as the 4.7-inch and 6-inch. They were both tremendous advances on their predecessors: the 4.7-inch could fire ten rounds a minute, compared to the old 5-inch's two, and the new 6-inch could fire seven to eight rounds a minute, compared with the old 6-inch's one.

Jellicoe still played rugby football, until one particular match against Portsmouth Corinthians ended his career on the field. It was a very rough game: one side finished with only eleven players, the other with nine. One player nearly lost an ear and Jellicoe received a blow on his Adam's apple which so badly injured his larynx that he lost his voice completely for six weeks. He took a course of Turkish baths at Bournemouth and his voice returned enough for him to conduct his gun trials, uncharacteristically for a Gunnery Officer, in a whisper.

On 5 July 1887 Jellicoe was temporarily appointed to HMS *Mercury*, Captain Darwin, for the Golden Jubilee Review at Spithead and for the manoeuvres which followed it. She was a small cruiser of the Mersey class, 3,730 tons, 13 guns, with a complement of 276 officers and men.

The chief driving force behind the 1887 Review was Lord Charles Beresford, then Fourth Sea Lord, who saw it not only as a great naval occasion and a chance to show off the Navy's strength, but also as an opportunity to demonstrate the Navy's weakness. He was one of the very few naval officers to realise the power of the press, and he sensed a definite awakening of public interest in the Navy. Press and public could be harnessed to the Navy's advantage.

The Review was officially organized by the C-in-C Portsmouth, Admiral Sir George Willes, who had the advantage of having arranged a smaller review the year before for visitors to the Colonial and Indian Exhibition. But it was Beresford who had the order restricting guests on board ships rescinded, who got the number of official press passes doubled from fifty to a hundred, and who took parties of MPs around Portsmouth dockyard to show them some of the Navy deficiences. Even so, there were important errors in organization: for instance the tides on the day chosen, 23 July, prevented the largest ships coming up harbour until 9 p.m. – any visitors who wanted to land before that time would have to be ferried ashore at great inconvenience and expense.

It was decided that no ships would be brought home from foreign stations. Some twenty-five extra warships were commissioned in Portsmouth. They were largely what Rear-Admiral Sir Sidney Eardley-

Wilmot called 'a motley collection of ancient constructions'; many of them had a small coal capacity, slow speed and short range, obsolete armament and ineffective armour. Beresford himself called them 'absolutely useless'. Sir Edward Reid, the naval architect, told MPs that only a handful of the ships they could see were fit for war. Admiral Hewett VC was even more blunt: 'Most of what you see is ullage.'

To commission the ships at all, the Admiralty had to press into service what officers and men they could find, depleting one ship's company to make up another, so that the result was two inefficient ship's companies. Many of the officers and men were inexperienced and there were several embarrassing incidents. The Royal Yacht *Victoria and Albert*, with the German Crown Prince and Princess on board, collided with the troopship *Orontes* on 13 July. The ironclads *Black Prince* and *Agincourt* collided, so too did the notoriously unhandy *Ajax* with *Devastation* on 19 July. The *Daily News* observed: 'Foreign visitors ought to be kept out of the way until our bumping races of ironclads have come to an end.'

On 23 July, the day of the Review, there was a gun explosion in the gun-boat *Kite*, which killed one man and injured several others. It later transpired that the dead man had had only two days' training in weaponry before the Review and none at all on the type of breech-loading gun which had exploded. It was no wonder that the French naval attaché was not impressed by what he saw. He reported that it was all just a spectacle for the general public, and of no interest to the professional naval officer. It certainly was a spectacle. It was a lovely day of 'Queen's weather'. There were 128 ships present, with numerous tugs and small craft. Every ship was dressed with flags. The flagship *Inflexible* led a royal salute of 21 guns. The Royal Yacht steamed up and down the lines, and Her Majesty waved her handkerchief. Officers pushed visitors below so they would not clutter up the Queen's view of their ship, while the sailors manned the yards. It was 'significant, imposing and beautiful' said *The Times*; 'The people love their navy and believe in it,' said the *Daily Telegraph*.

The manoeuvres which followed attracted as much interest as the Review. The Navy got daily press coverage, which must have delighted Beresford, although not all the comment was favourable. An unopposed 'bombardment' of Falmouth by Admiral Fremantle aroused alarm about the vulnerability of English coastal towns to French attack. A correspondent writing 'A Landsman's Log' in *The Times* described the difficulties of 'A' Squadron:

Inflexible had four mishaps. *Collingwood* broke down altogether and could only proceed with one engine. The *Sultan* was detained for one hour by injuries to the inside of her condenser. The *Rattle-*

snake had to go into harbour for repairs, having smashed the collar of her eccentric. Two of the torpedo boats had at one time or another to run in for repairs. The *Minotaur*, *Monarch* and *Mercury* alone came out scatheless.

Jellicoe returned to *Excellent* at the end of August 1887. He was appointed to the senior staff in May 1888, with Percy Scott as the senior staff officer. Perhaps Jellicoe had been at Whale Island too long; he began to find the work 'rather tame and decidedly uninteresting' after the excitements and novelties of being experimental officer. However it was what is known as a 'promotion job', and Jellicoe was sure to be promoted commander in three years.

In August 1889, long before the three years were up, Fisher, who was still Director of Naval Ordnance, asked Jellicoe to come to the Admiralty as his assistant. Jellicoe was in a quandary; it was a great compliment to be asked, but he was almost certain of promotion where he was, while he could not be sure of it in a newly-created appointment at the Admiralty. Fisher solved the problem by writing a minute to the Board of Admiralty making a case for having the best brains available in the Navy for work in Whitehall. The Board replied with a special minute virtually guaranteeing that Jellicoe would be promoted as early as if he had stayed in *Excellent*.

The whole episode had been nicely calculated by Jellicoe. It was a bold and confident officer who hedged at accepting a new appointment on the grounds that it might prejudice a promotion which itself was not certain. He might have been thought presumptuous, as a mere lieutenant. He might even have destroyed his chance of promotion altogether.

Jellicoe went up to the Admiralty as assistant to the Director of Naval Ordnance in September 1889. Once again, with the charmed luck he had, he had arrived in the perfect job *au moment juste*. It was a time when big changes were in the air. Mr W. T. Stead, who had caused a naval 'panic' almost single-handed in 1884 with a series of articles on 'The Truth about the Navy by one who knows the facts' in the *Pall Mall Gazette*, was writing another series on 'The Needs of the Navy'. In that year, 1889, a Navy Defence Act was passed appropriating £21 million to the Navy, spread over seven years. A new programme of ship-building was begun, for ten new battleships, nine first-class cruisers and thirty-three second-class cruisers. Fisher's energetic intriguing had greatly assisted the wresting of control of the Navy's guns and mounting design from the War Office. The size of Fisher's achievement can actually be quantified: in March 1881 there was not a single breech-loading gun in the fleet; by the end of 1889 1,293 were mounted in ships, not including all manner of quick-firing guns.

Fisher worked very hard indeed himself and expected as much from others. Jellicoe never had Fisher's Machiavellian flair for intrigue and bringing pressure to bear where it would be most effective, but he learned a great deal from him about committee work and how best to marshal support for a case in the corridors of power in Whitehall. Jellicoe was kept to his desk until 11 p.m. most nights, but he had the mental capacity and the application to do paperwork for long hours.

But it was not all desk work. Fisher had a staff of only three: there were two commanders who were engaged on the routine work of examining returns from ships in commission, practice shoots, and training personnel, while Jellicoe dealt with new ideas and improvements in guns, ammunition, mountings, shells and how and where they were installed in the new ships which were being built. This meant that Jellicoe had to get out and about, and he travelled the country constantly, visiting shipyards, armament factories and ammunition depots. He had his reward when he was promoted Commander on 30 June 1891. At the end of that year Captain Arthur Knyvet Wilson asked him to go as his Commander in the battleship *Sans Pareil* in the Mediterranean Fleet.

Chapter 3

Arthur Knyvet Wilson's invitation to Jellicoe to join him in *Sans Pareil* was a most significant sign that Jellicoe was a coming man in the Navy. Normally a captain commissioning a new ship would have preferred an experienced commander, but Jellicoe was newly promoted and had been three years away from a full sea-going appointment. Wilson's request was therefore a tremendous compliment to Jellicoe's ability.

Captain Wilson was himself one of the best seamen of his day. He had first gone to sea in the line of battleship *Algiers* in the Crimean War; he had been wrecked in the frigate *Raleigh* under Keppel, off Macao in 1857, and had served in action on the River Peiho in 1858. He had won a Victoria Cross in hand-to-hand combat at the battle of El Teb in Egypt in February 1884 – where he had no official function but, as he said, he just walked up to the front to see what was happening and was on the spot when the British square broke. He was probably the foremost torpedo expert of the Navy, an inventive and resourceful man with several technical innovations to his credit. He drove others as hard as he drove himself, and thought nothing of sending a ship or fleet to sea on Christmas Day if he thought duty demanded it. Churchill, who was First Lord to Wilson's First Sea Lord during the First World War, said of him that, 'He was, without any exception, the most selfless man I have ever met or even read of. He wanted nothing and he feared nothing – absolutely nothing.' To Wilson, '. . . Everything was duty. It was not merely that nothing else mattered. There was nothing else.' The sailors called him 'Old 'Ard 'Art'.

Sans Pareil was a battleship of 10,470 tons, and yet another Victorian grotesque with her very low freeboard forward and her enormous single turret housing two gigantic 16.25-inch 110-ton guns, her humped bulky superstructure mounting six 6-inch guns each side, two funnels set abreast of each other, and another turret with one 10-inch 29-ton gun right aft. She was actually a somewhat retrograde step in design, after the Admiral class of *Collingwood* and others, laid down under the Northbrook programme in April 1884. She was launched in May 1887 but not completed, because of delays over her main armament, until July 1891, when she commissioned for the annual manoeuvres. She paid off again into reserve in August, and recommissioned for the Mediterranean Fleet at Chatham on 9 February 1892. She left England on 6 March with Dr White, the Director of Naval Construction, on board as a passenger to note her behaviour, and reached Malta on the sixteenth. After making good some defects, *Sans Pareil* was detached on an independent cruise to the Levant to work up her ship's company. It was a valuable opportunity to exercise drills and evolutions in slow time; in company with the fleet, *Sans Pareil* would have been expected to take her time in all things from the flagship, a very difficult thing for a new ship to do.

The rank of Commander is crucial in a naval officer's career. It is the first promotion by selection, thus the first to show that an officer might be anything out of the ordinary. It is high enough to give a man glimpses of where he might climb to, but low enough for him still to be struck down by bad luck or an unfortunate choice of captain.

As commander, Jellicoe was Wilson's second-in-command and acted as intermediary between the captain and the ship's company. He was responsible for the work, welfare and wellbeing of the officers and ship's company, in this case some 430 men. He took charge of the ship's internal organization, watch bills, cleanliness, minor punishments and drills. He was on deck early in the morning, when the hands first fell in, and on his feet until late at night, doing rounds of the ship to make sure that all was well. As president of the wardroom mess he also ruled the lives of the officers and consequently had a decisive effect on their morale and efficiency. A good commander could make even the most rigorous commission and the most demanding captain a pleasure to serve under. A bad commander could make a ship a hell afloat.

In May 1892 *Sans Pareil* returned to Malta to rejoin the fleet. The C-in-C was Vice-Admiral Sir George Tryon, flying his flag in *Sans Pareil*'s sister ship *Victoria*. Tryon was another able officer and outstanding seaman, with a strongly overbearing personality. In a Navy where large numbers of ships performed as a fleet, Tryon was brilliant. He delighted in ever more intricate maneouvres, setting up ever more seemingly irretrievable situations for his ships, and solving them with ever more ingenious formations. His manoeuvres were sometimes so ingenious that his second-in-command, Rear-Admiral Markham, flying his flag in *Camperdown*, admitted he was completely baffled by them.

Tryon kept such a tight grip on his fleet that individual captains were always glad to get away on their own and Wilson, as senior Captain, was given most chances. On 15 August *Sans Pareil*, with the cruisers *Australia* and *Phaeton*, detached from the fleet under his orders to visit Livorno, Spezia and Genoa, where they arrived on 3 September to represent Great Britain and the Royal Navy at a great international festival to commemorate the voyage of Christopher Columbus to the New World four hundred years earlier. They joined fifty ships from thirteen nations – Italian, British, Austrian, American, German, French, Spanish, Portuguese, Greek, Dutch, Argentine, Mexican and Romanian.

The King and Queen of Italy arrived on 8 September escorted by the Italian Fleet. For some six days the ships carried out a hectic programme of official visiting, inspections, receptions, balls and dinner parties in a whirl of protocol and ceremonial (by 14 September *Sans Pareil* herself had fired 6,968 rounds in gun salutes). Though as Commander of the senior British ship Jellicoe was almost constantly on deck to receive and bid farewell to distinguished visitors of all nationalities, he still kept a sharp eye cocked for any chance to improve his ship. For instance there was the matter of boats, for pulling and sailing in regattas.

Malta dockyard had fobbed *Sans Pareil* off with two pulling cutters, fitted with air casings and excellent as lifeboats, but they were heavy and hopeless for racing. For a Victorian ship's company this was a much more important point than it seems today – Regatta results mattered for a ship's reputation, and the morale of the sailors was much boosted by them. But for sailors to win, they had to believe they could win, and nobody in *Sans Pareil* believed they could ever win anything in those two boats.

At Genoa, *Sans Pareil* lay at anchor off the outer mole, but with her stern secured to the mole by wires. The cruiser *Australia* was lying alongside her. One evening the wind freshened and by the time the sun went down a gale was blowing. All *Sans Pareil*'s wires parted except one 3½-inch steel rope. Jellicoe could see that unless he took some action *Sans Pareil* and *Australia* would crash sides together. Seeing his chance, he ordered the two heavy cutters lowered between the ships to act as fenders and, with any luck, to be totally smashed in the process. This duly happened and Malta dockyard supplied *Sans Pareil* with two light mahogany cutters, ideal for racing. Jellicoe had done his part, but his crews rather failed in theirs – in the fleet regatta in the Levant that autumn *Sans Pareil* had one first and one second in the pulling races and one first in the sailing. *Sans Pareil*'s crews could not have failed for lack of fitness. Being an 'unmasted ship' she was fitted with steam winches for hoisting the large boats in and out. When the gear broke down Jellicoe improvised a system of tackles so that the boats could be hoisted by hand. This greatly pleased 'Old 'Ard 'Art' and he often ordered the boats hoisted by hand even when the winches were available. Other ships later copied Jellicoe's system.

At the end of the year Tryon asked for Jellicoe for his own flagship

Victoria when she recommissioned at Malta in April 1893. Though of course he agreed, Wilson was very much upset by the request. He thought it 'a great blow' to lose his 'very able Commander'. 'The penalty we pay', he wrote, 'for selecting the best man is that some Admiral is sure to walk off with him when he gets the chance. It is, however, a promotion for Jellicoe, as it puts him in a more prominent position.' Wilson's feelings were understandable. He had chosen Jellicoe himself, suffered the inevitable hesitations and mistakes of a new and inexperienced commander, and, just as Jellicoe was getting into his considerable stride, the C-in-C stepped in and pinched him. When Wilson himself became an admiral and commanded the Channel Fleet he would never allow any application for any officer in another ship in the fleet to fill a vacancy in the flagship. Wilson strongly disapproved of the practice, which he thought no better than poaching.

Jellicoe himself had mixed feelings about leaving; in later years he said, 'I spent a happy year in the *Sans Pareil*,' but to refuse an invitation to the flagship would have been professional madness. Jellicoe was sent home to bring out *Victoria*'s new crew in *Achilles*, which he joined on 2 March 1893. *Victoria* recommissioned at Malta on 1 April 1893. Some said later that the signalman hoisted the ensign upside down that first morning, to start the ship's run of bad luck.

In *Victoria* Jellicoe not only had the normal duties of commander but, like everybody else on board, he also had Vice-Admiral Sir George Tryon. Tryon was a big man physically, with a loud voice, in which he frequently expressed his opinions. He thought deeply about the Service, had ideas in advance of his time, and might one day have been First Sea Lord. He was well known in social circles in Malta and at home in London. His staff had mostly served with him before. Men such as Maurice Bourke, his staff captain, Thomas Hawkins-Smith, his staff commander, and Lieutenant Lord Gillford, his flag lieutenant, thought they knew how to handle the admiral, although it always had to be borne in mind in the Victorian Navy that an officer's mental powers were deemed to increase with his rank, so that an admiral, *ex officio*, was more intelligent and knowledgeable than a captain, who was himself by virtue of his own seniority more intelligent than a commander. A man who tried conclusions with Tryon had to be very sure indeed of his ground, and even then it was nearly always wiser to hold one's peace.

Sir George Tryon took his fleet to sea at the end of May for a cruise in the eastern Mediterranean, calling at Marmarice, a harbour opposite the island of Rhodes, Haifa and then at Beirut. The Mediterranean Fleet then consisted of eight battleships, *Victoria*, *Sans Pareil*, *Edinburgh*, *Inflexible*, *Nile*, *Dreadnought*, *Collingwood* and

Camperdown (flag of Rear-Admiral Markham); three first-class armoured cruisers, *Amphion*, *Edgar* and *Phaeton*, and two third-class cruisers, *Fearless* and *Barham*. The fleet anchored in two lines off Beirut, Tryon heading the inshore line in *Victoria*, Markham the offshore line in *Camperdown*.

Tryon's fleet was as mixed as any in the Victorian navy. Of the eight battleships, *Victoria* and *San Pareil* were sister ships and comparatively modern, but the six others were all different; *Inflexible* had been flagship at the bombardment of Alexandria and still mounted muzzle-loaders, as did *Dreadnought*. The ships also varied greatly in manoeuvrability – *Dreadnought*'s turning circle was 430 yards, but *Edinburgh*, the unhandiest ship in the fleet, needed about four cables (800 yards).

At 10 a.m. on 22 June 1893 the fleet weighed anchor. *Victoria* headed the inshore division of herself, *Nile*, *Dreadnought*, *Inflexible*, *Collingwood* and *Phaeton*. *Camperdown* led the offshore division, with *Edinburgh*, *Sans Pareil*, *Edgar* and *Amphion*. As soon as the anchors were weighed – all ships weighed together – Tryon turned his fleet towards the sea as if to steam out in divisions, line abreast, *Camperdown*'s division leading.

At once Tryon carried out one of those unusual and spectacular manoeuvres with which he loved to astonish and mystify his captains. Tryon first took his division in line abreast through the intervals of Markham's division. Once clear, his own division steamed on a steady course at six knots. Meanwhile, Markham's division was ordered to steam on a slightly diverging course at seven and a half knots; as a result, Markham's division began to catch up. But by the time it had done so, its diverging course had taken it out to port, so that *Camperdown* eventually took station exactly abeam and to port of *Phaeton*, the port-hand ship of Tryon's division. All eleven ships then steamed in single line abreast northwards along the coast of Lebanon towards Tripoli, where they were due to arrive and anchor at 4 p.m. that afternoon. The form-up manoeuvre had been so satisfyingly contrived, and had been carried out so faultlessly – by captains who had not been briefed beforehand – that once again everybody believed that Tryon's hand had not lost its cunning.

At that time Jellicoe was laid up in his cabin with a very bad bout of dysentery – a disease endemic in Malta. Sufferers continued to drink the island's goats' milk which years later was found to be the very vector by which the disease's organisms were transmitted.

Shortly after midday, the flagship signalled the 'anchoring signal' for the day. The fleet was to anchor 'in columns of divisions – guides of columns [there was only one other column guide, *Camperdown*] north-west of the guide of the fleet [*Victoria*] ships in column north-east of their guides. The columns were to be two cables [400 yards] apart, the ships each two cables apart from each other.' This was a perfectly normal anchoring signal, indicating a normal anchoring pattern for the fleet. But at 2.20 p.m. the signal was made for the fleet to form columns of divisions in line ahead, columns disposed to port and six cables apart. This meant that the fleet steamed in two lines, *Camperdown* leading her division of five ships six cables (1,200 yards) to port of *Victoria*, leading her division of six ships.

This signal began to arouse misgivings in some of the ships. To change formation from the steaming formation to that signalled for anchoring, the two columns would have to turn inwards on each other. But the columns were only 1,200 yards apart and the minimum turning circle (because of *Edinburgh*) was 1,600 yards – twice 800. For the object to be achieved as Tryon had signalled, the two columns would have had to be at least ten cables or 2000 yards apart. As it was, the situation was fraught with danger. Tryon's intentions, as signalled, were basically unsound and unseamanlike.

This was realized at once by Captain Gerard Noel in *Nile*, immediately behind *Victoria*, who was sure there had been some error and signalled for a repeat of the anchoring signal. 'I thought we had taken it in wrong,' he said. It was repeated and, 'I still thought there was something wrong. . . .'

Two signals for the manoeuvre to be carried out were hoisted at 3.27 p.m. They were, 'Second division [Markham] alter course in succession 16 points to starboard', and 'First division [Tryon] alter course in succession 16 points to port', both preserving the order of the division. Captain Arthur Moore in *Dreadnought*, two ships behind *Victoria*, remarked, 'Now we shall see something interesting.' He did not mean it sarcastically. Like everybody else, he genuinely thought Tryon could pull something out of his sleeve. Some of the other captains thought that possibly Tryon meant *Camperdown* to come round and steam outside him. Jenkins, in *Collingwood*, concluded that because the manoeuvre as signalled was impossible it must have been made wrongly to Tryon's division and they would surely turn to starboard, in other words away from Markham's division.

Whether Tryon suffered a mental blackout or a momentary aberration in which he confused turning radius with diameter, or whether he was even more convinced of his own infallibility and even more irascible after lunch-time wine, nobody will ever know. His staff were certainly alarmed; something very similar had once happened before, in another ship, and they had managed to get the admiral to change his mind. Bourke was uneasy; he thought that *Camperdown* would go very close to *Victoria* but was reassured that '. . . the Commander-in-Chief had some way out of it'. But Hawkins-Smith

46

remonstrated with his chief until he was hotly told to hold his tongue. Tryon was not a man to argue with, and every ship except *Camperdown* acknowledged the signal by repeating it and hoisting the flags close up to the yard-arm indicating that the message was received and understood. It would have been a very bold man to press a point with Tryon.

Certainly, Markham in *Camperdown* was not such a man. He was no coward – he was a very competent officer with a distinguished record in Arctic exploration, but he admitted that he was mentally out-gunned by his superior. When the signal was reported to him, Markham said, 'It's impossible – it's an impracticable manoeuvre.' He told his flag-lieutenant to repeat the signal, but only 'at the dip', or half-way up to the yard-arm, showing that the signal had been seen but was not understood. At the same time he ordered the message semaphored: 'Do you wish the evolution to be performed as indicated by the signal?' (Wilson, in *Sans Pareil*, the second ship behind *Camperdown*, saw the semaphoring and decided it was Tryon and Markham deciding who should pass outside each other.)

While *Camperdown* was semaphoring, *Victoria* semaphored back: 'What are you waiting for?' Such was the grip Tryon had on the minds of his officers that even now Markham thought of a solution. Clearly the signal for his column to turn would be delayed by a few seconds, giving his column time to stand on a little further and then turn *outside* the commander-in-chief and form up on his port side. (This was not what the signal actually said, and would have meant Markham's column anchoring closer inshore than the c-in-c's, which would be unlikely. But in the short time available to Markham it was not a bad interpretation.) Convinced in spite of himself, Markham ordered the repeat to be hauled close up.

Both hoists were hauled down simultaneously (which was the actual signal to begin) at 3.31 p.m. and both leading ships put their helms over, *Camperdown* twenty-eight degrees to starboard, *Victoria* hard over to thirty-four degrees to port. Both ironclads headed in towards each other, their rams gliding through the water like giant fists ready to strike.

Even now disaster could have been avoided. But Markham believed, and said in evidence, that it would have been 'utterly wrong' to alter so as to pass outside the flagship. Tryon himself seems to have been stunned by the magnitude of his error as soon as it became obvious to him what he had done. Hawkins-Smith had always known it was going to be a close thing, whatever happened, and on his own initiative had ordered helm 'hard a starboard' (in the old parlance hard a *port*) as soon as the turning signals had been hauled down. Bourke, too, could see things going wrong and said to Tryon, 'We shall be very close to that ship, sir. May I go astern with the ports crew?' But Tryon stood silently, his eyes fixed on *Camperdown*, as though he were frozen to the spot. Bourke had to repeat his request loudly and with more urgency. It was not until the two ships were end-on to each other, and rapidly closing, that Tryon gave his permission. Shortly afterwards Bourke ordered, 'Full astern both engines.' 'Full astern both' had also been ordered in *Camperdown* (although in fact it would have been better had both ships gone full astern with their inner screws and full *ahead* with their outer; this would have brought them both round more quickly and, though they would have still collided, it would have been broadside on). Both ships also passed the pipe, 'Close watertight doors.'

Victoria had more helm on than *Camperdown*, and had swung round further at the moment of impact, so that it was *Camperdown* who struck *Victoria* on the starboard bow about ten feet abaft the anchor. Both ships were still making about five or six knots so that *Camperdown* delivered *Victoria* a colossal blow, at an angle of about sixty-eight degrees, which forced *Victoria* bodily sideways about seventy feet. *Camperdown*'s ram, some twelve feet below the water, penetrated *Victoria*'s hull to a depth of about nine feet.

Both ships still had way on, so that as they began to swing together *Camperdown*'s ram was wrenched laterally, enlarging the gap, and breaching the sideplating where it was connected to two important watertight bulkheads, just abaft the point of impact. When *Camperdown* slid free and began to pass aft down *Victoria*'s side, she had inflicted a wound nearly thirty feet across and extending to eighteen feet below the waterline, a great gash of over a hundred square feet through which tons of water flooded in. With the majority of watertight doors still open, because there had not yet been time to shut them, the blow was mortal and though efforts were made at once to bring up and rig a collision mat, *Victoria* began to fill with water forward and to heel over to starboard.

At the time of the collision Jellicoe was still in bed in his cabin, very seriously ill with his bout of Malta fever. That morning he had a temperature of 103 degrees. When he first felt the impact he did not think it serious, but got up at once and put on trousers and a coat over his pyjamas. His marine servant came in to tell him that there had been a collision and to help him up the ladders to the upper deck. Jellicoe passed a platoon of marines formed up in fours on the main deck, and their officer, Lieutenant Farquharson RM, noticed how pale and changed Jellicoe was by his illness. However, helped by Gunner Savage RMA, Jellicoe reached the upper deck and climbed to the after bridge, which was his post at 'collision stations', intending to supervise the hoisting out of the ship's boats. Lieutenant Leveson, the gunnery officer, was already there, but by the time Jellicoe reached the bridge all hydraulic power had already failed and nothing could be done.

Forward, the party rigging the collision mat had already been overtaken by the water flooding along *Victoria*'s fo'c'sle and had to abandon the attempt. The ship was still making way, and was heading towards the shore in the hope of breaching her in shallow water inshore.

Victoria's list to starboard was still rapidly increasing. Up on the bridge Tryon said to a young midshipman, 'Don't stay here, youngster, go to a boat.' But before the midshipman could obey or anybody could make a move the ship gave a sudden ominous lurch, much further over to starboard. It was only some eight minutes since the collision, but the ship already had about 2000 tons of water as extra dead weight forward. The whole of the fore-deck was submerged as far as the superstructure. Water began to pour in through scores of open scuttles and ventilators, until it was lapping at the forward turret embrasures. The ship was losing way and the quartermaster reported that there was no longer any power on the steering. It was becoming clear that *Victoria* would never reach shallow water.

On deck the ship's company fell in by divisions in an orderly manner. They had to brace themselves against the heeling deck, but they preserved perfect discipline. The ship's padre, the Reverend Samuel Morris, a Welshman, called out, 'Steady men, steady', and steady they were. The word to come on deck was never passed to the engine-room and boiler-room crews. Looking down through the iron gratings, the men could be seen still at their posts in the cavernous machinery spaces.

The list had reached more than twenty degrees and it was almost impossible to stand up without holding on to some support when the ship suddenly seemed to give up and turned right over. Captain Noel, on *Nile*'s bridge only about a hundred yards away from *Victoria*, said that it '. . . was almost momentary. She seemed to turn over in an incredibly short space of time.' The torpedo lieutenant, Herbert Heath, called out 'Jump, jump!' and the ranks on deck broke. It was every man for himself.

On the after bridge Jellicoe had said to Leveson, 'We had better go down the ship's side as she turns over.' They reached the jackstay of the torpedo nets, level with the upper deck, when the ship finally turned over and they actually walked down the ship's port side and into the water, where Jellicoe began to swim away to avoid being sucked down.

Many men, including almost the whole of the engine-room department, never got away from *Victoria*. Some were entangled in wires and jackstays and were dragged down with her. Others were killed by the smashing blows of the giant propellors, still revolving as the ship

49

turned over and sank. Shortly afterwards, there was an enormous water disturbance on the surface. Captain Wilson, watching horror-struck through his telescope on *Sans Pareil*'s bridge, said,

> A great rush of air came from the stern ports and as the water entered the funnels as she was turning over there was something like an explosion of steam, apparently due to the water getting into the furnaces. After she sunk, large quantities of air came up, keeping the centre over where the ship had gone down clear, and spreading the men and wreckage in a circle around.

As the ship went down, great quantities of debris rushed to the surface. Boats, fittings, gratings, wooden spars and baulks of timber, the ship's main derrick, furniture, fragments and debris of all kinds boiled on the surface for some minutes, killing or injuring many more men who might have got away.

Jellicoe was sucked down some way and was conscious of bodies passing him as he came to the surface and began to swim away. 'I felt the suction of her sinking,' he wrote, 'but was not drawn down. I noticed one of our steamboats near me bottom up with some officers and men holding on to her. I managed to get rid of my clothes in the water as they hampered me in my rather weak state.' Jellicoe had been in bed 'on slops' for seven days and was almost exhausted by his exertions when Cadet Roberts-West swam up to him and asked if he needed any help. 'I said I would be glad if I might put a hand on his shoulder, which I did.'

At 3.30 that afternoon the Mediterranean Fleet had been steaming in station in perfect order, on a bright sunny afternoon with a calm sea and visibility almost unlimited. Ten minutes later the flagship had disappeared and the remaining ships were milling about in disorder. Tryon had signalled all boats to keep clear, presumably to avoid them being sucked down as well, but some captains disregarded the order and sent boats away. Jellicoe was picked up by a boat from *Nile* and taken on board her. Meanwhile, a few hundred yards away, Midship-man Hugh Tweedie in one of *Dreadnought*'s whalers was trying to drag somebody's sea-chest into the boat, but it was too heavy. When he broke it open with an oar, the clothes he took out were marked 'J. Jellicoe'. But the silver inkstand Jellicoe won at Dartmouth went down with the ship (although the Admiralty later replaced it). So, too, did a photograph of his then fiancée. The ducking, Jellicoe claimed, cured him of his infatuation.

It also seemed to cure him of his fever. His temperature went down and he felt very much better. 'The curious thing', he wrote to his mother next day, 'is that my temperature today is normal, so the

50

ducking did me good.' On the twenty-third Jellicoe was transferred at Wilson's request to *Sans Pareil*, where his younger brother Edmund had been an appalled spectator of the disaster. 'I can't tell you my feelings', he wrote to Mrs Jellicoe, 'when I saw the *Victoria* going down and I knew that dear Jack was practically unable to help himself being so weak.' Of Roberts-West he said, 'It was very brave of him to help Jack and he ought to get a medal for it. How dreadful it would have been for Lou if Jack had not been saved and you would hardly have got over the shock.'

Twenty-two officers, including Tryon himself, and 336 men were lost in *Victoria*. The surviving twenty-nine officers, including Jellicoe, and 262 men were all court-martialled according to Service custom at a court-martial which began on board *Hibernia* at Malta on 17 July and lasted until the twenty-seventh. Jellicoe and most of the survivors were not called to give evidence. The chief 'trial', if it could be called that, was of Markham and some of the other officers in *Victoria* and *Camperdown*. All were acquitted, although few reputations were enhanced, and nobody liked *Camperdown*, thenceforth nicknamed 'Crampherdown', to steam astern of them afterwards. Roberts-West, who very probably saved Jellicoe's life, never really recovered from his experience of the immersion and his exertions in the water. His naval career petered out and much later, in the First World War, Jellicoe managed to save Roberts-West from the consequences of a failure to carry out his duty (which Jellicoe attributed to the after-effects of that day in *Victoria*).

Shortly after the tragedy, broadsheets of a long narrative poem suitable for recitation, of a kind very popular in the nineteenth century, went on sale, price one penny. Called 'The Loss of H.M.S. *Victoria*', it was written by W.A. Eaton (author of 'The Fireman's Wedding', 'The Ruined Home'. etc., etc.,) and was 'Recited by all the best Elocutionists' and 'No Special Permission is Required'.

> The sun shone bright, the gentle breeze
> > Rippled the sunny waters:
> Who would have thought four hundred men
> > Would soon find watery graves?

After a few such scene-setting stanzas, the reciter would come crisply to the point:

> The brave ship *Camperdown* steamed round,
> > (I cannot tell you how);
> Her ram struck the *Victoria*
> > And crashed into her bow.

51

The details of the accident were generally accurate:

> The Admiral upon the bridge,
>   Had her head turned for shore
> But now the water rushing in,
>   Told him all was o'er.
>
> Collision mats were of no use
>   To keep the water out;
> The crew with perfect discipline
>   Moved rapidly about.
>
> Now came the order 'Save yourselves,
>   The ship is going down;
> Bring up the sick and prisoners,
>   It's hard to let them drown.'
>
> The weight of the water pouring in –
>   The cannon on that side,
> Dragged down the vessel till she sank,
>   Head foremost in the tide.

Of the hundreds of men in *Victoria*, the reciter picked out one:

> Commander Jellicoe lay sick,
>   Of fever, in his berth,
> He felt he could not lie and die
>   Like a wild beast run to earth.
>
> He rushed on deck, and outward sprang
>   Into the boiling sea;
> For, where the vessel overturned,
>   The sea whirled dizzily.
>
> He might have sunk beneath the wave,
>   But a comrade struggling there,
> Flung his arm round him, cheered him on,
>   Where calmer waters were.

Jellicoe himself made a remarkable recovery. Captain I.G. Christie, an army officer who travelled home in the same ship, later wrote that Jellicoe '. . . was not, like some officers, inclined to mope and be down in the mouth, but was all over the ship doing physical jerks with a party of midshipmen who were taking passage to England'.

He did have some reaction, suffering from severe rheumatism when he went home on sick leave, but was fit again in October 1893 when he was appointed commander of the new battleship *Ramillies* which commissioned on the seventeenth. She was one of the Royal Sovereign class, designed by Sir William White FRS, laid down at Thomson's Clydebank in August 1890 and completed in March 1892. She displaced 14,000 tons, had a complement of 712 officers and men, a main armament of four 13.5-inch guns in barbettes, seven torpedo tubes and 38 other quick-firing guns mounted in the superstructure.

The Royal Sovereigns were handsome ships, with a high freeboard and reasonable living space for the sailors, but they rolled abominably. *Revenge*, the first of the class, once rolled so badly on passage to Gibraltar that the bridge superstructure was actually displaced and jammed the steering gear. At Malta, *Ramillies* first went into dock to have bilge keels fitted; she then went to Corfu for a 'shakedown' cruise, after which she returned to Malta to hoist the flag of C-in-C, Admiral Sir Michael Culme Seymour Bart, KCB, who had come out to the Mediterranean after Tryon's death.

Ramillies was therefore yet another of the flagships in which Jellicoe served, thus keeping him under a kind of service spotlight throughout his sea-going career. There was some justification for the remarks of Admiral Chambers, who came out to the Mediterranean as a commander some years later, that, 'Generally speaking, the coming men of the Navy formed two big cliques alternating between service in the Mediterranean and service at the Admiralty. One only has to examine the Navy Lists to see how the same names appeared year after year in the Mediterranean flagships gradually climbing the ladder of promotion.'

Certainly there was a hand-picked look about *Ramillies'* officers. For Jellicoe there were some very familiar faces among them: the captain was Francis Bridgeman, who had been commander in the *Excellent* when Jellicoe was on the junior staff; Herbert Heath and Arthur Leveson, Jellicoe's 'old ships' from *Victoria*, were once again torpedo officer and gunnery officer. These officers, with *Ramillies'* first lieutenant, Edward Inglefield, her watchkeepers Lieutenants Edwyn Alexander-Sinclair, Lionel Halsey, Godfrey Paine and H.G. Sandeman, and Seymour's flag lieutenant, Hugh Evan-Thomas, all reached flag rank. Most of them were full admirals, and Osmond Brock, who later relieved Leveson, became an admiral of the fleet.

Jellicoe himself spoke very highly of them all. They were in his opinion '. . . a complement of officers second to none in the Service – all most delightful companions and most excellent officers'. So too were the warrant officers, in particular the boatswain with the superbly apt name of Mr Trice, 'a splendid Warrant Officer and a delightful personality'.

In those days the Mediterranean Fleet was in the last decade of its Victorian peacetime splendour. Under Culme-Seymour the fleet moved around on its seasonal cruises to the Levant, to Italian ports, to the French Riviera, in stately progress like a Tudor monarch's court. Hulls were painted gleaming black, with white topping, and super-structure was dazzling white, with buff funnels and brick-coloured masts and yards. There was the fiercest competition between ships, to be the smartest in appearance inside and out, to be the quickest at drills and evolutions, to win the most races at the fleet regatta. The pressure of competition produced an equally fierce pride in the ship.

As commander, Jellicoe ran a very taut ship. He paid attention to the minutest detail, and was willing to work long hours. He was rewarded by success in every sphere. The ship did well at coaling, and in drills, in regattas, or shooting on the rifle range, in field gun's crew competitions and in the fleet athletic meetings. The officers 'shone at polo and other games and other sports'. Jellicoe's reminiscences of that time bring back the flavour of a golden era, which even by the outbreak of the First World War seemed as remote as the Crusades.

Jellicoe's main rival was his old friend Stanley Colville, commander of the second flagship *Trafalgar*, but some measure of the competition Jellicoe had to surmount is given by one particular *coup* by Cecil Burney, another of Jellicoe's friends, commander of the first-class cruiser *Hawke*. Having burnished every possible piece of metal on and around *Hawke*'s quarterdeck, Burney looked round for fresh conquests. His eyes lit on the two enormous anchor davits, on the fo'c'sle. He decided they should also be burnished – a colossal task, rarely, if ever, undertaken by any ship before. Burney piped the whole ship's company aft and told them that when the anchor davits shone like silver he would call the watch every afternoon for a fort-night – in other words all except the watch on deck would have the afternoon off.

Everyone in *Hawke* from the captain of the maintop to the cook's mate took his turn at burnishing during his spare time, and in an astoundingly short space both of the huge davits gleamed like silver. However at this point Culme-Seymour decided that this was taking spit and polish too far and ordered the davits to be painted white, which everyone in *Hawke* thought was the meanest jealousy on the flagship's part.

Unfortunately the Mediterranean Fleet's gunnery was nowhere near on a par with its paintwork. 'Gunnery efficiency in the modern sense was, I fear non-existent,' Jellicoe said, 'an annual competition prize firing was carried out off Malta at a range of some 1,600 yards,' but

54

'. . . gunnery took rather a back seat in considering the smartness and efficiency of a ship's company'.

This was the state of affairs Percy Scott, the peppery apostle of gunnery, found when he was appointed captain of the cruiser *Scylla* in May 1896 and joined the Mediterranean Fleet in June. It was six years since Percy Scott had last been in the Mediterranean – he had been commander of the battleship *Edinburgh* from 1886 to 1890 – and when he returned he expected, perhaps naively, to find 'great improvements in the routine, in gunnery and in signalling'. But to his surprise, 'Everything was just as it had been; no advance had been made in any way, except in the housemaiding of the ships. The state of the paintwork was the one and only idea. To be the cleanest ship in the fleet was still the objective for every one; nothing else mattered.'

Percy Scott was describing a most peculiar paradox, for normally in the Navy the cleanest ship will also be the best at gunnery. The Victorian Navy had achieved a state in which competence and initiative had become almost totally divorced from fighting efficiency. According to Scott, the quarter's allowance of ammunition '. . . had to be expended somehow'. The custom was to make the signal, 'Spread for target practice – expend a quarter's ammunition, and rejoin the fleet at a certain time.' Ships then radiated in all directions and held their own target practices. How the ammunition was expended did not matter; the important consideration was to get the practice over and rejoin the flagship at the time specified.

Jellicoe was particularly susceptible to Malta fever and had several bouts of it. Midway through the commission, when *Ramillies* was lying off Venice, Jellicoe was so ill that he had to be taken in the Admiral's yacht *Surprise* back to Malta, where of course he was put on a diet of milk. Eventually Jellicoe was sent home in a P & O steamer, so weak that he had to be carried on board. It is a measure of Jellicoe's standing in *Ramillies* that he was not invalided and replaced by another commander, but his place was kept open for him until he returned.

Malta fever indirectly cost Jellicoe the chance to go on an expedition up the Nile with Kitchener in 1896, where he would have joined in action such stormy petrels as Beatty and Beresford. Kitchener actually thought of Jellicoe and telegraphed to Malta to ask for his services to command one of the gun-boats. Unfortunately the telegram arrived while *Ramillies* was at sea carrying out target practice. Culme-Seymour replied, without consulting Jellicoe, that he could not be spared. When Jellicoe returned to harbour and found out what had happened he protested, but Culme-Seymour told him he felt sure that if he had allowed Jellicoe to go he would have gone down with fever. Jellicoe was bitterly disappointed; Colville went in Jellicoe's place, was severely wounded, but distinguished himself in action and was promoted captain, so that he became senior to Jellicoe.

But when he was not sick with Malta fever Jellicoe kept himself in tremendous physical condition. Culme-Seymour was also a considerable games player, and he and Jellicoe, playing as partners, won the Fleet Rackets Cup. Jellicoe played golf with the admiral at Salonika, on a course laid out by the Navy. He played tennis for the ship's team and won several sailing races at fleet regattas. It was a happy and successful commission, which Jellicoe always recalled with pride. 'After three years of a most happy commission I found it a real pleasure to meet men who had served in the *Ramillies* as we all shared the pride with which we remembered our time on board.'

Jellicoe came home at the end of *Ramillies'* commission and was promoted to Captain on 1 January 1897. After leave he was appointed on 9 January a member of the Ordnance Committee, a body which dealt with such matters relating to guns, mountings and ammunition which were still common to both navy and army. The chairman was a Royal Artillery officer, while the members were naval and army officers. The committee's boardroom was at Woolwich arsenal, but the members visited ordnance factories around the country and the firing trial ranges at Shoeburyness.

At first Jellicoe had rooms in London but later Major George Aston RMA, who was an old friend of Jellicoe's and had served with him in *Victoria* and in *Ramillies*, invited him to share his rooms at the Royal Naval College, Greenwich.

George Aston, who was Professor of Fortifications at the College, was another most able officer (he later rose to be a major general) with a keen and original mind. He and Jellicoe suited each other very well; they used each other as sounding boards for their own ideas, each acting in turn as devil's advocate against the other's theories.

Throughout his life John Jellicoe had a great talent for forming and keeping such friendships. He was simple and easy of approach, was never jealous, and had the gift of enthusiasm. His relationship with George Aston was a paradigm of his friendships with so many men. They shared their work and their play; in 1897 the two friends went on a holiday expedition to the Orkneys and Shetland Islands. They stayed in boarding houses, hired a boat and caught sea-trout, and walked most of the way round the shoreline of Scapa Flow, neither of them dreaming what a part this magnificently bleak sea and landscape would play in their professional lives.

Through an introduction (very probably by August Cayzer), the two went to stay with Sir George and Lady Cayzer at Delguise in Perthshire. Sir Charles was founder and co-owner of Cayzer, Irvine & Co. Ltd of Glasgow, and later of the Clan Line. He also had daughters

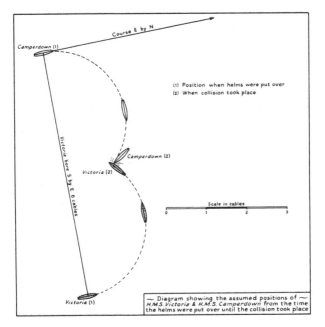

Course E by N

Camperdown (1)

(1) Position when helms were put over
(2) When collision took place

Victoria bore S by E 6 cables

Camperdown (2)

Victoria (2)

Scale in cables

0   1   2   3

Victoria (1)

— Diagram showing the assumed positions of —
H.M.S. Victoria & H.M.S. Camperdown from the time
the helms were put over until the collision took place

staying at home, in particular his second daughter, a very pretty girl called Gwendoline.

John Jellicoe was nearing forty, and Gwendoline Cayzer was not yet twenty. He was a post captain in Her Majesty's Navy, she was a teenager who had never moved out of her family circle – she had only just recently come out of the schoolroom and put up her hair. She was the daughter of a rich man; John Jellicoe had only his pay. She had met sea captains before, employees of her father's who had dinner with the family and paid their respects to the daughters of the house. But to Gwendoline none of them had the attraction of this small, wiry, sun-tanned man, obviously on top of his profession, brimming with nervous energy. His rank gave him a tremendous glamour – and he had been shipwrecked in the *Victoria*, and had fought in Egypt, when Gwendoline was still a child. With the big, bluff, cheery marine providing the perfect foil for Jellicoe, amid scenes of Victorian Scotland which could have been painted by Landseer and described by Sir Walter Scott, a mutual attraction began to blossom. Jellicoe later said that he found his visit to the Cayzers '. . . one of the greatest pleasures, and I left with the happiest recollection of the whole family'. Jellicoe was due, indeed overdue, to get engaged in the rank of captain. But in the meantime, towards the end of 1897, Vice-Admiral Sir Edward Seymour, who was just about to go out to China as c-in-c, asked Jellicoe to be his flag captain. It was another professional opportunity, and Jellicoe gladly accepted.

57

Chapter 4

Vice-Admiral Sir Edward Hobart Seymour came of a very distinguished naval family: three of his forebears had been admirals and commanders-in-chief; Culme-Seymour was his cousin. As a midshipman he had served in the Crimean War and, under his uncle Admiral Sir Michael Seymour, took part in the naval brigade's operations in Canton in 1857 (the other midshipman in his battery was Arthur Knyvet Wilson). As a lieutenant he took part in the British–French assault on the Taku forts in 1860 and again on the same forts during the Teiping Rebellion of 1862. Seymour was a very capable and competent officer, but cautious and reliable rather than spectacular; he always did his duty as he saw it. 'I never could understand why anyone minds taking responsibility,' he once wrote. 'You have only to do what seems proper, and if it turns out badly it is the fault of Nature for not having made you cleverer.' This admirably fatalistic view carried Seymour imperturbably through several campaigns, three of them in China (in each of which the Navy went to war and took the Taku forts), and a very long service career in which he rose to be admiral of the fleet. His rather severe features and black beard, gave him a somewhat austere appearance. He seemed distant in his manner and difficult to approach, but was in fact a very kindly and considerate man who got on very well with Jellicoe.

Seymour and his flag captain left England by steamer early in 1898. At Colombo they changed ships to a mail steamer which took them as far as Hong Kong; the admiral's yacht *Alacrity* then took them up to Chusan, to relieve Admiral Sir Arthur Buller in the flagship *Centurion*. *Centurion* and her sister ship *Barfleur*, the second flagship on the China Station at that time, were small battleships of 10,500 tons, built to be cheaper 'second-class' warships (although the mere passage of time has always provided the Navy with all the 'second-class' warships it has ever needed). They were specially designed as flagships in hot climates, with a shallower draught for the passage of some of the larger Chinese rivers, and wood-and-copper sheathed hulls to combat the exuberance of tropical marine growths. They had triple expansion engines which gave them about eighteen knots, with good endurance on a coal capacity which was not unusually large. They were armed with four 10-inch and ten 4.7-inch guns, and had a complement of 650 officers and men.

An admiral would only ask one of the most promising junior captains on the list to be his flag captain, so for Jellicoe *Centurion* was another compliment and another opportunity. As flag captain he had command of a larger and newer ship than his seniority would normally have entitled him to, and with the admiral's flag and authority behind him he acted as the admiral's deputy in routine matters connected with the administration of the fleet. (He also had to give up his living quarters to the admiral, which a more senior captain would have objected to.) At that time, the flag captain also acted as the admiral's chief-of-staff.

The political situation in China at that time was particularly complicated, even for China. After China's defeat by Japan in 1896 the European powers scrambled unscrupulously for territory concessions and markets. Chinese waters contained British, American, Russian, French, German, Italian and Austrian warships, all representing their national interests. But though China was a beaten and militarily prostrate nation, ominous political currents were stirring beneath the surface. Chinese scholars had been to Europe and returned to spread the word of socialism; the new principles were intellectually seductive to some, dangerously subversive to others. So there were in China those who were ready to rebel to bring in a new order, and others just as ready to use violence to preserve the old.

Seymour's first visit in April 1898 was to Chifu, a good harbour on the Shantung peninsula, on the gulf of Pe-chi-li in northern China. It was a time of international uneasiness because of a tense relationship with Russia, and this was a sensitive area because negotiations were then in progress for a British lease of the harbour and surrounds of Wei-hai-wei just along the coast. Already at Chifu was the second-in-command, Rear Admiral C.C. Penrose Fitzgerald (known as 'Rough' Fitzgerald) flying his flag in *Barfleur* (who also had a nickname, 'Far-Bluer', because of the unusual blue tinge in the paint on her ship's side). In company were the battleship *Victorious*, the cruisers *Endymion*, *Narcissus*, *Grafton* and *Iphigenia*, and the gun-boat *Pygmy*.

Wei-hai-wei was leased from the Chinese on 2 May 1898; it had actually been held by the Japanese who, to save face, had turned the place over to the Chinese on 1 May so that they did not have to hand it over directly to the British. Mr Hopkins, the consul at Chifu, went to Wei-hai-wei in *Narcissus* to arrange the transfer. Bluejackets and marines were landed to keep order, and Lieutenant Ernest Gaunt of *Narcissus* was appointed town mayor of the island of Liu Kingtao – Wei-hai-wei itself was actually a fortified town on the mainland, opposite the island.

The batteries, the island, town and dockyard had all been badly damaged during the Japanese siege and capture of the place. When Prince Henry of Prussia arrived in his flagship *Deutschland* on 30 May, he walked through the town with Seymour and Jellicoe and remarked that, 'It looks as if there had been an earthquake and all the people had run away.'

Centurion had arrived at Wei-hai-wei on 25 May 1898, and as chief-of-staff Jellicoe had at once to set about the task of setting up what was virtually a new, self-contained British colony. Contracts had to be placed for the repair of buildings and for the construction of a barracks for the marines on the mainland, a canteen for the sailors, a house for the mayor, a hospital, a pavilion for the recreation ground, and many other stores and facilities. There were Chinese soldiers who were supposed to prevent looting, but when in June some outlying camps on the mainland were raided by about 2000 bandits from the interior the Chinese soldiers actually helped the looters. Jellicoe landed a strong party from the fleet, in route-marching order, to occupy the camps and restore law and order. Among all his other undertakings Jellicoe also had a cricket ground laid out, with a coconut matting pitch. As he admitted, it was a ground which encouraged heavy scoring, with a hard pitch and a lightning-fast outfield. In a match between a team from *Centurion* and the destroyer *Handy* against *Victorious* and *Narcissus*, which took place on the usually ominous date for him of 21 June, Jellicoe scored 120 runs in an hour, his first-ever century.

They returned to Wei-hai-wei to resume the usual squadron routine. In the regatta on 31 August Jellicoe sailed his gig into second place for the Admiral's Cup and fourth in the Rear-Admiral's Cup. But fleet routine in China was always liable to be disrupted by sudden scares and incidents, messages of alarm, hurried raising of steam and putting to sea. In September there was a palace revolution in Peking. The Empress, alarmed by what she considered to be the radical views of the Emperor, deposed him and took over the reins of government herself.

Sir Claude MacDonald, the British minister in Peking, telegraphed Seymour to meet him at Taku, the forts guarding the entrance to the Pei Ho, the great waterway leading up-country to Tientsin and Peking. Those Taku forts ran like a *leitmotiv* through Victorian naval history, and were the scenes of many desperate fights, casualties and pro-motions, after which everything always returned as it was before. *Centurion* raised steam in two hours and, when passing Chifu, signalled by mast-head flashing lamp to *Victorious*, *Narcissus*, *Hermione* and *Fame* to join her at Taku as soon as possible. But by the time *Centurion* arrived Sir Claude had already left for Tientsin and he later sent a telegram to say that all was quiet.

Hardly had this furore died down when the Fashoda Incident took place, in October 1898. A Captain Marchand hoisted the French flag on territory in the Sudan claimed by Great Britain. So sensitive were relations between Britain and France that for a time war seemed likely, and on 29 October the Admiralty telegraphed Seymour to inform him that the situation was critical and forecasting that Russia would very probably side with France if war broke out.

Jellicoe advised Seymour that the whole China Squadron should assemble at Hong Kong, of which Great Britain had just obtained a ninety-nine year lease. He argued that it was useless to try and defend Wei-hai-wei; provided Hong Kong was held, Wei-hai-wei could eventually be recaptured. The country's chief trade was in the south. The only possible way to assemble a fleet bigger than the combined French and Russian squadrons was for all the British ships to go to Hong Kong, otherwise the British fleet might be defeated in detail and Wei-hai-wei and Hong Kong would be lost for good. The ships all went to Hong Kong to await developments. But meanwhile Kitchener had met Marchand at Fashoda and requested him to lower the French flag. He did so, the crisis was over, and by mid-November the China fleet had returned to Wei-hai-wei. Jellicoe's advice was sound, although it was never tested in war.

Jellicoe's autobiographical notes still preserve the flavour of life on board a man-of-war on a remote station at the turn of the century. It was certainly a full life. Jellicoe believed that the devil made work for idle hands to do, but all work and no play made Jolly Jack a dull lad. With the incessant drills there were also sightseeing trips; there were landing parties, but there were also children's parties; there was work on board, but there was a canteen and an officers' club ashore. Interest was kept up by making ship compete against ship at everything from gun drill to the seamen boys' football team.

At the end of November Seymour went to Shanghai in *Alacrity*, leaving Jellicoe to take *Centurion* on a cruise to Japan, where he was glad to meet his old friend Colville, now in *Barfleur*. They did a lot of bicycling, saw mixed Japanese bathing, and 'a very good geisha dance'. Afterwards *Centurion* went down to Hong Kong for Christmas. On Christmas Day 1898 the admiral and his flag captain made the traditional midday tour of *Centurion*'s messdecks to inspect the decorations and wish every mess a merry Christmas. Ahead of them the band played 'The Roast Beef of Old England' and 'Farewell and Adieu'. The men had gone to great trouble to decorate their living spaces for the festival, with coloured paper-chains, streamers, cut-out patterns and garlands. Every mess had its placard wishing everyone a merry Christmas. One mess had painstakingly carved hard ships' biscuits into letters which, threaded on a piece of spun yarn, spelled out 'Merry Christmas'. Another showed a certain macabre wit: a loaf of bread transfixed upon a bayonet, with the slogan 'The Staff Of Life On The Point Of Death.' For popular officers the Christmas round was a pleasant ordeal. So many pieces of cake, and figgy duff, and sips of rum were offered that it was difficult to stay sober and keep on walking, and at the same time avoid giving offence.

On New Year's Eve Lord Charles Beresford, who was on a commercial mission to China, and Dr Morrison, *The Times* correspondent, dined with the C-in-C to see in the New Year of 1899. At midnight the New Year was rung in by the youngest sailor on board ringing sixteen bells on the ship's bell. Prince Henry and the German squadron were also in Hong Kong; the German ships were all illuminated and fired off coloured rockets, and there was a great deal of cheering and singing.

The festivities continued into the New Year. *Centurion* gave a ball which was a great success once the question of precedence between HE the Governor of Hong Kong and Prince Henry was solved (the result was apparently a compromise). Jellicoe gave ten midshipmen tickets for the theatre. One of them wrote in his diary: 'Captain Jellicoe seems to please everybody because he is so polite, even to a humble midshipman.' This same humble midshipman also noted in his diary that, 'Captain Jellicoe has lately taken to bicycle rides with a select few of the fair sex, who afterwards come off to supper in his cabin.'

Jellicoe always admired the efficiency, cleanliness and internal layout of the German ships, and he developed a great friendship with Prince Henry. The Prince challenged Jellicoe to a shooting match on the rifle range on Stonecutters Island. Standing at 200 yards, Jellicoe beat the Prince fifty to thirty-six (out of a possible sixty); sitting at 300 yards, they tied thirty-five points each. Shooting was to remain one of Jellicoe's greatest sporting interests all his life.

Jellicoe recorded the happenings and oddities of a varied life. At Macao he ate frogs for the first time. At Canton he saw the coffin of the Viceroy's second wife which had lain for six years while lacquer was applied to it; the lacquer was already reputed to be two inches thick. At Manila he met Admiral Dewey, the victor over the Spanish in that same bay in 1898. At Port Hamilton they did prize-firing before returning to Wei-hai-wei, where in June Jellicoe won the squadron lawn tennis tournament. In a cricket match 600 runs were scored in one day, eighty-four of them by Jellicoe's younger brother Edmund, [who died on the China Station in 1905 while in command of the destroyer *Whiting*].

With the exception of his 1898 century at Wei-hai-wei, the time of the summer solstice was unlucky for Jellicoe, and so it proved again in 1899. The squadron left for Port Hamilton on 20 June and early on the twenty-first the weather closed in. At dinner the admiral happened to remark that the Bishop of Korea had asked him to raise a subscription in the squadron for the Korean Mission. Jellicoe said he would sooner subscribe to lighthouses on some of the islands; the remark was meant as a joke but it soon took on a new significance.

As a precaution in the very low visibility, Jellicoe had stationed a destroyer on each bow as a lookout. The rest of the squadron were in line ahead, led by *Centurion*, steering east along the coast. At 2.15 a.m. on 22 June the destroyer *Fame*, stationed on the port bow, reported land in sight to port of her. The squadron course was therefore altered three points to starboard, from east to south-east by east. But soon afterwards the starboard wing destroyer *Whiting* reported land ahead and, shortly afterwards, land to starboard of her. Clearly the squadron was steaming straight towards land. Jellicoe asked the Admiral for permission to alter course through 180 degrees and the squadron retired, feeling their way out of danger. It had been a very lucky escape. The entire China squadron had been within a few minutes of driving onshore. Jellicoe's precautions in posting the destroyers had saved his ships. In the morning it was found that a northerly current had pushed the squadron some ten miles ahead of their dead reckoning, whereas the sailing directions for that coast said that, if there was indeed any current there, it would be southerly. Jellicoe noted the date.

As this affair occurred on June 22nd the day on which, in 1893, H.M.S. *Victoria* was sunk in collision with the *Camperdown*, I began to look upon that day in the year as an unlucky one for me. Later, during the Boxer trouble in 1900, I was wounded at Peitsang on June 21st, and this rather confirmed my idea of this particular period in June as being unlucky. For this reason I was not very anxious to take the Grand Fleet to sea about June 22nd during the War unless some real necessity arose for so doing. Such is superstition!!

There was another navigational mishap a few weeks later when the squadron visited Korniloff Bay in Russian Tartary. The cruiser *Bonaventure*, commanded by Captain R.A.J. Montgomerie, had been ordered to berth separately. On her way she struck some uncharted rocks some 600 yards outside the five fathom (100 foot depth) line. She stuck fast and with a heavy swell running it seemed that she might well begin to break up. The rest of the squadron anchored as planned, and sent away boats to lay out anchors ahead, astern, on the bows and quarters of the stranded ships. The whole squadron co-operated to help their stricken member. As Seymour said, these sort of accidents '. . . have their bright side', because they showed '. . . the immense zeal in our service'. As he said there was '. . . no excitement of action with an enemy, no hope of promotion or distinction for war service, no prospect of prize money, or other reward exists; but the strongest emulation is there to save a ship of their squadron and assist her unfortunate crew'.

Jellicoe himself went off to help Montgomerie with salvage operations and he was on board *Bonaventure* for thirty-six hours, he and Colville eventually relieving each other as the hours went by. Luckily the swell went down, *Bonaventure* was not a large ship, and her hull was sheathed in wood which helped to protect her and made it easier to patch her up. She was 'tipped' by placing as much weight as possible aft so as to bring her bows up and at last, after four days' hard work, she was towed safely off. Seymour held a court-martial which decided that the fault lay with the survey of the bay. The squadron did their own survey and found many more uncharted rocks. It seemed a miracle that an accident had not happened before.

The China Station was vast and it was not possible for the c-in-c to visit it all, even in three years, but Seymour did his best, keeping his squadron constantly on the move. At Barracouta Bay in Russia Jellicoe caught a 33 lb salmon in a total catch of 186 lb of salmon and sea-trout. He shot pheasant, snipe and duck at Douglas Inlet in Korea. He was received by the Mikado and drank wine with the King of Siam; he had a cold buffet supper with a governor in Korea, consisting of meat (which somebody told Jellicoe was really dog, so he left it) and hard-boiled eggs, chicken, raw chestnuts, champagne and Kirin beer. At Amoy there was a dance on board the German warship *Hansa*, where Jellicoe met the Japanese consul's wife in her national dress, '. . . the first Japanese lady I had met at any entertainment. She looked very attractive.'

Jellicoe was pleased to meet remote relations at unexpected places. At Chifu there was Emmie Scott, wife of Bishop Scott, and a cousin of Jellicoe's. At Bangkok, the financial adviser to the Siamese government was Mr Rivett Carnac, and Jellicoe '. . . was interested to find out that his mother was a Miss Jellicoe, a cousin of mine'. Jellicoe dined on board the Royal Yacht on his fortieth birthday, 5 December 1899. Later he discussed Belleville boilers and Whitehead torpedoes with Prince Damrong, who '. . . had real knowledge of all subjects'.

The squadron fulfilled a never-ending programme of visits and functions. From Bangkok they went to Singapore, to Sarawak and Brunei, to Manila and back to Hong Kong, where Jellicoe played cricket for the Navy and made nineteen runs, not out. Off Wei-hai-wei they passed through the outer fringes of a typhoon; although she was many miles from the storm centre, *Centurion* was battened down fore and aft and the word was passed that anyone who fell overboard could not be picked up.

Centurion spent New Year 1900 at Hong Kong and stayed there

64

longer than usual while the ship's company carried out a musketry course and several exercises with landing parties on the mainland. By pure chance these preparations could not have been better timed, for Admiral Seymour was quite wrong in saying that there was '. . . no excitement of action with an enemy, no hope of promotion or distinction for war service'. He and his squadron were just about to undertake some of the most active service of any sailors in the Navy's history.

National defeat had encouraged national resentment in China against foreigners. The aim was to expel the foreigners, the 'Hairy Ones', from China. Rumours spread, and were believed, that all such misfortunes as droughts, floods and disease were signs of the gods' anger that China had allowed the foreigner to enter. Foreign intrusions, such as railways and factory machinery, were causing the spirits to deprive hundreds of thousands of Chinese coolies of employment. Railway construction had disturbed many graves which, in normal Chinese fashion, were scattered over the countryside so that inevitably some were desecrated by the iron horse. The educated Chinese hated Christianity in particular because it undermined ancestor worship. The proposed reforms aroused the hostility of those who had most to lose by them. At the same time the Empress's reactionary policies frustrated the aspirations of the young and middle classes who had hoped to profit from reforms.

Weak in armed forces, China turned to stealth and guerilla warfare where open force had failed. National unrest manifested itself in regional secret societies; the Society of the Gun, of the Sword, of the Knife, and in Shantung province the I-ho Chüan, the 'Fists of Patriotic Harmony', better known as the Boxers. Originally formed to overthrow the Manchu Dynasty, but suborned by the Empress and diverted to the expulsion of foreigners, the Boxers believed that, if properly initiated, they were immune to European bullets. If any of them were struck down they would rise again in triumph to continue the fight against their enemies. With a morale born of such faith, and while the peasants in the countryside silently approved, the Boxers began a reign of terror. Regular Imperial troops, who were supposed to keep law and order, first connived at and later actually assisted in Boxer outrages.

Until the very last moment, when the Boxer rebellion exploded on them, the European diplomatic community in Peking remained astoundingly ignorant of what was going on in the countryside, although there had been ominous signs since the beginning of the year. On 29 April 1900, the 'first day of the fourth moon', a curiously worded, almost incantatory Boxer placard was posted up in West City, Peking: 'Wait for three times three or nine times nine, nine times nine or three times three – then shall the devils meet their doom. The will of heaven is that the telegraph wires be first cut, then the railways torn up, and then shall the foreign devils be decapitated. If my tidings are false,' the placard concluded, 'may I be destroyed by the five thunder bolts.'

The tidings were not false. On 19 May the *North China Herald* published a letter which, even though the legation staffs thought it greatly exaggerated, should still have been taken into account. The writer gave details of a plan to crush all foreigners, saying that the Court favoured the plan, the Manchu armies and the Imperial Guard, together with the I-ho-Chüan, would all take part, that all the upper classes in China knew of the plan and approved, and that the legations had had dust thrown in their eyes (which was true).

On 28 May, when the China Squadron was at Wei-hai-wei, Seymour received a telegram from Sir Claude MacDonald asking for a guard to be sent up to the legations in Peking. Next day Seymour learned that Fengtai, the station next to Peking on the railway up from Tientsin, and five other stations on the line to Hankow, had all been burnt. By 30 May the cruiser *Orlando*, the sloop *Algerine* and thirteen vessels of other nationalities had arrived off the Taku forts. *Orlando*, *Algerine* and the other vessels sent up a party of marines to Peking, 337 men strong, including seventy-nine British marines, three sailors from *Orlando* and a Nordenfelt quick-firing gun.

Although he had not much hard information, Seymour was growing uneasy about the general situation. As a precaution he took all his ships to Taku, where they could be ready for any emergency. He himself arrived in *Centurion* with *Whiting* in company on 1 June, to join the international squadron of French, German, American, Austrian, Italian and Japanese ships which had also gathered off Taku. A huge mud bar across the mouth of the Pei Ho river estuary prevented any ship drawing more than 12 feet from crossing, and larger ships in any case had to anchor miles offshore. To get troops from the ships to Tientsin it was necessary to embark them in small boats and make a passage of some two hours through the gulf of Pe-chi-li, under the guns of the Taku forts at the entrance to the Pei Ho and up-river for some forty miles. Since the countryside was hostile on both banks it was a long and extremely dangerous passage.

When he arrived off Taku, Seymour had telegraphed to the minister in Peking that he could send up another 200 marines and bluejackets if required. The minister replied the next day that the marines already sent had entered Peking quietly and unmolested, and affairs generally were much more peaceful. The reply was in fact much too optimistic; indeed the legation staffs, isolated in Peking, seem all along to have been remarkably obtuse about the dangers that faced them. They were still sending reassuring telegrams when the countryside for miles around was in a state of uproar, communications were breaking down, missionaries and Chinese christian converts were being kidnapped and murdered, and mission stations and railway stations were being burned. Waving their flags bearing the inscription '*Feng Chi Mieh Kiao*' ('By Imperial Command exterminate the Church') the Boxers were being organized for the offensive; some were sent to Peking, some to attack missionaries and Chinese christians, and others to stay and prepare to defend their own homes and villages against the foreign devils.

Seymour had no official status, but he was the senior officer afloat and took over all charge by general consent – in any case, none of the other admirals flying their flags off the Pei Ho pressed their own claims to lead in his stead. On 3 June Seymour landed at Tongku, above Taku, to see for himself, and learned that there had been murders and other outrages in the province. The next day he sent a field gun's crew from *Centurion* to relieve the ten men of *Algerine* who had been there nearly a week (the absence of ten men was a serious handicap to a small ship) and on the fifth reinforced *Algerine*, lying just below Taku, with 100 men from *Centurion*.

Meanwhile in Peking itself foreign representatives from the various legations held a meeting and decided that those nations which had warships in the Pei Ho should telegraph to their respective governments asking that the naval forces should relieve Peking, if it were cut off and the anti-foreign party should get the upper hand, as it seemed very likely to do. When Lord Salisbury signalled this request to Seymour, on behalf of the British government, Seymour replied that it was unwise to '. . . distress ships for men' (that is, to render ships inefficient by taking away their men). Seymour suggested sending troops up from Hong Kong, using the cruiser *Terrible* as a troopship.

After a conference of senior officers on board *Centurion* on 5 June, Seymour sent Jellicoe up to Tientsin to decide the best way of taking a naval brigade up to Peking, if it became necessary. Clearly the road, which was no more than a rough cart track, was not feasible; the river was possible, but it was shallow and winding and the journey would take a long time. But there was also the railway – it was only seventy miles from Tientsin to Peking, and troops could be in the city by rail in a matter of hours.

The legations in Peking were still extraordinarily out of touch with reality. It was known in Peking on 8 June that Boxers had burned railway bridges at Yangtsun, about twenty miles from Tientsin, that the railway line was out and, worse still, that Imperial troops under General Nieh, who were supposed to be protecting the line, had returned to their camp. Yet on the afternoon of 9 June, when Jellicoe left Tientsin to return to Tongku, he was assured by the legation that the railway was still intact.

In fact, not only was this information quite wrong but the situation in Peking had deteriorated that day. There were riots in the city and an attack on a party of students attached to the British legation, who only escaped by firing on their attackers. The grandstand on the racecourse, a place very much associated with foreigners in the Chinese mind, was burned down. A Chinese Christian was roasted in the ashes.

When Jellicoe reached Tongku that evening he was called to the telephone and told by Mr Carles, the British consul in Tientsin, that he had heard from Sir Claude MacDonald that unless help were sent urgently to the legations it would be too late. The Dowager Empress was saying openly that foreigners must be expelled from Peking. Regular troops were awaiting orders to attack the legations.

Jellicoe was astonished by this news, which went against everything the legation had been saying earlier that day, but he reacted very quickly. He sent a signal by searchlight to *Centurion* down-river: 'Very serious news, submit landing party be prepared at once.' He saw the head of the Tug and Lighter Company and arranged for all available tugs and lighters to be sent down river as soon as the tide permitted. He sent Commander Charles Granville of *Centurion* to the Railway Company to tell them to have trains ready to transport a thousand men by dawn on 10 June. In a few hours, and from a standing start, Jellicoe had made all the preliminary preparations for landing a large naval brigade on foreign soil. At 9 p.m. he himself embarked in a launch lent by the Americans and, with a pilot, went down-river. When he passed *Whiting* and *Fame* anchored in the stream he dropped off the pilot in *Whiting* and told both destroyer captains to raise steam at once. At 11.30 he arrived on board *Centurion* to tell the admiral what he had done.

Jellicoe had assumed that a naval brigade would be sent ashore, but in fact the matter was not as simple as that. Besides *Centurion*, Seymour had with him the cruisers *Orlando*, *Endymion* and *Aurora*, and by disembarking large numbers of sailors and marines he might be putting those four ships at risk. After all, the Navy's main business was afloat. Seymour's first duty was to his ships, which might have to put to sea at any moment to safeguard British interests somewhere else. Throughout the nineteenth century the Admiralty were always reluctant to use highly trained specialist sailors ashore as infantry in foreign parts. But Seymour knew that European, American and Japanese citizens, including women and children, were being menaced in Peking. They were defended by about three hundred marines against thousands of rioting Chinese. In any case, Seymour reckoned that he had only to deal with an undisciplined rabble of Boxers, armed only with the rudimentary weapons they could scrape together.

At a conference in *Centurion* earlier that day, attended by senior naval officers of the nationalities present, Seymour had read them Sir Claude MacDonald's alarming telegram and said that he was prepared to land the maximum available force and that he hoped they would co-operate. He would lead the force himself, with Jellicoe as his chief-of-staff. Seymour was not afraid of responsibility and to him his duty seemed absolutely clear. Although his decision to dispatch a relief force up to Peking has been criticized in the light of later knowledge, clearly at the time he did the right thing.

Shortly after midnight the sailors and marines began to muster on the upper decks of their ships for the issue of arms, ammunition and webbing equipment. Every man wore boots and gaiters and carried hard rations and a water-bottle. Field guns' crews and rifle platoons were detailed off; officers were allocated their duties; the doctor and his staff prepared field dressings and first aid equipment. This was a job the Navy knew well. They had landed scores of naval brigades in the nineteenth century, and at that very time a large naval brigade was on active service ashore in the Boer War.

By 1 a.m. the landing party, with two field guns and provisions and water for two days, had embarked in a tug which arrived alongside *Centurion*. The landing parties from *Endymion* and *Aurora* embarked in *Fame* and in their own boats, to be towed up-river. Jellicoe's arrangements were working well. The British contingent were able to go up-river on that tide, but the other nationalities had to wait until the next.

The British reached Tongku at 4 a.m. and occupied the first train, which moved off at 5 a.m. and reached Tientsin at 7.30. They were joined by another two trains and later by a fourth train. The total strength of Seymour's expeditionary force was 116 officers and 1,956 men, and nineteen guns – British, German, Russian, French, American, Italian, Japanese and Austrian. The largest contingent was the British, with sixty-eight officers, 640 seamen, 213 marines and twelve guns, the smallest the Austrian with one officer and twenty-four sailors. The expedition also included Mr Clive Bigham, honorary attaché to the Peking legation, as intelligence officer; Mr Archibald Currie, C.E. of the Peking–Tientsin Railway, as engineer; and Mr C.W. Campbell, British consul in Wuchow, as interpreter. There were also a hundred Chinese coolies. A fifth and last train carried supplies, tools and emergency gear such as spare sleepers.

Tientsin station was new and smart, but the expeditionary force felt the glowering hostility of the Chinese all around them. However, the trip would not take long. As Clive Bigham wrote, they '. . . looked forward to a journey of a few hours perhaps, or at the most a day'.

With well over two thousand men, five locomotives and over a hundred coaches and trucks, it was a considerable force which eventually moved off to the north, across a vast, hot, dusty plain, shrouded in heat haze. As the sun rose the temperature climbed to 104 degrees. The weather had been dry for months and a hot wind blew dust everywhere. Up to Yangtsun, twenty miles north-west of Tientsin, where the railway crossed the River Peiho on a massive iron bridge, the journey was uneventful. The locomotives were watered. Regular Chinese troops in the neighbourhood seemed friendly or at least neutral. However, north of Yangtsun the line was damaged and there were frequent stoppages for repairs. Dead bodies of Boxers lay by the track, which suggested that Imperial troops had been defending the railway. That evening the force stopped at Lofa, some miles north of Yangtsun, and there the third and fourth trains with Germans, Russians and French joined the party, to bring Seymour's expeditionary force up to full strength.

Thirty men were left to guard Lofa, where a fort was built and christened Fort Endymion, while the main party pressed on in the morning; 11 June was uneventful and the expectations that the naval force would be able to reach Peking without much ado seemed to be vindicated. At 6 p.m. there was a first brush with a handful of Boxers who made menacing passes and a couple of charges at the trains but were soon driven off.

On 12 June the trains reached Langfang, less than thirty miles from Peking, where there were signs of Boxer activity. The station building was badly damaged, rails torn up, holes dug in the permanent way and the water tanks destroyed, so that the locomotives had to be watered by sailors forming long lines from the wells and passing buckets from hand to hand. The wells were thought to be poisoned, so no water could be drunk without first being boiled. The hot, searing wind from the Gobi Desert shrivelled the skin, dried every leaf and blew fine, choking dust into every crevice of the trains. When the trains moved, the sailors sat in rows sweating in the intense heat, with their neckerchiefs tied over their mouths. They spent the day watering the engines, or working on the line, or keeping guard. At night they slept as they could on the bare wooden boards of the compartments. Many preferred to sleep on the sand in the open. Jellicoe and Clive Bigham shared a saddle, using it as a pillow.

On 12 June a Chinese on a donkey brought bad news. The Imperial Army were preparing to resist the expeditionary force at the south-eastern gate to Peking. But first the force had to get to Peking and that was growing ever more difficult. Lieutenant Gordon Smith of *Aurora* was sent on ahead with forty-five men and two days' provisions to try and reach Antung, thirteen miles nearer Peking. He bivouacked in a village five miles further on that night but was attacked next morning by about 450 Boxers. They were driven off, but in so doing Smith's party used up most of their ammunition and had to retire to the trains.

70

At Langfang, meanwhile, the state of the line was so bad that it was clear the force would have to stay for some time while repairs were made. Another fort was built, called Fort Gefion, after the German ship whose sailors were left behind to man it.

The whole expedition was daily becoming more difficult and dangerous. It was obviously impossible to protect the whole line from Tientsin to Peking with the forces available; all Seymour could do was to try to safeguard the line back to Lofa and hope that General Nieh's troops would protect the rest. While repairs went on at Langfang, the engines had to go back to Lofa for water. A company of British marines had another brush with the Boxers and drove them off.

On 14 June Seymour wrote to Sir Claude MacDonald from Langfang: 'Am confident of entering city. Hope in a few days.' A postscript added at 10 p.m. was much less sanguine, but concluded: 'All will yet be well.' The reason for Seymour's loss of confidence was a sharp engagement with the Boxers. It was easily the most serious thrust so far and, but for some luck and some quick thinking by Jellicoe, it might have been much worse.

The place where the trains had halted was not good for defence. Some quite thick copses of birch and alder came down within thirty yards of the line and there was a village not far away. Hidden by the trees and favourable 'dead ground', and aided by some very poor watchkeeping, the Boxers crept to within a short distance of the trains before leaping to their feet and beginning their charge. A picket of nine Italians was completely surprised and lost five men before they could get back. Lieutenant J.L. Fownes Luttrell was having a wash with another officer at a well 200 yards away when they heard the alarm. Neither of them was armed and it was '. . . only by doing a record quarter of a mile' that they got back in front of the Boxers who were covering the ground at terrifying speed, waving their weapons and yelling: 'Kill, kill, kill!'

The sailors had been having their midday dinner and were caught in an unready, unbuckled state. Jellicoe reacted first and had a Maxim gun mounted on a truck at the front of the train, which opened fire as the Boxers advanced. Bigham wrote:

They came on us in a ragged line, advancing at the double from a village some quarter of a mile to the left flank. Not more than a couple of hundred, armed with swords, spears, gingals (two man blunderbusses) and rifles, many of them being quite boys. To anyone who had been some little time in China it was an almost incredible sight, for there was no sign of fear or hesitation, and these were not 'fanatical braves' or the trained soldiers of the Empress, but the quiet peace-loving peasantry — the countryside in arms against the foreigner. As they approached they dropped to their knees, lifting up their hands to heaven to invoke the God of War. Then they charged until they dropped again as our volleys began to tell. In twenty minutes they were in full retreat, leaving some sixty dead on the field.

But it was an anxious twenty minutes while it lasted. With their red ribbons and head-bands showing they were true initiates, the Boxers came on waving swords and pikes, jog-trotting into the machine-gun fire. Their leaders sang, danced and gesticulated in front of their men. Some collapsed when hit, and others kowtowed, actually going through the ritual of immunization and being shot dead while they were doing it. The sailors thought it was slaughter to shoot human beings down in this extraordinary manner.

Several Boxers had to be shot and stopped, literally dead in their tracks, or their impetus would have carried them on. Some staggered on after several bullets. Once down, they shammed dead until their opponent had passed, when they leaped up with fresh cries of 'Kill, kill, kill!' One midshipman was hit on the breast-bone by a sword stroke from a Boxer warrior who jumped up with a savage cry as the young man was passing. Luckily the sword point had been broken off in an earlier fight. The Boxers seemed as immune to pain as they thought themselves to death. They tried to bite or strike those who bent down to offer them first aid. An apparent corpse would suddenly leap up and swing a heavy two-handled sword.

The attack never got past the first train. The Boxer dead lay in rows, in heaps, all around. The five bodies of the Italian picket were re-covered, already disgustingly mutilated.

When Bigham pointed out the rows of Boxer dead to his Chinese servant, the man showed that it was not only the Boxers who believed they were immune to European bullets and that, if they were struck down, they would be whisked away to fly up in the night and join their ancestors in glory. 'These', said the man, when he was shown some badly wounded Boxer prisoners, 'are not *real* Boxers, only make-believe; or, if they are real, in a few days they will get up healed, disappear miraculously, and then come and fight again.' Seymour and his officers began to realize that a campaign against opponents with these beliefs was going to be a dispiriting business.

These feelings deepened at 5.30 that afternoon when a messenger arrived on a rail-trolley from Lofa to say that Fort Endymion was being attacked by a large number of Boxers. Admiral Seymour took the rearmost train back and helped the defenders repel a really dangerous assault by well over two thousand yelling Boxers. About a hundred Boxers were killed, against two of *Endymion*'s sailors wounded, one

72

mortally. Afterwards, the admiral came back to Langfang that evening to continue his letter to Sir Claude MacDonald in less rosy terms.

The advance to Peking had now come to a complete stop. No mileage at all had been achieved in the last two days. It was obvious to Jellicoe that it was not going to be possible to rush a relief force to Peking in the face of these sporadic attacks even by such an ill-organized rabble. The whole expedition had been mounted on incorrect intelligence, and launched in far too optimistic a spirit. Had Seymour's force faced a properly led and planned counter-offensive, it might well have been wiped out. On 15 June Jellicoe and his opposite number in the Imperial German Navy, Captain von Usedom (who became Jellicoe's great friend) reorganized the manning of the trains: the British and Americans were in train No. 1, British and Japanese in No. 2, German, Russians and Austrians in No. 3, French and Italians in No. 4, with the coolies and engineering repair staff still in No. 5.

It was at this critical middle part of the expedition that Jellicoe showed his tremendous worth as chief-of-staff and as commander of the British naval contingent. He was never down-hearted; he conveyed the sailors' indomitable cheerfulness to the c-in-c and represented the admiral's optimism to the sailors. He was the most admirable go-between – he co-operated with the officers of the other nationalities, joking away international tensions between the various parties, and soothing ruffled feelings. He was a superb organizer, always on the spot, whether it was a machine gun to be assembled in position or a working party to manhandle sleepers. His lifelong passion for physical fitness paid off yet again. No matter how hot the sun, how dry the wind, how short the water or how long the march, Jellicoe was always there, with his quick step and his urgent command.

An impression of Jellicoe in China was written by Mr Whittall of the *Pall Mall Gazette*, who accompanied the expedition as a press correspondent and first met Jellicoe on the station platform at Tientsin, before the trains first set out on their journey:

It was to Captain Jellicoe that I was referred for permission to accompany the relieving force, and I can see him now as he put a few terse questions to me before granting the required permit. A man below middle height, alert, with that in the calm brown eyes which spoke of decision and a serene confidence in himself, not the confidence of the oversure, but that of a real leader of men. A man whose features would have been unpleasantly hard but for the lurking humour of the eyes and for certain humourous lines about the mouth that on occasion could take the likeness of a steel trap. A man to trust instinctively and one to like from the beginning. Those were my first impressions of him as he stood that June morning watching the troop-trains discharge their freights on the dusty North China platform. Later, when I came to know him, he inspired me with the same feeling of affection with which he was regarded by everyone with whom he had occasion to come into close contact. There was, and is, a magnetism about the man which stamps the personality of him who is indeed a commander, rather than one who commands.

The critical day, when all Jellicoe's forebodings began to be fulfilled, arrived on 16 June. A train was sent back under Lieutenant zur See Hilmers to fetch supplies from Tientsin. Hilmers returned in the evening to report that he had not been able to reach Tientsin – the line to Lofa had been damaged, but not seriously; the line beyond Lofa, which was supposed to have been guarded by Imperial Chinese troops, had been completely destroyed. Seymour's line of communication was cut off, and the expedition could no longer think of relieving Peking. In fact, unless stores and ammunition could be replenished, the expeditionary force could not stay for much longer where they were.

On Sunday 17 June the line was repaired enough for No. 1 train to run back through Lofa to Yangtsun, which was completely destroyed. Boxers in the town prevented the townspeople from supplying the expeditionary force with anything. Food was short, and the water ration was cut to two pints per man per day for all purposes. Seymour was about to give up the relief of Peking when on the eighteenth he received another plea for help from the British and French ministers there. He therefore asked the Germans to push forward again and hold the line as far as Langfang, but another large bridge had been destroyed and it was beyond the capabilities of Seymour's force to repair it. The relief could not go forward, and as the days passed it began to seem that they could not go back either.

Later on 18 June events took an even more ominous turn. While retreating from Langfang von Usedom's sailors were attacked by Boxers and detachments of troops from the regular Chinese army, who were now openly siding with the Boxers. The attack by some four thousand Boxers and Imperial troops was the most serious the expeditionary force had yet sustained – casualties were seven European killed and fifty-seven wounded. Von Usedom's train was surrounded and cut off until another train with 150 marines and some Russian sailors arrived to support them and helped to drive the Boxers off. Four junks were captured on the river near Yangtsun, which later were to be invaluable. To complete a thoroughly miserable day, the first rains of the season began – the skies clouded and the rain came down in torrents. The cheering Chinese were able to point gleefully to the sky and claim that the gods were rewarding the Boxers with rain for driving away the hairy foreign devils.

74

A council of war was held on 19 June, and to add point to the deliberations the rumble of heavy guns could be heard from Tientsin. It was impossible to continue by train; there was no road transport for the wounded; food and ammunition were both short and no more could be got up from Tientsin. The river was the only hope; it was shallow, muddy, studded with sand-banks and spits of land; it was winding and the force would have to cover two miles to make one; there were many villages on the river-bank and each one would be occupied by the Boxers, or by regular troops. But the river it had to be.

Everything was burned except what the men could carry. Each man had a blanket and ship's biscuit for two days, with his rifle and other equipment. The wounded were put in the four junks. The expeditionary force mustered on the left bank of the river and at 3 p.m. began to march off, southwards. Towed by men hauling on ropes from the bank, the junks were very difficult to steer. They often grounded in the shallows and had to be poled and heaved off. Sudden eddies of current whisked them around and whirled them out into midstream. Only two and a half miles had been covered by nightfall, when the men camped for the night. When the sun went down the air temperature plummeted, and the night was bitterly cold after the great heat of the day.

On 20 June, when the sailors got up stiff and cold after a night under their blankets, they had to face their first real opposition. Every village was armed against them and each one had to be cleared with a bayonet charge. The Chinese had also brought up a one-pounder quick-firing gun which kept up a harassing fire. When the Chinese had been driven out of one village, they merely retreated and took up positions in the next, while more Chinese on the other side of the river kept up an enfilading fire on Seymour's men as they advanced. It was weary and dangerous work, and by 6 p.m. only eight and a half miles had been covered. It was better than the day before, but Tientsin still seemed a long way off.

The next day was 21 June, and Jellicoe's fateful time of year had come round again.

Chapter 5

On 21 June the sailors had breakfast consisting of a cup of cocoa and a biscuit, and broke camp at 5.30 a.m. They faced another long day of forced marching and fighting, hauling their wounded in the junks, through the hostile countryside. The enemy were on both banks of the river and the previous day Seymour's column had been troubled by crossfire from the other side. Soon after the start a party of Germans, Russians and Austrians under Captain von Usedom crossed to the right bank to provide covering fire.

The plan was for both parties to advance along the banks together, but in practice it was impossible for them to keep level with each other. There were villages on both banks, so both parties had to fight at different times, taking cover, charging and storming a village with the bayonet, and then pressing onwards. The British and French on the left bank also had to haul the junks, while von Usedom's party might be delayed in clearing a village. Thus one flank was constantly leaving the other exposed to attack.

At about ten o'clock that morning some 150 horsemen rode up towards the British left flank. At first it was hoped they were Russians, but they were in fact Chinese. At about the same time two field guns opened fire on the column from the next village immediately in front. Clearly the Boxers were mustering in strength for an attack.

The British and French returned the fire with a few shells and then hurried on to get their guns under cover in the village. Most of the infantry stayed outside the village, sheltering behind a railway embankment. Von Usedom came across the river to confer with Jellicoe and Seymour. This was potentially the most dangerous situation yet: von Usedom's men were lying in the open; the French had occupied the first village (there were in fact two villages, separated by a short stretch of open ground) though not quite to its further outskirts; the British were outside the village, with their guns; both columns were surrounded by the Boxers, who now had cavalry, and a considerable force of troops in the second village, Peitsang, supported by field guns. Jellicoe and von Usedom agreed that there was nothing for it but to clear both villages at the point of the bayonet.

Jellicoe brought up a nine-pounder gun to shell Peitsang, and ten sailors from *Centurion*'s company ran forward to join the left of the

French line. Two rounds of common shell were fired into Peitsang with the nine-pounder and then Jellicoe's party charged into the village with a cheer. They went on in what Jellicoe called 'good style', while the enemy fell back behind Peitsang, taking cover behind a bank from which they returned a hot fire. Another party of the enemy were also firing heavily from the opposite bank. Jellicoe thought these were von Usedom's men firing by mistake, but in fact the Germans did not move off until some time after Jellicoe's party.

Jellicoe himself came along on the right beside the river and at the outskirts of the first village, where the open ground began, he found the French still in position and a few of his own men remaining behind the houses. 'The fire at the corner was very hot', he wrote in his diary. Jellicoe tried to get the French to come on and then went on himself with his own men following him. As he came round a corner of a building he was hit on the left side of his chest. The shock of the bullet's impact was so great that it turned Jellicoe half round in his tracks, and he thought his left arm had gone. He sat down on a stone where Petty Officer Cross, the gunnery instructor from *Centurion*, found him. Cross cut away the sleeve of Jellicoe's tunic and the shirt beneath it, and helped Jellicoe behind a house where he lay down.

After a short time Dr Sibbald came up and bandaged the wound. He told Jellicoe he thought he was finished; Jellicoe thought so too, and scribbled his will on a piece of paper. It said: 'I leave everything to my mother and my fondest love & hoping she will give remembrances to Fred, Joe, & my dear sisters and to my coxswain & boats crews & servants who have served me so faithfully. JR Jellicoe, Captain.' He folded the paper and gave it to his coxswain. By then he was spitting up quantities of blood, and when another surgeon, Pickthorn, came after a short time to rebandage him, he asked if he too thought the wound was mortal. Pickthorn had more tact than Sibbald, and merely said that it was very dangerous and injected morphia. The chaplain, Harrison Smith, came along later to comfort Jellicoe in what he and everybody else clearly thought were his last moments.

But Jellicoe did not die. After an hour he was carried down to the river and put in Admiral Seymour's sampan. He was still conscious enough to gain a clear impression of what was happening. Jellicoe's men and the French went on and cleared the enemy out of Peitsang but suffered heavy losses: one lieutenant was shot in the leg, just behind the place where Jellicoe was hit; the admiral's coxswain and several others were also shot. The heavy fighting went on all day, and Jellicoe could hear it from where he was lying. 'Hottest at about 5 p.m.' he wrote in his diary, 'after which we could get on no more. Enemy in strong force and good position. Cavalry threatening our left flank and rear all day, and repeatedly shelling.'

As the evening drew on, the situation looked especially grim for Seymour's expedition. The men were getting up at 4 a.m. and after spending the whole day marching, fighting and hauling the junks they did not halt until 7 p.m., for a scratch meal of cocoa and ship's biscuit. With delays caused by clearing villages of the enemy, and then, as likely as not, having to wait for the other side to catch up, the column was only making about six miles a day. As Bigham said, 'It was the most toilsome and disheartening work imaginable.' Even Seymour's spirits began to falter. With his chief-of-staff badly, perhaps mortally wounded, with his mixed force of many nationalities miles from safety and cut off from reinforcement, '. . . even the admiral', wrote Bigham, 'who had been the life and soul of the expedition, and who by his bravery, unselfishness and courtesy, had made himself popular with the foreigners as he already was with his own men, seemed a little despondent'.

That evening, Seymour's column bivouacked beside the river, having made good just the six miles that day. They were watched by the enemy's cavalry and field artillery continued to shell them occasionally. At a conference with von Usedom, whom Seymour had asked to take over Jellicoe's duties as chief-of-staff, it was decided to bring von Usedom's party back across the river to join the rest and to push on during the night to a village called Hsiku, further downstream. There the column would leave the river and march overland to Tientsin as soon as a relief party reached them.

The field guns and Maxims were embarked in the junks at midnight. One nine-pounder from *Endymion* and several Nordenfelt machine guns had to be left behind, and were thrown into the river. At 1 a.m. on the twenty-second the column began to move off; there was what Jellicoe called '. . . some confusion and noise at starting, but things quieted down after a bit'.

Jellicoe and the other wounded had to lie in the junks and listen, hoping that all would go well, which it did until about three o'clock that morning when there was brisk firing from a village on the left bank. Marines sallied out and stormed the village in fine style, but with so much cheering and noise that Jellicoe and the other wounded thought it must be the arrival of the relief party. Shortly afterwards there was another setback. The junk carrying two nine-pounder guns had been leaking, probably damaged by the recent firing; it now sank, and the guns were lost.

At about half past four, when Seymour and an advance party had gone ahead with Mr Campbell, an incident took place which reached the newspapers at home. It was described with accompanying drawings in the *Illustrated London News* the following September as '. . . an example of Chinese treachery'. Seymour's column had seen

78

fires at one or two places some distance off the river-bank, which were obviously signals reporting their progress. Seymour and Campbell were in fact opposite Hsiku, which was on the right bank, when they saw two unarmed Imperial Chinese soldiers coming out of a house by the river, and clearly wishing to communicate with them.

Seymour halted to hear what they had to say, but they merely enquired who Seymour was and where they were going. Seymour said he was going to Tientsin on a peaceful mission. The two Chinese beckoned Seymour on, saying that everything was all right, and themselves walked leisurely back to the house they had come from. However no sooner had they reached it than some Chinese hidden behind a bank on the other side of the river opened fire on the admiral and his party. It was a carefully planned ambush, but the enemy had been too hasty. According to Jellicoe, 'The fire was so hot that it was a marvel that anyone escaped; but no one was hit. They got under cover and returned fire.' In Jellicoe's opinion, 'Had the enemy waited a bit longer before opening fire, till more of the force had passed, it would have gone hardly with us.'

As it was, the leading junk carrying the wounded was badly hit in the crossfire, and three men were killed. The junk itself swung out into the river and might have grounded on the other side, leaving the wounded in her to be captured, but two bluejackets, Able Seaman Edward Turner of *Centurion* and Seaman George of *Orlando*, swam out to her, caught her line, and towed her back. Jellicoe was in the third junk which also came under a hot fire, but once again he survived and was actually well enough to get up and land, taking shelter with a good many other wounded in a small donga. Meanwhile, the Marines and B Company from *Centurion* under Captain Johnstone RMLI of *Centurion* were sent across the river higher up to clear the enemy out of Hsiku village, which they '. . . did splendidly without loss'. They were able to approach without being seen and charged with a great cheer, which was echoed by those watching from the other side of the river.

Rifle fire was directed at a 47-mm Hotchkiss gun sited at the north corner of what appeared to be a large fort close to the village, and two 10-cm guns beside the river. Captain Johnstone's party had cleared the village and found themselves under the shadow of the great walls of the fortress. They were joined by a party of Germans who had crossed lower down, and together the two detachments stormed into the fort, while the enemy inside fled for their lives. After some desultory firing, Captain Johnstone found himself in charge of a vast fort, whose giant walls enclosed a huge rectangle, 1000 yards long by 700 yards wide.

This capture was the greatest stroke of luck for Seymour's column. Without so much as suspecting it was even there, they had taken the Imperial Chinese army's main arsenal. Its walls were defensible, and there were plenty of buildings to shelter the wounded. There were tons of rice, bandages and medical stores. The magazines were crammed with field guns, machine guns, rifles, shells and millions of rounds of ammunition. The whole contents of the arsenal were later conservatively valued at over £3 million.

After such a loss, the enemy understandably counter-attacked in great strength. That afternoon a force of seven thousand (according to prisoners) charged three times and were beaten off each time, never getting closer than five hundred yards from the walls. The attackers lost heavily but they also caused some casualties among the defenders, including Commander Bucholtz of the German ship *Hertha*, who was killed. 'The Admiral found a room for himself and one for me in an inner camp where I was fairly comfortable,' Jellicoe wrote, 'though the constant shelling was unpleasant, and we lost a few men by it.'

That evening the reporter Mr Whittall, who had been so impressed by Jellicoe's personality when the expedition set out, came to see how he was. Jellicoe was badly wounded, and still thought he might die – he had lost a great deal of blood and was still in pain with the bullet in his left lung. He had been carried to and fro that day, put on board a junk and then landed to take shelter; it had been a long and terrible day for him, and it might yet be his last. However, despite all that he still had no patience with Mr Whittall's bedside manner. When Jellicoe asked how things were, Whittall tried to be optimistic. He wrote:

Foolishly, perhaps I tried to make the best of affairs and said I thought we should cut our way back to Tientsin or even the coast if the foreign settlements had fallen.

I don't think I shall ever forget the contemptuous flash of the eyes he turned on me or the impatient remark –

'Tell me the truth: don't lie.'

I had thought to lessen the anxiety I knew he must be feeling, but if I had known him as I learned to know him later on I should have told him the plain truth straight out. He thanked me and, indicating his wounded shoulder with his eyes, remarked: 'Hard luck just now.'

Seymour's most urgent concern was to get news of his column's predicament back to Tientsin. On the evening of 22 June he sent Captains Richard Doig and Henry Lloyd, both of the RMLI, with a hundred marines to try and make their way into the foreign settlement by a detour to the north and along the railway. Mr Currie went with them as a guide. The party started off after dark but when they reached the railway they were seen; alarm bugles blew up and down the line, and the Boxers attacked and caused four casualties. The party was forced to return to the arsenal.

The Boxers were always formidable opponents, by no means the undisciplined and ill-organized rabble the Europeans had expected. Throughout Seymour's expedition the Boxers had made excellent use of cover, in the trees which grew beside the river, in tall clumps of reeds, in graveyards and behind irrigation banks and channels. They were always ready to punish a mistake, and on the night of 22–23 June, Seymour made a serious error in not having the whole length of the arsenal walls guarded. At daybreak the Boxers made a most determined counter-attack and a fierce struggle took place actually inside the arsenal. About fifty Boxers were killed, but the defenders also lost Captain Beyts RMA of *Centurion* who was killed; command of Beyts' marine company was then taken over by Mr George H. Cockey, engineer of *Centurion*. As late as 5 p.m. that day single Boxers were still being discovered hiding in long rushes inside the arsenal.

Seymour's column had now had a chance to explore the arsenal and get some idea of its extent and the riches it contained, which included ten tons of rice. But rice was not much to European tastes and the expedition's food supply was now very low indeed. Conditions inside Hsiku were almost intolerable. 'It is impossible to describe the nastiness of life in the arsenal,' wrote Midshipman William Ross, 'quarter rations, rice and sand-storms, rice puddings absolutely brown from the dirty water they were cooked in. The bones of a mule boiled into soup were greatly relished.'

Seymour could not move on from the arsenal unaided, because his wounded now totalled more than two hundred. Various attempts were made to get a courier through to the foreign settlements, but the whole countryside was closely watched and they all failed. Finally on 24 June, Clive Bigham's Chinese servant was sent off with a cypher message for the British consul. He was captured by the Boxers and tied to a tree but fortunately had had the presence of mind to eat his message. He was released, captured again by Imperial troops, and arrested by a French outpost before finally reaching the British consulate and delivering his message verbally.

On the twenty-fourth it was the Boxers who missed an opportunity. A fierce sand-storm blew all day, so strongly that, as Seymour said, 'You could only bear to look to leeward and then could see but a few yards, and had we been attacked from windward, the enemy would have had a very great advantage.' But the day passed quietly enough, with a little sniping and shelling. More guns were mounted and some Chinese forts down-river were bombarded.

Early on the morning of Monday 25 June the fort below the arsenal was seen to be firing towards the direction of Tientsin, so it was bombarded from the arsenal. The fort then shifted its fire on to the arsenal, but shortly after 6 a.m. its guns fell silent; European troops were reported in sight. At 7 a.m. a relief column under the Russian Colonel Shirinsky, formed from different nationalities and guided by Bigham's Chinese servant, arrived outside the arsenal. Seymour's column now began to prepare to leave the arsenal and to destroy its contents. The whole force crossed the river and bivouacked on the left bank, ready for an early start. Lieutenant Lowther-Crofton and Gunner Mr Charles Davidge of *Centurion* remained behind to set fire to the ammunition and other storehouses in the armoury; they lit fires in five places and great clouds of smoke arose, with frequent explosions. The two then crossed the river, mounted ponies which were waiting for them, and joined the main body.

The return march began at 3 a.m. on 26 June. The men were tired and hungry and just about exhausted as a fighting force. They carried their wounded in litters, four men to a litter. Seymour himself, with his alpenstock, and jutting beard led his column back to Tientsin, which they reached with no further alarms or excursions at about 9 a.m. As Seymour later wrote in his report:

> The primary object of the expedition, viz. to reach Peking and succour the Foreign Legations has failed. Success was only possible on the assumption that the Imperial troops, with whose Government we were not at war, would at least be neutral; their turning their arms against us, and certainly conniving in the destruction of the railway (probably actually joining in it) made failure inevitable. For the undertakings of the expedition, for its conduct and its issue, I am responsible.

The expedition had had sixty-two men killed, of whom twenty-seven were British, and 232 wounded, of whom ninety-seven were British.

The arrival of Seymour's column was witnessed by Emma Scott, Jellicoe's cousin, who wrote about it in a letter home:

> I shall never forget to my dying day the long string of dusty, travel-worn soldiers, who for a fortnight had been living on quarter rations, and fighting every day; officers almost unrecognizable with a fortnight's beard and layers of dust, but so glad to get back and have a handshake; while the men were met by kind ladies with *pails* of tea which the poor fellows drank as they had never drunk before some bursting into tears – like children. Alas, the saddest part was the long line of stretchers with their poor, motionless figures inside, which turned into the Hospital gate. I was there, waiting for Jack Jellicoe. The Admiral, with his never forgotten courtesy, had sent a special message to prepare me for his arrival. He was shot through the lung five days ago, and at first thought to be killed; but most

mercifully he took a turn for the better, and was quite on the mend when they brought him in. I soon washed him and got some clean clothes and made him comfortable, and then I did the same for half a dozen other officers, all his company, who had wounds. . . .'

Among the force who relieved Hsiku were Commanders David Beatty of *Barfleur*, and Christopher Cradock of *Alacrity*. Beatty had already been wounded in action in Tientsin but had volunteered to join the party. A great deal had happened in Tientsin and off the Taku forts since Seymour and his expedition had been inland. *Barfleur*, the second flagship, had arrived on 11 June, the day after Seymour left, to join the international flotilla off the Taku bar. The same day Beatty landed with about fifty seamen and marines and two Maxim guns to assist in the defence of Tientsin, whose garrison had been depleted to provide a force to go up to Peking. There were practically no guns or artillery, but a force of two thousand Russian troops arrived from Port Arthur on 13 June, bringing the garrison up to a strength of about 2,400 men, with nine small field guns. They were besieged by about fifteen thousand Imperial troops with modern quick-firing guns and unlimited ammunition, supported by hordes of Boxers who made up in bloodthirsty enthusiasm for any lack of military precision. There was fierce fighting in the town, particularly around the railway station. Beatty received his wound near the railway on 19 June, but nevertheless insisted on joining the force which relieved Seymour's expedition at Hsiku.

The situation grew graver every day. Tientsin was besieged and likely to fall. The Chinese were reported to be laying mines in the channels, and bringing fresh troops down from the north. Supplies and reinforcements could actually be seen going into the Taku forts. Seymour had lost touch with Tientsin. The railway between the city and the mouth of the Pei Ho might be cut at any time.

On 16 June a conference was held on board the Russian flagship, presided over by the Russian Admiral Hiltebrandt, who was now the senior officer afloat. It was decided to occupy the Taku forts, either by force or by consent. An ultimatum was sent to the commandant of the forts and the Chinese viceroy of the province. This was a very bold decision, probably much bolder than those who made it knew at the time. The forts had successfully been stormed in 1860, but another Anglo–French attempt a year earlier had been repulsed with heavy losses. There were two forts on each side of the estuary; all four had been rebuilt and modernized by German engineers and re-equipped with heavy Krupps quick-firing guns.

Four new Chinese destroyers, each German-built and each mounting six three-pounder quick-firers, lay under the shelter of the guns.

The water over the Taku bar, which was twelve miles offshore, varied between two and seventeen feet, depending upon the tide. The only ships which could cross it were the two modern destroyers *Fame* and *Whiting*, the sloop *Algerine* and a collection of gun-boats, some modern, some old – *Iltis* (German), *Gilyak*, *Bobre* and *Koreetz* (Russian), *Lion* (French) and *Atago* (Japanese).

About nine hundred men embarked in the gun-boats, which weighed anchor at nightfall and took up station in line astern opposite the forts on the northern bank, while the confident Chinese guns' crews could be seen grinning down at them. The ultimatum was due to expire at 2 a.m., but at 12.50 a.m. the forts opened a hot fire on the ships. Seven of the nine replied, while *Fame* and *Whiting* steamed onwards until they were abreast of the four Chinese destroyers, where they slipped two whalers with boarding parties. *Fame* and *Whiting* came alongside two of the destroyers and the whalers boarded the other two; all four were captured after very little resistance. (One of the destroyers was later commissioned as HMS *Taku*, and the other three were given to the Russian, German and French navies.)

Apart from the Russian *Gilyak* who rashly switched on her search-light, giving the Chinese a good aiming point, the gun-boats were surprisingly little damaged by the fire from the forts. About 3 a.m. a British landing force under Commander Christopher Cradock floundered through deep mud towards the northern forts. At dawn the gun-boats could see their targets and their gunnery improved; as one fortunate shell detonated a magazine, the first fort was stormed at the point of the bayonet and the second surrendered shortly afterwards.

Another lucky shot detonated the magazine in one of the larger forts on the south bank, which blew up with such violence that it could be clearly seen from the ships off the bar twelve miles away. In the fort the air was so thick with dust that the attacking party could hardly see. By 7.30 a.m. the gunfire had died away, and all four Taku forts, the key to any campaign in northern China, had been taken by nine very small and mostly obsolete ships, at the cost of 172 casualties. Had the forts held out, as they should have done, the people in the legations, Seymour's expedition, the garrison in Tientsin, indeed every European in northern China, would very probably have been massacred.

On 21 June the cruiser *Terrible* arrived off the Pei Ho from Hong Kong with three hundred officers and men of the Royal Welsh Fusiliers and forty Royal Engineers. These, with another 250 seamen and marines, 150 United States marines, and twenty-three Italians, all under Commander Cradock, reached Tientsin on 23 June, having to fight their way through Boxer opposition and a blinding dust-storm – the same storm which afflicted Seymour in Hsiku. More reinforcements, 1,200 Russians, a detachment of the 1st Chinese Regiment from Wei-hai-wei, fifty men from *Terrible* and one of the ship's 12-pounder guns, also arrived on 24 and 25 June. Considering the strength of the surrounding Chinese, these additions should merely have been extra hostages to fortune. But the Europeans thought they had relieved Tientsin and, thanks to the Chinese, they had, but only after several more days of fierce fighting, in which the Naval Brigade distinguished themselves – Midshipman Basil Guy, of *Barfleur*, won a Victoria Cross in Tientsin on 12 July.

On 11 July the officers and men of *Centurion* returned to their ship, and Seymour with his staff also returned to his flagship. The greater part of the Naval Brigade returned to their ships between 14 and 20 July, but a small Naval Brigade of two hundred bluejackets from *Centurion, Barfleur, Terrible, Endymion, Aurora, Phoenix* and *Fame*, with four guns and three hundred officers and men of the Royal Marine Light Infantry, were included in General Gaselee's international force of some twenty thousand men and seventy guns which moved out of Tientsin towards Peking on 4 August.

After hot actions at places with familiar names such as Peitsang and Yangtsun, Gaselee's force reached Peking on 14 August and entered the city with much less fighting than had been expected. The people in the legations had also fared better than expected, due to a brave defence in which the Royal Marines played an outstanding part – Captain Lewis Halliday RMLI of *Orlando* won a Victoria Cross in defence of the British legation on 24 June.

While these events were taking place, Jellicoe was still in the hospital at Tientsin recovering from his wound. Emma Scott wrote home on 27 July: 'Jack is still here recovering: the doctors don't want him to join his ship again if she is going into action, she passed through on Tuesday on her way to the Yangtse and we just had a glimpse of the Admiral.' Mrs Scott's letter goes on to record the sadness that followed the excitement, the quiet that was the aftermath of violent action:

Yesterday I went with Jack to the funeral of two of his men, who after a long fight succumbed to their wounds. *You* know the scene well enough, the flag over the coffins; the quiet lovely service; the three volleys fired by the sailors, the bugle call and then the return to the ship. How pathetic it all is! The little cemetery here is on the quiet hill-side where so many *Centurions* already lie. Well, they died for their Queen and country, and *that* remains, all through the ugly struggle with pain and death in the hospitals; truly if you are to die let it be fighting! How one does realise that sentiment now. Though I suppose for the relations at home it is better to have news of the days of suffering and dying, it is pathetic to have to sit down by their beds and write the last letters home.

85

The dead of the Naval Brigades could not have had a better epitaph. Sadly Emma Scott herself died of dysentery, contracted during her ordeal in Tientsin, on 7 September. She had finished her letter above with these words: 'Though we have lost everything you must not think we grieve about that, we always felt out home was too perfect, and have tried to keep it ready to let it all go. We shall build a sufficient nest again some day somewhere.' Someone else had written a note to her letter: 'She was always ready to "let it go". Her "perfect home", her "sufficient nest" was not to be on earth.'

Jellicoe's brave, sensitive and talented kinswoman died, but he survived. With his extraordinary resilience of body and mind, it seems he had already begun to recover by the time he was carried in his litter into Tientsin. Two Admiralty telegrams received by his mother and father at home in the Isle of Wight were both optimistic: 'Captain Jellicoe reported shot through lung. Doing very well.' and later, 'Commander in Chief China reports this morning Captain Jellicoe progressing favourably expect him to resume duties before long.'

Jellicoe was taken down to Taku as soon as he could be moved, stayed there two days, and was then taken to Wei-hai-wei for a month's convalescence. When he rejoined *Centurion* she went to Shanghai, where Jellicoe was treated by a Japanese masseuse. The course of massage and electrical heat treatment did him a good deal of good and by October, some three months after the wound, he could raise his arm halfway up to the horizontal; he was particularly pleased that he could once more get a gun up to his shoulder. Eventually the use of his left arm was completely restored, but for the rest of his life he suffered occasionally from rheumatism and cramp associated with the old wound, and the bullet was lodged permanently in his left lung — an X-ray in 1934 showed it still there.

The relief of the legations in Peking was by no means the end of the Boxer Rebellion, but from then on the war in China became more military than naval. Troops arrived from various quarters, under the supreme command of Field Marshal Count von Waldersee, while the naval detachments withdrew to their ships which continued to patrol the coasts, safeguarding refugees, protecting life and property, and preventing the Imperial troops from joining in the campaign against the Allied powers.

Relations between the Allies still tended to vary between cool and touchy, and at the end of September 1900, by which time Jellicoe was well on the mend and back to duty in *Centurion*, an incident occurred which made the whole Navy chuckle.

At a conference on 29 September the Allied admirals decided to occupy the Chinese forts at Shanhaikuan, the place at which the Great Wall of China came down to the sea. It was an important point on the approaches to Peking, especially in winter when the Taku estuary, the normal entrance to Tientsin and Peking, was likely to be frozen over; Shanhaikuan then became the nearest open water to the road to Peking. It was known that the Russians had ambitions to take over the forts as part of their campaign in Manchuria.

What Jellicoe called 'an elaborate scheme' was drawn up for sailing seventeen Allied battleships from Taku to Shanhaikuan, but in the meantime Jellicoe sent the aptly named gunboat *Pigmy*, 755 tons, Lieutenant John F.E. Green in command, up to the forts to call on them to surrender. *Pigmy*'s complement was seventy-three men and she only had six guns, the largest a four-inch breech-loader, so her sortie was intended to be more of a reconnaissance than an armed landing. She also had on board as passengers Sir Walter Hillier, a political officer, and Colonel Powell of the 1st Gurkhas, who was on von Waldersee's staff.

Pigmy arrived off the forts at noon on 30 September, and Green, Hillier and Powell went ashore to see the Chinese general commanding the forts. He was perfectly charming, even gushing. He would not resist, he would evacuate the forts, in fact he was keen to leave as soon as he could get his men and their equipment together. Green could not leave the forts unoccupied, so he sent Lieutenant Briggs ashore with eighteen men to take possession of them, while he steamed back to Taku to report the surrender. Jellicoe put fifty extra bluejackets on board *Pigmy* and sent her back. She could only make thirteen and a half knots at full speed, but due to prodigious efforts by her stokers *Pigmy* arrived back at about 10 that night, by which time the Russians had also arrived and were landing troops by searchlight from the cruiser *Rurik*.

When the Russians thundered on the gates and demanded to be allowed to enter the forts and hoist their flag they were told to wait until dawn, and they were advised in the meantime not to move about too much by night, for their own safety, because the Chinese had mined the whole area. The Russians later lodged a formal protest and claimed that the British had fired on them. Nevertheless the Russians had still not been admitted to the forts by the next morning, when Seymour arrived in *Centurion* with several other ships in company. Another three thousand Russian troops arrived by train at noon, so *Pygmy*'s men had acted just in time. When the Allied navies heard that the Russians had been frustrated by a handful of men from a little ship called *Pygmy*, roars of laughter eventually rolled around the world. The French were puzzled as well as amused: they could not understand why one of the British ships was being addressed by signals as '*mon cochon*'. *Centurion*'s signalmen had found that the international code had no hoist for 'pigmy', so they used two hoists, one for 'pig' the other for 'my'.

After several conferences, ruffled international pride was soothed. All nationalities were to fly their flags over the railway station and over No. 1 Fort, nearest the sea. The other forts were allocated at the rate of one to each one or two nationalities. The British shared No. 4 Fort with the Japanese, and Jellicoe landed another sixty men to occupy it.

Centurion left Shanhaikuan on 5 October, when the situation appeared to have been stabilized, apart from sporadic looting by troops of several nationalities. They left, as Jellicoe wrote home, '. . . after a good deal of difficulty, as I dropped a man overboard at the start; and, having picked him up and got away, I was chased by a French and German steamboat with letters'. 'By the way,' Jellicoe added, 'I don't think I told you that I received a very nice letter some time ago from the daughter of the Russian Port Admiral at Vladivostock asking how I was etc. I saw a good deal of his wife and daughter last year there; and the daughter wrote when she heard I had been hit.'

Centurion resumed her interrupted commission. Jellicoe was soon playing cricket at Hong Kong. There were the same visits to ports, official calls and ceremonial, the usual drills and sailing races, football matches and dances. But it was not the same; nearly a third of the old *Centurions* had been killed or wounded ashore in China and there seemed to be so many new faces, who knew not Joseph. It was like a new commission, and Jellicoe lamented after the old.

Whatever criticism there might be of Seymour's action in launching his abortive expedition up-country, the Admiralty thoroughly approved. They wrote to him on 1 October expressing Their Lordships' '. . . high appreciation of the tact and judgement' displayed by him. They were of the opinion that 'great credit' was due to Seymour for the manner in which the expedition was conducted, in view of the great difficulties and the overwhelming numbers of the opposing forces. They desired that Seymour should express to Jellicoe and several others mentioned in dispatches '. . . their unqualified satisfaction at receiving such high commendation of their conduct'. Seymour had already written personally on 27 June to the senior officers of the other navies concerned, thanking them for their support and brave conduct.

Seymour was awarded a GCB, Rear-Admiral Bruce, the second-in-command, a KCMG. Captains Bayly (*Aurora*), Burke (*Orlando*), Callaghan (*Endymion*) and Jellicoe were all awarded CBs. Lowther-Crofton, Charrington (*Alacrity*), MacKenzie (*Whiting*), Phillimore (*Barfleur*) and Engineer Cockey were all awarded DSOs. A long list of other officers were promoted, or noted for promotion, and many, including Jellicoe, were awarded gratuities for services in China. However, the services of petty officers, sailors and marines were not rewarded on the same scale. Some won the Conspicuous Gallantry Medal, which was often inadequate for the bravery of the action, and it was to meet this objection that the Conspicuous Service Cross was instituted in 1901 which in 1914 became the Distinguished Service Cross.

After such excitements and awards, the rest of the commission was something of an anticlimax. At last, on 25 June 1901, *Glory* arrived at Wei-hai-wei with Vice-Admiral Sir Cyprian Bridge on board, who relieved Seymour as C-in-C the next day. Seymour's captains dined him out on his last evening and *Centurion* sailed for England on 26 June. On her last morning the band played 'Home Sweet Home' and the long, white, paying-off pendant fluttered over the waters of the bay. As always, most of those who watched, those who were going and those who were staying, had lumps in their throats.

The ship called at Hong Kong and sailed, after farewell banquets from the governor and the China Association, on 3 July, reaching Singapore on the eighth. They coaled at Pulo Weh, a small island in the northern tip of Sumatra, and again at Colombo, where at Mount Lavinia, Seymour and Jellicoe visited Boer prisoners-of-war, who said they still expected to win the war in South Africa. Leaving Colombo they met the full force of the south-west monsoon, which one evening washed Jellicoe out of his cabin on the upper deck. They coaled again at Perim and went on to Suez where Seymour was incensed to find his ship placed in quarantine, having to hoist *two* yellow flags and not take in a pilot, because there had been plague in China. The ship was also in strict quarantine at Port Said, Malta and Gibraltar which, as Seymour said, '. . . was equally tiresome and ridiculous'. The ship coaled again at Malta, where Jellicoe succumbed to his old bugbear of fever and was confined to his cabin for most of the remainder of the voyage home. Sub-Lieutenant E. Altham, who was newly promoted, having just passed his seamanship examination, wrote that it was '. . . perhaps some sort of reaction from his wound, and it was with careful footsteps and lowered voices that we passed the Flag-Captain's upper deck cabin. We saw nothing of him during the voyage and understood he was a very sick man'.

On Saturday 18 August 1901 *Centurion*'s wardroom drank to the traditional Saturday night at sea toast, 'Sweethearts and Wives', for the very last time in the commission. Next day, on a fine summer's morning, the ship arrived at Spithead. A recovered Jellicoe could hear the Sunday church bells ringing across the water from the Isle of Wight, and everybody on board feasted their eyes on the rich, intense green of England which can only be properly appreciated by those who have been away for four years.

On Monday morning Lord Selborne, the First Lord of the Admiralty came on board to receive the ship and to pass on His Majesty the King's message of approval and welcome home. Seymour left the ship the next day and his flag was hauled down. On 11 September the admiral, the flag captain, and the officers and men of *Centurion* were dined at the Guildhall by the mayor and corporation of Portsmouth. 'Such leave takings are things not easily forgotten,' Seymour wrote. 'These endings of the chief phases of our lives are the milestones of our existence!' A memorial to *Centurion*'s dead was later erected in Victoria Park, Portsmouth.

For Jellicoe, *Centurion*'s commission was one of the most important milestones of his career. He left her not only with a CB, but with a greatly increased reputation both inside and outside the Service. He was almost famous. 'Yes! I know Captain Jellicoe more or less,' Commander Bertram Chambers wrote home in August 1902, from the cruiser *Andromeda* in the Mediterranean. 'He is said to be one of the smartest men in the service, and I suppose taking him all round he is about the most capable.'

The doings of Jellicoe and the other naval officers who had taken part in the China operations received a great deal of press notice. Although the Boxer Rising was somewhat overshadowed by events still taking place in South Africa, it still had full, not to say lurid, press coverage at home. Dr Morrison, *The Times* correspondent, was in Peking during the siege. It was not true, as the *Daily Mail* reported, that all the men, women and children in the legations had had their throats slit open, but actual events were dramatic enough.

Beatty described the operations in China as '. . .the maddest, wildest, damnedest, rottenest scheme that could emanate from the brain of any man'. It was an accurate enough description, except that the events in north China did not actually emanate from the brain of any man. They were more of a series of impromptu escapades, unrelated and unconnected to each other, which took place with very little prior planning and no overall co-ordinating strategy. It all unfolded like a story written by G.A. Henty for *The Boy's Own Paper*. For the general reader, the Boxer Rising had everything: small garrisons of gallant Europeans beleaguered by hordes of yelling barbarian Asiatics; a young midshipman winning the Victoria Cross by bringing in a blue-jacket from under the very walls of an enemy stronghold; rescues in the nick of time; hand-to-hand fighting; cavalry charges; mortal wounds and desperate encounters; steam trains; field guns' crews; wide open desert spaces; and Chinatowns.

The Boxer Rising was also remarkable for the number of different personalities taking part who later achieved eminence in various fields. Herbert Hoover, a future president of the United States, superintended the construction of the defence barricades in the foreign settlements of Tientsin. Among the Japanese officers was Togo, who commanded the Japanese Fleet at Tsushima. The German officers included von

Holtzendorff, who was later chief of the German naval staff when the Germans began their unrestricted submarine warfare in 1917; von Pohl, later c-in-c of the High Seas Fleet; von Lans, who commanded the 1st Battle Cruiser Squadron in the High Seas Fleet; and von Naedorn, who commanded the naval defences in the Dardanelles in 1915. When the time came, Jellicoe was to have an unusually full personal acquaintance of many of his opponents and the Boxer Rising certainly impressed him with the smartness and efficiency of the German Navy.

For the Royal Navy, those who took part included Beatty, Cradock, who died so gallantly at Coronel, Warrender, George Callaghan, Roger Keyes (who commanded the destroyer *Fame*) and many others. Even an obscure sub-lieutenant from *Barfleur*, Edward Coverley Kennedy, who was mentioned in despatches and promoted to lieutenant, won his own immortality in command of the armed merchant cruiser *Rawalpindi* in 1939.

But *Centurion* not only brought Jellicoe to public notice. Professionally, it was a key appointment for him; he was able for the first time to show that he was much more than a very competent sea captain. He had had the day-to-day running of the ship and its handling in all weathers, with all the practical problems and difficulties of operating a man-of-war on a detached station. But as flag captain he had also been the link between flag and squadron. He had had to deal tactfully with other captains, most of them senior to himself, and to oversee a mass of detail about the other ships in the squadron, their movements, handling, coaling, manoeuvres, gunnery practices, drills, defects and overhauls. He had to act as buffer to protect his admiral from trivialities, and, although Seymour was the politest of men and his courtesy was never-failing, it fell to Jellicoe to mitigate the effect of the admiral's reproofs on the reproved. Jellicoe was a master at promoting peace in the squadron, keeping up harmony between flag and fleet. He was, as they say, one of nature's gentlemen.

At the same time, *Centurion* had given Jellicoe priceless experience of politics and international relationships. He had now served with officers of other navies, seen their problems and their difficulties, watched their behaviour under stress, and had a chance to sum up their national strengths and weaknessss. From Sir Claude MacDonald and the other political officers he had been given some insight into the workings of politics. He had learned that what seemed simple and desirable to the fighting man at his gun was not always feasible for the politician. For a future admiral, *Centurion*'s commission in China provided extraordinarily fortunate and varied breadth of experience.

Chapter 6

After such success in *Centurion*, Jellicoe could expect interesting offers for his next appointment. While he was at home in the Isle of Wight on foreign service leave he had a letter from Admiral Sir William May, whom Jellicoe had first met when May commanded the torpedo ram *Polyphemus* in 1885. May was now Third Sea Lord and Controller of the Navy, and he asked Jellicoe to come to the Admiralty as Assistant Controller. The post was new, and Jellicoe of course was delighted to accept.

The Controller was a member of the Board of Admiralty, with particular responsibility for the building, fitting out and repair of ships for the Navy, also for the provision and testing of equipment. The Controller had under him the Director of Naval Construction, the Engineer-in-Chief and the Director of Dockyards; the Director of Naval Ordnance was also responsible to him as far as guns, mountings and equipment were concerned. In short, the Controller was concerned with the 'nuts and bolts' of the Navy's *matériel*, in ships, guns, machinery and equipment.

Jellicoe went up to the Admiralty in November 1901, although his appointment was not actually confirmed until March 1902. His job, as assistant to the Third Sea Lord, was to bring to the shipyards and factories the experienced eye of a man who had actually taken ships to sea, and would do so again. He was able to give them the benefit of a seaman's opinion, to introduce practical sea-going suggestions, to bowl out anomalies, to point out errors in layout or in fitting. He also inspected the building plans and blueprints of new ships and equipment for the same purpose.

Jellicoe's work involved a great deal of travel around the country, and particularly to Glasgow, where he once again met the Cayzer family. He often stayed at their house at Ralston, just outside Glasgow, and renewed his friendship with their second daughter, Gwendoline. Charles Cayzer was a self-made man in the true Victorian pattern; he had a sharp eye for a profit, he drove a hard bargain, and he had a talent for fast financial footwork, but he also had a most pleasant voice and persuasive manner, with which he put across his business propositions and his points of view. He was a good judge of men, only very rarely picking wrongly. He was ambitious, hard-working and intelligent, with a flair for seeing an opportunity. From humble beginnings he had worked himself and his family up into a position of tremendous power and wealth.

He was born in 1843, the son of a schoolmaster of Poplar in east London. At seventeen he went to work for the trading company of William Nicol & Co., who were also agents for the British India Line in Bombay. Cayzer spent some years in the Bombay office and served a long apprenticeship in the shipping industry; at one time he had his own ship's chandlers' business in Liverpool and was for some years chief cashier of Gray, Dawes & Co, the London agents for the British India Line.

However Charles Cayzer did not intend to spend his life as a clerk, working for others. He realized that manufacturers in Scotland and the north of England would welcome a direct steamship route from Glasgow and Liverpool to Bombay, and in 1878 he formed his own firm of Cayzer, Irvine & Co., taking delivery that year of his first ship, the 2,080-ton iron screw brig *Clan Alpine*, so called '. . . because the steamers are being built in Scotland, and it's a distinctive title, easily remembered,' he said. The ship, like many others Cayzer owned, was built by Alexander Stephens of Glasgow. Throughout his business life Charles Cayzer made skilful use of the 'Scottish connection', making friends and doing business with the handful of Presbyterian Scots who had such influence in the Far East and Glasgow.

In spite of constant money difficulties, much shuffling of bills and mortgages, great comings and goings of partners and shareholders, and a long-lasting trade depression in the 1870s and 1880s, Charles Cayzer survived. He began to run ships to South Africa as well as to India. Clan Line Association Steamers, with Cayzer as a partner, was formed in September 1881, with offices in Glasgow. Clan Line Steamers Ltd was incorporated in July 1890, with Cayzer himself holding a majority of the shares in the thirteen vessels the line then owned. Under Cayzer Clan Line expanded; he chose his captains and officers carefully, and treated them well, urging them to handle Clan Line ships as though they were their own property, and uninsured property at that, which in general they did.

Charles Cayzer was married in Bombay in 1868 to Agnes Elizabeth Frickey, niece of a ship's captain who called at Bombay. Agnes, a brave girl, came ashore when her uncle's ship departed, to marry a young man she could not have known very well. They had ten children, of which nine survived, six sons and three daughters. His third son August, known to the family as 'Gus', went to HMS *Britannia* as a cadet in January 1890, but left the Navy in 1902.

When John Jellicoe met him, Charles Cayzer was the pattern of the Victorian family patriarch. He was elected Conservative member for

Barrow-in-Furness in 1892, and knighted in the Diamond Jubilee Honours List in 1897. In 1886 he leased [and later bought] the great Victorian mansion of Ralston, in Abbey parish, Renfrewshire, on the outskirts of Glasgow as it then was. There, self-willed and autocratic, he loved to lead family life and to entertain. (Whenever a new baby showed signs of self-will and of demanding the constant attention of all, the non-Cayzer members of the family, including Lady Cayzer, used to say 'It's a true Cayzer, just like grandfather.')

Early in 1902 Charles Cayzer invited Jellicoe to go with his family on the acceptance trials of the new flush-decked steamer *Clan Macgregor*, built by Archibald McMillan along the Clyde at Dumbarton. While on board Jellicoe was skylarking with the younger Cayzers when he slipped and sprained his knee rather badly. Naturally he went to Ralston to be nursed. It proved to be a most fortunate knee sprain. Jellicoe was forty-three years of age, and it was high time he married and settled down. The ladies of Malta and Hong Kong, and of Vladivostok, could eat their hearts out in vain. Jellicoe wrote later:

During this week I came to the conclusion that my future happiness depended on my persuading Gwendoline to marry me. I proposed on February 9th and to my joy was accepted. We were married at Holy Trinity, Sloane Street on July 1st and my married life was one of the most perfect happiness. My dear wife was ever a most helpful companion in whatever appointment I found myself. Our love grew if possible stronger as the years passed by and she was besides a most loving mother to our dear children. I do not think many men could have been so fortunate in their married life as I was.

Florence Gwendoline Cayzer, the second daughter, was a very pretty girl, more than twenty years younger than her husband. She was a strong-willed member of a strong-willed family – she had money of her own, and a mind of her own. She was always intensely loyal to her husband, and in later years, when he was criticized by people she thought were not fit to tie his bootlaces, she longed to write strongly worded letters to the newspapers herself, although, in deference to her husband, she never did so. Both husband and wife brought fresh contacts to each other. Gwendoline learned as much from John Jellicoe and his fellow naval officers as he did from Charles Cayzer's world. Gwendoline was outspoken and did not mind what she said, although she was always careful of Jellicoe's prospects when she was entertaining officers senior to him, or their wives; she was never a wife to blast her husband's career with some unconsidered remark over the dinner table, or some slighting reference during a tour of a ship. She was energetic and took great pains over her appearance, which always took her a very long time to prepare. An exasperated Jellicoe used to exclaim that he could get the whole Grand Fleet to sea in less time than his wife needed to get ready to go out.

After a honeymoon in Taplow, the couple settled above Harrods, in Knightsbridge, which then had flats on the third, fourth and fifth floors of the main building. In 1902 the Jellicoes paid rent of £400 a year for a flat with two sitting-rooms and five bedrooms, plus servants' rooms. At that time a captain on promotion was paid 22s 6d (£1.12½) a day, or £410 a year, rising to 45s (£2.25) a day when he was within the top fifty names in seniority on the captains' list. When he was married Jellicoe was ninety-ninth on a list of 211 captains. Such a flat was expensive for somebody of Jellicoe's income, but Gwendoline had money settled on her by her father. Jellicoe commuted by train to the Admiralty each day, and here their first child, a daughter, Gwendoline Lucy Constance Rushworth Jellicoe, was born in 1903.

By modern standards Jellicoe was late in marrying but, as contemporary fiction and correspondence show, he was only following quite normal social practice of naval officers of that time. The Admiralty did nothing to encourage marriage, not even recognizing an officer's wife or child until his death, and then not over-generously. Some confirmed bachelor admirals, such as Old 'Ard 'Art Wilson, actively discouraged marriage, holding that a man should be wedded to the Service. It was not at all usual for officers to marry before the rank of commander and many waited, like Jellicoe, until reaching captain. But there is no doubt that a married captain was a better captain for a ship's company, many of whom would themselves be married and would look to their officers for understanding of their problems.

Jellicoe was not allowed to enjoy home life for long. In August 1903 he was appointed to sea, relieving Francis Bridgeman as captain of the cruiser *Drake* in the cruiser squadron commanded by Rear-Admiral Sir Wilmot Fawkes, who flew his flag in *Drake*'s sister ship *Good Hope*. As the senior captain in the squadron, Jellicoe led the second column.

Drake was an armoured cruiser of 14,100 tons, designed by Sir William White, built at Pembroke dockyard and completed in 1902. The four ships of her class (*Leviathan* and *King Alfred* were the two others) were excellent steamers and could go twenty-four knots when pressed, but they were a little cranky in a seaway. At 500 feet they were among the longest warships in the world at that time, but their four thin funnels gave them an old-fashioned look. They were certainly undergunned compared to their nearest German equivalents, as was tragically demonstrated when *Good Hope* was sunk off Coronel in 1914. Their main armament was two 9.2-inch guns in single turrets, one forward, one aft; but they also bristled with minor guns, including sixteen 6-inch and twelve 12-pounders, in side casements.

The Cruiser Squadron was a development of the old nineteenth-century Flying Squadron, intended to give sea-going experience to young officers and seamen. When *Drake* and *Good Hope* joined in 1903, the squadron still included its original members, *Brilliant* and *Rainbow*, both built in 1890, with *Minerva* and *Hyacinth*, who were normally on boiler steaming trials and rarely seen. However they were replaced by four of the new County class cruisers, *Donegal* and *Kent*, followed later by *Berwick* and *Monmouth*. These ships all had fourteen 6-inch guns, all but four of which were mounted in maindeck casemates. The lower casemates were so near the waterline that the guns could not be fired in rough weather – another disadvantage which was so fatally demonstrated in *Monmouth* off Coronel.

Drake was actually one of the ships Jellicoe had visited whilst he was assistant to the Controller. But shore visiting and sea time were two different matters – there was nothing like the sea for finding defects. Jellicoe himself seems to have had early misgivings about his ship, for on the first day of the commission he assembled his officers and warned them to make sure that all watertight doors which should be shut *were* properly shut.

Jellicoe's warning was timely, because it soon transpired that rivets had been omitted during *Drake*'s building and in any seaway quantities of water leaked through the armoured deck. Repairs were carried out in Portsmouth dockyard, while *Good Hope*, *Donegal* and *Kent* sailed on 2 December 1903 for Lisbon, to take part in the celebrations to welcome King Alfonso of Spain on his first visit to Portugal. *Drake* joined on 17 December at Las Palmas where the squadron spent Christmas day and ate Christmas fare brought out by *Drake*. *Drake* played *Good Hope* at cricket, in a temperature of over a hundred degrees, before sailing for the West Indies on Boxing Day. *Berwick* and *Monmouth* joined the squadron on passage. Heavy gun practice and cruiser search formation station-keeping were exercised before the ships arrived at Bridgetown, Barbados on 5th January 1904.

During these exercises it was found that although weather and sea were moderate for the trades, neither *Drake* nor *Good Hope* nor any of the other cruisers could keep their 6-inch gun-ports open without flooding the decks. When the squadron returned to England, Fawkes, Jellicoe and Fawkes' flag captain, Charles Madden, attended a conference at the Admiralty. The First Lord, the Controller and the Director of Naval Construction were also present. As a result of the sea-going officers' reports, the next class of cruiser, the Defence class, had all their main armament on the upper deck.

Drake's commission under Jellicoe was a tense, somewhat nervy period, dogged by defects in the ship, and always influenced by the necessity to keep up the very highest standards in everything at all times. *Drake* had none of the happy atmosphere of *Ramillies* or *Centurion*. One of the midshipmen, Lionel Dawson, who also served in *Drake*'s next commission under Prince Louis of Battenberg and Captain Mark Kerr, noted that under them *Drake* '. . . was a very much more free-and-easy ship than had been the case during her first commission, few of whose officers remained'.

Jellicoe's commander was another gunnery officer, Charles Martin de Bartolomé, who ran a very taut ship indeed. He had a face and figure distinctly reminiscent of Napoleon, and his characteristic attitude of '. . . chin sunk, hands behind his back, with the thumbs twiddling, and legs wide apart' warned that '. . . squalls were in the offing'. He rarely went ashore himself and had to have the most convincing reasons before he would permit any other officer ashore. The gunnery lieutenant was Bernard Collard, another coming man in the gunnery world, so *Drake*, as Lionel Dawson, said was '. . . a very "Gunnery" ship'.

In the West Indies the squadron joined the North American and West Indian squadron under Admiral Sir Archibald Douglas, flying his flag in the cruiser *Ariadne*, with what Dawson called 'a conglomerate collection' of small cruisers, two auxiliary sloops and a small yacht, *Columbine*, used as a dispatch vessel. The squadron was typical of several the Navy maintained in foreign waters around the world in those days.

On general drill days the two squadrons would compete against each other, normally in the cool of the early morning, a very pleasant time in the West Indies, in anchor drill, clearing for action, and boat pulling. The two sloops often performed sail drill against each other. It was a leisurely peacetime existence in which the squadron spent some three months cruising around the islands, visiting Trinidad, Grenada, St Lucia, Dominica, Antigua, St Kitts and Jamaica, where Jellicoe took the chance to change his captain's gig for a faster boat, in which he won several races.

On 2 March 1904 the squadron arrived at Bermuda for a stay of some three weeks. So, too, did Mrs Jellicoe and her younger sister Constance Cayzer, a quiet and gentle girl, much less direct than either of her two sisters. She had come out for a holiday and to keep her elder sister company, but she also met Charles Madden, the flag captain. The romance flourished, and two years later they were married.

During their stay in Bermuda the ships often went to sea for various exercises, including minelaying, counter-mining and prize firing. In *Drake*, as in most of the Navy, fire control was still in a primitive stage. According to Dawson:

It was my lot, as Midshipman of the fore turret, to take my stand on its roof – outside the turret – to observe the range signals and other firing orders which came from the foretop (where was the gunnery officer), should the Heath-Robinson-like apparatus of pulleys and dials worked by him from his lofty eminence fail to function inside the turret. As this was nearly always the case, I count myself fortunate in that I have preserved my ear-drums intact. [However] . . . inside the turret the officer in charge made up for a somewhat elementary knowledge of its mechanism by the loudness of his orders.

Drake did '. . . fairly well in gunnery competition' as Jellicoe said, '. . . but I found it necessary to take a pretty firm stand as regards insisting upon the use of Captain Percy Scott's aiming device for heavy gun instruction, the use of the devices being still opposed by many gunner officers'. Percy Scott was no respecter of persons or glad sufferer of fools, and his forthright language had made him many enemies – many people dismissed him as a crank or as a self-advertiser, a fatal taunt in the Navy. But in the Mediterranean he had made his cruiser *Scylla* a seminal name in the history of naval gunnery. He fitted telescopic sights to his guns, devised a new type of sub-calibre gun for target practice, a 'Dotter' which trained gunlayers to keep their sights on their targets despite the rolling of the ship, and a 'Loader' machine for practising gun drill. With these and constant practice, *Scylla* won every cup and broke every prize firing record in sight. Nevertheless Scott's ideas were regarded with 'something akin to horror' by the older officers and by the older seamen, who were in their own way as conservative as any barnacled admiral. It needed strong pressure, sustained over a long period, from Jellicoe and other officers who believed in Scott's innovations before they became generally accepted.

For the ship's companies cruising meant coaling and cleaning ship. Coaling was also carried out as an evolution, in which ships competed to embark the most coal in the shortest time. Everyone tried hard, sometimes too hard, to beat their opponents. The sheer pressure of competition made some captains cut corners, with occasionally embarrassing *dénouements*. Captain F.E.C. Brock in *Donegal* longed especially to wipe the squadron's collective eyes at coaling, and when the ships were ordered to coal to capacity for the trip back to England in March Brock, as usual, took charge of the whole proceedings, keeping his chief engineer on tenterhooks while he compared his total of coal embarked with the chief engineer's reckoning.

When Brock calculated that the ship was complete with coal, the chief engineer pointed out that they were still a hundred tons short, but Brock insisted on sending the 'coaling finished' signal and getting the commendation from the admiral he longed for, having completed before the rest. As a result, when the ship had done three hours of machinery trials to prepare for the passage and was ready to sail, the chief engineer had to come and tell his captain, the day before they were due to sail, that they did not have enough coal to reach England. A chastened Brock and his chief engineer were invited to repair on board the flagship and a lighter had to come out with more coal. When *Berwick*, who were *not Donegal*'s chummy ship, next produced a squadron's *Sod's Opera* the hit of the show was a song called 'If the Captain wants to coal, let him coal', which scandalized the admiral but had the rest of the squadron falling about in the aisles.

The squadron sailed from Bermuda on 19 March and reached Plymouth on the twenty-sixth. Once again the sea state, which was only moderately rough, prevented any of the cruisers opening their gun-ports. *Drake* again needed repairs, this time to her steering gear, which were taken in hand by Portsmouth dockyard later in the year. The steering gear was actually ashore when the Dogger Bank episode occurred on 22 October – the Russian Fleet, on its way out to the Far East (and defeat at Tsushima), fired on some Hull fishing vessels, thinking they were Japanese torpedo boats, thus causing yet another war scare. *Drake*'s steering gear engine was replaced in a great hurry, but the affair blew over. As Dawson said, 'The best war scare of recent times found us definitely caught at a disadvantage.'

Much more numerous were *Drake*'s defects in the watertight integrity of bulkheads and doors. Jellicoe himself believed that many warships, and in particular *Drake* and her sisters, were no longer watertight below decks because of the ever-increasing number of electrical leads, voicepipes, water and fuel pipes, passing through them. Air tests showed that Jellicoe was quite right, and his reports caused improvements to be put in hand.

But Jellicoe also had unexpected personnel problems. Even he fell foul of the Great British Parent. Life in a ship's gunroom was always tough for the most junior midshipman and clerks. Some sub-lieutenants ruled their mess by fear and the rod. Most weeks an evening of unpleasant party games, known as 'gunroom evolutions' was inflicted on its members. Sometimes, as in *Drake*, this ragging came perilously close to organized bullying. In *Drake* 'conduct books' were examined every Sunday forenoon and penalties were inflicted for transgressions. According to Dawson, the junior sub-lieutenant revelled in the production of crimes, real or imaginary, and his juniors went in such fear every Sunday morning that they would sometimes hide in the stokeholds. Some boys, who had as many as three dozen cuts over the backside in one morning, were incapacitated for some time afterwards. One of the midshipmen described 'gunroom evolutions' and the 'conduct book' punishments in a letter to his parents, who, horrified, complained to the Admiralty. Jellicoe had had no idea such a state of affairs existed in his ship and the resulting investigation and re-appointment of certain midshipmen (who, ironically, included Dawson who had actually been one of the main sufferers) came as a very unpleasant shock indeed.

A similar state of affairs existed in the gunroom of the flagship *Good Hope*, where midshipmen were cruelly terrorized. It is curious how individual ships carry on reputations and traditions from one commission to another, even though all the personalities have changed. Five years later another midshipman, Charles Morgan, joined *Good Hope* when she was in the Atlantic Fleet. The conditions on board her (renamed *King Arthur*) were later graphically described in his novel *The Gunroom*, though it aroused a storm of disbelief and ridicule and was hotly refuted by some officers.

After leave and refitting the Cruiser Squadron carried out tactical and strategic exercises in the Channel until the end of May, and then early in June left for the Mediterranean for manoeuvres with the Mediterranean Fleet, the cruisers being under the command of Admiral Sir Baldwin Walker. *Drake* was still bedevilled by defects, and she had to be docked at Malta afterwards because a propellor shaft casing had worked loose. The squadron sailed for home again on 5 July 1904 and went to Portland to prepare for manoeuvres on a large scale with the Home Fleet and some additional vessels specially commissioned, all under Arthur Knyvet Wilson. The opposition was provided by the Combined Channel Fleet under Lord Charles Beresford at Torbay.

In September the squadron took part in one of the largest amphibious exercises ever carried out. The cruisers escorted ten transports, loaded with twelve thousand officers and men of the army, two thousand horses, sixty guns, three hundred vehicles, a few motors and a large number of bicycles, from Spithead to Clacton in Essex, where they were to be landed against shore opposition. The cruisers and transports weighed on the evening of 8 September and put to sea, the force organized in two divisions in line ahead, a cruiser ahead and astern of each division, *Drake* and *Good Hope* on the beam, four cables off. It was significant that no arrangements were made for scouting or for protecting the convoy from hostile warships, because none were expected. The whole operation was based on the experience of the South African wars, during which the Navy had several times to put soldiers ashore and supplied them, but had never faced any seaborne opposition at all. Transports and escort arrived off the beach in good order, but the landing was full of incident. Some of the horse-boats' wheels were locked, and the boats grounded half-way out and stuck. The horse-boats were old and mostly in poor order. As the weather worsened, some of them began to break up and a few of the released horses swam out to sea and had to be chased by picket boats.

The sailors from the cruiser squadron who, like all sailors, adored anything to do with horses, had the time of their lives rounding up horses, riding them ashore, fishing out half-drowned riders and re-uniting them with their chargers.

Jellicoe left *Drake* on 21 November 1904 and was relieved by Doveton Sturdee. The ship recommissioned under Mark Kerr early in the spring of 1905, when the regime was much easier as Dawson noted. Jellicoe had only been in *Drake* just over a year, so clearly he had once again been plucked out of his ship, to be spirited away to higher things.

On 19 October 1904 Jackie Fisher wrote to Lord Selborne, the First Lord. It was just two days before Fisher became First Sea Lord. He had an idea for the future of the Navy, which he wanted '. . . the five best brains in the Navy below the rank of Admiral to thresh out! and associated two other brains for the consideration of the types of future fighting vessels'. Fisher guaranteed that '. . . these seven brains may be absolutely relied upon for secrecy. I have tested each of them for many years!'

The seven were Captain Henry B. Jackson FRS, about to become Controller of the Navy; Captain John R. Jellicoe, about to become Director of Naval Ordnance; Captain Reginald Bacon, Naval Assistant to the First Sea Lord; Captain Charles Madden, about to become Assistant to the Controller; Captain Wilfred Henderson, who, Fisher wrote, '. . . has all the signs of the Zodiac after his name!'; Mr William Henry Gard MVO, Chief Constructor of Portsmouth dockyard; and Mr Alexander Gracie, of Fairfield Shipbuilding & Engineering Co., who was '. . . the best Marine Engineer in the world!'

These seven brains on 'special service' were later augmented into a full committee which sat to consider new designs of battleships and battle cruisers. The result was HMS *Dreadnought*, an advanced design of battleship which rendered all her opponents, and all the Navy's own existing battleships, obsolete overnight. Fisher had said that she was to be ready in a year and to Jellicoe, who became Director of Naval Ordnance early in 1905, fell the task of providing her main armament of ten 12-inch guns, which he did by robbing two battleships already building, *Lord Nelson* and *Agamemnon*, of their 12-inch guns and mountings. This manoeuvre of Jellicoe's enabled *Dreadnought* to be finished in time – it actually took longer to build a ship's gun mountings than to build the ship herself.

Once again Jellicoe was in the right place at the right time; he took part in what was nothing less than a revolution in the Navy. Fisher intended to revolutionize the Navy's mentality as well as its *matériel*, its minds as well as its ships. He began at the beginning, by changing the system of training young officers so that all officers (except, as it turned out, the Royal Marines) started off their naval service together and took the same basic course at the new colleges of Osborne and Dartmouth. (The full scheme, whereby executive and engineering officers became virtually interchangeable, except for necessary physical criteria such as eyesight, was never really implemented until 1956 and has still not been fully realized today.) He introduced schemes for promoting officers from the lower deck, which in theory had always been possible in the Victorian Navy but was in practice so rare as to be almost impossible. He reorganized fleets and ships so as to concentrate the best and biggest battleships in the areas of greatest strategic significance, the North Sea and the Channel, so that these two seaways became the centre of naval emphasis for the first time since the seventeenth century. He paid off more than 150 sloops, gunboats, second- and third-class cruisers which were scattered around the world, '. . . too weak to fight and too slow to run away', as Fisher himself contemptuously said of them, leaving only a few necessarily on the west coast of Africa and the rivers of China. He used their crews to form a Reserve Fleet in 1906, which later became the Home Fleet. The very names of the new fleets – the former Home Fleet became the Channel Fleet, which itself became the Atlantic Fleet – showed a new emphasis and a new purpose. Meanwhile, the vast shadow fleet of interesting old relics was brusquely and unsentimentally sold off for scrap. He also began a reform of the organisation and capabilities of the royal dockyards which, like most of the Navy, had slumbered very peacefully since Trafalgar.

In all these great events Jellicoe's judgement was sound. He seemed to sense the direction of the true current of affairs in the Navy; he did not exclaim, like some, at the scrapping of old and obsolete ships, nor, like many more, at the rise in the status of sooty and plebeian engineers, nor, like a great many more, at the coming of the *Dreadnought* which, by making all previous designs of battleship obsolescent, seemed to place the Royal Navy back on a par with some of its weakest rivals. Jellicoe knew these things had to be, and gave them his fullest support.

Jellicoe had, in fact, been chosen by Fisher specifically for the purpose, and he relieved Rear-Admiral Barry as Director of Ordnance in February 1905. The previous October Fisher had written to Lord Selborne, 'You think I'm fickle about Barry – *I am not*! I love him as much as ever!' But, Fisher went on, good as Barry was, Jellicoe was '. . . *just the least bit better!*'

Jellicoe certainly played his part. For a four-ring captain, fresh from sea, he had a remarkable influence in Whitehall. He knew from past experience how to conduct himself in this world of committees and conferences, where battles were fought on paper, or face to face, and the weapons were a telling turn of phrase, a tone of voice, or the timing of a remark. On these battlegrounds Jellicoe did extremely well. He had a steely quality in him, and was not easily deflected in argument.

During his term as Director of Naval Ordnance Jellicoe, with Fisher's help, finally succeeded in wresting away from the War Office control of the supply of naval guns, and much of the responsibility for their design. Realizing that control over design ultimately depended upon technical experience, he set up a department of qualified 'Inspectors of Steel' to oversee the manufacture of naval guns. As the sizes and ranges of guns grew larger, so too did the problems of spotting and fire control. Jellicoe paid special attention to this, as he said, 'It occupied my mind and time a good deal.' He encouraged several officers who were studying the problem, particularly Lieutenant F.C. Dreyer, another coming man in the gunnery world, who had taken the battleship *Exmouth* to the top of the fleet list in gunnery practice. 'To his inventive genius and strenuous labours', wrote Jellicoe, 'the system adopted and at present in use in the Navy is largely due.'

Above all, Jellicoe used every ounce of his influence to support Percy Scott, who was appointed Inspector of Target Practice in March 1905, with the job of going round the fleet attending gunnery practices and suggesting improvements. For many years ships had carried out annual so-called 'prize firings' in which ships steamed up and down firing at canvas targets. The number of hits obtained and the number of rounds expended were noted and an order of merit made out for each fleet or squadron. Everything depended upon individual admirals or captains. Some orders of merit were not published for months, by which time everybody had lost interest. A few ships took gunnery seriously and did well. Most carried out firings as necessary chores, as quickly as possible. Some ships evaded them altogether. The essence of 'prize firing', in Scott's view, was competition – the good ships must be identified and praised; the bad ships had to be exposed as duffers. But in 1904 the Admiralty changed the name to Gunlayers' Competition and increased the firing range so much that the gun-layers often could not see their target and the contest became one of luck rather than skill. The result was chaos. Nobody knew who had won or lost, which gave ammunition to those who opposed competitive firing in any case (for no clearly expressed reason, but very probably because it did expose the inefficient). In any case, there was still a great deal of feeling against anything to do with Percy Scott, his methods and his inventions. Jellicoe wrote:

There was a strong prejudice against competitive gunnery practices; indeed so great was this opposition, that efforts were made while I was D.N.O. to persuade me to abandon the Gun Layers' Test; efforts

103

which I resisted most strenuously and successfully, I am glad to say. I was convinced then, and remained convinced, that competition is the greatest possible incentive to efficiency.

The work as DNO was as hard and long as in Jellicoe's previous appointments at the Admiralty. Jellicoe's staff consisted of an Assistant Director of Torpedoes, three commanders or lieutenants for gunnery work, three for torpedoes, and a Royal Marine officer for general duties. Once again Jellicoe worked late into the night, and he always walked miles every day to and from his office. He and Gwendoline had taken a small house in Chelsea, at 25 Draycott Place, where their second daughter, Agnes Betty Gardner Jellicoe, was born in 1905.

On 8 February 1907 Jellicoe was promoted to rear-admiral and on 15 April the First Lord, then Lord Tweedmouth, wrote to him to ask if he would accept the appointment of rear-admiral in the Atlantic Fleet in succession to Admiral Egerton: 'Since you have been at the Admiralty you have done such admirable work and have been such a tower of strength in your department that I and all my colleagues look upon your absence with dismay. I am sure however that you will make a great success of your command in the Atlantic and I most heartily wish you God Speed and Good Luck.' Tweedmouth asked Jellicoe to keep the letter to himself until he had had a chance to tell the King the news before it appeared in print. Jellicoe kept the letter and the envelope, which he characteristically marked, 'To be shown to relatives only.'

On 25 August 1907, at Portsmouth, John Jellicoe hoisted his flag in the battleship *Albemarle*, with William Goodenough as his flag captain. Goodenough, son of a famous naval father who reached the rank of commodore, was Jellicoe's man, heart and soul: 'To serve under him, to live with him and to feel his confidence was a delight,' Goodenough wrote. The C-in-C was Admiral Sir Assheton Curzon-Howe, who flew his flag in *Albemarle*'s sister ship *Exmouth*. There were two opinions about Curzon-Howe. Reginald Bacon, Jellicoe's biographer, said that he '. . . was one of the most polite men who ever served in the Navy. He had, moreover, the knack of communicating that most desirable virtue to officers who served under him. He commanded the *Cleopatra* in the years 1892–95 and for the rest of their lives the lieutenants of that ship were paragons of politeness.' Perhaps Bacon was indulging some elaborate sarcasm, for William Goodenough wrote of the C-in-C that he was '. . . not always easy to serve, for his temper was at times quick, but those were the moments not to try to serve him too much'.

But Jellicoe was not troubled by the admiral. His year in *Albemarle* was yet another appointment in his seemingly inexorable progress upwards; in fact it is a fair comment on Jellicoe's career to say that he went from flagships at sea to the Admiralty onshore, but was never far from the reins of power, at sea or onshore. He never knew what it was to serve, for instance, in an obscure cruiser off west Africa or in the Pacific for three years. He had been picked by Fisher to command the main fleet in the future battle which Fisher knew in his bones must come. But there was a whole side of naval life which Jellicoe had never experienced.

Jellicoe had already been made CVO in 1906 and in October 1907, after a Royal Review at Cowes, he was appointed KCVO and knighted by King Edward VII on board the Royal Yacht. Now Sir John Jellicoe moved smoothly into his new duties, although, as Goodenough said, 'The duties of the second-in-command of a Channel Squadron, or Atlantic Fleet, as I think it was called at the time, were not heavy. Sir John was able to take, if not exactly a rest, at least opportunities for a broader view that [*sic*] his mental occupation with naval material had given him'.

After the strains, tensions and politicking of Fisher's Admiralty at a time of great upheaval and turmoil, the Atlantic Fleet was comparatively peaceful and uncomplicated, a return also to simple sailoring. It was the old life of salutes and ceremonial, of illuminations and dinners, exercises and night firings, sport onshore and regattas afloat. It was refreshingly close to Jellicoe's life at sea as a lieutenant. There were fleet manoeuvres, dummy fleet attacks, and torpedo boat exercises under Lord Beresford. There was snipe shooting at Arosa Bay and days out in the cork woods and steep valleys of the Calpe Hunt country just over the border from Gibraltar. Jellicoe still played rackets, reaching the finals and being runner-up in the fleet handicap championship. He kept himself very fit, as though preparing himself for an ordeal to come, which at the time he could only have guessed at. 'With the zest that he possessed for enjoyment,' wrote Goodenough, 'cricket, golf, a day with the Calpe hounds, or a walk over the hills from Berehaven, he was in the full tide of physical strength and health.'

Jellicoe's recollections later, and his letters written home at the time, give some idea of the flavour of fleet life in 1908, at the height of the seemingly golden Edwardian era. There was the same competition to clean and paint and burnish a ship until she outshone her sisters, but there was also a harder, more purposeful atmosphere than the Victorian Navy had ever known. Gunnery ranges were increasing. The Atlantic Fleet carried out shoots at 8000 yards and more, there were frequent night firings during which Jellicoe visited each ship in turn to watch their performance. The same emphasis was placed on sailing and rowing races, with Jellicoe still keen to improve his own chances: 'Service sailing race on the 11th for Rawson cup won by *Albion*'s

105

pinnace. My boat no good,' he noted disgustedly, at Berehaven. 'Rig new – masts in wrong place – difficulty in staying.'

He handled his c-in-c with consummate tact. One day, when the entire fleet was anchored in Lagos Bay, inside Cape St Vincent, Jellicoe saw that the weather was deteriorating. Wind and sea both got up, but no signal came from the flagship to raise steam. Jellicoe wanted to signal to ask permission but was afraid that the signal would be intercepted and read by other ships, thus suggesting a criticism of the c-in-c for not having given the orders already. So Jellicoe *wrote* to Curzon-Howe and sent the letter across by boat, and soon the fleet signal was passed ordering all ships to raise steam.

Jellicoe showed the same sure touch with great and small, old and young. One afternoon when the ships were lying in Arosa Bay, a boat with a small boy and a young woman on board was rowed round *Albemarle*. The boy was Don Alfonso Ozores, who had persuaded his Scottish nanny to go out and have a look at the fleet. When the boy saw a man watching them from the quarterdeck he called up to say how much he would like to come on board; the man invited them up and showed them round. Much impressed, the boy invited his host to his own home and was even more struck by the fuss, the tossing of oars and the ceremonial, as his visitor's boat came alongside. When the boy asked, his guest said he was the Admiral. The family learned who their guest was when he signed their visitors' book. Ever afterwards he sent them a card at Christmas. During the war, when many Spaniards had German sympathies, Don Alfonso Ozores was '. . . always for the Allies heart and soul', because '. . . he could not bear the idea of Jellicoe being beaten'.

The fleet assembled at Berehaven in the summer of 1908 and sailed on 5 July for Quebec, for the tercentenary celebrations of the founding of the city by Samuel Champlain. The Prince of Wales (later George V) sailed independently in the new Dreadnought-type battle cruiser *Indomitable*.

It was one of the most hectic weeks of Jellicoe's life – 'Sleep was rather difficult to get', he wrote. There was a dinner with the French admiral, the premier of Quebec Province, the mayor and dignitaries ('My French lasted out well'). The Canadians, '. . . especially the Mayor, were charming, and he swore eternal friendship to me'. There was a pageant representing Champlain landing from the *Don de Dieu* and a state dinner at The Citadel ('Full dress for dinner and very hot it was'). Then there was a Review on the Plains of Abraham ('. . . not large and there was hardly room for us all'). Jellicoe led the Naval Brigade in the march past – 'The day was very hot and I expected we should have some casualties from sun-stroke, as we were in blue clothing and the officers in cocked hats, but there was a nice breeze and no-one got knocked out.' In the evening there was a State Ball, '. . . about 3,000 present; there was an awful crush'. The Prince went aboard *Arrogant* and steamed up and down the lines of the fleet – 'The ships were manned, of course, and cheered and saluted.' There was a state service at the cathedral, a dance in the French flagship, a fleet fireworks and naval display, an athletics sports meeting, a garden party at the lieutenant governor's house, and the Prince of Wales gave a dinner in *Indomitable*. All these junketings were recorded in letters home, which the wives had to read with whatever tolerance they could muster. 'If you fall in love with the same people you fell in love with before, I can't help it,' Mrs Goodenough said to her husband. 'If you fall in love with their *daughters*, I can't bear it.'

The French admiral gave Jellicoe a farewell photograph of himself, and souvenirs for Gwen and the children. The Prince of Wales also gave Jellicoe '. . . his photo in a magnificent silver frame as a souvenir of what he called a "strenuous time"'. The ships sailed on 29 July, *Albemarle* going to Hawke Bay on the coast of Labrador as a precaution, to maintain wireless communication with *Indomitable* for forty-eight hours after she had passed it.

Albemarle sailed on 1 August and had to pick her way through fogbanks and icebergs. There were nineteen in sight at one time and Jellicoe calculated that the biggest weighed 2,500,000 tons. 'Not a nice thing to knock up against. We had a very narrow shave of hitting one at 10.30 p.m. on the 2nd. It was pitch dark and we sighted a large one only 400 yards off and right ahead, and had to put the helm hard over to clear it.' Jellicoe was in his pyjamas and just about to turn in when the junior officer of the watch came to tell him. The iceberg was then almost alongside on the port beam. 'By George!' he said, 'it's a beauty! I'll be up.' He and Goodenough spent the rest of the night on the bridge.

When he arrived in England Jellicoe went on six weeks' leave. He did not go back to *Albemarle*; while in Quebec he had received a letter from Reginald McKenna, the First Lord, offering him the post of Third Sea Lord and Controller.

Chapter 7

As Controller, Jellicoe stepped for the first time fully into the arena where the Navy and politics met, and fought, and from now on his present actions would provide hostages for the future. In later years, when Jellicoe complained quite rightly of the Navy's deficiencies and unpreparedness for war, his critics could reply that he was only accusing himself; if there were deficiencies, if there was unpreparedness, then surely Jellicoe as Third Sea Lord and then as Second Sea Lord before war broke out had been one of the very few people in a position to put matters right? These were understandable and, up to a point, justified charges which Jellicoe never recognized himself and never answered. He had done his best, according to his lights, and so he had. But it is almost unique in naval history for a naval officer to be a dashing, successful, innovatory commander in action at sea, and also a skilful Whitehall warrior at a desk. Judging by his achievements in both fields, Jellicoe was more successful than any other officer of his time, perhaps of all time. But it was not quite enough to satisfy the country. In short, Jellicoe was now approaching the period in his life when too much was expected of him.

Jellicoe received McKenna's letter on 18 July 1908, at Quebec, and sat down next day to answer it. It was, of course, once again a marvellous chance, and the greatest of compliments to have had such an invitation. 'I am very sensible,' he wrote, 'of the great honour you do me [and] wish I could share the opinion you so kindly express as to my fitness for that position. My inclination – in common with that of most of us – is for sea-going, as compared to Admiralty work.' Nevertheless Jellicoe accepted with many thanks. In such a dutiful and cautiously polite letter, Jellicoe also went on to lay down what seemed to be conditions for his acceptance. With the information he had, though he admitted it could not be complete, Jellicoe concluded '. . . that it will be necessary for this country to lay down three or four battleships a year for some little time to come (completing them in two years), if we are to retain the two-power standard in this class of vessel. A strong programme of destroyers and a moderate one of small cruisers will also be necessary . . .' Jellicoe concluded, 'I feel that it is better that you should be in the possession of the facts of the case as they appear at present to me, before you definitely decide to give me the appointment.' Jellicoe was no politician, but this was worthy of the wiliest politician. He might have been at sea, or riding to the Calpe hounds, or quaffing toasts with French-Canadians, but he must still have kept a sharp eye on what was happening at home. These views, as Jellicoe must have known, descended like manna upon McKenna, who had himself been appointed only in April of that year. Jellicoe's letter could not have been more fortunate nor more happily phrased in view of the political struggle to come, which Jellicoe seems almost uncannily to have foretold.

In December 1905 the Conservative and Unionist government had proposed what was known as the Cawdor programme, to lay down four Dreadnought battleships, or battle cruisers, every year. A Liberal administration had taken over later that month, which in the spring of 1906 had begun to question the need for such an ambitious programme. It was argued that Great Britain already had such a lead in warship building that the Cawdor programme was unnecessarily expensive. This was certainly true at the time, and the Admiralty was not able to defend a policy of laying down three more Dreadnoughts in 1906 – two Dreadnoughts were laid down in 1906–7.

After a long-drawn-out cabinet crisis in January and February 1908, the proposed increase in the Naval Estimates for 1908–9 was halved. When McKenna relieved Tweedmouth as First Lord in April, he agreed with the Sea Lords that four and possibly six Dreadnoughts should be laid down in 1909. To Fisher, then First Sea Lord, this increase was '. . . perhaps the greatest triumph ever known'. But his triumph was short-lived.

When Winston Churchill entered the Cabinet in April 1908 as President of the Board of Trade, he and Lloyd George, Chancellor of the Exchequer, began to challenge the Admiralty's building programme. Churchill himself believed at that time that a war with Germany was morally unthinkable, and commercially and ethically impossible. The money should rather be spent upon social reforms. Churchill never wavered in his belief in naval supremacy, and his desire to cut down Dreadnought building was not to try and reduce the country's naval superiority – it was just that he believed that the country's naval superiority was unassailable for the forseeable future. 'I do not defend unpreparedness,' he once said, 'but with a supreme Navy all unpreparedness can be redeemed. Without it, no preparations, however careful, can avail.' When, on 8 December, McKenna recommended to the cabinet a programme of six Dreadnoughts, Churchill and Lloyd George combined to attack the proposal and to defeat it. On 21 December, Lloyd George was gleefully writing to Churchill to thank him for '. . . the assistance you rendered me in smashing McKenna's fatuous estimates'.

Jellicoe had been feeling his way into his new job as Controller – he had actually started in October – but had been watching events with increasing alarm. Eventually, as the gunnery and supply expert, he pointed out what nobody else seemed to have noticed, namely that '. . . the governing factor in our rate of production of capital ships lay in the time required to construct the necessary turret mountings'. It was the same problem as in the first Dreadnought: the ship herself could be built more quickly than the guns which were to go into her.

Jellicoe had also found out privately, and now told the Board, that Krupps in Germany could produce gun turrets more quickly than any firm in England. No doubt, Jellicoe said, British firms would *say* they could do better, but,

> We could only judge by actual performances; and, as a matter of fact, in the case of the last 17 large ships built which carried 9.2-inch and 12-inch mountings, the *average delay in delivery of the mountings beyond contract dates was 6 months*. We had as a matter of fact found it necessary to order the turret gun mountings of the later ships well in advance of the time for placing the contract for the ships themselves.

In fairness to the armament firms, however, Jellicoe did make the point that they were prepared to increase their gun mounting plant if they were sure they would get increased orders, but it was unreasonable to expect them to instal extra plant unless they could see a real chance of the orders being placed.

These arguments of Jellicoe's were added ammunition for the Sea Lords, who had by no means accepted defeat. In the New Year of 1909, as early as 3 January, Lloyd George was writing to Churchill: 'The Admiralty mean to get their 6 Dreadnoughts . . . the Admiralty have had very serious news from their Naval attaché in Germany *since our last Cabinet Committee* & that McK is now convinced we may have to lay down *8* Dreadnoughts next year!!!' Lloyd George said he feared '. . . all along this would happen'.

The Admiralty forecast that it was quite possible Germany would have twenty-one Dreadnoughts (including battle cruisers) by the spring of 1912, and would certainly have seventeen, whereas the Royal Navy would have eighteen. This forecast was based on figures actually published by the German Admiralty, and secret information was also available from other sources that the Germans were just about to accelerate their building programme. Krupps were stepping up production, ordering new machinery for making six turrets simultaneously, and were secretly hoarding nickel – a strategic material necessary in the processes of hardening steel.

In January 1909 the Admiralty therefore asked for two ships to be added to the 1909–10 programme, to make up eight, the last two ships to be laid down at the end of March 1910. Lloyd George and Churchill still thought four in the 1909 Estimates was quite enough. The whole controversy was accompanied by a rising chorus of press comment, with Conservative and Liberal newspapers leaping up and down on the sidelines encouraging their own and jeering at their opponents. 'We want eight and we won't wait,' yelled the Conservative press. The other side were labelled 'pacifists' or 'Little Englanders', 'Econo-maniacs' accused the *Daily Express* – 'Panic-mongers' was the retort.

When, in the spring of 1909, McKenna asked for six Dreadnoughts and was only offered four, he sent in his resignation; the Sea Lords intimated that if it was accepted they too would resign. At this point Sir Edward Grey, the Foreign Secretary, realizing that Reginald McKenna was not the man to resign lightly or frivolously, examined the documents on the matter and went to see Asquith, the Prime Minister. On 24 February a special meeting was called in Sir Edward's room at the Foreign Office to discuss the whole question again. It was a stormy occasion. When they all rose from the table and, according to Jellicoe, who was present, were discussing the German facilities for manufacturing gun mountings, Lloyd George suddenly burst out bitterly: 'I think it shows extraordinary neglect on the part of the Admiralty that all this should not have been found out before. I don't think much of any of you admirals and I should like to see Lord Charles Beresford at the Admiralty, the sooner the better'. Jellicoe later said:

I was on the opposite side of the table, and heard the remark perfectly distinctly. Mr McKenna who apparently heard part of it immediately said 'You know perfectly well that these facts were communicated to the Cabinet at the time we knew of them, and your remark was "It's all contractors' gossip" (or words to that effect).' This was enough to crush Lloyd George, at least for the time being.

The upshot was that Lloyd George was defeated, and eight Dreadnoughts were approved for 1909–10. As Churchill said, the Admiralty asked for six ships, the economists offered four, and they all finally compromised on eight. It was a victory for the Navy although, in the light of Lloyd George's later attitude towards the Navy during the war, it might have been something of a Pyrrhic victory.

Many years later Churchill admitted that he was wrong. He and the Chancellor were right, as he said, in the narrow sense, but absolutely wrong in relation to the deep tides of destiny. He gave the greatest credit to Reginald McKenna for the resolute and courageous manner in which he fought his case and withstood his own party. When

Churchill and McKenna eventually exchanged posts, Churchill was to 'welcome with open arms' the ships of which he had tried so hard to deprive McKenna.

While all this press furore and political brouhaha were going on, while McKenna grappled in Cabinet with Lloyd George and Churchill, while Fisher locked horns with Beresford, causing many other naval officers to split into warring factions, while important letters, notes, and minutes were penned, while influential men took other influential men to lunch at their clubs, while speeches were made in the Commons, in the Mansion House, or over private dinner tables, Jellicoe quietly worked on as Controller. He kept a strong grip on his department, himself working twelve, sometimes fifteen or sixteen hours a day. According to a tribute to him in the magazine *Engineering*, Jellicoe was a 'strong Controller' and no other had been more popular or commanded greater respect as an administrator. 'He never worried, fussed or drove his subordinates. His words were few but to the point. And he had never been known to make a request or give an order twice.'

Jellicoe himself described his years as Controller as 'difficult', and that was certainly no overstatement. He took a crucial part in what amounted to an arms race between Great Britain and Germany. The size of British ships, and their guns, steadily increased; as the German Navy followed suit and began to build bigger ships, so the Royal Navy followed with even bigger ships until both navies became engaged in a 'Dreadnought race' which continued until, and was partly responsible for, the First World War.

In 1908 and for some time afterwards it was difficult to obtain accurate information on German construction, especially of battle cruisers. Jellicoe's secret sources suggested that the new German ships had a horsepower much greater than the early British battle cruisers. He knew that, in terms of ship construction, horsepower, weight of armour, guns, speed and size, were all linked by certain immutable rules; other things being equal, an increase of horsepower meant an increase in size of ship. Variations in one component had to be compensated for in the others: for the same size of ship, bigger guns meant less armour or slower speed, likewise heavier armour meant smaller guns or slower speed, and higher speed meant smaller guns and lighter armour. This was a truth of ship-building which even Churchill on occasion found difficult to grasp and Jellicoe, as Second Sea Lord, had to point it out to him.

Of the battle cruisers already building, the Invincible class had a displacement of 17,250 tons, the New Zealand class one of 18,800 tons. Jellicoe had the size, armament and horsepower of the next design, the Lion class, greatly increased to a displacement of 26,350 tons. As Jellicoe said, 'It was fortunate that this was done, as it turned out the corresponding German ship, the *Moltke*, displaced 22,640 tons, whilst the next ship to her, the *Seydlitz*, displaced 24,610 tons.' The 'Dreadnought race' was by then well under way.

It was a time when developments in all departments of man-of-war design were making rapid progress. Armour plating was increased from the 10–11-inch thickness of *Dreadnought* to 12 inches thick in the Orion and King George V classes. Guns increased in size from 12-inch to 13.5-inch, the weight of projectile from 850 lb to 1,250 lb and later to 1,400 lb. To improve underwater protection, *Hercules* and later ships had three engine-rooms abreast of each other, so that after damage the ships could still steam at a reasonable speed on the centre engine-room alone. Bigger (21-inch instead of 18) torpedoes with much greater explosive warheads were introduced. In the teeth of opposition from the Admiralty civilian departments Jellicoe obtained approval for two floating docks capable of docking capital ships. He could see that the Navy's bases were concentrated in the south of England, and moveable docks would give the fleet much greater flexibility, he pressed hard for the completion of Rosyth as a naval base and dockyard. Jellicoe thought that the docks would not be ready before 1917, but McKenna bet him £5 that one would be finished by the end of 1916. 'I took him up,' Jellicoe said, 'and lost the bet, I am glad to say.'

Despite the pressures of work, Jellicoe's years as Controller gave him and Gwendoline some of the most pleasant domestic interludes of their whole married life. They took a large house called Thornton, on the Stanmore side of Harrow Weald in Middlesex, about a mile from Harrow Weald church. Thornton was a Victorian gentleman's residence with a tree-lined drive of its own leading off the main Uxbridge Road, eight bedrooms, servants' quarters, stables at the back, a tennis court and a large paddock in the front of the house. The house itself was red brick, with high, pointed gables and large windows; the main living-room was wood-panelled and looked out on to the garden. The property was sheltered at the back by Mutton Wood, which was on the edge of the Bentley Priory estate.

Every morning Jellicoe walked down to Harrow Weald Station, then a pretty little country station, and caught the train to Euston and thence a cab to the Admiralty. The Jellicoes' fourth daughter, Norah Beryl Cayzer Jellicoe, was born at Thornton on 30 March 1910 and christened in the local church; the third daughter, Myrtle Grace Brocas Jellicoe, had been born at Sir Charles Cayzer's house in Belgrave Square in 1908. On summer evenings Gwendoline and the children would meet the train and Jellicoe would push the perambulator up the hill and home.

113

Besides walking, Jellicoe also got some exercise by playing golf, and took lessons from the professional at Stanmore golf course which was only a quarter of a mile away on the other side of the Uxbridge Road. One of his playing partners and fellow learners was Eldon Manisty (later Paymaster Rear-Admiral Sir Eldon Manisty), who first met Jellicoe in *Ramillies* when Manisty was an assistant clerk; they also served together in *Centurion* when Manisty was the admiral's secretary's clerk). Jellicoe's golf was of the 'tip and run variety'. He used to strike the ball with all his might and then hasten after it as fast as he could walk. 'We played a beginner's match,' said Manisty. 'He played too quickly for me, and though I began well, remembering and carrying out the teaching I had just received, his pace was too much for me and I think we both finished badly.' Among the Jellicoes' neighbours was Sir William Schwenck Gilbert, of Gilbert and Sullivan, who had a house and a hundred-acre estate not far away at Grimsdyke. Another of their friends was Mr Royle, who kept a private school at Stanmore, and his family.

The growing rivalry between Great Britain and Germany, though not as blatant as it was to become after the Agadir incident in 1911, had already in 1909 begun to strain relations between Jellicoe and von Usedom, now admiral of the dockyard in Kiel. Von Usedom still signed himself Jellicoe's 'true friend', and even 'comrade in arms'. Jellicoe sent cards with Christmas wishes two years running, but von Usedom did not acknowledge either until February 1909 when he decided he had delayed long enough. 'I have tried so [to write a reply] several times but found it so very difficult as being not able to express myself in a foreign language about matters of such a complicated nature as the misunderstandings between our two nations that I found myself obliged to give it up.' Von Usedom's is the letter of a man who is anxious to preserve his friendship, but feels it being swept away by great national tides which were beyond his or his friend's power to control. His attitude is interesting in that it reveals the friendliness of European naval officers towards each other. It would have delighted King Edward VII, who worked so hard for unity and good relations between the European nations.

Von Usedom referred to:

... the so-called race of our nations in building such ships, which I always said quite absurd (I mean the race not the ships), because we are wanting [i.e. lacking] the most essential supposition for building many big ships that is the money, and that therefore there is no possibility for us and never will be of our attacking you or trying an invasion of England ... If we are obliged to have [allies] then let it be the British and none other. I think we have seen

114

enough of worthy allies in 1900 ashore [the Boxer Rising]. . . .

But we don't want to be a *quantité négligible* and are therefore building a fleet as large as we can pay for. That Germany is not able to build a fleet like yours or one of much more than a third part of yours cannot be doubted, as we are obliged by our open frontier on all sides to have an army ready of more than two millions of soldiers.

Besides that I can't find a single reason for our two nations to go into a war with another, our trade to England being greater than to any other country and so far as I am informed, it is the same with you.

Von Usedom went on to say how valuable the recent visit of King Edward to Germany had been, to congratulate Jellicoe on his deserved elevation to Sea Lord, to hope that Lady Jellicoe and the children were doing well, and signed himself '. . . your old comrade in arms'.

The two friends met for the last time when Jellicoe and his wife visited Kiel in 1910, though it was an occasion clouded by awkwardness. The Germans had stipulated that Jellicoe was to go in uniform and that he might not visit any German man-of-war without first getting the permission of the c-in-c. Jellicoe's first reaction was to cancel the trip, but McKenna urged him to go, and, as it turned out, the visit went quite well. The Jellicoes stayed at the Hotel Seebadeanstalt Dusternbrook, with rooms giving a good view out over Kiel harbour. Prince Henry, Jellicoe's friend from China days, gave them dinner in his yacht and took them out for a sail. Jellicoe went to an annual reunion dinner of veterans who had fought against the Boxers in China. He met von Usedom again and found him very lame from the old bullet wound in his leg which he got at Langfang and later broke in Peking. Jellicoe encountered several old friends and comrades in arms, including von Lans, who had distinguished himself at the Taku forts.

Jellicoe also met the Kaiser, who arrived in his Royal Yacht *Hohenzollern*, when he went on board to pay his respects. Later he raced with the Kaiser on board his yacht *Meteor*, which Jellicoe enjoyed very much indeed. They discussed the beams of battleships and problems of dock accommodation for ships of large beam – esoteric subjects of conversation for a sailing race. Jellicoe told the Kaiser he thought the German Navy were lucky because they could have ships of wider beam, less vulnerable to torpedo attack, because they had larger docks, whereas the Royal Navy was limited by the width of the docks and the government's reluctance to build bigger ones. The Kaiser '. . . remarked that he had adopted the wiser course of first constructing wide docks and afterwards building his ships'. Doubtless Jellicoe wished he could inscribe this remark upon tablets of stone in Whitehall.

Jellicoe left the Admiralty in December 1910 to take up the command of the Atlantic Fleet. As Controller he had demonstrated tremendous organizing energy and he had got the ships built. In his two years as Controller twelve battleships and armoured cruisers, eight protected and unarmoured cruisers, seventy destroyers, torpedo boats and submarines, and more than ninety warships of various kinds had been added to the Navy's strength, with another thirteen battleships and armoured cruisers, ten protected and unarmoured cruisers and fifty-nine smaller vessels all either building or at design stage ready for laying down.

But there was one important thing left undone. In October 1910 Jellicoe initiated some firing trials with heavy guns, using the old battleship *Edinburgh* as a target. The trials showed that when the shells hit their target at an angle they often knocked holes in the armour through their momentum, but then broke up instead of penetrating and exploding inside in some vital part of the target. This was a most serious defect. Jellicoe asked the Ordnance Board to endeavour to produce an armour-piercing shell which would penetrate at an oblique impact and go on in a fit state for bursting inside. Jellicoe could not press the matter himself because he moved to his new appointment. It was left to his successor, Rear-Admiral Charles Briggs, whom Fisher described to McKenna in November 1911 as '. . . a servile copyist, and d—d timid into the bargain!' (He had previously written of him, in November 1909, as '. . . simply an automaton signing papers'.) Rear-Admiral Archibald Moore was Director of Naval Ordnance from 1909 until 1912. Of him and Briggs, Fisher wrote: 'Both as timid as rabbits and as silly as ostriches'. Neither officer pursued the matter of efficient armour-piercing shells with anything of Jellicoe's energy or expertise, so nothing was done, and the Navy entered the war with the shells of which Jellicoe had complained.

Sir John Jellicoe hoisted his flag as Acting Vice-Admiral in command of the Atlantic Fleet in succession to Prince Louis of Battenberg on 20 December 1910. His flagship was the pre-Dreadnought battleship *Prince of Wales*, completed in 1904. His flag captain was Captain Ronald Hopwood, his commander the notable gunnery officer F.C. Dreyer, his secretary Fleet Paymaster Hamnet Share, and his flag lieutenant Bernard Buxton. There were six battleships in the Atlantic Fleet: *Prince of Wales* herself, *Formidable, Implacable, London, Venerable* and *Queen*. Second in command was Rear-Admiral Carden, flying his flag in *London*. There was also a cruiser squadron of four armoured cruisers under Rear-Admiral Hamilton, flying his flag in *Drake*, and two light cruisers.

Command of the Atlantic Fleet was one more step upwards in the progress Fisher had ordained for Jellicoe. On 23 October 1910, a few weeks before Jellicoe took up the appointment, Fisher wrote to Balfour who had expressed misgivings that perhaps some naval officers were not as flexible in their thinking as the times warranted. 'The ablest man who has spent his life in thinking in terms of 9-inch guns and torpedo destroyers', said Balfour, 'will not easily adapt himself to 13- or 14-inch guns and submarines.' To Fisher such opinions from a politician amounted almost to a miracle. He wrote:

My absorbing thought for six years has been the one point you mention, to push young men to the high commands who will think in submarines and 13½-inch guns! Such a one – the first fruits of ceaseless importunity – goes as Commander-in-Chief of the Atlantic Fleet next month – Sir John Jellicoe. Phenomenally young and junior. He will be Nelson at Cape St Vincent until he becomes 'Boss' at Trafalgar when Armageddon comes along in 1915 or thereabouts – not sooner! Others follow in his footsteps. The 'fossils' hate submarines and the big gun! . . .'

This is the earliest reference to Fisher's explicit ambitions for Jellicoe, although in 1914 he wrote to George Lambert, the Civil Lord of the Admiralty, claiming to have written that Armageddon would occur in 1914, and that Jellicoe would be 'Admiralissimo' as early as 1905.

Even when Fisher was succeeded as First Sea Lord by Wilson, he went on intriguing on Jellicoe's behalf. He worked especially hard on Admiral Sir Francis Bridgeman, who had been Jellicoe's captain in *Ramillies* and who was now commanding the Home Fleet, to convince him, as Fisher himself put it, '. . . that he [Bridgeman] is very happy and he perfectly understands that his mission is to put Jellicoe in the forefront of the battle, like Uriah the Hittite, only not with the same result!'. He wrote to Jellicoe in January 1911 to tell him that Bridgeman '. . . is prepared and wishes to lean wholly on you as regards war operations'.

Meanwhile, after Christmas leave, the Atlantic Fleet went to Vigo for exercises with the Mediterranean and Home Fleets, the Mediterranean Fleet being commanded by Admiral Sir Edmund Poë, another 'old ships' of Jellicoe's, who had been Jellicoe's lieutenant in the old *Newcastle*. The exercises included a night action between fleets in close contact with each other, which made a profound impression upon Jellicoe, who decided that the difficulties of making out a friend from foe and the uncertainty of the result confirmed the opinion he had held for a long time, that a night action between fleets was '. . . a pure lottery, more particularly if destroyers took part in it'. Jellicoe carried his prejudices against night actions with him in command of the Grand Fleet.

It was during these exercises that Jellicoe received an Admiralty telegram that Betty, his second daughter, had died of a mastoid infection. The news came as 'a great shock', since she had been quite well when she came with her elder sister Lucy and Lady Jellicoe to see him off from Portsmouth. The little girl was buried in St John's Churchyard, Stanmore.

After the fleet exercises the Atlantic Fleet went to Gibraltar for gunnery practice, in which Dreyer made his name with Jellicoe. Dreyer had already been Jellicoe's assistant when he was Director of Naval Ordnance and had distinguished himself as gunnery officer of *Exmouth*, flagship of the Channel Fleet. Clearly Jellicoe marked Dreyer out as the man to have as his flag captain in time of war.

At Gibraltar *Prince of Wales* had a short refit and Lady Jellicoe came out to stay to help her recover from the shock of her daughter's death. Together they had a very pleasant holiday in Tangier. From Gibraltar the Atlantic Fleet came home to join the Home Fleet off Swanage, and the assembled fleets went to Spithead for the Coronation Review on 24 June 1911. Sir John and Lady Jellicoe were in Westminster Abbey for the Coronation ceremony on 22 June.

The fleets dispersed on 28 June, and after more exercises with the Home Fleet the Atlantic Fleet went to Rosyth, to prepare for joint exercises with the German Fleet in Norwegian waters. Jellicoe was looking forward to the meeting. He hoped it would have a very necessary good effect on relations between the two countries, and it would also be a good chance to assess the state of the German Navy and its personnel. Ever since his China days Jellicoe had had what he called '. . . a decided admiration and considerable liking' for German naval officers and men. He very much respected their efficiency, he took every chance of meeting them, and was a personal friend of many of their senior officers.

Unfortunately there now occurred what was known as the Agadir incident – it had more resemblance to musical comedy than to high naval strategy, but it did have a most dramatic effect. On 1 July 1911 the German gun-boat *Panther* arrived at the Moroccan port of Agadir, which the French claimed, ostensibly to protect German nationals and interests there but really as a mark of German displeasure at the way Britain, France and Spain were disregarding German claims to territory in Africa. It was an extremely provocative action, and diplomatically and militarily somewhat foolish. One gun-boat could not possibly gain for Germany the port of Agadir, so it was not a demonstration of strength. But that one gun-boat was quite enough to alert the other European powers to German territorial ambitions.

The Agadir crisis, like all the other crises, eventually blew over, but it had the immediate effect of causing the combined exercises with the German High Seas Fleet to be cancelled. At first Arthur Knyvet Wilson, the First Sea Lord, wrote privately to Jellicoe to say that if the meeting did take place nothing but official courtesies were to be exchanged and no hospitality was to be offered or accepted. Jellicoe replied that it would be a great mistake for the meeting to take place at all with such restrictions and it would be better to cancel it. To Jellicoe's disappointment – for he was quite right: the meeting would have helped relations and might have provided useful intelligence about the present state of the German Navy – the exercises were cancelled. Jellicoe took the Atlantic Fleet to Berehaven to await events and then, when the crisis had evaporated at the end of July, to Portsmouth to give summer leave.

Jellicoe himself stayed with his in-laws at St Lawrence Hall in the Isle of Wight. It was Cowes Week and he visited the battleship *Albion*, on board which as a guest was Jellicoe's old friend Prince Henry of Prussia who, of course, at once tackled Jellicoe about Agadir in general and the cancelled meeting in particular. Among other things, Prince Henry said that the Kaiser was very angry and disappointed. Prince Henry obviously thought that the cancellation had been intended as a direct snub to the Germans – which, of course, it had.

Jellicoe was under strict orders not to discuss Agadir so he merely said that the Admiralty had ordered his fleet to its home port to give leave and he was not aware of the reason for the change in plan, though he much regretted it. As Prince Henry remained Jellicoe's friend, and as Jellicoe himself later raced on the Kaiser's yacht *Meteor* (although the Kaiser was not actually on board), Jellicoe seems to have retrieved a delicate situation with great tact.

The fleet regatta was held at Berehaven in September 1911 and *Prince of Wales* won the 'Cock'. Jellicoe was still a keen and indefatigable competitor: despite an acute attack of lumbago, which was so bad that he had to have his back 'ironed' with a hot flat-iron, he got up from his bed of pain to win the veteran officers' skiff race in a close finish with *Good Hope*'s veteran skiff stroked by Jellicoe's old friend and sparring partner Cecil Burney, who had succeeded Hamilton in command of the cruisers in May.

Later the fleet went to Gibraltar and did well at battle practice, which pleased Jellicoe very much. Lady Jellicoe and the children came out and stayed at a rented house, the Villa Plata, and '. . . spent a very pleasant time there'. Jellicoe won the officers' competition at 500 yards at the Naval Rifle Meeting, and to complete a clean sweep for *Prince of Wales* Dreyer won the 200 and 600 yards competitions.

In November the King and Queen visited Gibraltar for a few hours, on their way out to India for the Great Durbar in Delhi. Jellicoe anchored his fleet outside the harbour and decided to try and get all the ships' companies to cheer at the same time, by signal from *Prince of Wales*. The result was 'fairly satisfactory'.

119

In October 1911 Churchill and McKenna exchanged cabinet posts, to McKenna's intense annoyance, and Churchill became First Lord of the Admiralty. In December Jellicoe received a telegram from Churchill offering him the command of the Second Division of the Home Fleet – once more relieving Prince Louis of Battenberg. Jellicoe had not yet served in a Dreadnought battleship or battle cruiser (*Prince of Wales* was a pre-Dreadnought); the Home Fleet consisted almost entirely of Dreadnoughts and it was obviously to Jellicoe's professional advantage to serve in a Dreadnought, and to command a fleet of them.

Yet, strangely, Jellicoe demurred. He was always an ambitious man, in the sense of wanting to rise as far as fortune and his own capabilities would take him, but his ambition seems to have faltered for once. It was another great compliment to be asked, and clearly it was important to have first-hand experience of Dreadnoughts. But Jellicoe was enjoying his Atlantic Fleet command; he preferred service away from England to service in home waters; he had his wife living ashore in Gibraltar, and he had an almost independent fleet command. With time at sea, and time with his family, life was good. He replied that he would rather retain his command of the Atlantic Fleet.

Churchill was new to his post, but already feeling his oats. Jellicoe received what he called a 'somewhat peremptory telegram' telling him that his Atlantic Fleet command was at an end anyway, and no other appointment was open to him except the Home Fleet command offered. 'Under the circumstances,' said Jellicoe, 'I had no option but to accept.' On the face of it this was a much less enthusiastic acceptance of a new appointment than was normal for Jellicoe.

But before he went there was one more adventure, which showed Jellicoe at his best. In the early hours of 13 December, on a very wet and windy night, the P & O steamer *Delhi*, with the Duke of Fife, the Princess Royal and members of their family on board, ran aground two miles south of Cape Spartel, on the west coast of Morocco. A messenger came to the Villa Plata to waken Jellicoe and tell him at 3.15 a.m. At once Jellicoe went on board *Prince of Wales* to take charge of the situation. From his own bald account of the episode, a vivid picture emerges of Jellicoe issuing a stream of orders, reacting to the latest news, anticipating events, always thinking ahead clearly, rapidly and accurately: he ordered *Duke of Edinburgh*, *London* and *Weymouth* to get up steam; told Rear-Admiral Cradock to shift his flag to *Duke of Edinburgh* and go to sea in her; had extra 6½-inch and 4½-inch wire hawsers, and all the grass ropes they could get hold of, sent from the other ships in the fleet to *Duke of Edinburgh* and *London*; wrote to the governor asking for military rocket apparatus to go over to Tangier in *Weymouth*, in case it was difficult to get at the ship from seaward; wired the minister at Tangier to ask his permission to land the gear and requesting him to have mules ready for transporting it; telephoned for a lifeboat and ordered dockyard tugs to be ready to tow her; and offered a volunteer lifeboat crew from *Prince of Wales*, which was gratefully accepted by the port captain.

Duke of Edinburgh sailed at 6.30 and the others followed as soon as they could. Cradock arrived near the wreck and anchored at 9 o'clock. A very heavy sea was still running. It took most of the day for *Duke of Edinburgh*'s cutters, very gallantly assisted by boats from the French cruiser *Friant* (they went inshore in conditions under which Captain Kemp of *Duke of Edinburgh* told Jellicoe later he would have hesitated to send his own steam-boats) and finally by the lifeboat from Gibraltar, to get the royal party and other survivors ashore. The rest were brought ashore the next day. The only casualties were three men drowned from one of *Friant*'s steam-boats. Jellicoe and his fleet received signals of thanks from the King and from Queen Alexandra. The steamer *Delhi* became a total loss.

Jellicoe came home and hoisted his flag in command of the Second Division Home Fleet in *Hercules* at Portsmouth on 19 December 1911. The flag captain, flag commander, secretary and flag lieutenant all went to *Hercules* with him. Burney relieved him in command of the Atlantic Fleet – '. . . an appointment', Jellicoe said, 'that gave me great pleasure'. Jellicoe went on leave almost at once, and spent Christmas with Lady Jellicoe in Madrid. They stayed with the ambassador, Sir Maurice de Bunsen, dined at the embassy on three nights including one 'very smart dinner' attended by Princess Henry of Battenberg, Don Carlos and his wife Princess Clementina of Bourbon, together with the French, Italian and Austrian ambassadors, and many dukes and duchesses present. Jellicoe left Madrid on 30 December, and while Lady Jellicoe went back to Gibraltar he himself came home. On New Year's Day he went to the Admiralty where he saw Churchill for five or ten minutes. 'He asked my views on the way of relieving a Controller of work and asked if I did not think some of his work should be taken from him. I said emphatically "no". It is only necessary to give his Naval Assistant more power and it would be most unwise to let such work go out of Naval hands. He did not seem to agree.'

That meeting did not seem to augur well for the future.

Chapter 8

In 1912, when he was First Lord of the Admiralty, Winston Churchill visited the training ship *Mercury* to inspect the boys under training. There is a picture of him, clearly stopping to ask a question of a slightly abashed barefooted boy at the end of the front rank. Churchill's stance, and the thrust of his body, are eager; the angle of his top hat is jaunty; and there is the suspicion of a smile on his lips. This is not a naval officer attending familiar divisions and exchanging predictable platitudes with the right-hand marker. This is plainly an outsider, quizzically amused by all he saw, keen to learn and to be instructed, but at the same time remaining to be convinced. He is asking a question, not just of this boy, but of the whole Navy.

It was this impish quality of sceptical amusement at their profession which often disturbed naval officers in their dealings with Churchill. He and Jellicoe, for instance, although their careers ran in harness for some years before the First World War, never really understood each other. Each respected the other, but their relationship never warmed. Churchill thought, or persuaded himself to think, even when evidence was lacking, that Jellicoe was truly the dashing, Nelsonian fleet commander everybody, and especially Churchill, longed to have as C-in-C when hostilities began. Churchill wanted to believe that Jellicoe really was the man whose merits Fisher so constantly trumpeted.

Jellicoe, for his part, never seems to have overcome his misgivings at so much power over the Navy being entrusted to so young a man, and a man who appeared so disrespectful of Service customs. To Jellicoe Churchill always seemed too quick to jump to a point, too ready to leap to a conclusion, too willing to consult junior officers before senior. Jellicoe never properly grasped Churchill's stature as a politician, never realized the tremendous driving ambitions under the exuberance, nor the formidable powers of leadership concealed behind that round, innocent, cherubic face. Each man blamed the other for their own misunderstandings. Churchill seemed to want to punish Jellicoe for not being the man he believed him to be, and in later years Jellicoe had genuine reason to resent Churchill's remarks in his writings on aspects of Jellicoe's stewardship as a Sea Lord and as a fleet commander. Jellicoe had some excuse for thinking them mischievous to the point of being malicious, and a good deal of Jellicoe's own writing was in answer to Churchill's charges.

Fisher seemed to suspect the possibility of awkwardness between the two men and, always ready to pour out paeans of praise for his protégé, wrote to Churchill in February 1912, after Churchill had visited Jellicoe: 'You don't say a word of your visit to Jellicoe – *but he does*! He is *much impressed with your grasp of the whole business*, and as Jellicoe very seldom indeed gives praise, I think you must have talked well!'

For Fisher, Jellicoe's appointment to the Home Fleet was, of course, one more step nearer the millennium. He wrote to Mrs Reginald McKenna on 5 December 1911:

> The greatest triumph of all is getting Jellicoe Second-in-Command of the Home Fleet. He is the future Nelson SURE! Now I will give you the whole effect of what has happened in one word. 'JELLICOE'! I say *Nunc dimittis*! For in two years he will be Commander-in-Chief of the Home Fleet at the same time as Battenberg becomes First Sea Lord owing to Bridgeman's age retirement. The Battle of Armageddon comes along in September 1914. That date suits the Germans if ever they are going to fight. Both their Army and Fleet will then be mobilised, and the Kiel Canal finished, and their new building complete. *So I sleep quiet in my bed*! – as to all else whatever! All is swallowed up in Jellicoe being NOW Second-in-Command of the Home Fleet. I've had a lovely letter from Callaghan about Jellicoe which adds to my heavenly feelings on the subject.

Fisher might have had 'heavenly feelings' about Jellicoe but Bridgeman, the First Sea Lord, took a much more realistic view of his talents. Bridgeman had been virtually pressed into service as First Sea Lord, after only about a year as C-in-C Home Fleet, by Churchill, who insisted to Bridgeman that he could never work with Arthur Knyvet Wilson but he could work with Bridgeman. Bridgeman himself said that he had moved from the Home Fleet partly so as to give Jellicoe his chance. He wrote to Fisher on 4 December 1911,

> Directly I go, up he comes automatically to command of the 2nd Division, and a splendid opportunity for him! He has had no experience of fleet work on a big scale, and is so extremely anxious about the work in it, that he really does too much. He must learn to work his captains and staff more, and himself less! At present he puts himself in the position of, say, a glorified gunnery lieutenant. This will not do when he gets with a big fleet. He must trust his staff and captains, and if they don't fit, he must kick them out! I am sure you

will agree with me on this view, and I wish, if you get the opportunity, you would drop him a hint. He would take it from you, but perhaps not from me.

This was a most shrewd summing-up of Jellicoe's most serious fault, made by a man who had known Jellicoe for very many years. A 'glorified gunnery lieutenant', though it must have been doubly offensive to Fisher, was a very accurate description indeed. Although Fisher must have had opportunities, as Bridgeman said, he does not seem to have taken them. One of the great flaws of Jellicoe's career in command remained his unwillingness to delegate.

Nevertheless, Jellicoe had been plucked out to be Second-in-Command and by the nature of things he would, as Fisher said, inevitably be C-in-C. Fisher wrote to Viscount Esher on 2 April 1912: '*I owe more than I can say to McKenna.* I owed nearly as much to Winston for scrapping a dozen Admirals on December 5 last so as to get Jellicoe Second-in-Command of the Home Fleet. If war comes before 1914, then Jellicoe will be Nelson at the Battle of St Vincent; if it comes in 1914, then he'll be Nelson at Trafalgar!' To talk of 'scrapping' admirals was typical Fisher hyperbole. Jellicoe was twenty-first in seniority on the active list of admirals, and had indeed been appointed over the twenty ahead of him, but they were by no means 'scrapped'.

The Home Fleet went to sea in January 1912 for exercises with the Atlantic Fleet, calling first at Arosa Bay. Jellicoe slipped easily into the sea routine of exercises, cruises and ceremonial. The ships in his Second Division showed that the Navy, as always, was in a state of transition. Besides the two Dreadnoughts, the 12-inch-gunned *Hercules* and her sister ship *Colossus*, there was also *Lord Nelson* and *Agamemnon*, sometimes called 'semi-Dreadnoughts' because they had approximately the same tonnage as Dreadnoughts, but had a mixed main armament of four 12-inch and ten 9.2-inch guns. The rest of the Division were four of the old pre-Dreadnought King Edward VII class, *Britannia*, *Dominion*, *Hibernia* and *Hindustan*. These four were replaced later in the year by three new Super-Dreadnoughts, *Orion*, *Thunderer* and *Monarch*, each of 22,500 tons and armed with ten 13.5-inch guns in five twin turrets.

Jellicoe's family and service life settled into a familiar pattern. There were exercises on the way back to England; a stay at Portland; a visit from Churchill in the Admiralty yacht *Enchantress* (and an argument between him and Jellicoe on the design and future use of the planned 15-inch-gunned fast Queen Elizabeth class battleships); gunnery practice in Torbay; a royal visit in May when the King went to sea in the C-in-C Sir George Callaghan's flagship *Neptune*, and Churchill in

Hercules, after which Fisher wrote to Viscount Esher: 'Jellicoe has an unbounded admiration of Winston! He says he's wonderful!'; torpedo and night gunnery practices off Colonsay in Scotland; and annual manoeuvres in the North Sea, in which Jellicoe departed, without orders, from the single line ahead formation and took successful independent action with his squadron in the rear of the enemy. Callaghan later approved of Jellicoe's decision. Jellicoe's initiative is revealing because he himself was to be accused of running the Grand Fleet too rigidly to the rule of 'Follow Father' and of making his fleet orders too inflexible. After Rosyth the squadron went to Lamlash on the Clyde for battle practice, and Gwendoline and the children came up to stay and rent a cottage nearby. The Second Battle Squadron, largely due to Dreyer, headed the list in the Navy in both battle practice and the gunlayers' test, which many had wanted to abolish and which Jellicoe had fought hard and sucessfully to keep.

In the autumn of 1912 several battleships of the Home Fleet, including *Hercules*, went to Berehaven to carry out, or to witness, trials of a system firing big guns by director control, using gear invented by Percy Scott. It was the most important naval event of that year, and one of the most important in the whole pre-war decade. It now seems obvious that a ship's main armament is more efficient in battle if as many guns as possible can fire together to make up a salvo, and if they can all be aimed and fired using measurements and observations taken coolly and quietly from a position high in the ship, for better visibility, and well away from obscuring spray and smoke, and out of the immediate earshot of the shattering blasts of the guns themselves. This seemingly obvious application of some of the principles of ordinary physics was fiercely resisted by many officers. Most gunnery officers were ready to concede the advantages of salvo firing, but some of the most distinguished gunnery officers in the Service were also just as convinced that good training and a high morale among the men could not only overcome but could far surpass any results achieved by 'new-fangled devices'. Ironically, it was some of the very best gunnery officers, those who got the best results from their guns' crews by the old system, who fought most fiercely against the introduction of the new.

Jellicoe was certainly not amongst these 'diehard' gunnery officers, and for years he had taken a long-sighted view of director control. While he was in *Prince of Wales*, director gear jointly designed and built by Peter Scott and Vickers was fitted in the brand-new battleship *Neptune*. Early in 1911 she went to Aranchi Bay in Sardinia for a month's working up, while Percy Scott himself '. . . fooled about with his patent director control gear', as one of *Neptune*'s midshipmen succinctly described it. But Jellicoe was subsequently so impressed by the rapidity and accuracy of *Neptune*'s fire — so rapid that McKenna remarked that battleships would use up all their ammunition in half an hour at that rate – that in March 1911 he advised the Admiralty to fit such gear in all ships.

In spite of Jellicoe's recommendations, prejudice against director firing remained so strong that Jellicoe wrote to a gunnery conference in Whitehall to point out that the increased battle practice ranges had resulted in far fewer hits. According to Jellicoe, gunnery officers and ratings were still too uncritical. It was quite common to hear them saying: 'There were very few hits – but the shooting was first rate!' Jellicoe urged that the old methods of scoring, indeed the whole framework of judging a ship's gunnery performance, should be over-hauled. It simply was no use plotting the 'hits' a ship could have theoretically got, or might have got, and the only criteria should be actual holes in actual canvas targets. In view of Jellicoe's opinion of night action, it is interesting to note that he also recommended that it was time remote control arrangements were fitted to searchlights.

When Churchill became First Lord he was urged to improve naval gunnery from two familiar quarters. Fisher, though retired and ostensibly growing roses in Norfolk, appointed himself Churchill's unpaid senior professional adviser, a sort of peripatetic *éminence grise* who fired off periodical letters, each one sparking with all the inimitable invective at Fisher's command, from various points around Europe and the British Isles. On 5 March, from Naples, he was advising Churchill that he '. . . MUST be Ruthless, Relentless, and Remorseless in administration, if you want in battle to HIT FIRST, *hit hard* and *keep on hitting*. . . . The gunnery of the Fleet is not in a satisfactory position at present. Many of those in authority hold very dangerous opinions.' Fisher went on to say who those were and he was no respecter of persons. May, (C-in-C at Devonport) was that 'bit of wood painted to look like iron'. Sir Arthur Moore was a 'fossil'. 'Dear old Bridgeman' was like Gallio (an easy-going Roman proconsul, the man who dis-missed the case against St Paul), while Battenberg was 'too much a bureaucrat'. The solution was clear: 'My counsel is, send for Jellicoe. . . .'

A week later the advice was the same. The gunnery of the fleet was '. . . *in a parlous state*. Send for Jellicoe and Percy Scott.' Actually Churchill had no need to send for Percy Scott – his problem was, at times, to get rid of him. Percy Scott still had the knack of seeing something so obvious that nobody else had noticed it and then point-ing it out in such a way that he got everybody's backs up. For example, he noticed that in the latest Dreadnoughts the fore-mast which carried the director position was placed behind the forward funnel, so that the spotting officer would be blinded by smoke and asphyxiated by fumes. 'I took the liberty', said Scott, 'of pointing out this amazing blunder to the Admiralty and got myself very much disliked for my pains.' The Admiralty, under pressure from Churchill, did authorize a repositioning in the fore-mast of the new battle cruiser *Lion*, but the new mast was such a weak stick that, as Percy Scott maddeningly pointed out, it vibrated too much under way for proper observations to be taken. Eventually, the infuriating Scott observed, alterations to the tripod masts would have to be carried out, at great extra expense to the country — and so they were.

Percy Scott had convinced Churchill about the need for remasting ships by means of a simple model, like a child's toy; anybody could see from it at a glance the absurdity of putting the mast behind the funnel. But Churchill told Scott that the Board were very much opposed to his system of director firing, and were quite certain that it would never be adopted. Nevertheless, Scott would not desist, and the Royal Navy owes a very great deal to this indefatigable, tactless and talented little man. He continued to argue for trials and, what is more, insisted that they be *competitive* trials, one ship pitted against another, and may the best system win.

Percy Scott's director system was installed in the 13.5-inch-gun Dreadnought *Thunderer* (Captain H.F. Oliver), although her officers kept their enthusiasm for the new invention well in check. 'We were by no means pleased at having this unpopular system thrust upon us,' wrote *Thunderer*'s gunnery officer, Lieutenant Altham (afterwards Jellicoe's biographer), 'but our Captain, with his broad outlook and deep-rooted sense of fair play, was determined that we should "give the thing every chance".'

On 14 August 1912 Percy Scott embarked in *Thunderer*, accompanied by Rear-Admiral Sir R.H. Peirse, his successor as inspector of target practice and who had himself devised a form of director in 1885, and the ship sailed for Berehaven for a two months' programme of intensive tests and calibration firings of the main 13.5-inch armament and the 4-inch secondary armament. Under the eye of the maestro himself, *Thunderer*'s guns and director crews were worked up to full efficiency in the 'follow the pointer system': the spotting officer laid on corrections on a dial, which was repeated in the turrets, so the sight-setter conformed to the movements of the master dial, and all ten turrets followed the same directions. The challenger, representing the old system in which every gun was individually laid and aimed, was the new Super-Dreadnought *Orion*, with 13.5-inch guns, flying the flag of Rear-Admiral Sir Herbert King-Hall. *Orion* had the best practice results of any 13.5-inch-gun ship in the Navy, so she would provide the best possible opposition.

The first trials, on 14 October, were inconclusive: the conditions were misty and overcast, with a force 3 wind and a slight sea. The real test came the following month, when it was stipulated that sea conditions had to be rough enough to make both ships roll five degrees each way, both ships would steam at 12 knots, both should open fire at the same moment upon a towed target 9,000 yards away, and both would cease fire after three minutes.

Time after time *Thunderer*'s salvoes, sometimes of five guns, sometimes of the full ten, rolled out and smothered the target. She fired thirty-nine rounds in the set time, scored thirteen hits, two ricochets on the target, and ten 'possible' hits on an imaginary ship around the target. According to Altham's account,

> '... in the *Thunderer* the Director Layer had learnt the trick of forecasting the roll so that it would bring his sight on to the target while giving the gun-layers time to line up their guns to the electrical indicators. At the word of command, and next time the cross-wires in his telescope came 'on', he pressed his trigger and four, five, and on one occasion the whole broadside of ten guns blazed in unison.

Meanwhile *Orion*'s gun-layers, well trained though they were, could hardly find the target at all, as they 'hunted the roll' of the ship, 'trying to adjust their own guns to the movements of the ship. *Orion* fired twenty-seven rounds in independent fire, scored two hits, one ricochet and one 'possible'.

The results were a crushing victory for *Thunderer*. Estimates of her superiority varied: a Vickers engineer said she put two to three times as many hits on the target as *Orion*; the *Daily Telegraph* also said three times; but *The Times* said five times, and *The Tatler* seven times. Percy Scott himself said six times, which was correct. Whatever the actual figure, there could be no doubt about *Thunderer*'s superiority, and Percy Scott was, for the time being, content. In his eyes his director system had been completely vindicated and its superiority established, thanks, he said, to Sir John Jellicoe and Winston Churchill.

In fact the director system was very far from being universally accepted. 'A very large number of officers were sceptical as to its value compared with the alternative system,' Jellicoe wrote. 'After the *Thunderer* trials there was considerable opposition to it and the great majority of ships were not fitted with it.' Incredibly, Jellicoe noted that the system was not liked even in some ships which had been fitted with it.

The truth was that if gunnery trials were carried out at slow speed, if funnel smoke was kept to the minimum, if there was little spray or movement of the ship, if conditions were as near as possible to the old artificial gunnery firings, then individual fire by turret *was* often more accurate. Many otherwise very competent gunnery officers were quite unable to see that these unreal conditions would not be repeated in war. By the outbreak of war only eight battleships had been fitted with the director system and then only to their main armament, although all except two had been fitted with them by the time of Jutland.

While *Hercules* was being refitted in Portsmouth dockyard, Jellicoe transferred his flag to *Colossus*, commanded by William Goodenough, and was in her for what Goodenough called '. . . a happy three weeks. . . . Sir John was at the height of his powers. I do not mean that he declined later, but he had reached that high plane on which he remained for so many years.'

In November 1912 Jellicoe rehoisted his flag in *Hercules* and took his squadron to Portland, '. . . where some interesting long range firing at 14,000 yards was carried out by H.M.S. *Colossus* in the presence of the Board of Admiralty.' Goodenough later wrote of the firings,

The plans and arrangements, made by staffs and experts, were many. Then came an opportunity of a clear range. The fact that a merchant ship was between us and the target was of no consequence. The plans went to blazes. The Admiral hoisted the 5 flag and we opened fire. Was it a long range? The present officers will smile tolerantly when they hear that it was not more than 14,000 yards. But it was an advance.

Goodenough might have been deprecating about the range but as Jellicoe rightly said at the time, 'This was by far the longest range at which Battle Practice had ever been tried and the results were very good.'

On 5 December 1912, when Jellicoe had not quite served a year in the Home Fleet, Churchill wrote to offer him the post of Second Sea Lord. Bridgeman's health, he said, was 'far from good'. Actually there was little wrong with Bridgeman's health; it seems that, just as Churchill had pushed him up to be First Sea Lord, so now he was elbowing him out. Battenberg was to be First Sea Lord in Bridgeman's place. Churchill greatly looked forward to having Jellicoe as a colleague and was satisfied that his acceptance of the offer of Second Sea Lord would be in every way conducive to the interests of the Service at an important period in naval affairs. Meanwhile he asked for the utmost secrecy to be observed.

Jellicoe, for his part, made the ritual obeisances and caveats of a man leaving a sea appointment to go back to the Admiralty: '. . . with great reluctance that I leave my command' and '. . . work at sea is very attractive to me', but he fully appreciated the honour, thanked Churchill for his kind remarks, trusted he would justify Churchill's confidence, and accepted the offer. He asked if he could inform his staff before the news was made public. Typically, Jellicoe remembered that his personal staff's future arrangements and prospects were bound up with his own and would naturally be affected.

Once more Gwendoline packed and followed, with the children. The Jellicoes rented a house in Westbourne Terrace for a short time and then bought 29 Sussex Square, just north of the Bayswater Road. Jellicoe could once again walk to and from his office two miles away. Hyde Park, for the children to play in, was just across the road. It was at the house in Sussex Square that another daughter, the fifth, Prudence Katherine Patton Jellicoe, was born in 1913.

Until now Jellicoe had only had dealings with Churchill at a wary distance, except when Churchill came bounding up the gangway, eager to see all that was to be seen. After that there would be a respite from that ebullient, cheeky, personality until the next visit. As Second Sea Lord, Jellicoe was in frequent and almost daily contact with Churchill, which was quite a different matter. It did not take Jellicoe long to find out that Churchill '. . . was very apt to express strong opinions upon purely technical matters; moreover, not being satisfied with expressing opinions, he tried to force his views upon the Board', Jellicoe admitted that Churchill was a very clever and able First Lord '. . . in some directions, but his fatal error was his entire inability to realize his own limitations as a civilian with, it is true, some early experience of military service but quite entirely ignorant of naval affairs'.

It was putting it much too strongly to say that Churchill was 'quite entirely ignorant of naval affairs'. By the time Jellicoe became Second Sea Lord, Churchill had exerted himself to learn as much as he could about the Navy from as many people in the Navy as he could – indeed, some admirals would criticize him for being too unselective about his sources of information. However, Jellicoe had a lot to put up with from Churchill over the years and much of what he says is justified. For instance, Jellicoe admired Churchill's 'wonderful argumentative powers' when putting a case for the Navy before the cabinet or the committee of imperial defence. 'He surpassed in this direction the ablest of lawyers and would make a weak case appear exceedingly strong.'

While Churchill was deploying his formidable debating expertise on the Navy's behalf, Jellicoe was content: 'We wanted the naval case well put to the Government.' But when Churchill began to exercise those same powers upon Jellicoe and the other Sea Lords, then Jellicoe was alarmed: 'It became a positive danger.' 'Naval officers', said Jellicoe, 'are not brought up to argue a case, and but few of them can make a good show in this direction. Moreover, if one is apt to be over-ridden in argument, as was the case with one of the Sea Lords on the Board at that time, it made the position very difficult for the remainder of the Board.'

Although Jellicoe was too discreet to say as much, the member of the Board so frequently over-ridden was almost certainly the First Sea Lord, Prince Louis of Battenberg, who seems to have been promoted beyond his capabilities. The main brunt of Churchill's pressure therefore fell upon Jellicoe. His dealings with Churchill more than once followed a similar pattern of discussion, disagreement, incompatibility of outlook, followed – occasionally years later – by recriminations.

One such subject for disagreement was oil fuel. While he was in *Hercules*, Jellicoe had been asked by the Admiralty to serve on the Royal Commission on Oil Fuel, which was to enquire into the question of future supplies of oil fuel and the possibilities of producing oil from coal and other materials. The Commission was chaired by Lord Fisher (one of whose nicknames was the 'Oil Maniac' from his ceaseless advocacy of the fluid's beneficial strategic properties), and had several distinguished scientists as members. The Commission decided that, though coal would stay as the Navy's main motive fuel for the time being, the fuel of the future would be oil. They recommended ways of obtaining oil, including the acquisition of oilfields, methods of storing it, cheaply and safely, in peace and war, ways of using it, including internal combustion-engined ships. All in all, it was an historic set of decisions for the Royal Navy.

It was Churchill who had proposed the appointment of the Royal Commission and it was he who had announced its findings to the House of Commons in July 1913. But his subsequent behaviour almost led Jellicoe to resign. The Commission had recommended a stockpile of four years' war consumption, which Jellicoe thought was 'totally unnecessary'. He proposed reserves of from three to six months' war consumption. Churchill thought both these demands extravagant, and only agreed to four-and-a-half months' reserve, to be accumulated over a period of time, after Jellicoe threatened to resign. Jellicoe was very much annoyed when Churchill wrote in *The World Crisis* that '. . . these conclusions stood the test of war'. In fact in 1917 German submarine attacks on tankers brought about a most critical oil situation. The country as a whole had about three weeks' supply, and some fuelling bases were down to less than a week's supply.

In 1912 and 1913 there was a shortage in the Navy of lieutenants and other officers of junior rank, and varied suggestions were made as to how to relieve the situation. Churchill proposed that paymaster officers should take over the duties of lieutenants, including officer-of-the-watch at sea. This was not an outrageous suggestion, as experience in two wars was to show. Officers can be trained to keep watches remarkably quickly, given reasonable intelligence, good eyesight and a little confidence from experience, but to Jellicoe and his colleagues this was an anathema. Jellicoe pointed out that '. . . no officer could properly take charge of one of H.M. Ships at sea unless he was certified as fit to do so, and that Accountant officers from their training could not possibly be so certified.'

Jellicoe was quite right that officers-of-the-watch needed a watch-keeping certificate. But he was quite wrong in saying that accountant officers, or any other non-executive officers, could not be trained to obtain a certificate. Jellicoe was echoing the old, proud, conservative view of the officers in sail, faintly contemptuous of those who were not executive officers, and unshakably sceptical that any but executive officers could ever handle a ship at sea. Churchill, understandably, 'took great exception' to Jellicoe's opposition and '. . . said that I was always trying to thwart him. I replied that I only did so when his proposals were of an impossible nature.'

In May 1913 Jellicoe went to Berlin for ten days, and Gwendoline accompanied him. They stayed at the Adlon Hotel. had lunch with the Chancellor, went to the opera, had dinner with the Kaiser and Kaiserin, and attended the wedding of the Kaiser's daughter, Princess Victoria Luise. She was a charming girl; Jellicoe sat next to her at dinner, and was much struck by her. After dinner the Kaiser and von Tirpitz had a long conversation with him about the Royal Navy: the Germans criticized the common entry for all officers, introduced by Fisher; Jellicoe replied that the Germans would have to do likewise soon, if only to improve the status of their engineering officers who were in a very inferior position relative to the executive branch.

Jellicoe had a trip in a Zeppelin, took tea at Tirpitz's house and invited him to come over to England; Tirpitz replied that if he did someone would surely murder him. Later, Jellicoe went to another reunion dinner of officers who had fought in China during the Boxer Rebellion. He had a very pleasant evening and when he asked, in conversation, who were the 'coming leaders afloat' in the German Navy, he was told Admiral Scheer was certainly one of them.

In July 1913 Jellicoe enjoyed what he called 'a very pleasant inter-lude from Admiralty work', when on the fourteenth he was tempor-arily appointed to *Thunderer* in command of the Red, or attacking fleet, for the annual manoeuvres. Sir George Callaghan, flying his flag in *Neptune*, commanded the Blue or defending fleet. Jellicoe had his staff appointed in good time, for the manoeuvres involved a great deal of extra work over and above Jellicoe's normal duties as Second Sea Lord: he had to prepare all the plans for deployment of his fleet and virtually to draw up a special signal book to cover eventualities.

All the battleship and cruiser squadrons, and all the destroyer flotillas in home waters, some 350 warships in all, were to take part.

The exercises were kept unusually secret – nothing was published in the press beforehand, and commanding officers were not allowed to invite guests on board their ships after a certain date prior to the start of the exercise. The object was to estimate the possible damage a raiding hostile fleet could inflict, and to test the possibilities of hostile troops being landed on British soil.

Jellicoe's Red Fleet assembled at the Nore, where part of his force included four fast transports, *Rohilla*, *Rewa*, *Dongola* and *Plassy*, in which three battalions of infantry and a battalion of marines, about 2,500 troops in all, were to be conveyed up the east coast and landed somewhere near the Humber. The umpire was Admiral of the Fleet Sir William May, who, as C-in-C Home Fleet a few years earlier, had paid a good deal of attention to the study of tactical problems posed by a mixed fleet of Dreadnoughts, pre-Dreadnoughts, armoured cruisers and destroyer flotillas. Despite Fisher's remarks, May was one of the few pre-war officers to try new ideas in fleet manoeuvres. Flying his flag in the armoured cruiser *Euryalus*, he sailed from Sheerness to supervise the exercises on 23 July.

Next day Jellicoe was off the Humber and lured his opponents out by pretending to steam towards Flamborough Head. Troops were landed on Humberside and began, in theory, to destroy shore installations, the Blue force being hopelessly outnumbered. Two days later a strong Red force appeared off the Tyne and began disembarking troops north and south of the river. Although annual naval manoeuvres were intended to test the country's defences and to demonstrate how sound they were, they often had precisely the opposite effect on the populace. While merchantmen in the North Sea were complaining about dazzling lights and vessels moving among them at high speed, the city councils of Grimsby and Hull were so alarmed at what they thought was their vulnerability that they asked for forts to be built guarding the river entrance.

Eventually the manoeuvres were cancelled prematurely, because of the risk that they might betray information of real value to the Germans, besides alarming the general population. The fact was that Jellicoe had done too well: he was on top of his form, at the peak of his mental, physical and professional fitness, and he had never been so sharp, so quick and accurate in decision. There is no doubt that he had completely wiped Sir George Callaghan's eye and, arguably, if the battle of Jutland had been fought in July 1913, it might have been the comprehensive victory the nation yearned for.

Jellicoe was so good that he probably misled Churchill, who had been in *Thunderer* himself for the latter part of the manoeuvres, into believing that he was more of the dashing, brilliant, cavalry-type naval commander than he actually was. Churchill wrote to him on 27 July:

'Only a line to congratulate you on the brilliant and daring manner in which you executed the difficult task entrusted to you in the manoeuvres. You have every reason to be contented with results which leave your naval reputation second to none among the naval officers of the active list.' At the same time, looking forward to August 1914, those manoeuvres of 1913 very probably sealed Sir George Callaghan's fate; if he had had any chance of continuing to command the Grand Fleet in war, it had now gone.

One of the most serious quarrels between Churchill and Jellicoe arose over naval air. From his first days as First Lord, Churchill had begun to press for a naval air service. Three times he was rebuffed by the Treasury before he obtained financial sanction, and even then the road continued to be rough and stony. In December 1912 he told Battenberg that the air department and naval aviation generally '. . . require to be continuously gripped and studied under one hand' so that a well-considered and properly thought-out policy could be evolved and carried out, the new Director of the Air Department, Captain Sueter, could be given the supervision and support he needed, and liaison between the Navy and the Army could be as close and harmonious as possible. The duties of First Sea Lord were very heavy, so Churchill wanted Air to be 'definitely and absolutely assigned to the Second Sea Lord'. Sir John Jellicoe was '. . . the very man to shake the whole thing together and unless you differ,' he wrote, 'I should propose to assign this duty to him.'

Jellicoe was certainly very interested in the possibilities for the Navy of aircraft and airships and was happy to be involved with their early introduction, but in his mind the naval air service had to be properly constituted and under proper naval discipline and was not to be a wild and unaccountable offshoot. For Jellicoe naval discipline and loyalty to the Service, which included his seniors and juniors alike, were indivisible. This was a principle on which Jellicoe felt very strongly indeed – once he struck out some comments of his own on Seymour's conduct of operations in China, because he feared it might be thought he was being disloyal to his chief. Loyalty and discipline were supremely important to Jellicoe and he was afraid that, in the matter of the naval air service, Churchill was about to try and overthrow all these principles. This was not what Churchill meant at all, but Churchill should have known his man better. He had, after all, been specifically warned; Fisher had written to him from Naples in March 1912, advising him to send for Jellicoe, '. . . engage him in private talk – he is fearfully sensitive as regards loyalty' (in that case to the First Sea Lord, Bridgeman).

It all began almost from nothing. It was true that Churchill sometimes had a very cavalier attitude to naval seniority and susceptibilities.

Some naval officers responded with a certain coolness. Rear-Admiral Dudley de Chair, who was then Naval Secretary, spoke for many naval officers when he described one of his earliest meetings with Churchill. He had already very bravely, some might have thought rashly, refused Churchill's invitation to go down to Portland in *Enchantress*, on the grounds that he already had an engagement to go to a matinée and he wrote: 'I thought it was ignominious for me to be "vetted" by a young politician, who knew little or nothing of the personnel of the Navy.'

Churchill was quite likely to consult a junior officer in his senior's absence, and as Jellicoe said, 'He was at his worst in this respect in connection with the Naval Air Service, then in its infancy.' In November 1913 Churchill visited Sheerness in *Enchantress* and while he was there went on board *Hermes*, the parent ship of the naval air service, which was lying at anchor in the stream. A current question of debate was the use of some land for the air service on the bank of the Medway. It was not a very important matter, on the face of it; Captain Gerald Vivian, *Hermes*' commanding officer, had already given a decision on it and thought the matter closed. However, one of Vivian's subordinates, a lieutenant, held differing views and happened, in the course of conversation, to mention them to Churchill. Churchill at once agreed with the lieutenant, and told Vivian the lieutenant's views were to be carried out.

This was already bad enough. Worse, considering the personalities involved, was to follow. After Churchill had left, Vivian naturally took his young subordinate aside and told him, quite properly, that he was not to go chatting to the First Lord in such a way. The lieutenant hotly replied that his opinions had been approved by the First Lord and went on to say that if he did not get what he wanted he would write to the First Lord because the First Lord had told him so.

Whether or not Churchill had really encouraged a junior officer to transgress so blatantly against the authority of a senior, the fat was now properly in the fire. Vivian complained to the commander-in-Chief at the Nore, Admiral Sir Richard Poore, who in his turn complained to Jellicoe, saying that the First Lord's methods were bound to undermine discipline. Jellicoe agreed that such 'procedure was of course entirely subversive to discipline'. Jellicoe was '. . . anxious that the force [the Naval Air Arm] should be properly disciplined, and rather feared there was danger that the First Lord's methods might do harm in this connection'.

The affair was rapidly gaining momentum and importance, uncovering real sources of grievances between the First Lord and the rest of the Board. Churchill heard of the outcome of his visit and asked Jellicoe to hand over to him any dispatch from Poore on the subject, but Jellicoe had diplomatically returned Poore's letter to him, and enclosed a letter of his own, advising Poore to rephrase some of the stronger language in it. When Churchill heard this he 'went dancing mad' and ordered the GPO to find the letter and return it to him. This was quite illegal, but it was done. Churchill read Poore's letter but later claimed that he had not read Jellicoe's enclosures.

That morning, de Chair arrived at his office and began to open letters when a private secretary came in and told him that Churchill was '. . . very angry with the Commander-in-Chief at the Nore for some letter he had written, that he intended to make the said c-in-c haul his flag down, and that he was going to order this to be done at once, without any reference to the Sea Lords'. The First Lord was, apparently, 'quite unmanageable', and de Chair was asked to go and see him. He found Churchill in a 'very excited state' walking up and down and dictating a telegram to the Secretary of the Admiralty. After de Chair had remonstrated with Churchill and asked him to put the matter before the whole Board, Churchill replied, 'Do you think I am going to humiliate myself before the Sea Lords? I will not be insulted. Either his flag comes down or I go. I refuse to discuss the matter further.'

All the parties involved, not just Churchill, used the threat of resignation as a kind of Homeric epithet, like princes and warriors of the Trojan War addressing each other in the vaunting language of epic hexameters. De Chair thought he should resign in protest, but before doing so he should warn the Sea Lords and see if they could stop Churchill '. . . doing such a mad thing'. According to de Chair, Jellicoe said to him, 'Don't resign. If the First Lord persists in this action we will all resign, and you can come with us, and it will make it all the stronger.'

In the event nobody resigned, not even Poore who 'under vast pressure' was induced not to – he was convinced by the Sea Lords that Churchill was something 'off his head' over the matter and he should not take so much notice of it. At Battenberg's suggestion the lieutenant apologised to Vivian and to Churchill. In a few days it was all over.

But it had one most important outcome, for the naval air service. Jellicoe told Churchill that he could not agree with his methods and resigned his control over the naval air service, which went to the Fourth Sea Lord, Admiral Pakenham. This served to remove control over naval aircraft just that little, perhaps crucial, distance from the centre of naval power. It may have been one small step more towards the eventual loss by the Navy of its own air power, which close personal control by such a personality as Jellicoe might have prevented.

Another long-running source of contention between Jellicoe and Churchill was the ship-building programme for 1914 (the programme for 1913 had, of course, been decided before Jellicoe became Second Sea Lord). Churchill was still expected by the radical wing of his party to reduce the Navy Estimates; that was, in fact, the main reason he had been appointed First Lord. The Board was in general agreement about light cruisers and destroyers, but when it came to capital ships Jellicoe '. . . found what I feared was a tendency on the part of the First Lord to reduce the number of battleships to be constructed from four to three'. Churchill argued on the basis of the number and calibre of guns alone, whereas Jellicoe argued that the only true basis for comparison was displacement; by that measurement the German ships would be markedly superior.

Lloyd George opposed the Estimates, as he had done before, but this time he and Churchill were on opposite sides of the table. Churchill insisted he would resign if the main features of the programme were not approved. And if he resigned, then, by the ritual heroic protocol of the age, all the Sea Lords would also have resigned. At this prospect the cabinet gave in; they cut out three light cruisers and some torpedo boats, to save face, and approved the rest.

His disagreements with Churchill had been so frequent and occasionally so acrimonious that Jellicoe himself eventually began to wonder whether command of the First Fleet, that consummation so devoutly wished by Fisher and himself for so long, might never come his way at all. When Jellicoe first came to the Admiralty as Second Sea Lord, Churchill had indicated 'pretty clearly', in Jellicoe's words, that he intended to offer him the command in succession to Callaghan and often, as the months went by, referred to the succession as though it were already settled and no longer even a matter for argument. 'But', as Jellicoe wrote to Admiral Sir Frederick Hamilton on 17 June 1914, 'up to date he has not offered it, and as we so constantly disagree, it is quite possible that he may think I am not the right person for it.'

Jellicoe was writing from Aix-les-Bains, where he and Gwendoline had gone to take the waters and have a short holiday; Jellicoe also wanted treatment for an old rugger injury in his knee. They had a very pleasant three weeks playing tennis, enjoying the medicinal waters, and driving out into the surrounding countryside. While they were there they heard the news of the assassination of the Archduke Ferdinand and his wife at Sarajevo, and as the international situation seemed to be darkening they came home early in July.

Disagreement with Churchill continued, to the end. Before he left, Jellicoe had been given by Churchill a copy of a report on the subject of seizing and occupying one of the German islands, Sylt or Borkum, for an advanced base if war with Germany broke out. The report, by Rear-Admiral Lewis Bayly, Jellicoe's old flat-mate George Aston and another officer, favoured the occupation of Borkum. Jellicoe did not, and said so – both islands could be shelled by long-range guns from the mainland and could not be held for long, nor would there be any point in holding them, because any ships based in the islands could also be shelled.

Jellicoe was much annoyed, yet again, when Churchill returned to the charge on this subject in *The World Crisis*; Jellicoe wrote:

> How an attack on Borkum could possibly assist fleet operations in the Baltic or lead to the German Fleet being driven altogether from the North Sea [as suggested by Churchill] is an argument that is difficult to follow. To suggest that we could mine them in their harbours *as the result of the capture of Borkum* is ludicrous, as is the idea that the capture of Borkum, even if it could be held, would have assisted us in a military attack on Schleswig-Holstein.

Jellicoe made the good point that general views on a possible operation, and detailed plans, were quite different things. Often what seemed a good idea in theory proved quite unfeasible in practice. 'The Dardanelles tragedy', said Jellicoe, 'was largely due to Mr Churchill being allowed to start operations without a properly worked-out plan.'

That year of 1914 the Admiralty, largely at Churchill's instigation, decided to cancel the annual naval manoeuvres and instead exercise the mobilization of the whole fleet, including the reserves. The mobilizations began on 15 July, and ships began to assemble at Spithead the next day. They consisted of the First Fleet, whose ships were fully manned and in full commission; the Second Fleet, which was partly manned and had been brought up to full complement; and the Third Fleet, which had been manned by reservists who had drawn their kits and proceeded to their various ships during the previous week.

A grand review of the fleet was held on 17 and 18 July. It was, in Churchill's words, '. . . incomparably the greatest assemblage of naval power ever witnessed in the history of the world'. There were fifty-seven capital ships present, and the king was there to inspect various ships of every class. On 19 July the fleet put to sea for exercises. The whole fleet raised steam, weighed anchor and steamed in one long line ahead past the Royal Yacht, each ship being 'manned' and giving three cheers for the King as she passed. There were so many ships that it took six hours for them all to go by, at an average speed of fifteen knots. Meanwhile seaplanes and aeroplanes flew overhead, the first time aircraft had taken part in a fleet review.

After the review some of the reservists returned to their homes, but the First and Second Fleets were kept in full readiness, while Churchill and the Board considered the situation. Eventually, after some days, when the international situation was clearly deteriorating, the ships of both fleets were assembled at Portland. On 29 July 1914 the First Fleet put to sea and steamed to the south-west until they were clear of land, before altering to the eastward. They were going to Scapa Flow. As Churchill said, 'The King's ships were at sea.'

Chapter 9

Not everybody believed that war was inevitable. On 28 July 1914 Jellicoe went to a dinner at the United Services Club, given by Lord Morely. Amongst the guests were Kitchener, Churchill, Lord Haldane and, sitting next to Jellicoe, Lord Bryce, who had just been ambassador in the United States. When Jellicoe remarked in conversation that the European horizon 'looked to be very clouded' Lord Bryce was surprised and asked what he meant; Jellicoe said that it looked as if they might be at war with Germany before long. 'War with Germany?' said Lord Bryce. 'Absurd. Why, any British government that did such a thing would be thrown out of office immediately.'

Nevertheless, Jellicoe had already been briefed by Churchill and Battenberg that in the event of war they thought it necessary that the C-in-C Home Fleet should have an assistant, and Jellicoe had been selected for the appointment. They asked him to arrange with Sir George Callaghan the ship in which he would fly his flag. Jellicoe had not had time to do so when, on 30 July, he turned over his duties as Second Sea Lord to Vice Admiral Sir Frederick Hamilton and prepared to join the fleet as second-in-command. The following day Jellicoe had a long talk at the Admiralty with Churchill and Battenberg and it was made clear to him that in 'certain circumstances' he '. . . might be appointed Commander-in-Chief in succession to Sir George Callaghan'. This, Jellicoe said, came to him as a great surprise. He protested against such a change on what might well be the very eve of war. But nothing was settled and Jellicoe left the same night by train for Wick, on his way to Scapa Flow, thinking, he said, that the change *might* take place, but had not been finally decided.

If that is what he thought, he was mistaken. It is very probable that Churchill had intended, almost from his first day as First Lord, to replace Callaghan with Jellicoe. He had clearly made up his mind on 30 July, before Jellicoe left for Scotland. Callaghan was nearly sixty-two years old; his appointment had already been extended by a year, and came to an end in any case in October 1914. To replace him, repugnant though it was to Jellicoe, and outrageous though it seemed to many other admirals, was a bold decision and the right decision. Before Jellicoe left King's Cross Station an officer from the Admiralty gave him a sealed envelope, to be opened in Sir George's presence if war should break out. It was Jellicoe's appointment as commander-in-chief.

While Jellicoe was travelling north emergency measures were being put into effect all over the country which, as Churchill wrote '. . . began to astonish the public. Naval harbours were cleared, bridges were guarded, steamers were boarded and examined, watchers lined the coasts.' The battleships of the Home Fleet, soon to be called the Grand Fleet, had arrived at Scapa and Cromarty, the battle cruisers at Rosyth.

Sitting in his first-class compartment Jellicoe had plenty of time to think, but nobody of whom to take advice. He knew that he was professionally, mentally and physically fit to take command of the fleet. He was younger than Callaghan. He probably had more experience, more recently and over a longer period, of the latest weapons. Not to be mealy-mouthed about it, although Jellicoe was a very modest man he was shrewd enough and realistic enough to know that he was a better fleet commander than Callaghan. But it was not so simple. Callaghan knew his own fleet, its officers and ships, intimately, and they were all looking to him to lead them into battle. Besides, he was an old friend of Jellicoe's. He had been Jellicoe's superior officer. Jellicoe owed him many kindnesses and much good advice. To a man with Jellicoe's fierce devotion to loyalty, the very idea of sacking Sir George at such a time seemed unthinkable.

Jellicoe was due to go aboard the cruiser *Boadicea* at Wick to take him across the Pentland Firth to Scapa, but he was delayed by fog. At 10.30 p.m. on Saturday 1 August he sent a telegram to the First Lord, addressed 'Personal' to Churchill by name.

Detained Wick by fog. Am firmly convinced after consideration that the step you mentioned to me is fraught with gravest danger at this juncture and might easily be disastrous owing to extreme difficulty of getting in touch with everything at short notice.

The transfer even if carried out cannot safely be accomplished for some time.

I beg most earnestly that you will give matter further consideration with First Sea Lord before you take this step. Jellicoe.

To Prince Louis of Battenberg, Jellicoe sent the same telegram with the addition of another sentence: 'You will understand my motive in wiring is to do my best for country not personal considerations.'

The telegrams make it clear that, although Jellicoe wrote much later that he had left London '. . . with the impression that the change was not one that had been finally decided upon, but that it might take place', by the time he arrived at Wick he was quite sure it was intended to take place. To emphasise his point, on Sunday morning Jellicoe sent another telegram addressed to Churchill and Prince Louis:

Reference my personal telegram last night. Am more than ever convinced of vital importance of making no change. Personal feelings are entirely ignored in reaching this conclusion. Jellicoe.

This time he had an answer, received at Scapa Flow at 8.30 that evening. From First Lord, Personal: 'I can give you 48 hours after joining fleet. You must be ready then.'

Churchill had already written to the King on 31 July, that should war come he should have to submit the name of Sir John Jellicoe for the supreme command. Churchill said he had reached, with regret, the conclusion that Callaghan was not equal to the strains which war would entail on the c-in-c. Churchill reminded the King that His Majesty himself knew well enough the purely physical exertions which the command of a great fleet demanded. They must have a younger man. These were not times '. . . when personal feelings can be considered unduly'.

Churchill wrote again on 1 August to the King to ask him 'respectfully and most earnestly' to approve Jellicoe's supercession of Callaghan. The same day he answered a note from Lady Jellicoe: 'I am deeply touched by the message you convey. We have absolute confidence in his services and his devotion. We shall back him through thick and thin. Thank God we have him at hand.'

Although Jellicoe could not have known of these exchanges, he should now have left the matter alone. He should have known that further remonstration would achieve nothing. But after considering Churchill's message on Sunday evening he sent a reply at 11.30, by code. It was marked 'Personal' to the First Lord, and repeated to the First Sea Lord.

Yours of second. Can only reply am certain step contemplated is most dangerous beg that it may not be carried out. Am perfectly willing to act on board Fleet flagship as assistant if desired to be in direct communications. Hard to believe it is realised what grave difficulties change of Commander-in-Chief involves at this moment. Do not forget also long experience of command of Commander-in-Chief. Jellicoe.

The situation, with this flow and counter-flow of imploring telegrams, was now straying perilously close to farce. *Boadicea* had finally left Wick with Jellicoe on board late in the forenoon of 2 August, so

Jellicoe had actually reported himself to Callaghan on board *Iron Duke* by the time he sent his Sunday evening telegram. Knowledge of the event to come had made Jellicoe's interview '. . . both embarrassing and painful, as I could see that he had no knowledge of the possibility of his leaving the fleet, and obviously I could not tell him'. Apparently Sir George also remained oblivious of the fact that Jellicoe was sending coded telegrams to the First Lord and the First Sea Lord from his flagship.

At 9.15 on Monday morning Jellicoe sent yet another telegram, again to Churchill and to Prince Louis, by name.

> Quite impossible to be ready at such short notice. Feel it is my duty to warn you emphatically that you court disaster if you carry out intention of changing before I have thorough grip of fleet and situation. I am sure Hamilton, Madden, or any admiral recently in Home Fleet will be of my opinion. Jellicoe.

Now Jellicoe was perilously close to impertinence. At 11.30 the same morning he added a rider:

> Add to last message. Fleet is imbued with feelings of extreme admiration and loyalty for Commander-in-Chief. This is very strong factor.

But time and the worsening situation had exhausted Churchill's patience. His next message, dispatched at 12.45 p.m. on 3 August, allowed no rebuttal. It was addressed to Admiral Jellicoe (Secret and Personal).

> Expeditionary Force will not leave at present and therefore fleet movements connected with it will not immediately be required. I am sending Madden tonight to be at your side. I am telegraphing to the Commander-in-Chief directing him to transfer command to you at earliest moment suitable to the interests of the Service I rely on him and you to effect this change quickly and smoothly, personal feelings cannot count now only what is best for us all, you should consult with him frankly. First Lord.

At about 4 a.m. on 4 August Jellicoe received orders from the Admiralty to open the envelope containing his appointment which he had been given on the train. He went on board *Iron Duke* at once – his account does not say in which ship he received the news – to find that Callaghan had also received his orders to turn over the command.

It must have been an absolutely crushing shock for Callaghan. On the eve of war, when everything he had worked for was about to be put to the test, he was removed because he was too old, not good enough, not fit. Jellicoe said that Callaghan behaved, '. . . as always, as a most gallant officer and gentleman, and his one desire was to make the position easy for me, in entire disregard of his own feelings'. But Admiral Sir Herbert King-Hall, writing of the way Callaghan was '. . . summarily and somewhat cruelly superseded', said, 'It was a stunning blow, and he never properly got over it.'

Jellicoe and Callaghan agreed that Jellicoe should formally take over command the following day, but as the fleet had been ordered to sea it was decided that Callaghan would haul down his flag at 8.30 a.m. on the fourth. He left in the cruiser *Sappho*, and sailed away into obscurity; in spite of his talents and devotion as an officer, he is now virtually only remembered for the fact that Jellicoe relieved him as C-in-C at the outbreak of war. Jellicoe wrote him a consoling letter later, and the King, as Callaghan said, '. . . did a great deal to put me right with myself. . . .' Callaghan went to serve in the Admiralty for a time, before becoming C-in-C at the Nore.

The fleet watched him go with dismay and none was more dismayed than Jellicoe. On the seventh he wrote to Hamilton:

I hope I never have to live through such a time as I had from Friday to Tuesday [i.e. from 31 July to 4 August]. My position was horrible. I did my best but could not stop what I believe is a grave error. I trust sincerely it won't prove to be so. Of course each day I get more into the saddle. But the tragedy of the news to the Commander-in-Chief was past belief, and it was almost worse for me.

It was almost worse for the rest of the fleet, to whom Callaghan's departure suggested confusion at the worst, and at the very least uncertainty. Jellicoe was well known in the Service but many flag officers resented his arrival, and there was even a feeling that Jellicoe might have somehow engineered it. A protest to the First Lord was briefly mooted. The King thought Callaghan had been badly treated. Beatty, when he first heard of the proposed change, telegraphed Churchill that it '. . . would cause unprecedented disaster'. He thought the 'moral effect upon Fleet at such a moment would be worse than a defeat at sea'. But all the protests and talk came to nothing, because there was nothing more to be said or done. Jellicoe was the right choice, undoubtedly. Churchill had made the right decision, but it took a man of real moral courage to do it. Some of the ratings in the ships' companies must also have been bewildered by the change, if they ever thought about it at all. But for most it was all much too high above their heads.

That morning the fleet put to sea from Scapa. It was a stately process. All ships shortened in cable, weighed anchor, and pointed ship, according to the orders of the flag or senior officer of each unit. For the destroyers the unit was the flotilla; for cruisers the squadron; for battleships usually the division (half a squadron). Ships put to sea in reverse order of size; destroyers first for screening, then cruisers for the outer screen, then the larger armoured cruisers for the close escort, and finally,the battleships (the battle cruisers were normally at Rosyth). *Iron Duke* usually put to sea last, being connected to the Admiralty by telephone buoy, thus remaining in touch until the last moment.

Jellicoe's immediate task was to take his four battle squadrons with escort north and east to within a hundred miles of the Norwegian coast and then make a sweep south and west. That evening of 4 August the ultimatum to Germany not to cross the Belgium frontiers expired, with no satisfactory assurances from Germany, and so at 11 p.m. – midnight Berlin time – the Admiralty sent the 'War Telegram' to all ships and shore establishments: 'Commence hostilities with Germany.'

In the morning Jellicoe received a message from the King:

At this grave moment in our national history, I send to you and through you to the officers and men of the fleet of which you have assumed command, the assurance of my confidence that under your direction they will revive and renew the old glories of the Royal Navy, and prove once again the sure shield of Britain and her Empire in the hour of trial.

The fleet responded with a thrill of loyalty and pride. As Lieutenant Stephen King-Hall in the cruiser *Southampton* wrote of the King, 'I for one believe he writes his messages to the Navy himself.'

King-Hall spoke for many officers in the fleet when he jotted down, on 5 August:

We know nothing as to the *casus belli,* or how matters are proceeding on the Continent. It is quite *impossible at present* to grasp the stupendous fact, that after a century of peace the British Navy has embarked on a great maritime war. It is useless to speculate on the outcome. God willing, I shall live to see our Empire emerge triumphant, though I feel that it may be a very 'waiting and watching' war.

When the fleet returned to Scapa on 7 August, having met no German warships but having sunk a quantity of German trawlers, Jellicoe had a chance at last to sit down and write to his mother. It is a revealing letter on Jellicoe's thoughts about his new appointment and on the future. It was addressed from *Iron Duke*, written in pencil, shortly before the fleet entered harbour:

My own darling Mother, I hope you have not been anxious about me, but I have of course been without a moment. I was sent north as Second-in-Command, and at the last moment was told I might have to take command. I protested strongly against the folly of changing the Commander-in-Chief on the eve of war, and after arriving up north telegraphed twice a day imploring the Admiralty not to do it, as I was sure it was a fatal error. I put on one side my strong objection to superseding a very old friend at such a moment, the idea of which so distressed me that I felt quite ill, and could not sleep at all. It was so utterly repugnant to my feelings. But the Admiralty insisted, and 4 hours before the fleet left I was ordered to transfer my flag as acting Admiral to the Flagship, and poor Sir George Callaghan left her utterly broken down. It was a cruel and most unwise step. But it is done, and I've had to make the best of it and try to grasp the work and get hold of all the many details at the shortest notice. I really wonder that I kept my head at all when I think of what I went through. But I am all right, Mother dear, and every day makes it easier. I cannot give you any news of our movements as all letters are censored and read (except of course my own), but I must set an example. Officers and men are not even allowed to head their letters with the name of their ships. I've done it for this letter, but you will understand if I don't do it again.

I've got Charles Madden with me as Chief-of-Staff and he helps me so much. We are entering harbour to coal now but shall be out tonight again. I dare not stay in harbour at night if I can help it for fear of destroyer attacks. I have of course the greater part of the Navy under my immediate command. The war may last some time. I should say it depends largely on what happens on shore.

You won't be anxious about me I hope, Mother dear. God will protect me and I look to Him to help me to do my duty to my country. I feel that our cause is just. The war has been forced on us, and that right will prevail in the end. I hope that dear Father is well, and that you will be able to arrange for a satisfactory man in place of Waterson, also that the high prices will not affect your comfort. I imagine that we are much better off than Germany as far as that goes. The Germans seem to be laying mines all over the sea to the danger of merchant ships. It is a cruel form of warfare which will recoil on their own heads. We have had no fighting up here as yet. I have had to capture and sink a lot of German trawlers as they have carrier pigeons on board and send information away I expect, but of course I take the crews off. I am simply overwhelmed with work and try to sleep when opportunity occurs as it is so vitally important to keep in health and my mind clear, so I know you won't expect long and frequent letters. I have asked Gwen to keep you informed about me, and Admiral Leveson at the Admiralty to contradict any false reports that get about. I will close now, dearest Mother. Give my fondest love to Father, Grace and Eddie, Fred, Alice and the dear Aunts. Every your most loving son, Jack.

The letter, though carefully phrased, as much to avoid worrying his mother as to transgress against censorship, gives an accurate summary of many of Jellicoe's problems. As he said, he had the greater part of the Navy under his immediate command. The main fleet consisted of nearly a hundred ships, besides all the store ships and colliers needed to maintain them. There were twenty-one Dreadnoughts in the 1st, 2nd and 4th Battle Squadrons, and eight pre-Dreadnought battleships of the King Edward class in the 3rd Battle Squadron. There were also four battle cruiser Dreadnoughts in the 1st Battle-Cruiser Squadron under Vice-Admiral Sir David Beatty, which moved down to Cromarty in October 1914 and then in December to Rosyth. There were eight armoured cruisers in the 2nd and 3rd Cruiser Squadron, four light cruisers of the 1st Light Cruiser Squadron and 42 destroyers of the 2nd and 4th Flotillas. Two other flotillas of destroyers based at Harwich under Commodore R.Y. Tyrwhitt were nominally under Jellicoe's command and theoretically part of the Grand Fleet, intended to join it at sea in the event of an action. In practice the Harwich force never did join the fleet.

It was no wonder that Jellicoe was, as he told his mother, '. . . simply overwhelmed with work'. Considering the size of his fleet, he had a comparatively small staff: Madden, as chief-of-staff, headed what might be termed the 'operational' staff, concerned with the strategic use and tactical deployment of the fleet. With him Jellicoe also brought Captain R.W. Bentinck who became chief-of-staff to Vice-Admiral Sir George Warrender in the 2nd Battle Squadron; and several other war staff, signal and wireless officers, including Lieutenant Fitzherbert, the flag lieutenant. From Callaghan's staff Jellicoe took over Commodore A.F. Everett, who headed the personnel and material staff, dealing with logistics, and several other war staff, wireless and signal officers. Captain F.C. Dreyer relieved Captain Lawson as flag captain and in command of Iron Duke in October 1915. Also on Jellicoe's staff, heading the supply and secretariat department, was Fleet Paymaster Hamnet Share, the C-in-C's secretary, who also, of course, had served several times with Jellicoe before.

Some of the staff officers knew each other already, some did not, but

147

they all quickly found themselves struggling to keep their feet in the tides of paperwork which flowed daily in and out of the flagship. At least a hundred telegrams, and often many more, were received and sent every day. The cypher officers kept watches twenty-four hours about. In the c-in-c's office seven officers, six chief and petty officers and other writers, with two printing presses and printers, were kept busy seven days a week.

Sir George Callaghan had left the fleet in an excellent state of training and discipline. But this was now wartime and the enemy might make a sortie at any moment. A thousand decisions had to be made, procedures laid down, routines settled, orders written and promulgated. Every day there were a score of ship movements: ships leaving and entering harbour, coaling, exercising, carrying out main or subsidiary armament shoots. For much of the time most of the fleet was at sea. In the first four months of the war, for example, the Grand Fleet steamed 16,805 miles. *Iron Duke* herself took in over 14,000 tons of coal, every pound of it loaded and shovelled by hand. She was only in harbour for one complete day of twenty-four hours in August 1914 and only for six complete days in September.

All this steaming was certainly not in pursuit of the enemy. As the early days of the war passed, everybody in the Grand Fleet was astonished that the Germans did not come out. Raised to a high state of anticipation by the fiery prophecies of Fisher, everybody had expected Armageddon at once. The British Expeditionary Force was safely conveyed across the Channel, entirely unmolested, by 20 August, and still the Germans made no move. On 12 August the Admiralty signalled to Jellicoe:

We cannot wholly exclude the chance of an attempt at landing during the week on a large scale by High Seas Fleet. Extraordinary silence and inertia of enemy may be prelude to serious enterprises . . . now that you have shaken off the submarine menace, or as soon as you can do so, it would appear necessary to bring the Fleet to the eastward of the Orkneys. . . .

Extraordinarily silent and inert though the enemy had been, Jellicoe had not shaken off the submarine menace, and his frantic steaming in the later months of 1914 was due to the fact that, incredibly, he had no secure fleet base. Scapa Flow, where the Grand Fleet lay, was in a vital strategic position, guarding the northern passage round the British Isles and out to the open North Atlantic. But as a fleet base Scapa Flow itself was almost totally undefended. Until it was, the fleet was forced to lead a nomadic, restless existence, never daring to stay in one place for too long, for fear as Jellicoe had said in his letter, of destroyer night attacks, and of submarine attacks at all times. It was the spectre of submarine attack that occupied Jellicoe's thoughts from the very earliest days of the war.

In August 1914 the Navy generally still had an innocent pre-Fall of Man conception of submarines and their capabilities. Their potential for destruction simply was not widely enough recognized. Many officers still thought them unfair, unsportsmanlike, a sneaky sort of weapon, 'damned un-English' as Arthur Knyvet Wilson called them, and no better than vermin. The view that submarines could be hunted down by surface ships, acting rather like nautical fox-hounds, was given tremendous encouragement on 9 August, when the cruiser *Birmingham* ran down, rammed and sank U-15. Jellicoe and the more cautious members of his staff were more impressed by the ominous range of the U-boat from its base, and the fact that it was very probably this same submarine which narrowly missed the battleship *Monarch* with a torpedo while she was carrying out gunnery firings off the Fair Isles the day before.

Jellicoe's feelings about submarines were soon fulfilled beyond his most pessimistic forebodings. Ironically, the first incident occurred after a time of great rejoicing, when the spirits of the Navy and the country had been given a colossal fillip after the puzzling anticlimax of the first weeks of the war by a rousing cruiser action off the Heligoland Bight. Two light cruisers and two destroyer flotillas from Harwich, supported by two battle cruisers from the Humber, attempted to lay a trap for German destroyers patrolling from Heligoland. The plan was to get between the enemy destroyers and their base at a time when the night patrol was being relieved by the day patrol, and devour them all.

When Jellicoe heard of the sortie on 26 August he thought the forces involved were too weak to operate in such a manner so close to the enemy coastline, and dispatched Beatty with the 1st Battle Cruiser Squadron and Commodore Goodenough's 1st Light Cruiser Squadron to lend assistance. From dawn on 28 August a somewhat muddled action was fought in intermittently poor visibility between ships who often had no idea of their true position, and mistook friend for foe. It was an affair of scattered salvoes, shrouding mist, missed signals and great confusion. At last, responding to appeals for help, Beatty ignored the bad visibility and the chance of minefields and charged through the mist to retrieve the situation.

Chaotic though it had sometimes been, the action in the Heligoland Bight was undoubtedly a success, all the more welcome for being the first of the war, and it was hailed as such. The Germans had lost three light cruisers and a destroyer sunk, with three more cruisers damaged, and suffered casualties of 1,200 officers and men killed, wounded, or taken prisoner. On the British side, the cruiser *Arethusa* and three destroyers were damaged, with thirty-five men killed and about forty wounded. Most significant of all, it had been a sobering experience for the German Navy and the Kaiser and made them even more cautious than before.

The press and Churchill were ecstatic; Beatty's and Goodenough's ships were cheered back into Scapa when they returned on Saturday, on a lovely calm evening, and everybody was delighted. King-Hall in *Southampton*, Goodenough's flagship, noted that the battleship *Orion* even sent over men to help them coal, and *that* had never happened before (or after).

But on Monday 1 September the fleet routine was, as usual, coaling, ammunitioning, storing, exercising. At about six o'clock that evening the cruiser *Falmouth* reported the periscope of a submarine in sight. This, as Admiral Bacon wrote, '. . . produced the same sort of excitement as would a cobra in a drawing room'. *Falmouth* at once opened fire without waiting for permission and after four rounds reported a hit. *Vanguard*, lying in the outer line of battleships, also opened fire on something she reported as a periscope. This was likely: the submarine was clearly trying to work out to the fringes of the fleet, having been thwarted in its attack. An 'E' class destroyer patrolling between the fleet and the Hoxa entrance also opened fire.

In a few moments the Grand Fleet was in a state of turmoil. The 2nd Destroyer Flotilla, lying at Long Hope at short notice for steam, was ordered to weigh at once and start searching. Every ship present was ordered to raise steam with all dispatch and to prepare for torpedo attack. Drifters, steam picket boats, motor boats, trawlers, yachts, anything small and handy which had steam up, all were organized to steam up and down the lines of warships at their highest speed, to confuse the submarine and, if it was sighted, to ram it. Colliers and store ships were ordered to go alongside battleships, as sacrificial buffers, so that a torpedo would sink them and not the battleship. All the ships in the outer lines were ordered to burn searchlights, to confuse and locate the submarine.

About half an hour after the first alarm, the cruiser *Drake* reported a submarine in sight, which dispelled the last remnants of doubt. The whole fleet was directed to weigh anchor by divisions and put to sea. By 9.30 p.m. the visibility had deteriorated and in fact much of Scapa Flow was hidden in mist. Night had fallen when, screws churning the Flow and funnel smoke adding to an already thickening murk overhead, the ships put to sea and began to feel their way out to the Pentland Firth in what had become a dense fog. There were no navigational marks visible, or lights lit, and visibility dropped at times to less than a hundred yards. At one time there was a great danger that collision would do more damage to units of the fleet than any U-boat could ever have achieved.

By midnight the vast anchorage was empty, except for the depot ship *Cyclops* with the telegraph and telephone cable to shore, and the lines of minor craft still steaming up and down searching the Flow for submarines. One destroyer flotilla was left behind to help in the search, while another was stationed, like terriers outside a rat-hole, to seaward of the Hoxa and Hoy entrances, waiting for the quarry to pop out. By dawn, when the destroyers had been ordered to rejoin, nothing had been found. Perhaps it was a U-boat. Or perhaps it was a seal. Meanwhile the fleet stayed at sea. The pre-Dreadnoughts of the 3rd Battle Squadron came back to Scapa on 5 September, but the Fleet went to Loch Ewe, another insecure harbour, and did not return until the twenty-fourth.

As if the great battle of Scapa, as it became known, was not enough, on 5 September the light cruiser *Pathfinder* was torpedoed off St Abbs Head, at the entrance to the Firth of Forth, by U-21, with the loss of 259 lives; she was the first warship to be sunk by a submarine in the open sea. On 22 September the Navy suffered a much worse blow, the first real catastrophe of the war. Three elderly cruisers, part of what was known as the 'Live Bait Squadron', were patrolling the 'Broad Fourteens'. Normally they would have been in company with Harwich destroyers off the Dutch coast, but on that day bad weather had forced the destroyers to return to harbour and prevented Admiral Christian, whose flagship *Euryalus* was short of coal, had damaged wireless aerials, and also needed to withdraw, transferring to another cruiser. Early on the twenty-second one of the 'Live Baits', *Aboukir*, was sighted, torpedoed and sunk by U-9. The other two, *Cressy* and *Hogue*, stopped to pick up survivors and were themselves sunk. In all nearly 1,400 officers and men, the majority of them reservists who had just joined up, were lost.

It was now high time, and past high time, that something was done to make Scapa Flow safe for the fleet. The insecurity began to haunt Jellicoe day and night. 'I *long* for a submarine defence at Scapa,' he wrote to Churchill on 30 September. 'It would give such a feeling of confidence. I can't sleep half so well when inside as when outside merely because I feel we are risking such a mass of valuable ships in a place where, if a submarine *did* get in, she practically has the British Dreadnought Fleet at her mercy up to the number of her torpedoes.'

On 16 October there was another 'battle of Scapa'. Once more the waters of the Flow were churned up by hundreds of screws, once more the air was blackened by smoke from a hundred funnels, once more the Grand Fleet put to sea and this time went to Lough Swilly, on the west coast of Ireland, over 300 miles from Scapa Flow, and did not return until 9 November. For a time in fact the North Sea was undefended, This the Germans never realized – indeed they never properly appreciated that Scapa was open to submarine attacks. It must have seemed to them incredible to the point of impossibility for such a state of affairs to exist.

Before the war politicians and press had clamoured for eight Dreadnoughts and insisted that they could not wait, but nobody had taken much notice of Scapa Flow. The anchorage had been hydrographically surveyed during Fisher's first term as First Lord, 1904–10, but no works were carried out. The Treasury begrudged the money, and it was felt that to fortify Scapa would be provoking Germany, the obvious enemy, too openly.

Scapa Flow was a landlocked stretch of water, about ten miles long and about eight miles wide at its broadest, roughly in the shape of a rectangle with its northernmost corner formed by Scapa Bay, a deep v-shaped indentation in the southern coastline of Mainland, the largest island of the Orkneys. A ring of islands enclosed the southern rim of Scapa Flow. Although very strong tidal currents swept through the Pentland Firth, to the south of the Flow — the tidal race 'The Merry Men of May' had been known to cause damage to quite large ships — the narrow entrances kept Scapa Flow virtually free of external tidal conditions. At certain states of the tide, the difference in height between the water inside and outside a place such as Holm Sound could be as much as six feet and the water poured through in a smooth torrent.

The main entrance to Scapa Flow was Hoxa Sound, which ran northwards up from the Firth, four to five miles long, one and a half miles wide at its narrowest and deep enough for the largest battleships. The 'tradesmen's' entrance was the nearby Switha Sound, also opening from the Pentland Firth and guarded by the island of Switha, leading into Long Hope Sound, which was the base for the trawlers, drifters, boomships and other small craft. Base ships for administration, communications, repairs, ship maintenance, ordnance and other equipment, hospital ships and supply ships were also accommodated in Long Hope. Gutter Sound and Weddell Sound were the anchorages for the destroyer flotillas and fleet auxiliaries.

The fleet anchorage for the big ships was in the south-western corner of the harbour, close to Flotta Island. In the outermost stretches of the Flow there was ample space for exercise grounds, with firing ranges of up to 10,000 yards for sub-calibre shoots. Full calibre shoots were carried out in the Pentland Firth. There were also ranges for running torpedoes, and calibrating guns.

The first armament placed at Scapa was some 12-pounder guns landed in Sir George Callaghan's time, mounted to guard the main entrances, and manned by Territorial gunners. But from mid-October the defences of Scapa at last were given higher priority. It was about this time that Beatty told Churchill: 'We feel we are working up to a large catastrophe. The menace from mines and submarines grows greater every day. We are gradually being pushed out into the North Sea from our own particular perch.'

Rear-Admiral F.S. Miller, who had been appointed to organize the defences of Scapa in August, began at last to have some of his demands met and some political weight put behind his decisions. The depot ships *Hannibal* and *Magnificent*, with gear and equipment for constructing defences, arrived from the south. Trawlers were stationed in long strings across Hoxa Sound, Switha Sound and Hoy Sound. By 24 October blockships were on their way. Instead of using derelict hulks filled with concrete, elderly but perfectly serviceable merchant ships were scuttled. Lacking ballast, their empty hulls were sometimes swept out of position by the currents, but they were better than nothing (although more than one officer looked down through the water at their hulls later in the war and thought of their priceless cargo-carrying capacities, lost for ever). The shore batteries were increased and guns were placed to defend the booms.

In November some fifty trawlers, fitted with guns and explosive sweeps which could be detonated from the towing ship, arrived to patrol the entrances. Electric contact mines were laid, and booms constructed of miscellaneous rafts and barges carrying torpedo nets. The work went on in haste. 'Every nerve must be strained to reconcile the fleet to Scapa,' signalled Churchill. Progress reports were called for every three days by Churchill and by Fisher, who had replaced Battenberg as First Sea Lord in October, after a disgraceful anti-German campaign in the press and the country had convinced the German-born Battenberg that he would serve the country better by resigning.

Despite Churchill's pressure, the short hours of winter daylight held up work and the defences of Hoxa Sound were only completed on 29 December. In January Jellicoe was complaining to Fisher that, 'It seems impossible to get the departments at Admiralty to realise that this is a base and the most important one in the country; that the fleet here is enormous and the number of auxiliaries is infinitely greater than at any other port. . . .'

The defences of the other channels had largely been completed by 19 February 1915. Though Jellicoe would not admit that Scapa was properly secure, at least it did not have that wide-open feeling of nakedness to submarine attack. One or two U-boats had sniffed around at the entrances but there had been no serious attack – a stroke of luck for the Grand Fleet which amounted almost to a miracle. Beatty's forecast of October 1914 of 'a large catastrophe' had, as it proved, been exaggerated, but it might so easily have been an under-estimate.

Jellicoe kept a pessimistically jealous watch over the comparative strengths of his Grand Fleet and the German High Seas Fleet. Any attempt by anybody to take any ships, or indeed anything at all, away from the Grand Fleet was always fiercely resented and sure to provoke a storm of protest from Jellicoe. Very occasionally he did over-react. When, for instance, machine guns were needed for the Naval Division going to the Dardanelles and the Grand Fleet was requested to supply some, Jellicoe thought that was '. . .weakening the Grand Fleet in principle'.

It is easy to criticize Jellicoe's caution, and his zealous hoarding of resources. But he knew very well that, as he said, he had the greater part of the Navy's force under his command. Those ships he could see, stretched out in lines at Scapa, were quite literally the country's main defence. Jellicoe's opponent could choose the day and the hour to strike and could arrange to have his maximum force available at the chosen time. Jellicoe had to be ready at all times and, unless he had prior warning, he would have to respond with whatever force he had.

Jellicoe also knew that the Grand Fleet was not the overwhelming, crushingly superior weapon which the country and the Navy and Churchill all believed it was. He was well aware that in certain matters, such as armour plating, underwater protection, watertight subdivision of compartments, gunnery control and some types of shell, the Grand Fleet was not even equal but actually inferior to the High Seas Fleet.

In November 1914 Jellicoe had fresh cause for anxiety about numbers. The Germans carried out a tip-and-run raid on Yarmouth, after which Fisher took two battle cruisers, *Inflexible* and *Invincible*, away and – quite correctly and successfully – sent them to the South Atlantic to dispose of von Spee's force off the Falklands. A third battle cruiser, *Princess Mary*, was stationed in the North Atlantic in case von Spee broke north. Jellicoe agitated for these ships' speedy return.

October had been a trying month, and the situation did not improve towards the end of the year. The battleship *Audacious* had been mined and sunk. *Iron Duke* and *Ajax* both had leaking condenser tubes. *Orion* had gone to Glasgow for examination of her main turbine supports. *Superb* also had turbine trouble, with stripped blades. *Conqueror* was refitting at Devonport, *New Zealand* was in dock in Cromarty, *Erin* and *Agincourt* had newly joined and were not yet fit to lie in the line, nor were *Empress of India* and *Benbow* properly worked up. 'It is astonishing how quickly our supposed superiority in Dread-noughts and Battle Fleet vanishes,' Jellicoe wrote to Fisher in January 1915. He reckoned that he had nineteen Dreadnoughts plus seven King Edward pre-Dreadnoughts, against sixteen German Dreadnoughts and eight Deutschlands plus another twelve pre-Dreadnoughts. It was hardly an overwhelming margin, and ships were having to go away for docking and refitting all the time.

Then there was the question of destroyers. Jellicoe knew the Germans had eighty-eight, to accompany the High Seas Fleet to sea, and he knew they would certainly all be there on the day the fleet did go to sea. He, on the other hand, had an average of just over forty, and six of those were normally away refitting at any given time. This, Jellicoe reckoned, '. . . was totally inadequate' and he threatened that, as the shortage of destroyers would make it impossible for him to crush the German Fleet, he would have '. . . to adopt the objectionable and difficult course of turning the Battle Fleet away when the attack takes place'.

Then there was the question of light cruisers. Jellicoe thought the six he had 'quite inadequate' to support destroyer raids, act with the battle cruisers in offensive sweeps, patrol the approaches to Scapa Flow, cover the van of the Battle Fleet at sea, and protect van and flanks in action, besides all the other duties cruisers were supposed to carry out. For example, they were supposed to stop and board merchantmen; but so scarce were the cruisers that battleships were having to do this. On one day in August 1914 no fewer than four battleships were absent on this duty.

This constant stream of complaints made Churchill restless. He did not share Jellicoe's pessimism, and thought Jellicoe looked too much on the black side. He could see that Jellicoe was always magnifying his own disadvantages, however small, and always crediting the enemy with more ships than they actually had. Churchill also tended to fall into his old error of comparing ships solely by the size of their guns; he could not accept Jellicoe's opinion that a ship was virtually useless until she was properly worked up. He accused Jellicoe of running the ships too hard and taking them to sea too often. Churchill began to be exasperated by Jellicoe and his old-womanish complaints – he must have seemed to Churchill like some old granny ceaselessly counting up the contents of her larder and comparing it unfavourably with her neighbour's across the street.

Fisher sensed the coolness growing between Churchill and Jellicoe, and did his best to patch it up. He urged Churchill to meet Jellicoe's demands if he could, to humour his attitude, because (he said) if the C-in-C grew depressed it might be infectious and spread throughout the fleet. Fisher noticed that Jellicoe wrote copiously to him, but not nearly so much to Churchill. 'I expect you'd better write now and again to the First Lord or he'll be jealous!' he urged Jellicoe. But in spite of Fisher's bridge-building efforts, there seems no doubt that Churchill was steadily revising his opinion of Jellicoe, downwards, from the day war broke out.

It was no consolation to Jellicoe, but his counterparts across the North Sea suffered one disadvantage which never troubled him – an unrealistically restrictive political control over their ships. The Kaiser wanted successful naval actions, but he wanted no loss of ships. His admirals were strictly warned they were to take no risks (the comparison with Hitler's warning to Raeder in the Second World War is inescapable).

In December 1914 the Germans took advantage of the known absence of *Inflexible* and *Invincible* in the South Atlantic to carry out another tip-and-run raid, this time on Scarborough, Whitby and Hartlepool. It was to be carried out by the battle cruisers under Admiral Franz von Hipper, supported by battleships of the High Seas Fleet under Admiral Friedrich von Ingenohl. The Admiralty, with the aid of Fisher's 'hunch' that the Germans were up to something, and with the priceless help of intelligence from German naval codes found on the body of a drowned signalman in the Baltic, planned to trap the German ships with Beatty's four battle cruisers from Cromarty, the 3rd Cruiser Squadron under Pakenham from Rosyth, the 2nd Battle Squadron under Admiral Warrender, and Goodenough's 1st Light Cruiser Squadron and the 4th Destroyer Flotilla, all from Scapa, where Jellicoe and his staff studied the evidence and worked out an admirably accurate rendezvous point which would give everybody the best chance of intercepting the enemy.

On 16 December, another day of poor North Sea visibility and more poor luck for Beatty, both sides fumbled their chances. At one point, by pressing onwards with a little more determination and a little less care for the Kaiser's warnings, Ingenohl could have destroyed or at least badly damaged Warrender's Battle Squadron and so gone some way to reducing the Grand Fleet to somewhere near the strength of the High Seas Fleet. Instead, he turned away as soon as he met Warrender's outlying destroyers, thinking he was about to run up against the whole Grand Fleet.

Beatty, for his part, had a good chance to annihilate Hipper's battle cruisers – '. . . a tremendous prize,' as Churchill said, 'the German battle-cruiser squadron whose loss would fatally mutilate the whole German Navy and could never be repaired – actually within our claws. . . .' But it was not to be. A misleading signal caused Goodenough, uncharacteristically, to break off contact with the enemy and return to his position in the screen. Hipper escaped under the cover of heavy rainstorms and by making a wide sweep to the north in very low visibility eventually returned unscathed to Heligoland.

The recriminations after the Scarborough raid were as loud and as widespread as the rejoicings after Heligoland Bight. Jellicoe was baffled by Goodenough's action – '. . . so totally unlike all he had previously done since the war began'. Jellicoe was 'intensely unhappy' about it all; it had been 'the opportunity of our lives'. Fisher thought '. . . all concerned made a mighty hash of it'. As for Beatty, '. . . It nearly broke my heart,' he wrote, 'the disappointment was terrific. . . . Truly the past has been the blackest week in my life. . . .' He too blamed Goodenough for not realizing that he was never meant to let go of the enemy. Perhaps he was right, but the true fault seems to lie more with Lieut-Commander Ralph Seymour, his own flag lieutenant. During the Scarborough raid, again in the engagement off the Dogger Bank in January 1915, and twice at Jutland, Seymour failed in the heat of the action to translate Beatty's intentions into a plain signal which allowed for no misunderstandings.

Jellicoe was prepared to see Goodenough relieved, but when the Admiralty ventured to criticize Beatty very mildly for not spreading his battle cruisers out sufficiently, Jellicoe sprang very smartly to his defence and had the criticism modified. In his own memoirs Goodenough did not mention the Scarborough raid at all.

Jellicoe and Fisher believed that the Germans would try another raid, or at least try something, at Christmas and so (shades of Old 'Ard 'Art Wilson) Jellicoe took the fleet to sea over the festive season. The Germans, wrote Jellicoe, although they keep Christmas '. . . even more than we do . . . will, however, expect us to all be drunk that day. . . .'

It must have been one of the most miserable Christmas Days anybody in the Grand Fleet had ever spent. The weather did moderate a little on the day, but in general it was foul, blowing a near-gale from the east most of the time. The ships cleared for action as Christmas Day dawned – very late in those high latitudes. 'We had Church at 11 a.m.,' Jellicoe wrote. 'Fortunately the weather was clear, so we could afford to be off deck a bit.'

Returning to harbour on Boxing Day the fleet ran into a whole gale from the south-east, and there was a near-disaster. As the leading battle squadron, showing no lights, came in the anchorage at 6 a.m., *Monarch* suddenly altered course to avoid a patrol vessel, and *Conqueror* ran into her from astern. Jellicoe sensed from signals intercepted in the flagship that something was amiss and led the following battle squadrons back out into the Pentland Firth, where even the large ships had an anxious time turning in the huge seas that were raging. *Conqueror* and *Monarch* were added to the list of missing Dreadnoughts having to go away for repairs, along with three destroyers also damaged in the storm.

On 28 December Fisher wrote to Jellicoe:

It gave me immense comfort to read that you were safely back in your Zareba!!! I HOPE TO GOODNESS YOU'LL STOP THERE! Also I hope you'll stop these insane cruises of your big ships in the North Sea, or we shall have the *Cressy, Aboukir, Hogue, Hawke* [cruiser torpedoed on 15 October] *Hermes* [seaplane carrier torpedoed off Calais on 31 October] all over again, and the Admiralty will deservedly be kicked out of office for allowing such utter murder by prowling German submarines, who are not going to be kept off by these Chinese methods of frightening them with a big ship!

That, in its way, seemed to sum up the old year of 1914 and to point the way for the new.

Chapter 10

After the disappointment of the Scarborough raid, Beatty wrote: 'I trust earnestly to have the opportunity in the *very near* future to obliterate it.' He had another opportunity off the Dogger Bank in January 1915, but once again it was not the victory it should have been.

As in December the Admiralty provided prior intelligence warning of a sortie by Hipper, with the battle cruisers *Seydlitz* (flag), *Moltke*, *Derfflinger* and *Blücher* (actually a heavy cruiser), plus four light cruisers and eighteen destroyers, to surprise and engage any British forces he discovered. Once again a trap was set, to be sprung by Beatty and his battle cruisers, supported by Goodenough's light cruisers; the pre-Dreadnoughts, and cruisers from Rosyth, were stationed in the North Sea to cut off any German movement northwards. Tyrwhitt, with three light cruisers and thirty-five destroyers, sailed from Harwich. Jellicoe and the Grand Fleet also put to sea, but were not within a hundred miles of the action, to his disappointment and complaint. Afterwards Jellicoe was sure that, if he had been sailed earlier, his battleships could have made sure of victory.

The action off the Dogger Bank on 24 January certainly was a success. It cost Ingenohl his command, and he was relieved by von Pohl, chief of the naval staff. But it was not the annihilating victory it could and should have been. Beatty was evidently not a lucky admiral; he seemed destined always to be afflicted by a battle cruiser version of Murphy's Law – anything that could go wrong, did go wrong. In this case he made the perfectly reasonable signal, as his ships were going into action, 'Engage the corresponding ships in the enemy's line.' Beatty had five battle cruisers – *Lion* (flag), *Tiger*, *Princess Royal*, *New Zealand* and *Indomitable* – to Hipper's four, and should have had a ship to spare. In fact *Tiger*, whose shooting in any case was bad, joined with *Lion* to fire on *Seydlitz*, leaving *Moltke* to fire unmolested on *Lion*. *Lion*, hit several times, was quite badly damaged and dropped back astern of the rest.

This was unfortunate enough, but there was much worse to come. Beatty sighted a submarine periscope and ordered his squadron to turn to port to evade the torpedoes. There followed another signalling muddle, which resulted in Beatty's four remaining battle cruisers, under his second-in-command Vice-Admiral Sir Archibald Moore, all attacking the already badly damaged *Blücher*. They duly sank her. Meanwhile Hipper, who had magical good luck, made yet another escape, but his flagship *Seydlitz* suffered two hits: one caused a magazine fire which nearly sank the ship. German casualties were *Blücher* sunk, *Seydlitz* badly damaged, and over a thousand more German sailors killed, missing or taken prisoner.

Publicly, Dogger Bank was hailed as another victory, but Beatty knew better. 'The disappointment of that day', he wrote to Keyes, 'is more than I can bear to think of, everybody thinks it was a great success, when in reality it was a terrible failure. I had made up my mind that we were going to get four, the lot, and *four* we ought to have got.' Similarly, heads ought to have rolled. But Beatty took full responsibility. There was no witch-hunt, although Moore was later quietly shifted to another appointment. Henry Pelly, however, remained in command of *Tiger* (whose shooting never did improve much).

Jellicoe had no doubt that whatever signals might have been made or appeared to have been made, Moore should have known Beatty's intentions – he should have known the *man*, and ignored the signals – and gone after Hipper's retreating battle cruisers. Keyes was not the only naval officer to be distressed by the '. . . spectacle of Moore & Co. yapping round the poor tortured *Blücher*, with beaten ships still in sight to be sunk. . . .'

Jellicoe also had misgivings on another point. Beatty had steamed to the rendezvous with Tyrwhitt and the others over an area which had reportedly been mined. Jellicoe felt that Arthur Knyvet Wilson, who was then serving, unofficially and unpaid, on a War Staff Group in an advisory capacity, and who was chiefly responsible for the rendezvous chosen, underestimated the effect of modern mines and submarines, and had routed Beatty's ships through dangerous waters. In a sense it was this apprehension about mines and submarines – the same cautiousness which in fact had made Beatty turn away – which separated the twentieth-century from the nineteenth-century naval officers.

It was not just the physical loss of ships sunk by submarines, though they were bad enough. Each loss caused ripples of alarm and disruption. Training programmes were put out of gear. The general uncertainty, the extra steaming days at sea, the added anxiety, all chipped away at the commander's capacity to act on the day of reckoning, The Day, or *Der Tag*, as the Germans called it.

Jellicoe prepared himself for *Der Tag* with almost monastic zeal. He went ashore with members of his staff, to walk furiously up and down hills and across moors. He played with a medicine ball on *Iron Duke*'s upper deck. 'It's splendid,' he told Beatty. 'I've already sprained a

Captain and Mrs Jellicoe, John Jellicoe's parents.

John Jellicoe as a naval cadet, aged twelve.

HMS *Newcastle*, a screw frigate launched in 1860, which was Jellicoe's first ship.

Cadets of Jellicoe's term in HMS *Britannia*, July 1872–74. Jellicoe is in the back row, second from left.

Staff of HMS *Excellent*, 1884. Fisher (seated, second from left), Percy Scott (standing right), Jellicoe (standing left).

HMS *Agincourt*, 1887, rigged with line masts.

HMS *Colossus*, 1887, the first battleship to be built of steel instead of iron.

Jellicoe at the time of his engagement to Gwendoline Cayzer in 1902 (from a miniature).

HMS *Victoria* sinking after a collision with HMS *Camperdown* in 1893. Jellicoe was a survivor. The photograph was taken by Staff Surgeon Collet of HMS *Collingwood*.

Jellicoe being brought back to Tientsin badly wounded in a litter. Admiral Seymour is walking beside him.

A picture of Jellicoe taken from a locket, *c.* 1918.

HMS *Albemarle*, in which Jellicoe was Rear-Admiral in 1907.

HMS *Prince of Wales*, in which Jellicoe hoisted his flag as Acting Vice-Admiral in command of the Atlantic Fleet in 1910.

Above: Churchill inspecting boys of the training ship *Mercury* in 1912.

Right: Churchill with Madden and Jellicoe (drawn by Matania).

Jellicoe saying farewell to Kitchener on board *Iron Duke*, 5 June 1916.

Above left: Jellicoe playing cricket at the age of seventy for the Admiral's XI *v*. The Nautical College at Pangbourne in Berkshire in 1929. *Above right*: The Jellicoe family in New Zealand in 1921. Standing left to right: Myrtle and Norah; seated left to right: Gwendoline, George and Prudence.

The Jellicoe family leaving New Zealand in 1924. From left to right: Norah, Lucy, Myrtle, George, Prudence, Lady Jellicoe and Lord Jellicoe.

finger and a knee. I recommend it to you.' Later in the war, Jellicoe was dissuaded with the utmost difficulty by his staff from turning out for *Iron Duke*'s gunroom rugger team. Yet his general health was not good and it deteriorated as the war went on. Already by January 1915 the strains and stresses of his command were seriously affecting his well-being. He did not have enough change of scenery, nor of company. 'Living over the shop', as he did in *Iron Duke*, he had to deal with a constant stream of telegrams, visitors, decisions; there were confrontations, situations demanding attention, plans to be considered for the future, every day and all day.

Jellicoe never properly got away from the cares of his command. Even his exercise ashore was taken at a hectic pace; his rounds of golf were played at the run, hardly pausing to stop to make a shot before sprinting on to the next hole. The Bishop of London, an old friend, once played a round with Jellicoe and after a few holes he had to cry a halt. 'Look here, Jack,' he asked Jellicoe, 'is this golf or a steeplechase?'

On 21 January Jellicoe began to suffer from the undignified but very painful and debilitating affliction of piles. It was at its worst during the Dogger Bank action, and on 25 January he suffered a very bad attack. 'I am not at all well,' he wrote to Beatty. 'Crocked up yesterday. Very bad attack of piles and general run down.' Late in January he had to go into hospital for an operation – under the name of 'Mr Jessop', the fact that he was sick being kept from the public. In his absence Burney took over the Grand Fleet – and, significantly, made a much less nervous C-in-C, as Rear-Admiral Duff of the 4th Battle Squadron noted in his diary.

Fisher sent up a specialist from London, and another specialist and a trained nurse from Edinburgh. 'Now do please take it easy and d—n Rosyth and everything else that worries you, and simply play bridge,' he urged Jellicoe. 'You are worth more than a hundred Rosyths or dozens of battleships, so put that in your pipe and smoke it, and take things easy!' Beatty also advised Jellicoe to rest. 'You must take the greatest care of yourself,' he said. 'What we should do without you the Lord knows.' But for Jellicoe himself, of much more importance was the well-being of the sailors of the Grand Fleet.

Scapa Flow, everybody agreed, had a flavour of its own. Scapa was a world of space and seabirds, of great cloudscapes and tremendous sunsets. The shoreline visible from the ships was grey and green, with low hills, and moors purple with heather in the late summer. In summer the days went on seemingly for ever. A man could sit on deck and easily read a newspaper at half-past eleven at night. In winter it was dark by half-past three, and stayed dark until late in the forenoon. Between November and March, and indeed at any time of the year, the winds at Scapa could blow for days and weeks on end. Ashore the few trees were bowed and swept back and stunted, as though borne over by the almost insupportable burden of the wind. On winter nights the Northern Lights burned and crackled in a great fiery curtain across the sky above Mainland.

Life at Scapa was not easy, but some ships had made it more difficult for themselves because of an early excess of zeal. At the outbreak of hostilities all ships were required to land boats, cutters, whalers, skiffs and a great deal of other wooden and painted gear, to reduce the risk of fire. Opinions as to how much combustible woodwork should be landed varied from ship to ship. Some 'blood and iron' ships stripped their wardrooms and cabins. One ship even stripped the corticene deck coverings off the messdecks; the Admiralty, when they heard of this, intimated that if this were repeated the corticene would have to be replaced at somebody's private expense. But other, rather more circumspect, ships had studied the reports of naval attachés in the Russo-Japanese War who had noticed that the Japanese ships had scrupulously stripped their ships at the beginning of the war and had later to replace everything at great expense. Similarly, in the Grand Fleet, ships which had landed, say, all their wardroom armchairs and fittings had to collect money to replace them later.

The fleet had to make its own amusements. Flotta island, which rose hog-backed and largely heather-covered from the waters of the Flow, was more or less 'seized' by the Navy. Engineer commanders used their ingenuity to construct stone piers. One of the battleships undertook to make a dug-out waiting-room close to the pier. The *chef d'oeuvre* was the golfcourse, for which each big ship designed and laid out one of the eighteen holes. According to King-Hall, the ships competed in this as in everything; one battleship was supposed to have spent £70, a large sum in 1915, getting turf from a famous Scottish course to make the green at their hole. King-Hall particularly remembered the greens provided by *Canada* and *King George V*, 'as smooth as a billiard table amidst the encircling heather'.

Everyone played as frantically as Jellicoe himself. Each afternoon a crowd queued to drive off from the first tee, and each pair drove off and ran after their balls, because the next pair would soon be driving over their heads. The players putted out as though the devil were after them and doubled off the green to the next tee, speeded by roars of 'Fore!' from down the fairway.

For the sailors, football pitches were laid out on rectangular patches of heather, which were as level and free from bogs as possible. There goalposts were put up and touchlines burned or hacked in the heather. Various ships had their own interdepartmental football leagues and there was also a fleet challenge knockout cup, as well as trophies for the battle squadrons, cruisers and destroyer flotillas.

For non-golfers and non-football players there were walking, fishing, boating banyans at weekends, and a little shooting after duck and the very occasional grouse – Flotta had four resident grouse named Matthew, Mark, Luke and John. Sometimes ships were allowed to go for a 'jolly' to the North Shore, at the northern end of the harbour, where there was a pier and a whisky distillery. Then there were always the bright lights of Kirkwall, the capital of the Orkneys. 'I should not select it for a cheery weekend,' wrote King-Hall. 'Still it is a town of sorts. . . . '

Two of the most important aids to fleet morale were the ex-Wilson Line frozen meat ships *Borodino* and *Ghurko*. *Borodino* was fitted out as a floating dry canteen, run by the Junior Army and Navy Stores, and dispensing extras and luxuries to supplement the official diet. There was 'a sort of Fortnum and Mason attachment for officers' where they could buy frozen game, salmon, trout, pâté, fruit, salted almonds, stuffed olives and other exotica. In wartime the Orkneys could not export their eggs and lobsters in the normal way, so the fleet had a plentiful supply.

Ghurko was the 'theatre ship', fitted out to hold an audience of six hundred, and she would go alongside a capital ship for a performance put on by the ship's concert party. Nobody had anything to spend their money on, so vast sums were expended on costumes (some sent up from Nathan's in London), props, musical instruments and scenery. The stage had the most elaborate lighting and equipment, and some of the performances were of a very high standard. Many ships' concert parties, with names such as the 'Agincourtiers' from HMS *Agincourt*, put on pantomimes, musical comedies and revues which were almost up to professional standards. The new fast battleships of the Queen Elizabeth class, when they arrived at Scapa, made a particular reputation for the standard of their concert parties.

The shows were attended by the admirals and captains (some officers wondered what would have happened if, say, *Ghurko* had been alongside *Vanguard* the day she blew up with so few survivors). Jellicoe always went to the shows if he could. Although he was slightly deaf, the legacy of a burst eardrum at Whale Island years before, and so found straight theatre hard to follow, he loved musical comedy and adored Gilbert and Sullivan. He loved nothing better than to sit with his staff and friends, the admirals and captains of his own and other ships, in the big armchair specially placed for him in the front row, smoking his after-dinner cigarette (always through a holder), while he roared at the fleet 'in-jokes' of the lower-deck comedians in *Dick Whittington and His Cat*, or a chorus line of midshipmen singing review songs such as 'We sit in the Sun, And wait for the Hun, Care of the GPO'. *Ghurko* had a full-sized boxing ring in which the fleet boxing tournaments were staged, and which Jellicoe also greatly enjoyed. Church services, lectures and cinema shows were also held in her; in terms of the Grand Fleet's morale, *Ghurko* was worth at least a couple of battleships.

But for most of the men in most of the ships for most of the time, it was a case of getting up one's own entertainment. They played deck hockey with home-made sticks and rope grommets, fashioned on board by the dozen because they were always being flicked over the side; there was throwing the medicine ball; weight-lifting; PT on the upper deck; deck golf; high cockalorum; inter-part tug-of-war; and, on the messdecks, the perennial games of uckers, a particularly rough and psychologically damaging form of ludo. The mail came on board regularly but there were often seemingly interminable days, especially in winter, when it blew and rained so hard that the mail drifters were unable to get alongside.

Lady Jellicoe, that formidably determined and extremely able lady, made the care and welfare of the fleet and their families her special concern. No trouble was too much for her to undertake, no source of possible revenue too remote not to be tapped, no politician or senior officer too august not to be buttonholed. With Lady French as joint President, Lady Jellicoe started the United Service League, to which over a hundred clubs for sailors and soldiers were affiliated, and which gave comfort, support and company for the women whose husbands and sons were away at the war. Lady Jellicoe also started and organized a fleet fund to provide comforts such as extra blankets, gramophones, books, Thermos flasks, packs of cards, socks and scarves. The work was done by volunteers, many of them officers' wives, who raised £150,000 in cash, and provided fifty thousand articles of clothing. Lady Jellicoe also travelled round the country to meet the mothers, wives and families of sailors in the Grand Fleet. She and thousands of other women on the home front made an astonishing contribution to the war effort which has never properly been acknowledged.

It was Lady Jellicoe's faithful letters which kept her husband up-to-date with family matters, the children's schools and holidays, their illnesses, and their longing to see their father again. Like every officer and man of his fleet, John Jellicoe desperately missed his family. Deprived of their company, he plunged more deeply into his work with a dedication which, for a man of Jellicoe's temperament and ability, came perilously close to obsession. Always reluctant to delegate, he was conscientious and painstaking to the point where he often involved himself in unnecessary detail. As the war progressed, Grand Fleet officers began to complain that the staff in *Iron Duke* was too large and too interfering.

Jellicoe was not a fleet commander on the pattern of St Vincent, who knew that he had so many men under his command that he could not be physically present among them all, so he must try to be in their thoughts, in anecdotes about his doings, in gossip about his eccentricities. Jellicoe did not inspire such stories. But he did inspire the most intense loyalty: '. . . the Commander-in-Chief's energy and wonderful influence permeated every mess and messdeck in every type of ship,' wrote King-Hall. 'The confidence of the Fleet was given unreservedly to J.J., and we trusted him absolutely.' When the Archbishop of York visited the Grand Fleet in June 1915 he later wrote to Jellicoe: 'I think we are both men who hate "gush", and try to keep our emotions under control: but I can only say that I thank God that you are where you are at this great time.'

Jellicoe's immediate subordinates, when they wrote to him formally, used the lofty Homeric address of a Bellerophontiad. Vice-Admiral Sir Lewis Bayly was one of the ablest admirals in the Navy; a tough man, hard-working, no sufferer of fools or temperer of winds to any shorn lamb. He had a rough tongue, in conversation and in signals. Apart from his short-sightedness in the matter of submarines – a failing which, after the pre-Dreadnought *Formidable* was torpedoed by a submarine in January 1915, cost Bayly his flag – he would have been a most valuable personality in the Grand Fleet. But Bayly, who commanded the 1st Battle Squadron, changed appointments with Burney, who commanded the Channel Fleet, in December 1914. On leaving, Bayly wrote to Jellicoe as though hailing him across the walls of fallen Troy:

> Never in opposition, though not always agreeing, you have always held out a helping hand, always offered a ready ear, to all of us when we thought we had something to say. I will joyfully serve under you anywhere or under any circumstances; you have given me that faith in you that one can only have in a man who is single-minded, and a master of his trade. You are both.

The relief of Bayly by Burney was not to the fleet's advantage. Burney was a competent officer, and of course a very old friend of Jellicoe's. Jellicoe defended him by saying he was 'a fine seaman', but he was slow of thought, very conservative and a little sleepy; the thought that some ill-chance might cause Jellicoe to be killed and Burney to take over supreme command of the fleet gave some officers severe palpitations. Burney would never turn a Nelsonian blind eye, seize a moment's chance, snatch a daring victory out of a stalemate. On the contrary, he could be absolutely relied upon to steam in a straight line at a steady speed until ordered to do otherwise.

George Warrender, commanding the 2nd Battle Squadron, was

another very old friend of Jellicoe's. He was no more enterprising than Burney, but Jellicoe justified him by saying that he had 'unique experience' in command and was excellent as a squadron admiral '*in peace*'. Warrender was rather deaf and absent-minded, and his health was not good, even Jellicoe was '. . . not always happy about him'. Warrender had not distinguished himself in the action after the Scarborough raid in December 1914. It was almost true that his French chef was better than his tactics.

Not to beat about the bush, most of the senior officers of the Grand Fleet were very worthy, but very uninspiring men, with the exception of Doveton Sturdee, the victor of the Falklands. 'Damn the staff!' was his motto. He had studied tactics deeply and was not afraid to advance his heretical views to Jellicoe. Sturdee disagreed violently with Jellicoe over the subject of the single line ahead in battle which formed the main plank of Jellicoe's Battle Orders. Sturdee argued long and very persuasively in favour of 'divided tactics', with a more flexible use of ships, such as had been tried in 1910–11 when Admiral Sir William May was C-in-C Home Fleet. The fleet manoeuvred in several separate squadrons with the object of concentrating upon a point in the enemy's line, overwhelming and outnumbering it at that particular point, much as Nelson had done.

These experiments ended when May hauled down his flag and they were not resumed. Sturdee continued to press the case until November 1915, when Jellicoe wrote to him, politely but firmly – indeed, considering the correspondents, in quite menacingly sharpish terms – reminding him that such discussion was beginning to affect morale and discipline and asking him, though not in so many words, to desist. Sturdee did so, although he continued to advocate divided tactics *sotto voce*.

There is no question that Jellicoe should have been far more ruthless with his juniors; he was far too ready to excuse and make the best of their shortcomings, and much too loyal to his friends of many years' standing. But to say this is to criticize not just Jellicoe, but the Royal Navy which produced him. By his upbringing in the Navy Jellicoe was far too inhibited to wield the knife, even had it occurred to him to do so. The Navy needed a fleet commander who was less of a pillar of the establishment and more of an 'outsider', one who cared nothing that an officer was 'a fine seaman' or had fought well against the Boxers. The obvious solution was to retire most of the admirals and promote from among the ranks of the captains. But the Royal Navy of 1914 was such a conservative service that compared with it even the apostolic succession seemed like queue-jumping, and such wholesale pruning would have been, quite literally, unthinkable.

Jellicoe did consistently inspire devotion where perhaps it counted most of all, on the lower deck. The stories of Bartimeus, who himself served in the Grand Fleet, generally have the ring of authenticity. In one, published in October 1917, a drifter carrying victorious regatta crews who had just won the Fleet Cock back to their ship in Scapa Flow, passes close under the stern of *Iron Duke*, where Jellicoe is walking up and down the quarterdeck. When he saw the silver trophy in the bows of the drifter, Jellicoe

. . . smilingly clapped his hands, applauding. . . . A wild tumult of frantic cheering burst out almost like an explosion from every throat still capable of emitting sound. There was gratitude and passionate loyalty in the demonstration, and it continued long after the figure on the quarterdeck had turned away and the drifter had resumed her noisy, triumphant tour of the Fleet.

'That's what I likes about 'im,' whispered a bearded seaman hoarsely, as they swung off on their new course. ''E's that 'uman!'

With all the other problems Jellicoe had to deal with in 1915, he had also to survive well-meaning biographers, who retailed cringe-making material about his boyhood. One example by Arthur Appin, in a book published that year, deserved a full salvo from *Iron Duke*:

There is a little story told of Master Jack soon after he learned to toddle which shows that his character was forming even at that early age.

'Jacky' had a habit of running ahead of his nurse and suddenly darting across the road. The spirit of adventure: probably he was ambitious to be a boy scout. Eventually finding that warnings were not heeded, the nurse told him that when she saw a policeman she would ask the Representative of Law and Order to take him away and put him in prison.

Presently a policeman appeared on the horizon of the pavement.

'Now, Master Jacky, you'd better behave yourself!' the nurse whispered warningly.

But young Jellicoe was not the least afraid of the man in blue. He advanced to meet him and solemnly looked him up and down.

'Nurse says you're to take me in charge,' he announced.

The constable, taken aback, smiled and asked the nature of the 'Charge'.

'Disobeying orders,' was Master Jack's reply. 'And I say, policeman, what ripping buttons you've got on your uniform!'

Another intending biographer of Jellicoe, Gerard Fiennes, might have produced a book of real insight but unfortunately he died before undertaking the work. He was one of many visitors who made the long train and boat journey up the length of the British Isles to Scapa – appropriately, the Scapa train in the Second World War was called *Admiral Jellicoe*. Although neither Jellicoe nor anybody in the Grand Fleet exactly encouraged visitors, it is a myth that the fleet lay throughout the war incommunicado, shut off in its misty, stormy northern fastness from all outside contact. There was in fact a steady stream of politicians, officers of allied or neutral navies, anybody indeed whom the government wished to impress or reassure.

The parties sometimes included the press, since there was no resident naval press correspondent with the fleet. Jellicoe and his fellow officers abhorred the press and personal publicity, or anything that smacked of self-advertisement, and they would never have volunteered a story. They discouraged press photographers, claiming quite wrongly that they could take just as good photographs in the fleet. Rear-Admiral Sir Douglas Brownrigg, the Naval Censor, who was largely responsible for organizing press visits and liaison, had a very difficult task indeed – it was not unknown for ships suddenly to go to sea, on a day they knew the press were invited, so as to avoid the encounter. Brownrigg had to handle his friends in the fleet with the most delicate of delicate kid gloves.

Neither Jellicoe nor his staff, in common with their naval generation, ever really grasped that the press could be an ally, that properly treated and properly organized it could be of immeasurable benefit to the Service. The officers never realized that much as they might disdain the attentions of the press, as they would themselves have phrased it, the sailors felt quite differently; the lower deck loved to read about their own doings. It was not that relations with the press were so bad, just that they hardly existed at all. This lack of mutual understanding was to cost the Navy and Jellicoe himself very dearly after Jutland.

Although Jellicoe remained cool towards the press and publicity, as Brownrigg says, once he had accepted a proposal, '. . . he threw himself into it heart and soul'. Brownrigg was glad to record that Jellicoe gave every assistance to a film on naval training called *Britain Prepared*. It was Mr Balfour who overcame what Brownrigg called '. . . the rooted objection of the Grand Fleet to this (or any other) form of publicity'. The film, directed by Charles Urban, was a great success and made money for naval charities.

King George V visited the Grand Fleet in July, and His Majesty and Jellicoe stood on the bridge of the destroyer *Oak* while she steamed up and down the great anchorage. It was, Jellicoe wrote in a letter to Lady Jellicoe, '. . . cold but fine. Fleet looked splendid, cheering very good. I doubt if ever he had a better reception. At 6 p.m. finished alongside *Druid* and had enormous tea there.'

Next day the King came on board and inspected *Iron Duke*. He spent the whole day going from ship to ship. 'The whole thing went splendidly, 85 per cent of the officers and men passed by close to His Majesty.' The King lunched with the vice-admirals, had a reception for the captains after dinner, and presented Jellicoe with a cigarette case before he left. Jellicoe noticed that while the King was there he used the cigarette case Jellicoe and others had given him thirty years before in *Excellent*.

On his last day the King '. . . inspected the Garrison and 6,000 men, the gunboats, destroyers, etc.'. Jellicoe had the men drawn up in a hollow square while the King made 'an excellent speech'. He called for three cheers for His Majesty, 'who was much affected'. (The Grand Fleet had a most moving effect on visitors; the Archbishop of Canterbury, who went over *Iron Duke*'s side to the strains of 'Auld Lang Syne' played by the band, said 'I never had a harder task of self-control.')

The King's visit, like a later visit of the Prince of Wales, was a brilliant exercise in what would now be called public relations. It was an enormous morale-booster for the fleet, and morale certainly needed boosting — it is the hardest thing in the world to keep up a fighting force's spirits in the face of prolonged inaction. The Grand Fleet certainly had to combat the weather and the sea, and life could never be dull, but they all longed for action against the enemy.

The events of 1915 unfolded: Churchill gave way to Balfour, Fisher to Jackson (there was a suggestion that Jellicoe might have relieved Fisher). There was the drama of the Dardanelles, the blood and heroism and tragedy of the Western Front. Some members of the Grand Fleet visited the trenches — some even won medals for gallantry while they were there — but to the fleet as a whole the great names of Ypres and Loos and Gallipoli were as the roll of distant drums. After the Dogger Bank action there was no further fleet activity for the rest of the year; German ships did venture out tentatively, but never in strength and never to any purpose.

Meanwhile, the fleet at Scapa had to wait, as the days turned into weeks and then into months. They faced the eternal round of drills, and coaling, and tactical exercises, and occasional sweeps into the northern part of the North Sea, and back to coal and drill again. 'The object of life', wrote King-Hall, 'was "WAR", and the C-in-C saw that this point was never overlooked.' Battleships went to sea by squadrons, to carry out full calibre shoots at a towed target at the western end of the Pentland Firth. Jellicoe's staff, '. . . the keen-eyed spies and marking party from the *Iron Duke*', watched the firings from *Oak*. It was gunnery, gunnery, day and night. On most days the little bays around the Flow would be occupied by ships practising with Percy

Scott's one-inch miniature calibre device, firing at a small target towed by a steam picket-boat. By night, the Flow would be lit up by flashes and searchlights of ships carrying out night firings.

It was a weary time for everybody, when boredom turned into frustrated rage. 'I feel we are so impotent,' wrote Beatty, at Rosyth, 'so incapable of doing anything for lack of opportunity, almost that we are not doing our share and bearing our portion of the burden laid upon the nation.' 'You'd think their women would *boo* them out,' said one of Bartimeus' characters. Nevertheless, it was Jellicoe's supreme achievement as a leader that he kept his fleet keen, on their toes, always ready. Frustration did not turn to disaffection. As a fleet commander, Jellicoe kept more men waiting and training contentedly for longer than any other admiral in naval history. He and his fleet were quite certain that some day, some time their chance would come.

In the meantime, Jellicoe did not lack for suggestions about possible actions to lure the German Fleet out, or at least to promote some sort of activity to break the prolonged deadlock. He resisted pressure from Churchill and Fisher to move the Grand Fleet to Rosyth and the battle cruisers down to the Humber. He thought the Humber as a base was 'quite impossible'. It would only hold about a dozen big ships, strong tides would sweep away any anti-submarine booms, it was easily mined by the enemy, and '. . . when there is a fog *anywhere*, it is sure to be there'.

Rosyth was also vulnerable to mining and submarines. At certain tide states it was difficult to get big ships to sea; in fact it was quite possible that it would take the fleet as long to get to grips with the enemy from Rosyth as it would from Scapa. Jellicoe knew that the naval blockade was defeating Germany, slowly but as surely as a stranglehold. He was like a wrestler with a firm grasp on his opponent's windpipe; tricky throws and flashy half-nelsons might excite the crowd, but they were irrelevant to victory.

Beatty agreed with Jellicoe on the subject of bases. 'I know that on all the large questions we are of the same opinion,' Beatty wrote, and that was true. The two men wrote to each other frequently, and their letters covered the whole scope of the naval war: fleet tactics, Admiralty decisions, proposals for joint exercises with the Grand Fleet and the battle cruisers, the dangers of mines, submarines and Zeppelins.

But the two did not meet often enough, and Beatty realized that. 'I should dearly like to see you again,' he said. 'There is so much to talk about and it is so much easier than writing.' He was absolutely right. Letters were all very well — they could be kept, re-read and consulted later — but there was no substitute for long and close discussion between two men who would have to work so closely together in battle. Those naval commanders who had close relations with their colleagues have been able to say, like a proud theme-song running through naval history, 'Everybody knew what they had to do without my telling them.' On the day, Jellicoe was not able to claim that.

Beatty would have liked a more affectionate relationship with Jellicoe. He admired Jellicoe, respected his enormous technical knowledge, and recognized his enormous prestige in the fleet. He would have liked to turn his respect and admiration into close friendship. But Jellicoe seems always to have held something back in his attitude towards Beatty. Both men had married women who had brought money with them, but that was almost their only point in common. Beatty, the younger man, was dashing where Jellicoe was cautious, more temperamentally moody than Jellicoe, and quicker to anger. Beatty had sartorial vanities, the cap tilted over one eye, the missing button on his reefer jacket, which Jellicoe would have abhorred. He was silver to Jellicoe's gold, but though men greatly respected and warmly admired Jellicoe, they loved Beatty.

On one point Jellicoe certainly began to have misgivings: the standard of the battle cruisers' gunnery. He knew Beatty's ships were not able to carry out the gunnery practice they needed at Rosyth. In one shoot in November 1915 *Lion* and *Tiger* both performed very badly. Beatty told Jellicoe it had been '. . . a terrible disappointment'. In the event, joint exercises with the two forces could not be organized. In any case the waters off Scapa were best for those, and Jellicoe did not want all his ships so far north if the High Seas Fleet did come out. 'I do not think you will be let down by the gunnery of the battle-cruisers when our day comes,' Beatty told Jellicoe, and he had to be content with that reassurance.

On 24 January 1916 the cautious and by then mortally ill Admiral Pohl was relieved of command of the High Seas Fleet by Vice-Admiral Reinhard Scheer, a most able and bold sea captain, the man who had been pointed out to Jellicoe before the war as a likely high-flyer. Scheer was given a clearer and freer brief for offensive action than his predecessors, but it was never his intention to engage the whole Grand Fleet at once. He knew that the High Seas Fleet would probably be no match in a toe-to-toe slugging contest.

However by stepping up a campaign of submarine and mine warfare he could so exasperate and irritate the British that parts of the Grand Fleet might be lured to sea. If he could defeat the Grand Fleet in detail by destroying parts of it, then eventually, some time in the future, the Grand Fleet might be whittled away by losses to a point where Scheer could risk a head-on, full-scale confrontation. But that lay very much in the future.

In February 1916 German destroyers made a sweep east of the

Dogger Bank. Three weeks later the High Seas Fleet made a sortie as far west as the Texel, in conjunction with a Zeppelin raid on the mainland. Neither sortie achieved anything, although the Grand Fleet, alerted through intelligence, put to sea each time. In March Hipper's battle cruisers, supported by battleships, put to sea but turned back because of bad weather. In April, to coincide with the Easter Rising of Irish Nationalists, Scheer took the High Seas Fleet to sea for a bombardment of Lowestoft and Yarmouth, but the German ships escaped without being brought to action. Beatty's ships got within 130 miles of Scheer, but Jellicoe was never nearer than 300 miles.

Although Jellicoe was as inflexibly cautious as ever, and was coming under ever greater criticism in 1916 because of his caution, which some said was contrary to all the Royal Navy's traditions, the teasings and feintings of the early months were perceptibly changing the atmosphere of the naval war, as though a faint breeze were stirring, bringing at least the promise of an end to the stalemate of 1915.

There were changes on the British side. As a result of the Lowestoft raid the 3rd Battle Squadron of pre-Dreadnoughts was moved from Rosyth to Sheerness, and the 3rd Cruiser Squadron from Rosyth to the Swin estuary, between Harwich and the Thames. They were to be replaced at Rosyth by the new 5th Battle Squadron of new, fast ships of the Queen Elizabeth class, a move that Jellicoe strenuously resisted for some time. As always, he wished the maximum strength under his own hand and felt that the stronger he made Beatty, the greater the temptation would be for him '. . . to get involved in independent action'. Jellicoe also objected to the use of the term Battle Cruiser Fleet, as applied to Beatty's squadrons. To him there was only one fleet, and that was the Grand Fleet. However, the 5th Battle Squadron did move down to Rosyth and were consequently not directly under Jellicoe's command when their day came at last.

Jellicoe was always suspicious of 'independent action', as his brush with Sturdee showed. He revised his Battle Orders in December 1915 and reissued them to the fleet in January 1916. Broadly speaking, they were much more of the same as before. They spread over seventy pages of print, and like their predecessors they attempted to provide for every contingency, foresee every eventuality, square off every corner, dot every 'i' and cross every 't'. Jellicoe insisted upon centralized command. He intended to fight a big gun battle, with his ships steaming in line ahead on a parallel course with the enemy and at long range. He would fight in daylight and not under any account by night, which he still regarded as a lottery weighted on the side of the weaker. He was still almost obsessively concerned with defensive precautions against torpedo attack, to which everything else, even the objective of sinking the enemy fleet, was secondary. Destroyers were urged to attack whenever possible, but their defensive roles were much emphasized. No matter what happened, Jellicoe never lost sight of the truth that he had in the Grand Fleet a weapon which must never be frittered away, which must preserve its overall superiority, for the preservation of the Empire and the Allied cause. At this distance of time it is evident that Jellicoe was quite right.

Jellicoe, for his part, was also planning an operation to entice part of the German Fleet to sea. Two squadrons of light cruisers would carry out a coat-trailing sweep from the Skaw down the Kattegat as far as the Great Belt. A squadron of older battleships would be in support in the Skagerrak, while further north, off the south-west coast of Norway, the Grand Fleet would be lying, with the Battle Cruiser Fleet ready to swoop down south if the Germans reacted in enough force. Three submarines were off the south of Horns Reef and two more off the Dogger Bank. The minelayer *Abdiel* was to extend the existing mine-field south of Horns Reef. The seaplane carrier *Engadine*, escorted by light cruisers, was also off the Horns, to give warning of Zeppelin activity.

It was a promising plan which might have set up a successful attacking position. But Scheer moved first, with a plan for a bombard-ment of Sunderland by a force of battle cruisers on 17 May. Sunder-land was a hundred miles nearer Rosyth than Lowestoft, and Scheer hoped to lure Beatty out. U-boats were stationed off Scapa and Rosyth to torpedo warships as they passed and to inform Scheer of their movements. A very important part in the plan was to be played by Zeppelins, who also would be stationed to report British fleet move-ments. But Scheer's plans were delayed, first by the need to complete repairs to *Seydlitz*, mined during the Lowestoft raid, and then for another six days by bad weather. By 29 May the U-boats were nearing the end of their fuel endurance, and the plan therefore had to be carried out by 1 June. Bad weather prevented Zeppelin reconnaissance on the twenty-ninth, but Scheer decided to go ahead the next day. If Zeppelin reconnaissance was still not available, Scheer had prepared an alter-native plan; Hipper was to go up to Skagerrak, to try and attract attention to himself, while Scheer with the High Seas Fleet followed some fifty miles astern of him.

The Admiralty had been aware that something was afoot since 17 May, when the departure of U-boats from their bases gave the first signs, later confirmed by the unusual number of signals decoded from U-boats in the northern part of the North Sea. There were also strong indications from neutral sources. During the morning of 30 May Room 40, the Admiralty centre for decoding German signals, reported a signal from Scheer ordering his U-boats to stay at sea, and another ordering the High Seas Fleet to prepare for sea and assemble in the Jade estuary. At midday the Admiralty were able to warn Jellicoe that there was a strong possibility that the High Seas Fleet would be putting to sea early on 31 May. At 5.20 p.m. Jellicoe received the order to raise steam; at 7.30 he was instructed to leave harbour as soon as possible. Thus Jellicoe's ships were already at sea on the evening of 30 May, some three hours before the High Seas Fleet, which sailed at 11 p.m. Hipper's ships sailed from the Jade at 1 a.m. the next morning. By 10.30 the great anchorage of Scapa Flow was empty once again, except for the solitary presence of the seaplane carrier *Campania*. By an oversight the sailing signal was not passed to her, and she either did not notice or ignored the activity and turmoil of the rest of the Grand Fleet putting to sea. Her officers and ship's company must have felt like men who woke up and found they had missed Trafalgar.

Chapter 11

Jellicoe sailed from Scapa on the evening of 30 May with the 4th Battle Squadron (Vice-Admiral Sir Doveton Sturdee, flying his flag in *Benbow*) and the 1st Battle Squadron (Vice-Admiral Sir Cecil Burney, flying his flag in *Marlborough*), the 3rd Battle Cruiser Squadron, of *Invincible* (flying the flag of Rear-Admiral the Hon. H.L.A. Hood), *Inflexible* and *Indomitable*, the 2nd Cruiser Squadron and 4th Light Cruiser Squadron.

On the morning of the thirty-first, Jellicoe was joined by Vice-Admiral Sir Martyn Jerram, who had relieved Warrender in December 1915, with the 2nd Battle Squadron and the 1st Cruiser Squadron. Jerram's battleships had sailed from Cromarty and took up their stations on the port end of the line, which, as they had joined from the starboard side, meant that they had further to steam. It also placed them on the side remotest from the enemy when the time came, whereas Burney's older and slightly weaker Dreadnoughts were nearest the enemy, a factor which might well have weighed with Jellicoe when the time came to deploy.

When drawn up in cruising formation, Jellicoe's battleships were in six divisions, in order from port hand to starboard:

1ST DIVISION	2ND DIVISION	3RD DIVISION	4TH DIVISION	5TH DIVISION	6TH DIVISION
King George V (Jerram)	Orion (Rear-Admiral A.C. Leveson)	Iron Duke (Jellicoe)	Benbow (Sturdee)	Colossus (Rear-Admiral E.F.A. Gaunt)	Marlborough (Burney)
Ajax	Monarch	Royal Oak	Bellerophon	Collingwood	Revenge
Centurion	Conqueror	Superb	Temeraire	Neptune	Hercules
Erin	Thunderer	Canada	Vanguard	St Vincent	Agincourt

Ahead was Hood's 3rd Battle Cruiser Squadron, Rear-Admiral Sir Robert Arbuthnot's 1st Cruiser Squadron of *Defence* (flag), *Warrior*, *Duke of Edinburgh* and *Black Prince*; Rear-Admiral H.L. Heath's 2nd Cruiser Squadron of *Minotaur* (flag), *Hampshire*, *Cochrane*, and *Shannon*; with the 4th Light Cruiser Squadron of five cruisers, with another six attached to the fleet; and three destroyer flotillas, the 4th, 11th and 12th, with a total of fifty destroyers and one light cruiser

175

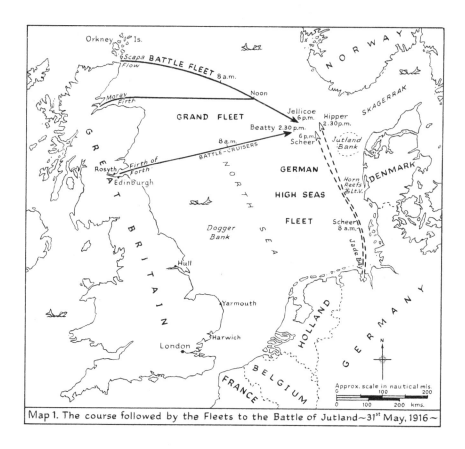

Map 1. The course followed by the Fleets to the Battle of Jutland ~31ˢᵗ May, 1916 ~

leader (*Castor*). The destroyer *Oak* and the minelayer *Abdiel* were also attached to the Grand Fleet.

Beatty sailed from Rosyth with the Battle Cruiser Fleet of *Lion* (flag), *Princess Royal* (Rear-Admiral O. de B. Brock). *Queen Mary* and *Tiger* of the 1st Battle Cruiser Squadron and *New Zealand* (Rear-Admiral W.C. Pakenham) and *Indefatigable* of the 2nd Battle Cruiser Squadron. Also with Beatty was the 5th Battle Squadron, of four new battleships with 15-inch guns, *Barham* (flying the flag of Rear-Admiral H. Evan-Thomas), *Valiant*, *Warspite* and *Malaya*. He had three Light Cruiser Squadrons, the 1st (Commodore E.S. Alexander-Sinclair in *Galatea*), 2nd (Goodenough in *Southampton*) and 3rd (Rear-Admiral T.D.W. Napier in *Falmouth*), with a total of twelve light cruisers. His destroyer strength was 1st, 9th and 10th, and 13th Flotillas, with two light cruiser leaders, *Fearless* and *Champion*, and twenty-seven destroyers. Finally, Beatty's force also included the seaplane carrier *Engadine*.

Thus, with Beatty's force, Jellicoe had a total of twenty-eight Dread-

176

noughts, nine battle cruisers, eight armoured cruisers, twenty-six light cruisers, five destroyer leaders, seventy-three destroyers, the minelayer *Abdiel* and the seaplane carrier *Engadine*.

By comparison the High Seas Fleet, which sailed from the Jade and the Elbe in the early hours of 31 May, had sixteen Dreadnoughts, with Scheer in *Friedrich der Grosse*, six pre-Dreadnoughts of Rear-Admiral Mauve's 2nd Squadron, which Scheer mistakenly allowed to come with him, thus reducing his fleet's speed to that of these slower ships, five battle cruisers under Hipper in *Lützow*, eleven light cruisers, and sixty-one destroyers. The Grand Fleet was superior to the High Seas Fleet in the numbers of Dreadnoughts, battle cruisers, cruisers and destroyers; in speed, although Jellicoe did not know that; in the number and size of heavy guns; and in the number of torpedo tubes. The German ships were generally superior in the thickness of armour and, as the battle was to show, in the efficiency of their armour-piercing shell, and in safety arrangements to protect magazines from flash after a hit – a lesson learned from *Seydlitz* in the Dogger Bank action.

By midday on 31 August, Jellicoe's and Beatty's ships were steaming towards a rendezvous in the North Sea. Jellicoe expected to be in position Lat. 57°45' N Long. 4°15' E by 2 p.m. and ordered Beatty to be sixty-nine miles south-south east of that position at that time. If Beatty had no news of the enemy by then, he was to steam north towards the main fleet. With hindsight, the distance of sixty-nine miles seems excessive, but this was the usual distance between the fleets in previous sorties. Jellicoe had always to keep his main force to the north, to cover any German attempt to strike out and lift the Northern Blockade. On the other hand, it did make it impossible for Jellicoe and Beatty to keep in touch with each other, even through their furthest scouting cruisers.

None of the British ships was bothered by submarines. The U-boat ambush failed almost completely. Only two sighted any British ships, and one U-boat fired two torpedoes, both of which missed. Some U-boats signalled reports but they were virtually useless. U-boats had no effect on the battle to come, save in Jellicoe's mind.

That morning, while the fleets of Jellicoe, Beatty and Scheer steamed towards a meeting-point in the North Sea, an important error was made in the Admiralty. Captain Thomas Jackson, the Director of Naval Operations, went into the decoding centre in Room 40 of the Old Admiralty Building to ask where direction finding placed the originator of call-sign DK, the call-sign actually used by Scheer's flagship *Friedrich der Grosse*. He did not vouchsafe the reason for his request. The staff of Room 40 were almost all civilians, whom Jackson and many other naval officers regarded as 'boffins'; they were useful in their own way and had been trained for a specific purpose, like gun-dogs, but they were not to be expected to have much knowledge of naval affairs and certainly not to be consulted on any problem of naval tactics or strategy. They had to be kept up to their job, which was decoding signals. Interpretation and assessment of those signals were essentially tasks for the naval officer.

Jackson was told that direction finding placed DK in Wilhelmshaven. Had he thought to mention why he wanted the information, he would also have been informed that DK was only *Friedrich der Grosse*'s harbour call-sign. When the ship went to sea, DK was transferred to a shore signal station and Scheer used another call-sign. But Jackson did not ask, and so drafted a signal to Jellicoe, which was received at 12.48 p.m., that wireless direction finding placed the German flagship in the Jade river at 11.10 a.m. that morning. The inference was obvious: the High Seas Fleet was still in harbour.

Jellicoe concluded that he still had plenty of time. There was no chance of meeting the enemy for hours to come. He eased off speed a little, to conserve his destroyers' fuel supply, always a source of worry to him, and spent time examining the bona fides of neutral ships passed by the fleet. It was altogether a most leisurely progess towards the action – had Jellicoe hurried he would have had a little more daylight for fighting, perhaps enough to be decisive.

Beatty and Jellicoe were both highly sceptical about the value of information sent them by the Operations Division. As Beatty said: 'What am I to think of O.D. when I get that telegram and in three hours' time meet the whole German Fleet well out to sea?' Jellicoe's reputation in recent years has suffered the grotesquely inaccurate criticism that he distrusted wireless telegraphy. It was not in fact wireless telegraphy Jellicoe distrusted, but some of the information passed by it.

At 2 p.m. Beatty was some ten miles from the position Jellicoe had specified for that time, and because of navigational discrepancies he thought he was sixteen miles from it. So he stood on, signalling to his force that he intended to turn northwards to steam towards the main fleet at 2.15. Beatty flew his flag in *Lion*, with the other 13.5-inch-gun ships of the 1st Battle Cruiser Squadron, *Princess Royal*, *Queen Mary* and *Tiger*, in close company. Some three miles astern was the 2nd Battle Cruiser Squadron, the 12.5-inch-gunned *New Zealand* and *Indefatigable*. Some five miles astern and to the north-west was Evan Thomas' 5th Battle Squadron, the new, 15-inch-gunned, accurate shooting squadron, of *Barham*, *Warspite*, *Valiant* and *Malaya*. They were stationed this far off because they were slower than Beatty's own ships and he wanted them to have that much of a head start if they encountered the enemy and had to steer for the fleet: to find the enemy and lead them under Jellicoe's guns was, after all, the main purpose in battle of Beatty's battle cruiser force. Perhaps Beatty also wanted Evan-Thomas' ships stationed so as to fit them more easily into the Grand Fleet's formation when they met. But, for whatever reason, the most powerful ships of Beatty's force were some way away, and on his disengaged side, when he most needed them.

Meanwhile, at 2 p.m. Hipper was some twenty miles east of Beatty's designated 2 p.m. rendezvous point, steering north-west with five battle cruisers of the 1st Scouting Group, *Lützow*, *Derfflinger*, *Seydlitz*, *Moltke* and *Von der Tann*, escorted by a screen of light cruisers of the 2nd Scouting Group and three flotillas of destroyers. At 2.15, when Beatty's ships were to turn due north, the most westerly of Hipper's ships was some sixteen miles away, hidden just under the horizon from *Galatea* and *Phaeton*, the most easterly of Beatty's ships. In another moment or so *Galatea* and *Phaeton* would have turned north and would not have made contact at that time.

Here, however, pure chance entered the battle. Between the two forces was a neutral merchantman, the Danish steamer *N.J. Fjord*, and both sides altered course towards her to investigate. So it was that at 2.20 *Galatea* hoisted the flag signal 'Enemy in sight', at the same time transmitting to Beatty by wireless 'Urgent: Two cruisers probably hostile in sight bearing ESE course unknown.' Had it not been for this contact, the first encounter would have been delayed until Jellicoe's ships were much closer. It was as though a trap had been sprung too soon.

Galatea's signal was received by Beatty, and by Jellicoe some seventy miles to the north. At 2.25 Beatty signalled his destroyers to take up their positions for a submarine screen when the course was altered to south-south-east, but meanwhile he stayed on his original course. He did not at once turn towards the enemy. At 2.28 *Galatea* fired the first shots of the battle of Jutland.

At 2.32, a delay of twelve minutes after the initial report (which Jellicoe later criticized), Beatty signalled by flags to his ships: 'Alter course leading ships together the rest in succession to SSE.' At the same time Evan-Thomas was signalling to his 5th Battle Squadron to alter course together two points to port (i.e. further from Beatty's course). As far as Jellicoe knew, the High Seas Fleet was still in harbour. The ships that *Galatea* was reporting were clearly light forces, which Beatty's ships could take care of. Nevertheless Jellicoe signalled his ships to raise steam for full speed at 2.35, and to report when ready to proceed. He increased speed to seventeen knots, and then to eighteen knots. *Galatea* reported a large amount of smoke 'as though from a fleet' at 2.39 and followed twelve minutes later with a report of seven vessels besides cruisers and destroyers. Jellicoe must have felt by the

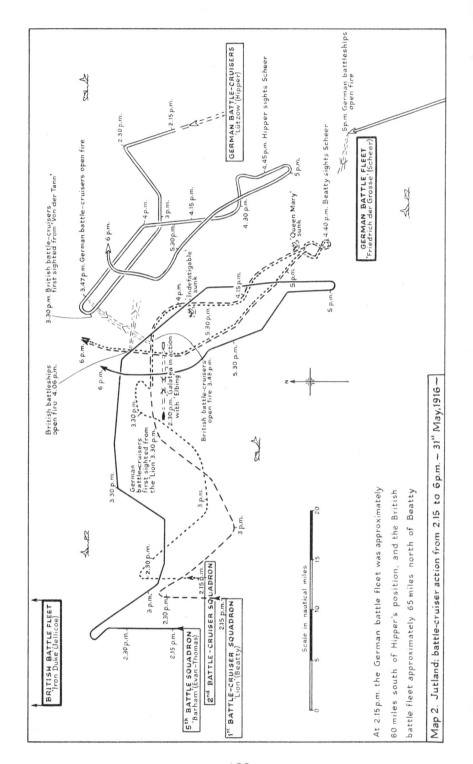

Map 2. Jutland: battle-cruiser action from 2.15 to 6 p.m. ~ 31st May, 1916 ~

At 2.15 p.m. the German battle fleet was approximately 60 miles south of Hipper's position, and the British battle fleet approximately 65 miles north of Beatty

BRITISH BATTLE FLEET Iron Duke (Jellicoe)

5th BATTLE SQUADRON Barham (Evan-Thomas)

2nd BATTLE-CRUISER SQUADRON

1st BATTLE-CRUISER SQUADRON Lion (Beatty)

GERMAN BATTLE-CRUISERS Lützow (Hipper)

GERMAN BATTLE FLEET Friedrich der Grosse (Scheer)

Scale in nautical miles
0   5   10   15   20

British battleships open fire 4.06 p.m.

3.30 p.m. British battle-cruisers first sighted from 'Von der Tann'

3.47 p.m. German battle-cruisers open fire

German battle-cruisers first sighted from the Lion 3.30 p.m.

2.30 p.m. 'Galatea' in action with 'Elbing'

British battle-cruisers open fire 3.48 p.m.

'Indefatigable' sunk

'Queen Mary' sunk

4.40 p.m. Beatty sights Scheer

4.45 p.m. Hipper sights Scheer

5 p.m. German battleships open fire

180

pricking of his thumbs that this might be the day they had all been waiting for. At 3.00 he signalled: 'Assume complete readiness for action in every respect.'

This signal was the first real indication to most of the ships that the enemy might at last be out. On every ship there was a well-drilled routine: guardrails were cleared away, shot-mantles were rigged covering vital points on the upper deck, fire-hoses were connected up and left to run on the upper deck, to keep it wet in case of fire. Hammocks, bedding, stools, tables, and anything else inflammable were removed from the main deck and struck down below. As a fire precaution, a limited amount of ready-use ammunition was got up from the magazines for the secondary armament. Extra cable stoppers were put on the anchor cables to prevent the shock of enemy fire letting the anchors go. Three or four extra large white 'battle ensigns' were flown – some ships had white ensigns painted on the sides of their control tops.

Back with the battle cruisers, Beatty signalled by searchlight to *Engadine* to send up seaplanes to scout north-north-east. *Engadine* did receive seaplane reports of the enemy, which she attempted to pass on to the battle cruisers, but none of them was received. The reporting seaplane returned and aircraft took no further part, after what might have been a promising start and was certainly a very promising tactical situation.

By that time Beatty's own tactical situation had worsened. The 5th Battle Squadron had been about five miles on Beatty's beam, on the disengaged side, when he altered course to south-south-east. By a combination of circumstances – the difficulty of making out the flag hoists on *Lion*'s yard-arms, the failure to send the signal also by light, a slowness of reaction by those on *Lion*'s bridge, who should have noticed what was happening, and by the refusal of Evan-Thomas, himself a somewhat stolid, orthodox officer, to take any action without being ordered – the 5th Battle Squadron did not immediately follow the rest of Beatty's ships. In fact the 5th Battle Squadron continued to steer a diverging course for another eight minutes. By the time the signal was at last flashed by light to *Barham* the already large gap between Beatty and Evan-Thomas had widened to about ten miles. Although Evan-Thomas did his best, working his ships up to the battle cruisers' speed of twenty-four knots and cutting all the corners he could, his ships were still some seven miles off when Beatty's ships opened fire. Most unfortunately, Beatty's force was split at the very moment when concentration was most urgently needed.

Beatty could have waited for Evan-Thomas to close up, and, with hindsight, it would have been better if he had. But that was not Beatty's way. There was the enemy, the same enemy who had by good luck and

181

a clean pair of heels eluded him in the past. He outnumbered them by six ships to five (although Beatty could not have been sure of that at the time) but in any case, even if it had been odds of a hundred to one against, Beatty would still have gone on.

Beatty's ships were steering south-easterly, to try and cross Hipper's wake and cut him off from his base. Seeing this, Hipper turned his ships through 180 degrees and also steered south-easterly, to frustrate Beatty – and also to lead him towards Scheer's battleships.

The Germans had sighted Beatty's ships at about 3.20 but had to endure a period of waiting, while the British ships outranged them. Commander Georg von Hase, gunnery officer in *Derfflinger*, watched the enemy close: 'Black monsters: six tall, broad-beamed giants steaming in two columns,' von Hase watched them change formation into line ahead. 'Like a herd of prehistoric monsters they closed on one another with slow movements, spectre-like, irresistible. . . .'

The British 13.5-inch guns had a 4,000-yard advantage in range over the German guns but this priceless asset was thrown away, as the British rangefinders continued to overestimate the range, and Beatty's ships came nearer and nearer without opening fire. At last, at about 3.47, both sides opened fire together, at a range of 15,500 yards.

Beatty's ships had grossly overestimated the range, some salvoes landing more than a mile beyond their targets, but the German gunnery was excellent. *Moltke*'s first salvo was just short of *Tiger* and the next straddled her. Within two minutes *Lützow* had hit *Lion* twice, and within four minutes *Princess Royal* had been hit twice and *Tiger* four times. Visibility had been clear for both sides, but within seconds the westerly breezes carried funnel smoke downwind from Beatty's ships to obscure the range. A destroyer flotilla thrashing up the engaged side, to get into position, added to the murk. Meanwhile the Germans enjoyed a clear view, the breeze blowing their smoke behind them.

The Germans had yet another advantage – Beatty had signalled *Princess Royal* to join *Lion* in engaging *Lützow*; with one more ship, the rest of the British Squadron should then have had an opponent each. But *Queen Mary*, the third ship, missed the signal and engaged the third German ship, *Seydlitz*, leaving *Derfflinger* free and unmolested. It was not long before von Hase noticed it: 'I laughed grimly,' he wrote, 'and now I began to engage our enemy with complete calm, as at gun practice, and with continually increasing accuracy.'

It was not until about 3.55, when the range had come down to 12,900 yards, that *Queen Mary*, the champion gunnery ship of the squadron, got two hits on *Seydlitz*, the first hits by a British ship.

Just after four o'clock, *Lützow* came within an ace of sinking *Lion*, straddling her with a very accurate salvo, one shell of which hit *Lion*'s 'Q' turret amidships, folding the front of the turret upwards and outwards 'like a sardine tin'. The guns' crew were all killed or mortally wounded. The cordite charges caught fire and, but for the presence of mind of the dying Major Harvey, the officer in charge of the turret, who ordered the magazine doors to be shut, an explosion would have followed which would have blown *Lion* in two. As it was, the handling crew, the doctor and his assistants, all died where they stood, but the flash stopped at the magazine doors and the ship was saved. Harvey was awarded a posthumous Victoria Cross.

A minute later *Von der Tann* landed three shells from a salvo of four on *Indefatigable*'s upper deck. From *New Zealand*, just ahead, watchers could see that *Indefatigable* was mortally hurt. A great cloud of black smoke gushed out of her after superstructure and she did not follow round at the next alteration of course. Then, after about thirty seconds, *Indefatigable* started to disintegrate, her whole frame exploding, starting from forward. Sheets of flame shot up above her funnels, followed by successive clouds of dark, dense smoke; debris was flung hundreds of feet into the air. Then, awed and horrified spectators in *New Zealand* saw a fifty-foot steam picket-boat rise 200 feet into the air and hang upside-down, but still intact. When the giant column of smoke had shredded away and the debris fell down, *Indefatigable* had disappeared. It seems certain that she suffered the terrible magazine explosion which *Lion* had so narrowly avoided. Of her complement of 1,019 officers and men, there were only two survivors.

Evan-Thomas, who had been catching up from the north-west, had been unable to see anything through the pall of smoke which seemed to hide the whole of Beatty's line. But at five past four he penetrated the smoke and at last saw his targets. He turned his ships to a course parallel to Beatty's and opened fire at the rearmost ships in the German line when the range was 19,000 yards. Within six minutes *Barham* had a hit on *Von der Tann*, and Hipper's ship came under a deluge of rapid, accurate 15-inch salvoes.

Lion had disappeared in a curtain of smoke, so *Derfflinger* and *Seydlitz* both concentrated on *Queen Mary*, who replied with rapid and well-laid eight-gun salvoes, giving as good as she got, scoring two hits on *Derfflinger* and straddling her several times with near-misses which drenched her upper decks with water, and incidentally helped to extinguish *Derfflinger*'s fires.

However, *Derfflinger* hit back with salvoes every twenty seconds and, at about 4.25, she straddled *Queen Mary* with a salvo of four, three of which hit. An officer in the conning tower of *Tiger*, next astern, saw the shells land and the splinters fly. The dull red glow of the shell-burst gave him the impression that *Queen Mary* was unhurt. Her armour had saved her. The next salvo also straddled her and she suffered two more hits.

There came another crimson glow amidships. The ship seemed to open out '. . . like a puffball or one of those toadstool things when one squeezes it'. As he watched, he could see a third red glow appearing forward. Then, the whole ship '. . . seemed to collapse inwards'; funnels and masts fell into the middle; the hull was blown outwards; the roofs of gun turrets could be seen shooting a hundred feet into the air. Then everything was hidden in smoke.

When the smoke pall cleared, the appalled onlookers in *New Zealand*, as their ship raced past, saw *Queen Mary*'s stern rear up from the sea, the propellors still revolving. *Tiger* had had to jink sideways to avoid the wreck. Great pieces of debris rained down on her decks as she passed close to the scene of the disaster. There were several more underwater explosions and the last remains of *Queen Mary* disappeared, taking 1,266 officers and men with her. From *Lion's* bridge, a signalman saw *Princess Royal* also vanish in the smoke and the leaping water columns of several salves. He reported her sunk. At this Beatty said to Chatfield, his flag captain, 'There's something wrong with our bloody ships today.'

While the battle cruisers were in action, the light cruisers had been steaming at full stretch to reach their position ahead, for their proper duty of reporting the enemy. By about 4.30 the most southerly of them, Goodenough's 2nd Light Cruiser Squadron, was about two miles ahead of Beatty's ships when they sighted the towering masts, fighting tops and funnel smoke of big ships, ahead and crossing to port, on a northerly course. These were Scheer's battleships. Hipper had done his job admirably – he had seemingly delivered a portion of the Grand Fleet into Scheer's hand. It had all worked out exactly as Scheer had hoped and prayed: for what we are about to receive, may the Lord make us truly thankful.

Goodenough was still standing on towards the enemy. He could now see more and more masts, rank after rank of tall grey fighting tops, coming out of the distance as far as the eye could see. This was no skirmish, no running battle with Hipper's ships. This was the main German High Seas Fleet, and this was *Der Tag*. This was IT.

At 4.38 Goodenough sent off the top-priority flash signal: 'Urgent. Priority. Have sighted enemy battle fleet bearing approximately SE, course of enemy N. My position Lat. 56°34′ N, Long. 6°20′ E.' Goodenough kept *Southampton* on her course to the south, towards the enemy, for as long as he dared – indeed for longer than was prudent. At 4.45 Beatty himself could see Scheer's ships. *Lion's* W/T had been put out of action and he had to signal via *Princess Royal*: 'Urgent. Priority. Have sighted Enemy's Battle Fleet bearing SE.' This was received by

184

Jellicoe as : '26–30 Battleships, probably hostile, bearing SSE, steering SE.'

Still Goodenough stood on southwards. His squadron was within 13,000 yards of the nearest German ships, who did not fire. Goodenough had the whole High Seas Fleet before him. As his signal officer said, 'This is the day of a light cruiser's life-time.' His commander, realistically, urged him to make his signal, 'You'd better make it now, sir. You may never make another.' The signal went out at 4.48, giving more details: 'Course of enemy's battle fleet N single line ahead. Composition of van *Kaiser* class. Bearing of centre, E. Destroyers on both wings and ahead. Enemy's battle cruisers joining battle fleet from northward.' In *Iron Duke* Jellicoe made the general signal, 'Enemy's battle fleet is coming North.'

At last, at a range of about 12,000 yards, Goodenough's ships turned away and the Germans, who had been unable to identify them until then, recognized their silhouettes and opened fire. At times *Southampton* was under fire at ranges of between 14,000 and 20,000 yards from no less than ten German battleships. But she bore a charmed life. As Goodenough said: 'I can do no wrong today.' Neither could his ship. *Southampton*'s upper decks were deluged with water from near-misses, and occasional shrapnel storms sang and hummed over her superstructure. *Southampton* was outranged and under fire for nearly an hour in which, as King-Hall later said, 'I can truthfully say that I thought each succeeding minute would be our last'. But by jinking and dodging, steering towards the last shellburst, and hoping for the best, Goodenough and his four ships got away, miraculously hardly scratched.

Now that the German Battle Fleet was in sight, Beatty's role had changed. Now it was his turn to try and lure his enemy on to the guns of Jellicoe's ships, approaching some fifty miles to the north. Recalling his cruisers and destroyers – an order which Goodenough disregarded — Beatty turned his battle cruisers northwards at 4.46 and very soon passed abreast of Evan-Thomas' battleships who were still steering south. Beatty hoisted a signal to Evan-Thomas to turn sixteen points to starboard in succession. This signal was hauled down, and thus executed, at about 4.57.

Barham was under fire from two German battleships as she turned and, arguably, it might have been better if Evan-Thomas had not waited to make his turn. But Evan-Thomas was not the officer to act without a signal and, whether he intended it or not, his run nearer the enemy did help to cover Beatty's turn northwards. But the turn to starboard took Evan-Thomas away from Beatty, and by the time it was completed Evan-Thomas was some three miles astern of Beatty's rearmost ship and on the port, or disengaged, quarter. Evan-Thomas had in fact to bear away to starboard, so that he completed a turn of some eighteen points in all, to follow in Beatty's wake. A turn to *port* would have been neater and quicker.

At 4.51 Jellicoe signalled to the Admiralty, 'Urgent, Fleet action is imminent.' This Jellicoe had deduced by instinct rather than from information received. For him it had so far been a frustrating afternoon of sparse signals, with long, aching voids of silence between them. At 3.40 he had had Beatty's urgent signal reporting five enemy battle cruisers and a large number of destroyers, bearing north-east, course unknown. Ten minutes later Beatty signalled that he was engaging the enemy. At 4.05 p.m., although he had not yet heard that the German Battle Fleet was at sea, Jellicoe signalled to Hood to join and support Beatty with his own battle cruisers; this signal, too, was made intuitively. Jellicoe just guessed that Beatty might be in need of assistance.

There was no news from Beatty until 4.45 when the report of '. . . 26–30 battleships, probably hostile' was relayed through *Princess Royal*. At 3.59 a signal from *Galatea* to Beatty was intercepted in *Iron Duke*: 'Urgent. Enemy bearing ESE. Course of enemy ESE. My position, course and speed. . . . ' From this Jellicoe's staff could put another position on their plotting chart, but there was still nothing like enough information. Jellicoe had scores of ships under his command that afternoon. At least one score of them had seen and been in contact with the enemy, but nobody except Goodenough reported. At 4.17 Jellicoe could not contain his impatience any longer and signalled direct to Evan-Thomas: 'Are you in company with Senior Officer, Battle Cruiser Fleet?' At 4.30 the reply came back, not answering that question but another: 'Yes, I am engaging the enemy.'

At last, Goodenough's three signals came, reporting the enemy's numbers and course, and Beatty's report signalled via *Princess Royal*. *Southampton* transmitted another enemy sighting report at five o'clock. Thus, between *Galatea*'s signal of 3.59 and Goodenough's last signal, Jellicoe received five enemy sighting reports. The garbled 4.45 report of '26–30 battleships' remained uncorrected and allowed Jellicoe to think that the enemy were in much greater strength than they actually were. Jellicoe believed that Scheer had put to sea with every battleship, Dreadnought and pre-Dreadnought, the German Navy had. Throughout the coming action, visibility was never good enough for Jellicoe to have a clear sight of his enemy and correct this misconception.

As time passed and it became more and more important for Jellicoe to receive accurate information, so he seemed to receive less and less. At 5.30 the cruiser *Falmouth*, flagship of Rear-Admiral Napier commanding the 3rd Light Cruiser Squadron, and the leading ship of

Beatty's force, actually sighted and exchanged identities with *Black Prince*, the leading starboard hand ship of the Grand Fleet. An exchange of information between these two ships could have brought Jellicoe up-to-date. But *Falmouth* merely told *Black Prince*: 'Battle cruisers engaged to the ssw of me', and *Black Prince* signalled to *Iron Duke* the totally wrong information: 'Enemy battle cruisers bearing south five miles.'

Between five o'clock and 5.40 there was another yawning silence. The two battle fleets were only about thirty miles apart and closing at a relative speed of some twenty-eight knots. They were in fact approaching each other at the rate of one mile about every two minutes. At 5.40 the faithful Goodenough piped up again with another invaluable signal, reporting the enemy battle fleet's alteration of course to NNW. But ten minutes later even Goodenough made a mistake. When his signal was drafted the reciprocal was mistaken for the true bearing and the enemy battle cruisers were reported south-west of the fleet instead of north-east. This, because of Goodenough's brilliant reporting earlier, took some untangling in the flagship; for some time nobody knew whether to believe it or not. At 6.03 Goodenough reported he had lost touch.

By then Beatty and Evan-Thomas had been in action again. Scheer believed Beatty was beaten and ordered 'General Chase'. Hipper's flagship, like Beatty's, had been damaged and its W/T aerials put out of action. Hipper was unable to inform Scheer of the true situation. At about 5.40 Hipper's battle cruisers appeared out of the haze, in full view of Beatty's ships, at a range of only 14,000 yards. In a brisk but fierce action *Seydlitz* was heavily hammered, and very nearly sank. Hipper was driven off to the eastward.

This engagement was seen and heard by Jellicoe's ships. At 5.40 *Minotaur* signalled: 'Report of guns heard south', and this was confirmed by *Hampshire* and *Comus*. Jellicoe knew the two fleets were closing rapidly and that the moment of encounter could not be far off. He asked his flag captain, Dreyer, to take ranges of objects on various bearings to find out which direction was best for the range-takers and spotters. Dreyer reported that the visibility was best to the south, and then, as the sun sunk lower, to the west.

At 5.50 the cruiser *Calliope* reported what appeared to be 'flashes of guns ssw'. It was at this point that *Black Prince* transmitted her false report of enemy battle cruisers to the south; the ships they could see were actually Beatty's, but in any case the signal was not deciphered for some time and Jellicoe's staff were spared the extra confusion. From *Marlborough*, away on the starboard wing, Burney had the message semaphored: 'Gun flashes and heavy gun firing on starboard bow.'

Jellicoe could hear it himself now, the far-off booming and thudding of Evan-Thomas' ships hammering *Seydlitz*. 'I wish someone would tell me who is firing and what they are firing at,' he said. Those were questions nobody on *Iron Duke*'s bridge could answer.

The battleships were still in cruising formation, in columns. The time was swiftly coming when they would have to deploy into battle order of line ahead. The question was, which way to deploy? If to starboard, where the noise of gunfire was coming from and where Jellicoe already sensed his enemy would appear, it would bring on the action all the more quickly. But it would deploy Burney's divisions, the oldest and weakest ships, nearest to the enemy. A deployment to port would mean that the Grand Fleet would be firing towards the better visibility, as Dreyer had predicted. If the German Battle Fleet was steering NNE as Goodenough had reported, a deployment to port would neatly cross the German 'T'. Further, it would place the Grand Fleet between Scheer and his bases. But it would also be a movement away from the enemy and would delay the onset of the action, which might be of vital importance. The day was already far on and the hours of daylight running out.

At 6 p.m. Rear-Admiral Gaunt in *Colossus* took the chance to semaphore to the ships in the other division: 'Remember traditions of glorious 1st of June and avenge Belgium.' It was a fine sentiment, but meanwhile Jellicoe was still being denied the information he needed. At six o'clock the message was flashed by searchlight to Burney: 'What can you see?' The reply was startling as well as disappointing: 'Our battle cruisers bearing SSW steering east, *Lion* leading ship.' This gave no information about the enemy, but it did reveal that Jellicoe's and Beatty's ships were much nearer each other than they had supposed. Zigzagging and manoeuvring under overcast skies with no chance for sunsights had led to navigational discrepancies of over ten miles, and Jellicoe had even less time than he thought. Furthermore, Beatty's ships had appeared well to starboard, by some forty-five degrees of where he had expected them. He had expected to meet the enemy dead ahead. Now, as his staff wrestled with the problems of Burney's signal, Jellicoe himself was sure the High Seas Fleet would appear to starboard.

By six o'clock *Lion* was in sight in the haze and *Iron Duke* flashed to her: 'Where is enemy's battle fleet?' The reply was: 'Have sighted enemy's battle fleet bearing SSW.' Jellicoe altered the Grand Fleet's course to south and then five minutes later to south-east. It was the only sign of indecision he gave. *Lion* reported: 'Enemy's battle-cruisers bearing SE.' Now, at last, the picture was beginning to form on the plotting table. At 6.10 *Barham* signalled by flags and by W/T: 'Enemy's battle fleet SSE.'

At 6.10 Jellicoe repeated his signal to Beatty: 'Where is enemy's battle fleet?' At last the lamp started to blink on *Lion*'s flag bridge. 'Have sighted enemy's battle fleet bearing ssw.' No range was given, but the time had now come for Jellicoe to make up his mind.

The yeoman of signals had been standing on the starboard side of *Iron Duke*'s upper bridge, spelling out the letters of *Lion*'s signal which was received at 6.14. Jellicoe was standing next to the yeoman, wearing his oldest cap with tarnished gold braid, a white muffler wound round his neck against the damp evening chill, and an old blue burberry raincoat with a belt tied round the waist over his uniform. His staff officers, Madden, Halsey the captain of the fleet, Forbes the flag commander, Bellairs the torpedo and war staff officer, and Herbert the flag lieutenant, all stood in the starboard after corner of the manoeuvring platform, watching Jellicoe. They heard his quick, distinctive footsteps on the deck as he crossed and stepped up on to the compass platform where Dreyer was standing. There was quiet for some seconds while Jellicoe looked down at the magnetic compass; the others could hear only the wind in the signal halliards and the rustling of the sea, pushing past the ship, far below. They watched him, studying his keen, sharp features, wondering what he would do. It was up to Jellicoe now.

Chapter 12

Jellicoe stared intently at the compass for some moments. Once he looked up and round to check the visibility. He had been given definite information of the enemy battle fleet so late that he now had only seconds to make up his mind, although, as Churchill said, a mistake now could lose the war in an afternoon. Standing next to Jellicoe, just aft of the magnetic compass, and watching him closely, Dreyer could see that he appeared calm and quite unmoved, totally absorbed in the solution of a most complex tactical problem.

To port or starboard, which should it be? With the experience of a hundred exercises, Jellicoe could see the whole problem in his mind's eye. His instinct was to deploy his line to starboard, to bring on the battle as early as possible. From *Iron Duke*'s bridge he could now see the gun flashes. The thundering noise from ahead and round to starboard was now heavy and continuous. He knew the enemy battle fleet would be encountered to starboard and well forward of the beam. Nobody had given him any ranges, but the visibility was not more than five miles, so the enemy must be close, so close that by deploying to starboard he might be laying his leading battleships open to attack from the German destroyers who were sure to be steaming ahead of the German Battle Fleet. There might already be an overlap, so that as Burney advanced enough German ships might already have crossed ahead of him to cross his 'T'. If that happened, then the deploying battleships would have to follow round to port, each division having to make a larger turn to port as it deployed than the eight-point turn they already had to make. It would take some twenty minutes to complete the deployment. For much of that time, the starboard wing with Burney's older and less well protected ships would be unsupported. The other divisions would each come under fire as they formed up.

A deployment to port would avoid all these possibilities and disadvantages, although it would certainly mean a delay before the battle line came into action. But Jellicoe must have felt in his bones that it was now his only chance of crossing the enemy's 'T'. He looked round and met the gaze of Commander Woods, the fleet signal officer, who was standing behind Dreyer at the back of the manoeuvring platform.

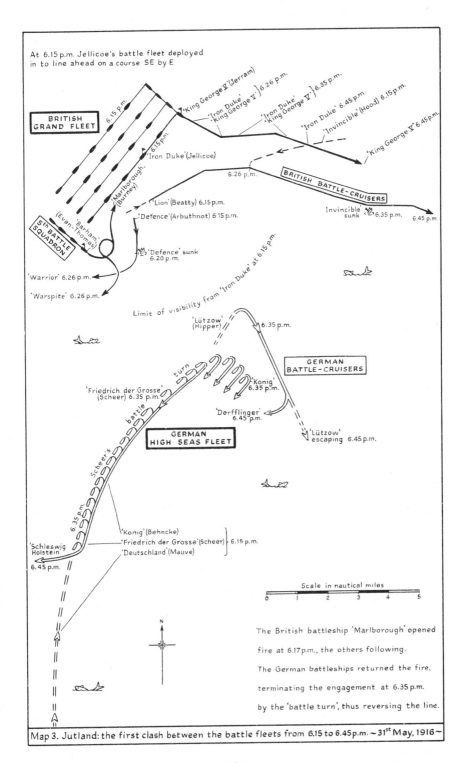

At 6.15 p.m. Jellicoe's battle fleet deployed in to line ahead on a course SE by E

BRITISH GRAND FLEET

6.15 p.m.

'King George V'(Jerram)

'Iron Duke' 'King George V' } 6.26 p.m.

'Iron Duke' 'King George V' } 6.35 p.m.

'Iron Duke' 6.45 p.m.

'Invincible'(Hood) 6.15 p.m.

'King George V' 6.45 p.m.

6.15 p.m.

'Iron Duke'(Jellicoe)

6.26 p.m.

BRITISH BATTLE-CRUISERS

'Marlborough' (Burney)

'Lion'(Beatty) 6.15 p.m.

'Defence'(Arbuthnot) 6.15 p.m.

Invincible sunk 6.35 p.m.

6.45 p.m.

5th BATTLE SQUADRON

'Barham' (Evan-Thomas)

'Defence' sunk 6.20 p.m.

'Warrior' 6.26 p.m.

'Warspite' 6.26 p.m.

Limit of visibility from 'Iron Duke' at 6.15 p.m.

'Lützow' (Hipper)

6.35 p.m.

GERMAN BATTLE-CRUISERS

turn

'Friedrich der Grosse' (Scheer) 6.35 p.m.

'Konig' 6.35 p.m.

'Derfflinger' 6.45 p.m.

battle

GERMAN HIGH SEAS FLEET

Scheer's

'Lützow' escaping 6.45 p.m.

6.35 p.m.

'Konig' (Behncke)

'Friedrich der Grosse'(Scheer) } 6.15 p.m.

'Deutschland'(Mauve)

'Schleswig Holstein' 6.45 p.m.

Scale in nautical miles

0 1 2 3 4 5

N

The British battleship 'Marlborough' opened fire at 6.17 p.m., the others following. The German battleships returned the fire, terminating the engagement at 6.35 p.m. by the 'battle turn', thus reversing the line.

Map 3. Jutland: the first clash between the battle fleets from 6.15 to 6.45 p.m. ~31st May, 1916~

'Hoist equal speed pendant south east.'

For a moment, when he heard the order given, Madden was amazed. For one ghastly instant he wondered whether his chief had suddenly gone off his head. Could Jellicoe possibly have cracked up, at this ultimate stage, under the strain? The equal speed pendant was a new signal, only recently included, and had never been tried before in the fleet. It meant deployment on the port wing, *remotest* from the enemy. Surely there must be a mistake?

But Woods, the practical signalman, knew that the signal code book did not have a simple signal for deployment to the south-east. The order, as given, would involve a signal unfamiliar to the fleet. However, there was a practical solution; a signal ordering a deployment one point to port of south-east could be made normally and unambiguously.

'Would you make it a point to port, sir?' he asked. 'So that they will know it is on the port wing column.'

Jellicoe took the point at once. 'Very good,' he said. 'Hoist equal speed pendant south-east-by-east.' So the three-flag signal, the blue and white equal speed pendant and the gaily coloured flags for Charlie and London (CL meaning SE by E), went fluttering up to *Iron Duke*'s yard-arm. (Jellicoe and Woods might both have been subconsciously aware of Pasco's amendment to Nelson's signal at Trafalgar, suggesting 'expects' for 'confides' because that word was in the signal book.)

To save time Jellicoe told Dreyer to 'Start the Deployment'. Down came the hoist, the signal to 'execute', while the order was flashed on W/T at the same time. Two blasts were sounded on *Iron Duke*'s siren and the helm was put over twenty degrees to port. The leading battleships of all the divisions conformed and turned eight points to port, except *King George V* on the extreme port wing who altered one point to SE by E. She was now the leading ship of the battle fleet. It was 6.15, only a minute after the yeoman had spelled out Beatty's signal that he had sighted the enemy's battle fleet. Jellicoe himself had not sighted a single enemy ship, yet almost entirely intuitively, and in less than half a minute, he had arrived at a solution which extensive post-war research, carried out over many years, demonstrated was not just the best but the only solution.

With so many ships involved, the deployment took some time and many ships had opened fire long before it was completed. *Marlborough*, down on the starboard wing and some way astern of *Iron Duke*, opened fire at 6.17 at a range of 13,000 yards on the German Battle Fleet which by then was almost on her starboard beam and steering an approximately parallel course. She was joined by *Barham* and the rest of the 5th Battle Squadron. When he first saw *Marlborough*, Evan-Thomas believed that Jellicoe was deploying the

Grand Fleet to starboard and prepared to take station ahead of *Marlborough*, but when he saw the deployment was to port he took up his alternative position in the rear. During the turn to port *Warspite* was hit, her steering gear jammed and she made a complete circle while under fire.

Warspite's manoeuvrings probably distracted enemy attention from the cruiser *Warrior* of Rear-Admiral Arbuthnot's 1st Cruiser Squadron. Arbuthnot had attacked the enemy line as he had always planned to do, but, in the poor visibility prevailing, very probably did not imagine that when the time came his ships *Defence* and *Warrior* would be the only targets visible to the enemy. *Derfflinger* and four Dreadnoughts opened fire on Arbuthnot's ships at ranges down to 5,000 yards. At 6.20 *Defence* was smothered in shells, and disappeared in a colossal column of smoke and flames. There were no survivors.

The Grand Fleet had the advantage of the best visibility – another result of the deployment to port – but the range was soon obscured by the smoke of Beatty's battle cruisers, racing across to take up their position at the van of the line. In what had become a very confused situation, Beatty's ships caused *Iron Duke* temporarily to reduce speed to let them pass, while Jerram in *King George V* had to steer further out to port to give himself more room. Beatty was in position by about 6.33, and the deployment was completed by about 6.40.

By then, Jellicoe could see three of the enemy battle fleet – at no time during the whole battle was he able to see more than four at once – and knew that his deployment had been successful. It was as if he had drawn a figure which, by its very geometry, was imposing its pattern on the battle; Jellicoe had actually done what every admiral planned to do in exercise and dreamed of doing in action. Scheer's leading battleships were steaming north-eastwards towards a line of flame-belching opponents which seemed to stretch from one horizon to the other. Even the delay in deployment to port turned out to be an extra advantage, allowing the Grand Fleet to extend itself even more comprehensively across Scheer's 'T'.

Iron Duke fired her first salvoes at 6.23 on a bearing of Green 80, range 11,000 yards. Her target was the sinking cruiser *Wiesbaden*, which each ship in turn had hammered as they passed. *Iron Duke* fired four salvoes, straddling with the third. Just after 6.30, very soon after she had turned to starboard to take her place in the line, *Iron Duke* opened fire on a battleship of the König class, bearing Green 70, range 12,000 yards. She hit with the second, third and fourth salvoes, with a total of at least six hits; it was calculated later that of nine hits achieved by the British battleships in this part of the battle, no fewer than seven were by *Iron Duke* herself. *Iron Duke*'s turret crews noted that the visibility was quite good; the enemy was lit up by the sun, whereas *Iron Duke* was very probably invisible in the mist. 'However that may be,' observed *Iron Duke's* gunnery officer, Commander Geoffrey Blake, 'the König battleships did not return *Iron Duke's* fire, although heavily hit. Nine salvoes, comprising a total of forty-three rounds, were fired at her in four minutes, fifty seconds.' It was very fast and very accurate shooting by the fleet flagship.

But meanwhile, ahead of the battle fleet, the battle cruisers had suffered another tragedy, almost identical to the other two. On seeing Hipper's battle cruisers approaching from the southward, Hood turned his 3rd Battle Cruiser Squadron on to a parallel course, and opened fire at 6.23, at a range of 9,000 yards. Hood's flagship *Invincible* began to score hits on *Lützow* and *Derfflinger*. Hood was just encouraging the gunnery officer, telling him that his fire was '. . . very good. Keep at it as quickly as you can. Every shot is telling', when four German battle cruisers and a battleship concentrated their fire on *Invincible*. She was hit several times, with no harm done, but at 6.33 a shell hit the fatal Q turret, pierced the roof and exploded inside. From *Lion*, the watchers heard several huge explosions in quick succession. Then, to their horrified amazement, *Invincible* blew up almost exactly in halves, so that the two portions of the ship sank together, until only the bows and the stern still showed above water, some distance apart. It was a grotesque and horrifying sight, but such was the confusion and so poor the visibility that many British sailors thought it was the end of a German ship and cheered madly as they passed the two shattered ends. There were only six survivors of *Invincible*'s 1,032 officers and men. There might have been more, but the advancing battle fleet ploughed through the spot where *Invincible* went down and many men must have been swept under. Some survivors were seen cheering and waving from the water as the battleships went by.

The German ships leading Scheer's line fired at what they could see ahead, but no ship in the British battle line suffered a single hit. However, they did experience an exciting few minutes, with the big ships manoeuvring to keep station and a score of smaller ships, cruisers and destroyers, jinking and dodging among them, trying to avoid the big ships and each other and find their proper places. Meanwhile the sea on all sides was churned into foam by shell-bursts, with tall spouts of water growing up everywhere. 'The general effect outdid the most imaginative picture of a Naval Battle that I ever saw,' wrote Lieutenant Briggs, in *Malaya*. 'It reminded us of those pictures of Spithead reviews you see up Queen Street,' said Alexander-Sinclair, commanding the 1st Light Cruiser Squadron, 'all ships and no water.'

All ships and no water was very much how it appeared to Admiral Scheer. He had been no better informed than Jellicoe, and the first real indication he had of the whereabouts of Jellicoe's battle fleet was the sight of it stretched out along the horizon. Scheer's own line was already dangerously extended. His twenty-two battleships were in a line nine miles long, compared with Jellicoe's twenty-four (the 5th Battle Squadron were not yet in station) tightly compressed into a line of less than six miles.

Scheer's ships were being battered to pieces, slowly and methodically. He could not turn aside and risk a slogging match on a parallel course with what was obviously a superior force. His van was already beginning to look ragged under the hits, and individual ships were starting to edge away like boxers flinching under too heavy punishment. Over to starboard Hipper's battle cruisers were in a sorry state: *Lützow* had left the line, *Derfflinger* was down by the bows, *Seydlitz* was damaged, *Von der Tann* had not a single turret left in action. Only *Moltke* was still fighting fit.

The wind shifted and began to carry funnel smoke and gun smoke and fumes forward in front of Scheer so that his view, never good, became much worse. Scheer was being hammered by an enemy he could barely see. Whenever the fog did disperse and show the horizon, all Scheer could see was the unbroken line of great dark shapes, shrouded in black smoke, through which bright flashes sparkled in rippling succession, as salvo after salvo was fired in a seemingly interminable thundering of violent noise.

In this moment of extremity, Scheer proved quite as resourceful as Jellicoe. He seized on the one possible way out of his predicament: he could not go on leading his ships against what seemed to be a solid wall of fire; he could not order them to turn in succession. Each ship as it reached the turning point would be in the focus of a storm of fire. At 6.33 Scheer ordered his famous *Gefechtskehrtwendung* or 'battle turn about'. His ships all spun round together through 180 degrees, and so steamed back the way they had come, except that their order was reversed, the last being first and the first last. The manoeuvre was well and neatly executed and was completed by 6.45, with Scheer's heavy ships all steering south-west, away from the Grand Fleet. At the same time, Scheer ordered the 3rd Destroyer Flotilla to go forward and attack under a smokescreen to cover the retreat.

On *Iron Duke*'s bridge, they noticed that the thunder of the guns was dying away; by about 6.40 there was a strange silence. Normal sounds flooded back. A south-westerly wind blew the German smoke towards the Grand Fleet. Jellicoe did not himself see the German ships turn away, and thought they had temporarily vanished in the deepening mist. Not for the first time that day, nor the last, he was very poorly served by those who should have kept him informed. The turn away was seen, but not reported, by *Falmouth*. Four battleships on the centre and rear of the line also saw, but did not report. Burney, in *Marlborough*, saw but said nothing. *Iron Duke*'s own transmitting station, receiving and correlating the information by which the guns were laid and trained, recorded a large turn away. Even Dreyer, in *Iron Duke*'s conning tower, noticed the turn but, preoccupied by his own ship in action, he assumed that Jellicoe had seen what he had and did not mention it. Evan-Thomas, at the end of the line, also saw but said nothing.

As the minutes began to pass and the silence lengthened, it was obvious something had happened. At 6.45 Jellicoe altered the battle line's course nearer to the enemy south-east. Ten minutes later, though he still had no fresh information, he altered further, to south. At the same time Jellicoe asked Burney: 'Can you see any enemy battleships?' Burney replied, unsurprisingly, 'No.' *Marlborough* had problems of her own: at 6.50 she was struck by a torpedo and her speed reduced to seventeen knots.

Scheer always had the speed to disengage if he wished, and the misty North Sea in the confusion of battle, with only an hour or so of daylight remaining, was an ideal setting for a disappearing act. Jellicoe had no intention of following in his enemy's tracks – that would risk mines and torpedoes, the very eventualities about which he had always been cautious. Jellicoe believed, wrongly as it happened, that the German battleships carried mines, and would jettison them as they retreated. Jellicoe had thought many times about just this state of affairs. His own interpretation of the situation was that he would need enough time, perhaps ten or twelve hours of daylight, and an ample margin of speed of some four to five knots to pin his enemy down. At the moment, he had neither.

Jellicoe's solution was to place his ships across Scheer's line of retreat back to his harbour bases. Scheer might or might not – probably not – steam to westward. But sooner or later he *must* steam eastward. Jellicoe would be waiting. At five past seven Jellicoe altered course to sw by s. Scheer was then about thirteen miles away, to the south-west, so this was a most promising course for a renewed action. But when *King George V* reported a u-boat dead ahead of *Iron Duke* and Goodenough reported that the enemy were once more steering east, Jellicoe brought his ships back to south.

Beatty meanwhile had lost touch with the enemy, after a strange gyration by *Lion* through 360 degrees (although Beatty always insisted in later years that it was *not* a complete circle but an 's' turn) which lasted from about 6.55 to 7.10 and this lost Beatty a good deal of ground. But the main failure was by the cruisers. What Jellicoe needed now, as always, was accurate and up-to-date information about the enemy, and here again he was very poorly served.

196

Of the Light Cruiser Squadrons, the 3rd (Napier) was at the head of the battle line but on the eastern or disengaged side of the battle cruisers. The 1st was astern, level with the rear squadron of the battle fleet and also on the disengaged side. Neither of these squadrons contributed anything. Of the two squadrons on the engaged side nearest the enemy, the 4th (Le Mesurier) headed southwest, but the visibility was obscured by heavy and dense smoke.

Only the inestimable Goodenough, as before, did the job he was paid for. As soon as the thundering of the guns died down at about 6.45 he led his squadron southwards and within a few minutes sighted the rearmost German ships. He also spotted that Scheer had reversed course and at 7 p.m. made another of his thrilling signals: 'Urgent. Priority. Enemy battle fleet steering ESE. Enemy bears from me SSW. Number unknown. My position . . .'

At 6.55 Scheer had ordered another sixteen-point turn to an easterly course and once again steered towards the Grand Fleet. He later told the Kaiser that he meant to attack regardless of the consequences, but it does not seem likely that having once broken away and considered himself to have done well in achieving this, Scheer would voluntarily place his ships in the same position from which he had just extricated them, inviting another chance of a catastrophe. It seems much more probable that Scheer, who was as badly served for reconnaissance as Jellicoe was, calculated that the Grand Fleet had already drawn to the south and east of him, and that if he struck eastwards now he stood a good chance of crossing behind Jellicoe and reaching safety. Perhaps he really was reluctant to leave the day and the battle without trying once more. Perhaps he did hope to head for home and also to deal the enemy a shrewd blow on the way and thus salvage something from the day. But if so, it was inexplicable that he should lead his line with his battle cruisers, who were the weaker ships and had already suffered much. He was in fact advancing towards the enemy with his weakest force extended.

Whatever Scheer's hopes might have been, his actual reception was as rough as before. The two rearmost divisions of the Grand Fleet sighted the leading German battleships at 7.10, at a range of about 10,000 yards to the south-west, and opened fire. Within five minutes most of the battleships of the British line had opened fire, Scheer's 'T' had been crossed, or rather he had volunteered to have it crossed, as comprehensively as before and by 7.15 the whole of the battle line was under fire at ranges varying from 11,000 to 14,000 yards. Beatty's battle cruisers, who were further from the enemy, also opened fire soon after 7.15 at ranges of between 15,000 and 20,000 yards.

This encounter was even more damaging for Scheer's ships than the earlier one. Jellicoe's battleships scored thirty hits, Evan-Thomas' five;

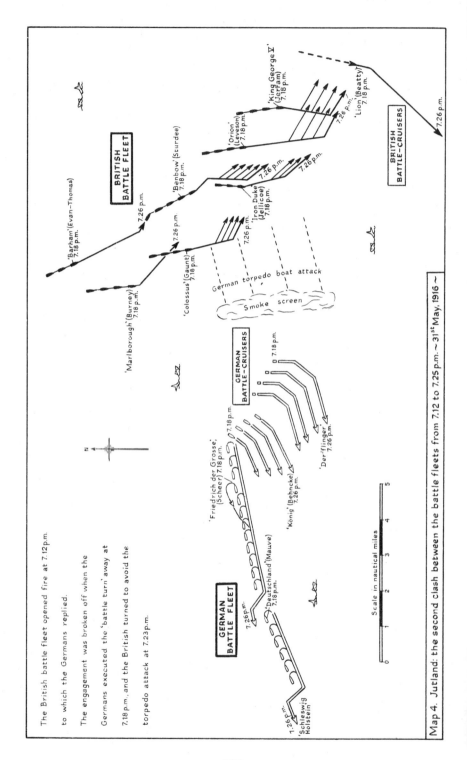

The British battle fleet opened fire at 7.12 p.m. to which the Germans replied.

The engagement was broken off when the Germans executed the 'battle turn' away at 7.18 p.m. and the British turned to avoid the torpedo attack at 7.23 p.m.

GERMAN BATTLE FLEET

'Schleswig Holstein' 7.26 p.m.

'Deutschland' (Mauve) 7.18 p.m.

'König' (Behncke) 7.26 p.m.

'Friedrich der Grosse' (Scheer) 7.18 p.m.

GERMAN BATTLE-CRUISERS

'Derfflinger' 7.26 p.m.

7.18 p.m.

German torpedo boat attack

Smoke screen

'Marlborough' (Burney) 7.18 p.m.

'Colossus' (Gaunt) 7.18 p.m.

'Barham' (Evan-Thomas) 7.18 p.m.

7.26 p.m.

BRITISH BATTLE FLEET

'Benbow' (Sturdee) 7.18 p.m.

'Iron Duke' (Jellicoe) 7.18 p.m.

7.26 p.m.

'Orion' (Leveson) 7.18 p.m.

'King George V' (Jerram) 7.18 p.m.

7.26 p.m.

'Lion' (Beatty) 7.18 p.m.

BRITISH BATTLE-CRUISERS

7.26 p.m.

N

Scale in nautical miles

0 1 2 3 4 5

Map 4. Jutland: the second clash between the battle fleets from 7.12 to 7.25 p.m. ~ 31st May, 1916 ~

198

of those, twenty-three fell upon Hipper's battle cruisers. In reply the German ships got two hits on *Colossus*. At 7.13 Scheer signalled to Hipper's ships: 'Battle cruisers, at the enemy. Give it everything.' By wireless, because the code book gave slightly different wordings, the message was 'Battle cruisers, turn towards the enemy and engage him closely. At him!'

Whatever the actual phrasing, the meaning was clear enough. Hipper's ships were to be launched upon a suicidal run towards the British Fleet. *Lützow* was out of action and the rest were badly battered, but they did their best, steaming at full speed in single line ahead. They got within 7,700 yards of the nearest British ship, *Colossus*, whose officers must have believed that their enemy was seeking to immolate himself upon their guns, when they made out Scheer's flag signal ordering them to attack the van. They altered to the south, and then west, and rejoined the main fleet. The 'death ride' mysteriously fizzled out. Hipper's battle cruisers had miraculously survived with no further damage.

At 7.15 Scheer ordered his destroyers to attack and lay a smoke-screen to cover the withdrawal of the battle fleet, which Scheer achieved by yet another turn together at 7.18. Although firing continued on the rearmost German ships as they retreated until about 7.40 p.m., Scheer had retrieved the situation for the second time. This time there would be no question of another tilt at the enemy.

Iron Duke herself had opened fire at 7.13 and fired four salvoes at an enemy battleship steaming away from her. Later, she trained turrets on an enemy battle cruiser but could not fire before she disappeared into the smoke. At 7.20 Jellicoe and his staff on *Iron Duke*'s bridge could see several German destroyers in the murk; clearly they were advancing to deliver a massed torpedo attack. Here, at last, was the new menace, the great threat of underwater attack, which had been studied by naval staffs ever since the Russo-Japanese War. Much debated in theory, here it actually was in real life, and Jellicoe countered with the moves he had laid down beforehand. At 7.22 he turned the battle line away two points to port, and three minutes later, when it had been calculated that the turn was not enough, another two points to port, so that the fleet steered south-east. He also ordered the 4th Light Cruiser Squadron to counter-attack.

Like many long-awaited bogeys, a massed destroyer torpedo attack proved to be much less dangerous than expected. Only two German flotillas, the 6th and 9th, made serious attacks, thirty-one firing torpedoes. Because of the light cruiser counter-attack, the destroyers launched their torpedoes at the comparatively long range of 7,000 yards and, because of the battle fleet's turn away, the torpedoes had run nearly 10,000 yards before they reached Jellicoe's battleships.

The surface tracks of the German torpedoes were much more visible than naval intelligence had led Jellicoe to believe. Eleven tracks were counted – one was sighted from *Oak*, travelling slowly 200 yards ahead of *Iron Duke*, and eventually sank about 2,000 yards on the port or disengaged side. At 7.24 *Iron Duke*'s six-inch secondary armament opened fire on the German destroyers abaft the starboard beam, range 10,000 yards. The main armament followed suit three minutes later with one salvo which the director gunner claimed sank a destroyer. Several other ships in the line had to avoid torpedoes. *Marlborough* evaded three, and *Colossus* one; *Revenge* had to swerve vigorously; *Hercules* and *Agincourt* had to sheer 60 degrees out of the line. But no ship suffered a torpedo hit.

Jellicoe's turn away, rather than towards, to comb the torpedo tracks, surprised and even shocked some officers in the fleet – the most shocked officers were those in the Battle Cruiser Fleet – and aroused one of the bitterest Jutland controversies after the war. But the action was wholly in keeping with Jellicoe's expressed intentions before the battle and his conduct of affairs during the battle. He had always made it clear that he would never pursue closely across the same water as a fleeing enemy. A turn away was the recognized practice in the fleet, agreed by all the squadron commanders with the exception of Sturdee. There was nothing surprising or exceptional about it. The performance of torpedoes in actual warfare was much feared but still unknown. Pre-war live practice with running torpedoes had not often been carried out because of the expense; it was still most unusual, even in war, because Scapa Flow had no facilities.

It could be argued that Jellicoe should have turned towards because his enemy was retiring, but Jellicoe did not know that his enemy was retiring. Once again, the reporting of enemy movements was poor. Four battleships towards the end of the line, *Valiant*, *Malaya*, *St Vincent* and *Revenge*, all saw Scheer turn away and none of them reported it. Even Goodenough, who had performed so nobly that day, saw the turn away at 7.30 and for some inexplicable reason did not report it.

Jellicoe was always conscious of the dangers of losing position by steering east or west. To steer north and south would be to draw down a steel blind between the High Seas Fleet and their home. To steer laterally would be like opening the shutters of that blind, for the enemy to slip through. It was already late in the day; night was coming on, when Jellicoe never had any intention of fighting. The König class battleships in the rear of the German line could make twenty-two knots, more than anybody else except the 5th Battle Squadron. It would have been a formidable task to pursue them and hope to overhaul them, to penetrate a smokescreen and possibly run against further destroyer attacks which Scheer might have launched had he become aware he was so closely pursued. A pursuit would certainly drive the German Fleet further to the west and give more time and space for a renewed action in the morning. But it was not impossible that Scheer might make another turn to the east and escape unmolested to the north or south of the Grand Fleet. Whether or not any of these arguments, for and against, passed through Jellicoe's mind at the time, he knew that he now held the master position between the German ships and their base.

At 7.30 Beatty was still pressing westwards in search of the enemy and at one time had the rear German ships in sight. At 7.40 he signalled that the enemy bore NW by W, distant ten to eleven miles. The sun was due to set that day at 8.19 and there would be a further forty minutes or so after that of deepening twilight during which gun action would still be feasible. The visibility then was about three or four miles in the dusk to the east, but much better, perhaps six or seven miles, towards the westering sun.

Beatty noticed that the nearest ships of the battle fleet, Jerram's squadron, were steering a much more southerly course than himself. At 7.47, when Beatty was some six miles ahead of the battle fleet he signalled to Jellicoe: 'Submit van of battleships [meaning Jerram] follow battle cruisers. We can then cut off whole of enemy's battle fleet.'

This signal probably caused more recrimination in later years than most other aspects of the battle of Jutland. Supporters of Beatty, who tended *ex officio* to be critics of Jellicoe, claimed that in effect it meant: 'If you follow me, sir, we can annihilate the enemy', but Jellicoe – cautious, stick-in-the-mud, opportunity-wasting, even cowardly, Jellicoe – refused to give Beatty the support he asked for and so let slip a chance of another Trafalgar.

When he sent the signal, Beatty had actually lost visual contact with the enemy. The nearest German ship was twelve miles and the nearest battleship thirteen miles away. But Beatty and his staff on *Lion*'s bridge were sure they knew where the enemy lay. Meanwhile Jellicoe had received another scouting signal from Goodenough, that the enemy had detached an unknown number of ships of type unknown which were steering north-west at 7.15, and he gave his own position. Beatty's signal arrived in Jellicoe's hands shortly before eight o'clock, when he ordered the fleet to steer west, speed seventeen knots (the most *Marlborough* could make). Jellicoe had hesitated to steer west earlier, but it seemed that the course which was inadvisible before was permissible now.

Jellicoe signalled by lamp to Jerram in *King George V* at the head of the line: 'Follow our battle cruisers.' No position was given. Jellicoe

201

had assumed that Jerram could see Beatty. In fact Jerram could not. He was unable to carry out the order, did not ask for clarification, and simply carried on steaming westward. So, ironically, Jerram's ships, which had been steaming too much to the south and to port of Beatty, were now, as a result of his signal, steaming too much to the north and to starboard of him. Beatty did not repeat his signal, and neither Jellicoe nor Jerram said any more.

By 8 p.m. the German Battle Fleet was steering south and crossing some twelve miles ahead of the British Battle Fleet. Beatty was some eight miles to the south-west and steering south-west; at that point he was in fact converging upon the head of the German line. At 8.09 Napier in the cruiser *Falmouth* sighted and reported ships bearing north-west; these were German cruisers of the 4th Scouting Group and there was an exchange of gunfire between the two cruiser forces for about ten minutes, after which the Germans turned away and vanished in the murk.

Beatty steered for the sound of the guns and at about 8.20 he opened fire to the north-west, range 10,000 yards, on Hipper's battle cruisers. In a short engagement, with some very good shooting in very poor light, Beatty's ships hit *Derfflinger* and *Seydlitz*. They might have done more but the six pre-Dreadnoughts of Admiral Mauve's 2nd Battle Squadron appeared, closing to a range of 8,000 yards and preventing Beatty from following Hipper, whose ships turned to the west and disappeared in the mist and falling darkness. A few minutes later Mauve's ships also turned away and vanished. Beatty's ships ceased fire at about 8.40 p.m. This, in fact, was the last time capital ships were engaged in the war.

There might have been another chance, but the next half hour was a chapter of missed opportunities. At 8.38 the cruiser *Comus* of the 4th Light Cruiser Squadron reported that she was firing at the enemy's battle fleet, bearing west. She, *Calliope* and *Constance* fired torpedoes at the German battle line, at 6,000 yards range. At 8.45 two more cruisers of the same squadron, *Caroline* and *Royalist*, sighted three German battleships bearing north-west, range 8,000 yards. Captain Ralph Crooke in *Caroline* reported his targets and began an attacking run. Jerram, who was only two miles astern of the cruisers, had also seen the ships in the mist but was sure they were Beatty's ships and signalled: 'Negative. Those ships are our battle cruisers.' But Crooke was convinced they were German and replied: 'Those are evidently enemy ships.' So Jerram allowed the attack to go on: 'If you are quite sure attack.' *Caroline* and *Royalist* both carried out torpedo attacks in which they each fired one torpedo, but both missed and the ships retired.

The next chance was missed by Commodore (F) Hawksley, commanding the Grand Fleet's destroyer flotillas in the light cruiser *Castor*. He and the 11th Destroyer Flotilla were just astern of *Caroline* when they saw and identified the German ships, but Hawksley did not attack, on the grounds that Jerram's ships still held their fire: 'He could not attack as it was not dark enough to make an attack unsupported by the fire of the fleet.' Enemy battleships might be able to hold off an unsupported destroyer attack with their secondary armament in reasonable visibility, but in the gathering darkness of that Jutland evening Hawksley stood a good chance of succeeding. For a moment, a golden chance to make himself a household name beckoned to Hawksley out of the mist, but he passed it by.

The third chance was missed by Jellicoe himself. At 8.28 he re-formed his battleships in single line and steered south-west to close the sound of Beatty's guns. *Comus'* report, *Caroline* and *Royalist's* action and, most important of all, a signal from Beatty at 8.59 accurately reporting the enemy's bearing, all gave Jellicoe information about the enemy's position. But, mistakenly, Jellicoe thought Beatty had been firing at ships to westward of him and not, as he had been doing, at ships to the northward and thus nearer Jellicoe himself. Furthermore, while Jerram had been doing his best to discourage Crooke, he had also given Jellicoe an erroneous report of Beatty's battle cruisers, when the ships he was reporting were actually German battleships, thus confusing the situation even further. As Jellicoe himself conceded, he should have closed the enemy battle fleet after *Comus'* report; he might have been able to give Scheer's battleships some parting knocks before nightfall. But the sequence of actions with *Comus* and *Caroline* and Beatty's battle cruisers all served to edge Scheer further away to the west and, incidentally, further from Jellicoe. As Jellicoe said, 'If it had only been about 6 p.m. instead of nearly dark, and clear instead of thick, we should have had a second Trafalgar.'

In Jellicoe's opinion, enemy destroyers in large numbers, and the impossibility of distinguishing friend from foe, made a night action a very risky gamble. Jellicoe knew that he was between the German Fleet and its base; he meant to steam south and then, possibly, up to the north again, until daylight. When darkness finally fell at about 9 p.m., Jellicoe disposed his battle fleet into night cruising formation, of three columns of divisions in line ahead, course south, speed seventeen knots. He stationed his destroyer flotillas astern of the battle fleet, to screen the rear and to give the destroyers the chance to attack enemy heavy ships with torpedoes should they attempt to approach the battle fleet. There was never any intention of fighting a night action; but there was every intention of another Glorious First of June in the morning.

In *Iron Duke*, biscuits and corned beef were broken out at the men's quarters. Cocoa was available from 9.30 onwards. The ship's company remained closed up at their action stations, with the guns' crews at their guns, but in a relaxed state, men being allowed to sleep in turn. Jellicoe himself retired to a bunk in a shelter beside the flag-bridge. It had been a very long day, and there would be another on the morrow. Jellicoe had been on his feet continuously since early that morning and it had been a day of enormous physical and mental strain: the anticipation of action, the anxieties of waiting for information, the pressure of decision, and, not least, the shock of heavy guns firing close at hand, would all have tested the endurance of a much younger man. With the coming of nightfall Jellicoe seemed to lapse into a more passive, much less alert state of mind; he had no plans for action of his own, and evidently believed that nobody else had. He left no instructions, and did not insist on enemy reports being transmitted at once to the flagship. Certainly, nobody disturbed him unnecessarily.

But it was not a quiet night. There were in fact seven night encounters, six of them short sharp and violent actions between destroyers or cruisers, beginning at 9.50 p.m. that night and ending at about 2.30 a.m., just after dawn, on the morning of 1 June. The British ships laboured under several disadvantages, some unavoidable, some self-inflicted, some connected with equipment, some the result of a state of mind.

The British ships had not been trained for fighting at night. When the sun came down, so too did a kind of curtain of caution over the whole fleet. Jellicoe's captains nearly all suffered from the same variety of mental night-blindness as he did himself. Even in daylight, the British ships preserved a peacetime sense of propriety: everybody always took their cue from Father in the flagship; nobody ventured to open fire, even on a clear and identified target, before Father; everybody assumed that Father, further up the line, must also have seen what they had just seen and therefore did not report it. Father always knew best.

The British ships had the further disadvantage that the recognition signal for that night had been betrayed by, of all ships, *Lion*, who flashed the correct code for challenge and response to *Princess Royal* on request. The letter groups were read by some German ship lurking beyond them unseen in the mist. It was always difficult enough to tell friend from foe at night; now, when a British ship challenged a stranger, she received the correct response, and naturally, hesitated before opening fire. The German ships had no such hesitations and, with their better searchlights, closely linked to the gun directors, they were able to open an accurate fire at once.

All these inhibitions, constraints and disadvantages on the British side were compounded by the failure of the Admiralty to pass vital signals about the High Seas Fleet's intentions. Thus everything seemed to conspire to let Scheer pass. Throughout the night his ships were constantly nudging to the eastward, trying to find a route through or round the line of Grand Fleet ships blocking the way; each time they sighted the Grand Fleet, without being sighted themselves, they recoiled to the west, before edging over to the east again. For much of the night Scheer was steering on a converging course, but at slower speed; thus his ships eventually fell astern of Jellicoe's and crossed astern of them. It was a very close thing. If Jellicoe had been a knot or two slower, if Scheer had been a knot or two faster. . . . If one or two vital signals had been passed in time. . . .

At 9.50 p.m. the British 4th Destroyer Flotilla was steaming north to take up its screen position at the rear of the battle fleet when it was sighted by the German 7th Flotilla who fired four torpedoes, but scored no hits, and swung away to the southward. Of the British destroyers only *Garland* sighted the enemy, and, what is more, her captain, Lieutenant-Commander Goff, made a report – one of the very few that night.

At about the same time, some distance to the south-west, the German cruisers *Frankfurt* and *Pillau* sighted the 11th Destroyer Flotilla, led by Hawksley in *Castor*, who were steaming north-eastwards to take up their screening position. The Germans fired torpedoes at close range, of about 1,200 yards, and then they too bore away without opening fire or using searchlights, so as not to draw their enemy after them towards their battle fleet. Unaware of the attack, *Castor* and her destroyers turned south and at 10.15 sighted three ships on the starboard bow, who gave the correct British recognition signal although they were actually part of the German 4th Scouting Group. *Castor* closed to 2,000 yards before the two leading German ships, *Hamburg* and *Elbing*, switched on searchlights and opened a fierce fire.

Castor replied with 6-inch and 4-inch gunfire and one torpedo. She was not well supported by the rest of the flotilla: only two destroyers fired torpedoes, and the others did nothing, either because they could see nothing, or because they believed that what they could see were friendly ships. Many of the flotilla captains were convinced that *Castor* was firing on her own side.

Hawksley had missed another tremendous chance to make his name. His enemies were half a mile off, showing their searchlights, which were perfect aiming points, but he thought it was more important to keep station with the battle fleet in case there was an engagement in the morning. So he fired no more torpedoes and neither did any of his flotilla. *Castor* was badly damaged and suffered a number of casualties, but Hawksley did get off an enemy report, via *Kempenfelt* because *Castor*'s own wireless aerials had been destroyed.

By the time a signal from Jellicoe was received asking Hawksley if he was engaging enemy destroyers, he replied simply 'No', and did not elaborate.

At 10.30 Goodenough's *Southampton*, who had seen more action that day that any other ship on either side, was in action again. Goodenough's squadron sighted the German 4th Scouting Group, as it was reforming and sorting itself out after the action with *Castor*. The Germans also sighted Goodenough's ships, on a parallel course, and both sides approached cautiously while trying to decide whether they were friend or foe. Goodenough and Commodore von Reutter in *Stettin* must have reached the same conclusion at the same time. Just as Goodenough opened his mouth to give the order to fire, the Germans switched on their searchlights and poured a very heavy fire on *Southampton* and *Dublin* at the extremely close range of less than 800 yards. *Southampton* and *Dublin* were both damaged and suffered casualties, while the German light cruiser *Frauenlob* was sunk by a torpedo. *Southampton*'s W/T aerials were shot away and news of this encounter was not signalled to Jellicoe (by *Nottingham*) until 11.30.

By that time, some of the leading ships in Scheer's line were very close to the Grand Fleet and butting up against it as they tried to find a way through. But the British ships either thought they were friendly, or if they did suspect them of being enemy, showed an astonishing reluctance to open fire. *Thunderer* saw *Moltke* at 10.30 but did not open fire because Captain Fergusson thought it was inadvisable to show up the battle fleet unless an obvious attack was intended; he took this decision himself without reporting to Jellicoe.

Agincourt also saw a large ship – actually the badly damaged *Seydlitz*, trying to creep home unobserved – but forbore to challenge her so as not to give the Division's position away. *Marlborough* and *Revenge* also saw her, did not fire, and did not report. *Marlborough* had her guns trained on *Seydlitz* at one time, range 4,000 yards, but the captain thought she was a British ship. The cruiser *Fearless*, leading the 1st Destroyer Flotilla, saw and identified *Seydlitz* as an enemy but, with that astounding deference for Father which characterized so many British captains, Roper thought that as the ships ahead had not fired and *Seydlitz* must certainly have been seen, it was advisable to take no action, as her course was leading her towards following destroyers. So these two damaged German battle cruisers ghosted through the lines of British ships – at one time *Seydlitz* was within a mere 1,600 yards of the nearest ship of Evan-Thomas's squadron and got clear away. At no time did any of these battleship captains tell Jellicoe what they had seen.

The fourth encounter, beginning at about 11.30 p.m., involved the High Seas Fleet itself. The 4th Flotilla, after its earlier brush, was steaming south when the shadowy shapes of ships were seen off to starboard, but on a converging course. *Tipperary*, the flotilla leader, challenged, and was answered by a furious storm of fire at a range of less than 1,000 yards. *Tipperary* had in fact challenged the German 1st Battle Squadron of Dreadnoughts. She and the next four destroyers fired their torpedoes but some of the captains of the rearmost destroyers, with that reluctance to get into action which bedevilled so many British ships that night, hung back and did not fire because they were not sure of friend from foe.

One of the rear German ships was momentarily lit up by searchlight. She was definitely identified as a battleship of the Helgoland class by Lieutenant-Commander Thomson in the destroyer *Petard*, of the 13th Flotilla away to eastward, and also by Captain Farie leading the 13th Flotilla in the cruiser *Champion*. But neither Thomas nor Farie passed this information to Jellicoe.

The confused and violent action went on for over half an hour. *Tipperary* and three more of her flotilla were sunk. Another four were badly damaged. The destroyer *Spitfire* collided with the battleship *Nassau*, port bow to port bow; though badly damaged, she eventually reached harbour. The German light cruiser *Rostock* was disabled by a torpedo, and *Elbing* was almost cut in two by the battleship *Posen*. Both were abandoned and scuttled. Torpedo hits were scored on four German battleships, so although the 4th Flotilla had been so badly knocked about that it had ceased to exist as a fighting unit, it had inflicted a considerable amount of torpedo damage on the German battleships and delayed them by about half an hour.

This half-hour's delay, and the position of the action, had they been reported to Jellicoe, might have turned the course of the battle. They would not have led to an action then, but they would have warned Jellicoe of the presence of the enemy's battle fleet and might have led to a decisive engagement at daylight. But in the event the failures to report the enemy continued, and eventually began to go from the regrettable to the incredible.

At 11.40 what appeared to be destroyer attacks on big ships to the west and then to the north were seen from *Malaya*. The flash of a detonating torpedo revealed one ship of the Westfalen class – it actually was *Westfalen*. All guns were trained and the gunnery officer asked permission to open fire; it was refused because Captain A.D.E.H. Boyle knew that Evan-Thomas was only two ships ahead, and believed he must have seen everything that *Malaya* had seen. If Evan-Thomas did not give the order to open fire, then fire would not be opened. Nor did Boyle report anything to anybody.

At 11.35 *Valiant* sighted two German 'cruisers' (in fact they were battleships) during *Castor*'s action. She passed the report by light to

Malaya who passed it to Evan-Thomas in *Barham*; Evan-Thomas thought the ships ahead of him must have seen the German ships and took no action, either to open fire or to report to Jellicoe. So these dear, devoted blockheads steamed steadfastly onwards through the night. They would have died for Jellicoe. But they would not send him a signal.

By about 12.15 a.m. on 1 June the leading ships of the High Seas Fleet were about three miles astern of the Grand Fleet, but slowly dropping astern and crossing to the eastward. But some thirteen British destroyers of the 9th, 10th and 13th Flotillas, led by *Lydiard*, were still between the High Seas Fleet and Horns Reef and in a position to attack. *Lydiard* sighted a line of large ships but, although they opened fire, took them to be friendly. Lieutenant-Commander Thomson, in *Petard*, was sure they were battleships and that they were German, but he had already fired all his torpedoes. *Petard* passed only 200 yards ahead of a German ship 'of the Wittelsbach class' which switched on searchlights and opened a heavy fire; *Petard* was damaged and her next astern, *Turbulent*, was sunk. All this activity was sighted from the bridge of *Marlborough*, about four miles to the north, where they concluded that they were watching German destroyers attacking the 5th Battle Squadron. They made no report.

By 1.45, when dawn was just beginning to break, the High Seas Fleet was less than thirty miles from Horns Reef and almost safe – almost, but not quite. In their path lay more destroyers, the 12th Flotilla under Captain A.J.B. Stirling in *Faulknor*, who made the only sighting report to Jellicoe by any destroyer that night: 'Urgent. Priority. Enemy's battleships in sight. My position 10 miles astern of the 1st Battle Squadron.' Stirling made two more signals during the course of his attack, but none of them reached Jellicoe.

Sighting large ships on his starboard bow, steering south-easterly, Stirling led his flotilla ahead of the enemy on their port bow. At about 2 a.m. *Faulknor* turned inwards, with the flotilla following in single line ahead. Six of the sixteen destroyers fired their torpedoes. One or possibly two hit the battleship *Pommern*, very probably in a magazine; she blew up 'literally to atoms' and sank with all hands. Stirling's ships then laid a smokescreen and escaped.

Captain Farie in the light cruiser *Champion*, leading the 13th Flotilla, heard the gunfire of Stirling's action and steered towards it at full speed. Only *Moresby* and *Obdurate* could keep up with her, with two more destroyers who joined from the 12th Flotilla. Four large ships were sighted to the west at about 2.30; Farie took no action and sent no signal, but Lieutenant-Commander Alison, in *Moresby*, recognized the ships as German Deutschland-class battleships and fired torpedoes, one of which sank a German destroyer.

208

There was one final brush with the enemy, at about 3.30, when it was broad daylight, though misty. *Champion* and four destroyers engaged four German destroyers: one German destroyer was hit by a torpedo, but the others disappeared in the mist. They were not followed, and needless to say not reported. So, effectively, ended the battle of Jutland.

Throughout the hours of darkness the flashes and periodical lightening of the skies to the north were seen from *Iron Duke*'s bridge, with the muttering and rumbling of the guns. The flashes started at about 11 p.m. on the starboard quarter and slowly moved across the rear of the battle line to the port quarter where they eventually died away. The men on *Iron Duke*'s bridge watched with wondering eyes, like astrologers of ancient times trying to read the heavens, pondering on what these portents might mean. It was decided that it was all caused by the rearmost destroyer flotillas fighting off attempts by the German destroyer flotillas to attack the battle fleet. Of all the scores of British ships which had sighted the enemy that night, including several who went into action, very few reported what they had seen and done. Only one signal, from Captain Stirling in *Faulknor*, mentioned the word 'battleships' and that signal was not received in *Iron Duke*.

Jellicoe himself must bear the responsibility for this almost unbelievable reticence among his captains. After all, training of his fleet was his affair and it was up to him to stress the importance of shadowing and reporting. But Jellicoe was as poorly served by the Admiralty, over whom he had no control. At 9.58 the Admiralty sent Jellicoe a signal which he received at 10.45 which gave a palpably wrong position for the German Battle Fleet. It put the rear German ships some eight miles south-west of the Grand Fleet, when Jellicoe knew they must still be well to the north-west of him. This, coupled with the midday signal which had placed the High Seas Fleet still in the Jade when they had been at sea for hours, made Jellicoe mistrust the value of the Admiralty's information.

At 11.15 Jellicoe had another Admiralty signal which read: 'German Battle Fleet ordered home at 9.14 p.m. Battle-cruisers in rear. Course SSE ¾ E. Speed 16 knots.' This signal was actually an amalgam of three signals, one of which had contained the vital information that airship reconnaissance at Horns Reef was urgently requested for the morning. Had the Admiralty sent this signal intact, there would be no room for doubt about the High Seas Fleet's destination. Of eight signals received by the Operations Room between 11 p.m. and 1 a.m., only one, concerning German submarines being hurried from German ports to attack, was passed to Jellicoe. Others, and especially ones ordering all German flotillas to assemble off Horn Reef by 2 a.m., were not passed on. So Jellicoe continued to steer south, believing the High Seas Fleet were making for the Ems Channel.

Dawn was breaking by 2 a.m., and by 3.10 when the sun came up Scheer was safely off Horns Reef. Jellicoe, still believing his enemy was to the westward, assembled his light forces round the battle fleet. By 2.38 a.m. the Grand Fleet was steaming north, ready for the battle Jellicoe expected to begin at any moment.

But it was too late. An Admiralty signal of 3.29, which was handed to Jellicoe just after 4 a.m., placed Scheer at 2.30 about thirty miles north east of *Iron Duke*, and only sixteen miles off the Horns Reef lightship. It was not a promising morning for fleet action: the sea was calm and milky, but there were hints of mist again and the visibility was generally hazy. But now Jellicoe knew that in any case his enemy had escaped. As late as 4.30 Beatty was signalling to his battle cruisers, 'Damage yesterday was heavy on both sides, we hope today to cut off and annihilate the whole German Fleet.' It was much too late. At 4.40 Jellicoe signalled Beatty: 'Enemy fleet has returned to harbour.'

Chapter 13

At first it was impossible to believe that the battle really was over. Jellicoe was certain he had placed the Grand Fleet between the High Seas Fleet and its base. But the sea to the west, which should have been full of German ships waiting for the *coup de grâce*, was empty. Where were they all? It was simply incredible that a whole fleet could so have spirited itself away in the night.

At about 3.20 a.m. there was the unmistakable rumble of gunfire to the south-west, and Jellicoe turned his ships hopefully towards it. Maybe the enemy had managed to steam further south than he had expected. But it proved only to be the battle cruiser *Indomitable* firing at a scouting Zeppelin, which sheered away to the eastward unscathed. Jellicoe brought his ships back to north. By 3.50 he could see the Zeppelin himself from *Iron Duke*'s bridge; other ships opened fire on it but it was much too high. It continued to shadow the fleet and was sighted at intervals later in the day. Just before four o'clock Jellicoe signalled by flags to the fleet, 'Cease fire.'

It was a misty morning with a calm sea; the atmosphere in the fleet, too, was calm and tranquil, broken by short-lived alarms for reports of mines and occasionally of submarines. For most of the men in the fleet, who had had very little or no sleep, the events of the night before had already acquired a dream-like quality. It was difficult to reconcile the violence and turmoil of the previous day with the peacefulness of this morning.

Some ships had badly damaged turrets and upperworks. There were many bodies, sewn in canvas, laid out in neat rows in the passageways and the makeshift sickbays. Goodenough told his ships '. . . they must throw their dead overboard at once. I hadn't a dead body on board by midnight and this feeling of being clear of it all by daylight was very distinct among the men.' From *Iron Duke*'s bridge, although their ship was undamaged, they could see evidence of the previous day's violence. They looked down on a considerable amount of wreckage, bodies of dead German sailors floating in the water and the shattered hull of the destroyer *Ardent*.

At 5.15 Beatty's battle cruisers and cruisers were sighted on the port quarter, that is, to the south-west, rejoining the Grand Fleet. At first he

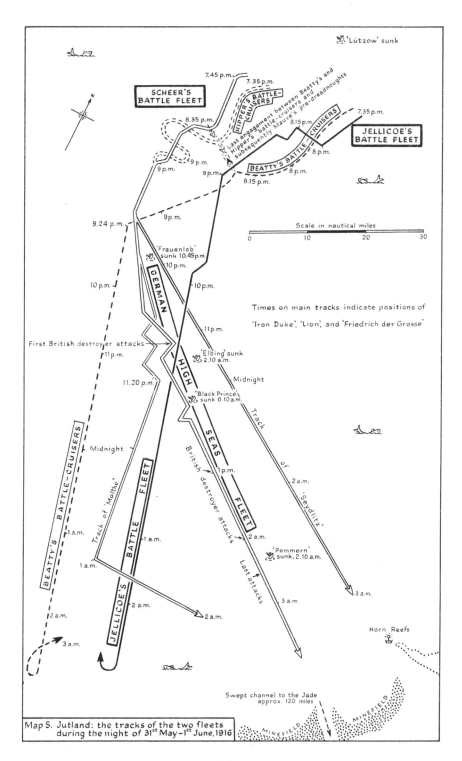

'Lützow' sunk

7.45 p.m.   7.35 p.m.   7.35 p.m.

SCHEER'S
BATTLE FLEET

HIPPER'S BATTLE-CRUISERS

Last engagement between Beatty's and Hipper's battle-cruisers and subsequently Mauve's pre-dreadnoughts

8.35 p.m.   8.15 p.m.   BEATTY'S BATTLE-CRUISERS   7.35 p.m.

JELLICOE'S
BATTLE FLEET

9 p.m.   9 p.m.   8 p.m.   8 p.m.

8 p.m.

BEATTY'S BATTLE-CRUISERS

9 p.m.   9 p.m.

8.15 p.m.

9.24 p.m.   9 p.m.

Scale in nautical miles
0   10   20   30

'Frauenlob' sunk 10.45 p.m.
10 p.m.

10 p.m.   10 p.m.

GERMAN

Times on main tracks indicate positions of 'Iron Duke', 'Lion', and 'Friedrich der Grosse'

11 p.m.

First British destroyer attacks
11 p.m.

'Elbing' sunk 2.10 a.m.

Midnight

HIGH

11.20 p.m.

'Black Prince' sunk 0.10 a.m.

Track of 'Seydlitz'

SEAS

Midnight

1 p.m.   2 a.m.

BEATTY'S BATTLE-CRUISERS

Track of 'Moltke'

British destroyer attacks

FLEET

JELLICOE'S BATTLE FLEET

1 a.m.   1 a.m.   2 a.m.

'Pommern' sunk, 2.10 a.m.

1 a.m.

Last attacks

3 a.m.

2 a.m.   2 a.m.   2 a.m.   3 a.m.

Horn Reefs

3 a.m.

Swept channel to the Jade approx. 120 miles

MINEFIELD   MINEFIELD

Map 5. Jutland: the tracks of the two fleets during the night of 31st May–1st June, 1916

212

and Jellicoe seemed at cross purposes. 'Where are you going?' Jellicoe asked him at 5.20. 'I have closed you in accordance with your orders,' Beatty replied. He asked permission, which was granted, to search for an enemy cruiser reported by *Dublin* nearly an hour earlier. Meanwhile, Jellicoe's ships made a cast south and east to look for *Lützow*, which was believed to be badly damaged, before turning north again. Nobody had reported the loss of *Indefatigable* and *Queen Mary* from Beatty's squadron. Nobody in *Iron Duke* seemed to notice their absence, although at 5.55 Jellicoe asked 'What do you know of *Indomitable*'s and *Inflexible*'s movements?' Beatty replied: 'They are with me.'

Slowly, Jellicoe and his staff were able to piece together a picture of what had happened and what state the ships were in. The cruiser *Warrior* was under tow by the seaplane carrier *Engadine* but was sinking. Later, when the weather deteriorated, her crew were taken off and she was abandoned. The destroyer *Acasta* was under tow by *Nonsuch*, and *Onslow* by *Defender*. *Warspite* was making for harbour, as was the cruiser *Chester*. *Sparrowhawk* was under tow by *Marksman*, but after some time the towing hawser parted and *Sparrowhawk* sank. *Marlborough* still could make no more than seventeen knots. *Malaya* had several holes below the waterline. *Barham* had two compartments flooded but her speed and armament were not impaired. The exact state of affairs was not known for a long time. As late as 8 p.m. that evening Jellicoe was asking Commodore (F): 'Have you heard anything of *Nestor*, *Onslow*, *Nomad* or *Turbulent*?' The reply was: 'No, nothing heard.'

The most astonishing news came shortly after 10 a.m., when Beatty signalled the approximate positions of the wrecks of *Queen Mary*, *Invincible* and *Indefatigable*. This crossed a signal from Jellicoe asking Beatty if all his cruisers and destroyers were accounted for, and also '. . . where are *New Zealand* and *Indefatigable*?' Shortly after eleven o'clock Jellicoe asked: 'When did *Queen Mary* and *Indefatigable* go?' To his amazement the reply was: '*Indefatigable* sank 4 p.m., *Queen Mary* 4.30 p.m.' This reply was not actually made until 12.27 and was the first Jellicoe knew of the loss of these ships nearly twenty hours before. Jellicoe knew that the German ships had had a hammering, although it was difficult to determine just how badly they were damaged. Now he and his staff began to appreciate for the first time that the Grand Fleet had also suffered heavy losses and casualties.

In the event of a fleet action Jellicoe had always been promised the services of the light cruisers and destroyers at Harwich commanded by Commodore Tyrwhitt. Tyrwhitt had been straining at the leash, and in fact put to sea on his own initiative on the afternoon of 31 May, but was recalled by the Admiralty to guard against a possible raid by

German forces on the south coast. Tyrwhitt was at last allowed to sail in the early hours of 1 June, when it was too late for him to take part in the battle. His presence and his ships would have been invaluable the night before; as it was, Jellicoe signalled that his force was not required except for destroyers to screen the returning *Marlborough*.

Jellicoe meanwhile was searching for information about his own ships. 'Do you know anything of *Duke of Edinburgh* and *Black Prince*?' he asked Rear-Admiral Heath, commanding the 2nd Cruiser Squadron. '*Duke of Edinburgh* is with me,' was the reply. 'I know nothing of *Black Prince*.' *Black Prince*, under fire from a whole line of German Dreadnoughts, had in fact blown up and sunk with all hands during the night.

Slowly, like the pieces of a great mosaic coming together, an impression of the battle began to emerge. Beatty signalled more details of the losses of his battle cruisers, the names of the destroyers still unaccounted for, and estimates of damage to *Lützow*. Evan-Thomas reported that his ships had scored a '. . . fair number of hits'.

Jellicoe had still not reported anything about the battle to the Admiralty. At 2.28 that afternoon he did signal that he had ordered *Marlborough* to report her damage direct to the Admiralty '. . . with a view to her being ordered to dock at Tyne so as to keep Rosyth for battle cruisers and *Warspite*. Am taking *Barham* and *Malaya* to Scapa with a view to repairing at Invergordon later.' Jellicoe had said nothing earlier and he never seems to have realized the effect of his unprefaced remarks about 'docks' and 'damage' and 'repairing'. The Admiralty had naturally intercepted a great number of signals and had some notion of the scale of the battle, but this signal of Jellicoe's must have added to the uncertainty and speculation ashore. Unknown to him, Jellicoe had won the battle of Jutland, but he had already begun to lose the aftermath.

The ships' companies were to have stayed at action stations all day, but at 2.40 the signal was passed to stand down. At that time the ships were still passing through the melancholy remains of the battle: many bodies, '. . . apparently German, two of which had on red lifebuoys with letters which began with S.M.', Pakenham signalled to Beatty. *Galatea* sighted what she identified as the bow of *Invincible*, and *Princess Royal* passed through '. . . a lot of oil and three hammocks, a body of a German officer and a German lifebuoy'.

The Grand Fleet had its own obsequies to observe. The battle cruisers held a burial service at 5.30. At 7 p.m. the bodies of those who had been most badly mutilated in action in *Barham* and *Malaya* were committed to the deep. All ships half-masted their colours while the flag hoist 'Silence and attention' was flown in *Iron Duke*.

At 9.40 that night a signal was received from the Admiralty asking for details; it was the first harbinger of all the wranglings and doubts and accusations which were to come. 'Enemy claims to have destroyed *Warspite*, *Queen Mary* and *Indefatigable*, two armoured cruisers with four funnels, two small cruisers and 10 destroyers. False reports will shortly be promulgated requiring prompt contradiction. Report losses ascertained and vessels not accounted for.'

By the morning of 2 June, when the Grand Fleet was nearing Scapa Flow, the battle of Jutland was over, but the battle of the dispatches had just begun. Reuter's in London reported an official German Admiralty communiqué giving details of a considerable German victory in the North Sea. Admiral Brownrigg, the Censor, held back publication of the report in the United Kingdom for the time being.

At 10.35 Jellicoe sent the Admiralty his first full statement:

VAC BCF reports *Queen Mary*, *Indefatigable* blown up by Enemy shell exploding in magazine. *Invincible* blown up, probably same cause but might be due to mine or submarine. She was blown in half. *Defence* similarly blown up. *Black Prince* unaccounted for and feared sunk. *Warrior* totally disabled and abandoned after being towed by *Engadine*. Believed to be still afloat. 2nd CS searching for her. *Tipperary* and destroyers *Turbulent*, *Fortune*, *Sparrowhawk* and/or *Ardent* lost, and five or six 4th Destroyer Flotilla are missing. *Broke* severely damaged making for Scapa Flow. Two light cruisers looking for her. Captain D12 reports by signal that his flotilla sank a battleship Kaiser class in night attack. VAC Battle Cruiser Force reports one battle cruiser thought to have been sunk, one severely damaged. Two light cruisers known to have been disabled. Enemy's destroyers were engaged but it is not known yet how many were sunk. Losses of our battle cruisers occurred during battle cruiser action. Visibility was very low and consequently battle fleet had great difficulty in keeping touch with Enemy's battle fleet which avoided action, but during the short time in action we apparently inflicted severe damage on some Enemy battleships. *Marlborough* only battleship injured in battle fleet action, injury due to mine or torpedo. *Warspite*, *Barham* and *Malaya* injured before our battle fleet came into action at 6.15 p.m.

With that grim catalogue, which certainly did seem to confirm German claims, the Admiralty had to be satisfied for the moment. Meanwhile Jellicoe's ships reached Scapa and entered harbour, in worsening weather, at about noon on 2 June. *Iron Duke* herself was secured to her buoy at 12.15 p.m. Jellicoe at once signalled to all ships to have steam for fifteen knots and at four hour's notice; senior officers were to report if any ship needed longer notice for steam. In other words, a battle had been fought, but the fleet had to look to the morrow. Hospital ships anchored, as ordered, near the battleships. All ships began fuelling and coaling, and preparing to embark ammunition. It was, in fact, business as usual, and by 9.45 that evening Jellicoe was able to signal the Admiralty: 'Battle fleet at four hours' notice and ready for action.' The Grand Fleet could have fought another battle of Jutland at once, whereas the High Seas Fleet had neither the intention nor the capability to put to sea for some time afterwards.

The Germans may have lost the engagement at sea, but they certainly won the propaganda battle ashore. The first of their ships returned to the Jade estuary on the morning of 1 June, feeling and saying that they had done extremely well. During the day the Germans broadcast worldwide the text of their version of the naval battle off the Skagerrak, and even that name had been chosen to leave readers in no doubt how far north and how far away from German ports the successful action had taken place. The German statement ran:

> During an enterprise directed northward, our High Seas Fleet encountered on 31 May the main part of the English fighting fleet, which was considerably superior to our own forces. During the afternoon a series of heavy engagements developed between the Skagerrak and the Horns Reef which were successful for us and which continued throughout the night.
>
> In these engagements, so far as has been learnt at present, the large British battleship *Warspite* and the battle cruisers *Queen Mary* and *Indefatigable* were destroyed, as were two armoured cruisers apparently of the Achilles type, one light cruiser, the new destroyer leaders *Turbulent*, *Nestor* and *Acasta*, a large number of destroyers and one submarine.
>
> Through observations beyond challenge it is known that a large number of English battleships suffered damage from our ships' artillery and from the attacks of our torpedo boat flotillas during the day and night engagements. Among others the large battleship *Marlborough* was struck by a torpedo as has been confirmed by prisoners. Several of our ships rescued portions of the crews of sunken English ships among them being the only two survivors of the *Indefatigable*. On our side the light cruiser *Wiesbaden* was sunk by hostile artillery fire during the day engagements, and the *Pommern* during the night by a torpedo. The fate of the *Frauenlob*, which is missing, and some torpedo boats which have not yet returned, is unknown. The High Seas Fleet returned to our ports during the day.

It was a cleverly constructed statement. It was not untrue. But it was less than the truth. Understandably, it did not mention the loss of *Lützow*, nor the light cruisers *Elbing* and *Rostock*, nor the extensive damage done to several other battleships and battle cruisers. It gave a great list of British ships sunk which, as the fleets returned to their bases, could be seen to be nearly true within the limits of war reporting at the time. The statement's wording suggested that German ships had inflicted a short, sharp but serious reverse on the Grand Fleet some distance away from Germany, and had then returned to their bases the same day, with a job well done. They had seen their enemy off and come safe home, with remarkably few losses of their own.

Brownrigg held the statement up as long as possible, but by midday on 2 June foreign radios had broadcast the message and some six thousand officers and men of Jellicoe's ships would soon be getting in touch with their families. So the German statement was released at about the time the Grand Fleet arrived at Scapa. As a result, the fleet had a reception ashore which puzzled, baffled and then angered them.

They had won a victory. Clearly it was not a complete victory. But they had steamed across a sea emptied of the enemy; the enemy had gone, so it must have been a victory. However, there were doubts. From signals, from rumour, from what they could see of damage to themselves and sister ships, obviously it had not been the complete, the crushing, the unanswerable, the apocalyptic victory, which the country had always expected. Nevertheless it had been a victory and the ships' companies were therefore amazed by the attitude of people ashore. It was not so bad for the Grand Fleet, which was comparatively unscathed and in any case returned to Scapa, far from crowds and busy seaports. But for the ships which went to Rosyth, or the Humber and the East Coast ports, the reception was gloomy and commiserating. The battered *Lion* was booed and jeered. This was not the greeting given to returning victors, but the sympathy and condolences extended to badly beaten losers; to their astonishment, the ships' companies returning found that everybody thought they had lost.

To counteract what was clearly becoming a dangerous and damaging tide of opinion, the Admiralty issued a communiqué. It was largely composed by Balfour, the First Lord, who was never a man to concern himself unduly with what the populace thought or believed, nor with the niceties of press relations, assisted by Jackson, Wilson and Oliver. None of these three admirals believed in press relations. Wilson, in fact, actually abhorred personal or any other kind of publicity. The Admiralty statement read:

On the afternoon of May 31st a naval engagement took place off the coast of Jutland. The British ships on which the brunt of the fighting

217

fell were the Battle Cruiser Fleet, and some cruisers and light cruisers supported by four fast battleships. Among these the losses were heavy. The German Battle Fleet, aided by low visibility, avoided prolonged action with our main forces, and soon after these appeared on the scene the enemy returned to port, though not before receiving severe damage from our battleships. The battle cruisers *Queen Mary*, *Indefatigable*, *Invincible* and the cruisers *Defence* and *Black Prince* were sunk. The *Warrior* was disabled and after being towed for some time had to be abandoned by her crew. It is also known that the destroyers *Tipperary*, *Turbulent*, *Fortune*, *Sparrowhawk* and *Ardent* were lost and six others not yet accounted for. No British battleships or light cruisers were sunk. The enemy's losses were serious. At least one battle cruiser was destroyed, one battleship reported sunk by our destroyers at night, two light cruisers were disabled and probably sunk. The exact number of enemy destroyers disposed of during the action cannot be ascertained with any certainty but it must have been large.

The communiqué was based on Jellicoe's first report of 10.30 on 2 June and such other information as was available to the Admiralty. There were, of course, no press correspondents on board *Iron Duke*; Jellicoe would not have permitted it. In the circumstances, considering the personalities of the men who composed it and the information available to them at the time, the communiqué was a very worthy, honest, fairly accurate (within the limits of war reporting) and even praiseworthy account of the battle.

But, of course, the ordinary reader took it as confirmation of the German version. Everyone assumed that the Admiralty would try to gloss over losses; this must be the very *best* view of what had happened, from the British point of view. It can be fairly said that much of the 'Jutland controversy' stemmed from this first Admiralty statement. No matter what information was given later, no matter how persuasively and correctly it was argued and proved that Jutland was a victory, the opinion of the man in the street never quite recovered from that first impression of defeat. That was what stuck in the popular mind.

Jellicoe was understandably angry over the Admiralty account and he was well aware of feelings running in his own ships. On 3 June he asked the Admiralty to amend the report, which, he said, quite rightly, '. . . magnifies ours and minimises the Enemy's casualties, and gives somewhat false impression of action generally'. Having made a serious error in their first announcement, the Admiralty tried hard to repair it. They asked Churchill to write an appreciation of the battle. But this made the press even more suspicious and hostile and the end result was worse than before.

The date of 3 June was the King's birthday and on arrival at Scapa Jellicoe had sent His Majesty a message of good wishes from the fleet. It is not impossible that Jellicoe hoped the King would respond with something to restore the fleet's morale; if so, he was not disappointed. The King rose to the occasion magnificently; his message of thanks was a masterpiece of tact and consolation. The King could not have known much more about the battle than any member of the public could have read in the official statements, but he put his finger on the main issues in a way that was immeasurably consoling. 'Though the retirement of the enemy immediately after the opening of the general engagement robbed us of the opportunity of gaining a decisive victory,' his message concluded, 'the events of last Wednesday amply justify my confidence in the valour and efficiency of the fleets under your command.' The King himself was a naval officer, and a very able one, and his praise was worth having. 'Immediately a new feeling of elation swept through the fleet,' wrote Admiral Bacon. 'Their King knew. God save the King.'

But there were very few other reasons for elation. Jellicoe was so disappointed that he wrote to Balfour saying that if he, Balfour, thought his handling of the battle had been incorrect he hoped he would not hesitate to order an inquiry. That same day, 4 June, the *Weekly Dispatch* printed an article entitled 'The lesson of it all', a fine piece of sustained polemic which ended with the clarion call: 'Give the Fleet over to the younger men' (meaning Beatty, or Madden).

Jellicoe was so stung by this he sent a telegram to the Admiralty on 6 June asking for immediate steps to be taken to prevent the publication of such statements, as they were '. . . most hurtful to discipline and morale and discouraging to the officers and men of the fleet'. Jellicoe also complained, justifiably, that some newspapers had jeopardized his fleet's security by publishing the time the fleet sailed and its bases. He also wrote to Jackson on the same lines: 'I do not wish to be captious but cannot something be done to censor the press articles? I have wired about some today and really it is too much altogether.' Jellicoe also thought it 'trying' that Churchill should be editing the Press Bureau's summary of the action (at the Admiralty's request) before his own report had even reached the Admiralty.

On Sunday 4 June Jellicoe and his staff went ashore to attend the funerals of men buried at Scapa. The weather had been foul ever since they returned and Sunday was another miserable day of high wind and sheeting rain; the wind had hardly slackened from gale force since their arrival, as though even the weather was harping on the same theme of gloom and despondency. On Monday the fifth, the same day that the Kaiser was congratulating Scheer on board his flagship at Wilhelms-haven, amid scenes of the wildest German jubilation, with waving flags, cheering crowds and awards of medals all round ('The Spell of

219

Trafalgar has been broken' said the Kaiser), there came another disaster for Jellicoe, which suggested that the fates themselves were conspiring against him.

Early in 1916 Field-Marshal Lord Kitchener had decided to visit Russia to discuss the supply of munitions and other matters personally with the Russian government. The cabinet approved, and the Admiralty informed Jellicoe on 26 May, asking him to detail a cruiser to take the field-marshal to Archangel. Jellicoe had nominated *Hampshire* on the twenty-seventh, but the ship was engaged in the battle of Jutland and did not return to Scapa with the rest of the fleet until 2 June. Kitchener himself arrived at Thurso on the morning of 5 June and came across to Scapa in the destroyer *Oak*. The weather was still atrocious, blowing a three-quarter gale from the north, with heavy rain squalls.

Kitchener came on board *Iron Duke* and went round the ship in the morning. He had lunch with Jellicoe, and the other flag officers were invited to come on board and meet him. Kitchener talked frankly with Jellicoe, of his misgivings about what he would be able to achieve in Russia, the difficulties he had had in making out a case before the cabinet, his general tiredness, and the strain he had felt in the last two years. There was much of what Kitchener said that Jellicoe himself could sympathize with. They also talked about Jutland; Kitchener was very interested in the tactics and the general story.

During lunch the weather worsened, and by teatime it was blowing a full north-easterly gale. Jellicoe asked Kitchener to put off his departure, but Kitchener was working to a strict timetable. He could only spend three weeks in Russia, so he must get away. Besides, he said, he was looking forward to this break from affairs of state and London.

Jellicoe and his staff considered the route that *Hampshire* should take. As it was only decided that afternoon there was no possible chance, as was later mischievously suggested, that it could have been betrayed to the enemy. It was decided that the westerly route, round Sule Skerry, would give more shelter in a north-easterly. The escorting destroyers would have a better chance to keep station, and there was little chance of mines; in any case, fleet auxiliaries used that route often, so it was cleared and under observation. The fierce weather in itself would be a safeguard against submarine attacks.

Kitchener and his staff said goodbye to Jellicoe and went on board *Hampshire* at about 4.30; the ship sailed an hour later, with her destroyers. As they rounded the western shore the wind shifted to the north-west so that the three ships were driving straight into the wind and sea. At about 7 p.m. Captain Savill in *Hampshire* ordered the destroyers to turn back, as they could not keep up. About half an hour later, when she was about one and a half miles off Marwick Head,

Hampshire struck a mine and sank in fifteen minutes, bows first.

It seems that Kitchener was below when it happened and he was escorted on deck. The captain was heard giving orders for a boat to be prepared, and Kitchener was seen on the upper deck. But when the ship sank only twelve men in a Carley float drifted ashore and survived. Kitchener was not among them, nor was his body ever recovered.

The incident had been seen from shore, and boats were out to search the area, but news was very slow in arriving. Jellicoe wrote:

> As the hours passed and no news was received of the rescue of any survivors, the anxiety became intense. With the arrival of daylight, and the certainty that this great man, who had served his country so faithfully and well in its great emergency, had met his death when under the care of the Navy, the anxiety turned into consternation and grief.

The mining of *Hampshire* was unlucky, at a time when Jellicoe seemed to have no luck, but when all the reasons had been explained and all the excuses made the fact remained that Lord Kitchener had been lost while the Navy were looking after him. Jellicoe felt it deeply and was plunged into despondency. 'My luck is dead out for the present, I am afraid,' he told Jackson. At times Jellicoe wondered whether he was physically still able: 'I often feel that the job is more than people over fifty-five [Jellicoe was fifty-six] can tackle for very long.' Having always discouraged visitors to Scapa, he now found himself plagued with them. 'What with journalists and Japanese admirals . . . it is very wearing. . . .'

The first few days after the return from Jutland may have caused something of a psychological breaking-point for Jellicoe. The unceasingly hostile weather, the anxiety and shock of Kitchener's death, the growing awareness with every day that passed of just how many chances had been missed at Jutland, all produced in him an unusually depressed state of mind. Until then hard work, applied intelligence, attention to detail, persistence, physical fitness, the ability to lead and to carry men's hearts with him had enabled Jellicoe to surmount every professional obstacle he had ever faced. The Navy had been to him like some great instrument which, however subtle and idiosyncratic, could always be played by one who knew how to perform according to the Navy's own ways. But the aftermath of Jutland showed Jellicoe that there were regions where success was not his to command after all. He had worked as hard as any man could, done his very best, trained his fleet to the peak of their capabilities to meet and conquer every eventuality he could foresee, but events had not turned out as he had expected. Furthermore, he was beginning to suspect that some of his subordinates had in certain respects failed him. Above all, he could not control the flood of ill-informed, hasty, irresponsible and sometimes malicious comment which was to beset him, with periods of only temporary respite, for the rest of his life.

However, Jellicoe concealed his feelings admirably, and nobody looking at him would ever know his doubts. Madden wrote to Lady Jellicoe on 6 June to say that:

'. . . the loss of the *Hampshire* and Lord Kitchener is a great blow and we all admire the splendid courage which J.J. showed when he heard of it and since: it positively made me feel sick and I can't get it out of my head: seeing the ships blow up on 31st had no such effect, as that was all in the day's work, but this is different. J.J. is very well and bright and commands in a greater measure than ever before the full confidence and great affection of all us officers, men and boys. . . .'

Lionel Halsey, Captain of the Fleet, also wrote to Lady Jellicoe:

I can only say that no words of mine can express what we feel for him — absolute admiration and the most perfect confidence. His work and responsibilities during the last 8 days have been more colossal than ever, but it appears to make no difference to him whatever, and I can't imagine any man on this earth who could compete with it all as he does. The joy of meeting the German Fleet, with the disappointment caused by the weather, the sad loss of good ships and splendid fellows, the consequent denial to him of causing the crushing defeat which the enemy would have got if the mist hadn't hidden them, and finally, the subsequent sinking of the *Hampshire* with K. on board would be enough for most men, but he is just the same as ever — and outwardly, anyhow, quite undisturbed. As you must already know, the whole fleet have always loved and respected their C-in-C, but now they simply worship him.

Jellicoe had the consolation of several letters, from Balfour and many senior admirals. Balfour reassured him that the public attitude towards the fleet had changed: 'Opinion has undergone a revolution, both rapid and complete.' Lord Selborne, Admirals May, Culme Seymour, Beresford, Cyprian Bridge and others all wrote to congratulate Jellicoe and to acknowledge that only the weather had robbed him of a greater victory.

On 6 June Jellicoe wrote to Gwendoline fairly summing up the battle and its aftermath:

Of course I am not satisfied, as given clear weather the battle would have been final and there would have been no German Fleet left,

222

whatever happened to us. But that can't be helped. It is ludicrous for the Germans to claim a victory. Victory always rests with the force that occupies the scene of the action, and we did this for the greater part of the next day, until it was quite clear that they had all gone home or as many as were left to go. If they had been so confident of victory they would have tried to go on fighting instead of legging it for home.

Many years later, this still appears the correct view of Jutland.

Jutland had taught the Navy a great many lessons and Jellicoe at once set about the task of learning from experience. He set up the first committee on 4 June and eventually there were several committees, composed of officers expert on their various subjects, on torpedoes, wireless, signals, searchlights, engineering, shells, armour protection, and above all on gunnery, with Dreyer chairing the battle fleet committee and Chatfield the battle cruiser committee.

If Jellicoe had done nothing else and retired forthwith, the Navy would still have been eternally grateful to him for the work he did after Jutland. Under his guidance the Royal Navy made the greatest leap forward in technique, equipment and organization, in the shortest time, of any navy of modern times. While the German Navy, the supposed victors, had already began to slip down towards harbour-bound immobility, deteriorating morale and eventual mutiny, the Royal Navy embarked upon a rejuvenating programme of tremendous change and reconstruction, in every aspect from director firing in ships down to destroyers, to the improvement of action information to the C-in-C.

There were improvements in spotting and fire control; star-shell was introduced (although shell improvements generally took longer and encountered a good deal of bureaucratic resistance); and alterations to ammunition supply arrangements, with flash-tight doors and interlocks, to prevent flash travelling down from a turret into a magazine and igniting the ammunition – almost certainly the reason why the three battle cruisers were lost. Additional armour was fitted, as urged by the fleet, although neither the Controller nor the Director of Naval Construction was convinced that it was needed. By 1917 Room 40 had been transformed into a proper intelligence centre, instead of a transit post for decrypted material.

Jellicoe also turned his attention to tactics. He issued a new set of Grand Fleet Battle Orders on 11 September 1916. There was a move towards less tight control from the centre, recognition that it was not always possible or desirable for the flag to keep such a close grip. The fleet would still fight in single line ahead, but the officers commanding the van or rear of the battle fleet were given much greater discretion to manoeuvre on their own initiative and combat enemy flotilla torpedo attacks. The fast 5th Battle Squadron was given a more advanced position in the fleet and, significantly, a special force was allocated to locate and keep in touch with the enemy after dark. The GFBOs were still very wordy, still a bulky and unwieldy attempt to lay down rules for very conceivable eventuality, but nevertheless they had changed under the pressure of action experience.

The King visited the fleet on 14 June, travelling across in the now traditional way from Thurso in the destroyer *Oak*. His Majesty steamed round the fleet and then spent the night in *Iron Duke*. The following morning he addressed a large number of officers and men from the various squadrons, and repeated the sense of his birthday message. 'You drove the enemy into his harbours, and inflicted on him very severe loss and you added yet another page to the glorious traditions of the British Navy. You could not do more, and for your splendid work I thank you.'

Later in the month, Jellicoe went down to London to visit the Admiralty and to see something of his family; he took Gwendoline and Lucy to the Exhibition of National Economy, and met the Queen. Lucy '. . . was presented and did a very good "bob",' he wrote to his mother. The children '. . . are all well, but Prudy had a little teeth trouble and has caught a cough with it'.

It was not only Prudy's teeth which were giving trouble. Jellicoe had become aware of growing feelings of animosity, rivalry and resentment between the Battle Fleet and the Battle Cruiser Fleet. Jellicoe called at Rosyth to see Beatty and his ships on his way south to London in June. According to Beatty, when Jellicoe came on board *Lion* on 24 June he was very depressed, sat in Beatty's cabin head in hands and admitted he had missed one of the best chances a man ever had.

That was an opinion with which Beatty agreed. His relationship with Jellicoe was always hard to sum up, and it became even more difficult after Jutland. The two men agreed on many things; on fleet tactics, they had far more ideas in common than in conflict. Beatty had the most profound respect and affection for his chief. Yet there is no question that the longer Beatty had to think about Jutland the more he came round to the view that Jellicoe had, by natural caution, thrown away a tremendous opportunity. It seemed that Beatty and Jellicoe agreed affably enough with each other when they were together and talking face to face. It was when they were separated, which they were almost all the time, and listening to their respective staffs – and especially Beatty's staff – that misunderstandings and recriminations were most likely to arise.

The Battle Cruiser Fleet came to think that they had taken all the risks at Jutland, and suffered almost all the casualties, without being properly supported. The Battle Cruiser Fleet had delivered the enemy into the Battle Fleet's very hands, which had then failed to dispatch the enemy properly. *We*, the Battle Cruiser Fleet, were dashing, successful, and much aggrieved. *They*, the Battle Fleet, were cautious, plodding, casting away golden opportunities gained through so much blood and effort by Us. If Beatty had been C-in-C, things would have been different. One or two senior admirals, who should have known better, agreed with this version of events to such a point that they guessed that Jellicoe had actually run away.

The Battle Fleet, for its part, felt that the Battle Cruiser Fleet was too much above itself by half, too fond of going off on hazardous jaunts which looked good in the newspapers but hardly helped the war along one jot. It was, after all, the Battle Cruiser Fleet's *job* to report the enemy fleet and lead it towards the Battle Fleet. When Midshipman Mountbatten dined with his cousin Prince Albert (afterwards King George VI) in *Collingwood*'s gunroom he was astonished and disturbed to find that everybody in the Grand Fleet thought the Battle Cruiser Fleet had let them down. Lieutenant Oswald Frewen, in the 4th Light Cruiser Squadron, wrote in his diary '. . . of the arrogant, slipshod and inhospitable Battle Cruiser Fleet'. Rear-Admiral Duff thought that the Battle Cruiser Fleet was 'swollen headed and truculent' and had intended to win the battle of Jutland all on its own without anybody else having a look in.

Feelings ran so high that when the Battle Cruiser Fleet visited Scapa in August 1916 Jellicoe took special pains to dispel these 'separatist' views, which could hardly be further from Nelson's ideal of a band of brothers. Jellicoe exerted himself to scotch the inclination, which he admitted existed, for the Battle Cruiser Fleet to look on themselves as a force apart. A great deal of social coming and going between the ships was arranged and Jellicoe himself started the ball rolling with a dinner given on board *Iron Duke* for the flag officers and captains of both fleets.

It was a curious meal, like a funeral wake at which the name of the deceased was never mentioned. If ever there was a time to discuss 'the battle' this was it; it must have been uppermost in the minds of everyone present. Yet by some extraordinary mutual tacit consent the subject was made taboo, and everybody talked about anything and everything else but 'the battle'. At one point Admiral Pakenham happened to lean forward and say something about it to his opposite number across the table, at just the moment when there was a general lull in the dinner table noise level. There was a long, awful, throbbing silence, followed instantly by a frantic babel of conversation to cover up the solecism. So throughout that meal Jutland lay like Amfortas' wound, unspoken and unhealed.

Beatty was not wholly persuaded by all the social activity, the tremendous welcome his ships received, the lusty cheers, the flood of invitations to dine, the bonhomie. He found it 'very overwhelming' and did his best to '. . . find out what is at the back of it all'. Perhaps Jellicoe overdid the cheeriness, but he did it for the best of motives.

By the end of July Jellicoe was, in his own words, quite played out. On 7 August he went on leave to Kinpurnie Castle in Angus, his father-in-law's house near Dundee. He disliked going intensely, he said, but as he admitted to Jackson: 'I feel so constantly tired that I am afraid of not doing justice to the Fleet should we succeed in meeting the enemy.' At first Jellicoe found it difficult to relax and unwind from the tensions of the war. He was not sleeping well, suffering from the reaction of the strains of Jutland. By the fifteenth he was feeling better for the change, and if everything stayed quiet he intended to stay for another few days. But it was not to be. As a precaution, Jellicoe had taken a Foreign Office cypher code with him and arranged for Jackson to send a telegram to Kinpurnie saying 'Important. He should get ready. Henry,' if anything happened. On 18 August that message arrived. The light cruiser *Royalist* was waiting off Dundee with steam up; Jellicoe was on board in half an hour and sailed to join the fleet, transferring to *Iron Duke* after dark.

The Grand Fleet, with Burney in temporary command, and consisting of twenty-nine Dreadnoughts of the 1st, 2nd, 4th and 5th Battle Squadrons, sailed from Scapa that morning. Beatty, with six battle cruisers of the 1st and 2nd Battle Cruiser Squadrons, sailed from the Forth at 6.20 p.m. The Harwich Force sailed, to rendezvous with the Grand Fleet, at 10.30 p.m.

Burney actually sailed some hours before Scheer, thanks to excellent intelligence. Scheer had sailed at 9 p.m. with eighteen Dreadnoughts, two battle cruisers (all that were seaworthy after Jutland), and some cruisers and destroyers. His intention was once again a bombardment – of Sunderland – and the hope of bringing a portion of the Grand Fleet to action. But he had been betrayed by intelligence and his opponent was much nearer and in much greater strength than he ever suspected.

The events of August 1916, a now almost totally forgotten incident in the naval war, might have given Jellicoe the chance to put into effect many of the improvements in the fleet since Jutland. But for the ill luck which dogged Jellicoe all that summer it might have been a decisive victory: this time Jellicoe had overwhelming strength, Beatty's battle cruisers were in much closer station, intelligence was quicker and more reliable, the visibility was better, and there was more time and more sea-room. It seemed that here was the chance to put right, once and for all, the things which had gone amiss at Jutland.

But again it went wrong. At 5.57 a.m. on 19 August the cruiser *Nottingham* was hit by two torpedoes fired from a U-boat off Holy Island. A third torpedo hit her half an hour later and she sank at 7.10. Jellicoe had to decide whether she had been mined and, if so, whether he was now leading his fleet into a minefield. A recent signal from the Admiralty told him the enemy were still two hundred miles away from him at 5.25, so he turned to the north. At 9 a.m., when he knew definitely that *Nottingham* had been torpedoed, and not mined, he turned south again.

By 2 p.m. the best estimate was that the two fleets were steaming at right-angles to each other and were only some forty miles apart. Jellicoe signalled his fleet to '. . . raise steam for full speed. . . . Assume immediate readiness for action in every respect.' At 2.15, when the blood was quickening and it really did seem that a decisive action was about to take place, Jellicoe made: 'High Seas Fleet may be sighted at any moment. I look with entire confidence on the result.'

Scheer, who had no idea of his danger, had several reconnoitring Zeppelins in the air and one of them, which had been shadowing the Harwich Force, reported a strong enemy squadron, including five heavy ships, coming up from southward. At 12.15, when Jellicoe only needed another hour's steaming to get between Scheer and his base, Scheer abandoned the bombardment of Sunderland and shortly afterwards led his ships to the south to search for this force, which he believed to be part of the enemy battle fleet, but which was actually the Harwich Force.

At 12.45 the Harwich Force also turned south, having failed to sight any German ships. Shortly after 2 p.m. Scheer had a report from a U-boat that the main British Fleet had appeared, steaming south. At 2.35 Scheer abandoned the operation and turned eastwards for home. He had decided that he had no chance of catching the enemy force to the south and it was too late in the day to go on and bombard Sunderland.

Unknowingly, Scheer had had a very narrow escape. He had been within fifty minutes or so of meeting Jellicoe's main fleet and having his 'T' crossed again. But by 3 p.m. Jellicoe knew that the trail had gone cold. A series of misunderstandings on the German side had miraculously extricated their ships from a very dangerous situation. At 3.53 Jellicoe ordered his fleet to turn north. U-boats lying in wait made several attacks; the light cruiser *Falmouth* was hit four times and sank some time later when under tow. It was, once again, a very disappointed fleet which returned to Scapa Flow.

Chapter 14

When *Iron Duke* secured to her buoy again on 20 August, when the telegraphs rang off to 'Finished with main engines', and the ship's company fell out from their sea-watches, Jellicoe came down from the bridge a very tired man indeed. He should have gone away, there and then, for a long leave in the Highlands of Scotland, with only his family about him, to shoot and fish and walk and think. He badly needed time and space and leisure to regain his vigour, to recharge himself, to clear his mind of his problems. His short leave at Kinpurnie had been interrupted and he was not to get any more. He had survived one testing time, and was just about to go straight on into another, with no break to refresh himself.

Jellicoe said he never read the newspapers much, but he must have been aware of the growing rumble of discontent about Jutland. The longer people had to think about that battle, the more enraged they seemed to become. His family certainly did read the papers and resented the suggestions that Jellicoe had failed to pursue the German Fleet vigorously enough. Jellicoe had sent home a full account of the battle as soon as he returned to Scapa, and to a certain extent it mitigated the effect of that first Admiralty statement, which did not mention Jellicoe's part at all.

The criticism of Jellicoe particularly affected his father-in-law, Sir Charles Cayzer, who was seriously ill. With Jellicoe and Madden as sons-in-law, Sir Charles had been delighted with the nickname of 'the father-in-law of the Navy'. Now the old man had to suffer what he considered the most infamous statements about his family and Jellicoe in particular, and it may have hastened his death. He spent his last days in the quiet surroundings of Gartmore, where he died in September 1916.

Jellicoe did not think of replying to his critics in public, then or ever; his stern sense of what was fitting forbade him. He was not tempted, even for a moment, by an offer from a journalist, Filson Young, who wrote to him on 9 June to say that he had obtained a considerable amount of information about Jutland, and asked Jellicoe to supply him with more, the source to remain strictly confidential. Jellicoe replied that he was quite prepared to meet criticisms himself, but in the proper place and the proper time. The press was not the proper place, in Jellicoe's view, at any time. Jellicoe sent the letter to Balfour, saying : 'I am not concerned to defend my action in the Press, or to let anyone do it for me. . . . I think it infinitely preferable that all the information on the subject that it is desired to give should be given by the Admiralty alone.'

This attitude of Jellicoe's, which was typical of the man and of his time, made him a curiously vulnerable target. He was so understanding, so approachable, so considerate to all, no matter how junior, when he was within his own naval surroundings. Perhaps he would have been less criticized if he had been a little less unbending, a little more forthcoming, to those outside the Navy. He did need someone to advise him about relations with the press. But that, for him, would have been unthinkable, and it is idle to criticize Jellicoe for not having the same attitudes towards press relations as a modern flag officer.

The action, or rather non-action, of 19 August cast a long shadow on both sides of the North Sea, having an effect on naval policies out of all proportion to the actual events at sea. For Scheer it meant the virtual end of sorties to sea by the High Seas Fleet. The German Naval Staff decided that the High Seas Fleet had no longer any chance of inflicting a decisive defeat on the Grand Fleet, and the emphasis of naval operations was switched to U-boat attacks on commerce. From 6 October U-boats were diverted from operations in conjunction with the fleet to resume submarine warfare under the Prize Rules, of visit and search.

Jellicoe himself was particularly impressed by two aspects of the events on 19 August: the success the Germans had with Zeppelins for reconnaissance, and the menace of submarines. He pressed the Admiralty for airships for the fleet. 'One Zeppelin is worth a good many light cruisers on a suitable day,' he said. As for the submarines, the only solution in his opinion was more destroyers. He estimated that he would need eighty-seven destroyers at the very minimum to give a degree of protection, allowing twelve destroyers to eight capital ships, two destroyers for every cruiser and one for every light cruiser. He actually had eighty-six destroyers at his disposal, fifty-five at Scapa and the rest at Rosyth, but only about seventy were normally available, the remainder being away refitting, boiler-cleaning, or required for other duties.

Writing to Balfour on 25 August, Jellicoe made no bones about the position. The shortage of destroyers '. . . calls for urgent pressure on the firms who are building destroyers, as until we get more, I cannot guarantee us from further heavy losses in cruisers, if not in Battleships, from submarine attack. . . .' To Jackson on the twenty-third he had already written that the only way to avoid losses in future was to screen all the cruisers and light cruisers, '. . . and I am afraid the number of TBDs won't run to it'. He followed that up with a memorandum to the Admiralty pointing out how short he was of destroyers and urging that their construction should be given priority above everything else except light cruisers.

There tended at this time to be a querulous, somewhat tetchy, note in Jellicoe's correspondence which was quite unlike the man himself. The Admiralty replied, very reasonably, that they had for some time been allocating all new destroyers to the Grand Fleet. They were already building destroyers just as fast as they could. They did, after all, have many other commitments, especially troop convoys, all over the world. There was no chance of destroyers being built more quickly. Jellicoe would simply have to be satisfied with those he had got and would be getting.

It was a sign of Jellicoe's tiredness and frayed temper that he could not be satisfied with this reply. On 13 September he returned to the charge, enlarging on the points he had made before. He had no fresh arguments; perhaps he believed that continual dropping weareth out the stone. He was disappointed. Oliver, the Chief of the Naval War Staff, simply minuted on the letter, 'This letter does not seem to call for a reply. Keeping up an argument will not provide any more destroyers.' When it reached Balfour on 3 October, he wrote even more curtly, 'Take no action.'

One potent reason for estrangement between the Grand Fleet and the Admiralty was the sheer distance, mentally as well as physically, from Scapa Flow to Whitehall. To travel from one to the other was a considerable undertaking. The seemingly endless hours sitting in a railway carriage gave men ample time to recast their memory of what they had seen and said, to rehearse a version which showed themselves in a more favourable or reasonable light, to imagine they had done rather better in an argument than they had, to remember slights where none had been meant, and to lend a remark a weight the speaker had never intended.

Early in September the Fourth Sea Lord, Captain Cecil Lambert, no supporter of Jellicoe's, visited Scapa and Rosyth. When he returned to London he reported to Jackson that Jellicoe was consistently and constantly critical of the Admiralty. Jackson too was a tired man, who had had a long and wearying summer. He wrote to Jellicoe on 11 September regretting that Lambert '. . . depicts your attitude as viewing everything that emanates from the Admiralty as wrong, whether it is really good, bad or indifferent'. Perhaps, Jackson went on, they had tried to meet Jellicoe's wishes too readily: 'Everything else has been starved, more or less, for the Grand Fleet.' Jellicoe's principal accusation: '. . . seems to be "when the Grand Fleet is ordered to sea [when the German Fleet is known to be out] that you are ordered to carry out impracticable or dangerous movements"'. This Jackson flatly denied and challenged Jellicoe to give examples.

Nor was that all. Lambert had noted and reported Jellicoe's strong preference for Madden, his brother-in-law, to succeed him as C-in-C if he should be killed or incapacitated. As reported to Jackson, Jellicoe not only thought Madden should succeed him he also believed that the others '. . . were hardly up to the mark – not fit to take your place if you are knocked out'. Jackson said he had always had a high opinion of Madden but '. . . to put forward the idea that he is the only man to take your place is I think rather strong'.

'Discontent spreads rapidly, especially downwards,' Jackson went on, in a remarkably plain-spoken letter, 'and may react when least expected. Popularity may sometimes be too dearly bought.' Jackson was not surprised that it weighed on Jellicoe's mind that '. . . we lack the initiative'. But that should not warp his judgement and make him accuse the Admiralty of not giving support and not 'playing the game straightly'.

At a time when there was so much to be done, when in Jackson's own words they were 'at a very critical period of the war', when both men had great demands on their strength, they now wasted their nervous energy in picking each other off with debating points, carefully slanging each other to the limits of Service convention. For Jellicoe was certainly not going to let such a letter pass, and he indignantly refuted all Jackson's points one by one. Some passages in his letter he underlined in red ink, 'I do not think I have ever been so insulted before,' he wrote.

Eventually Jackson attributed much of the disagreement to 'hot air' and the whole episode was somewhat uncomfortably shuffled over. It had achieved nothing, had merely drained away more of both men's remaining capital of energy and stamina and patience, and it certainly left Jellicoe unconsoled and resentful.

Of much more importance to them both was the conference held on board *Iron Duke* on 13 September. It was attended by Jellicoe and Madden, and by Oliver, who had come up specially from London. They discussed the naval future in the light of the events of 19 August. This obscure non-action was, in fact, one of the turning points of the naval war in home waters. Jellicoe stated that without more destroyers, and there were no more, he could not guarantee to protect the east coast ports against tip-and-run bombardment raids. The fleet could not even interfere with a German landing in the south, at least in its early stages, unless the situation was very pressing and dangerous. Jellicoe felt that the main fleet should not venture south of Dogger Bank. Mines and submarines had changed the whole face of naval war. The day of the great clash between fleets of Dreadnoughts was over – Jellicoe even suggested disbanding one battle squadron. The war had reached a stalemate.

The Admiralty agreed that heavy ships were to keep north of the latitude of Horns Reef unless circumstances were exceptional — an attempted invasion, or a really good chance of a daylight action in clear weather against the High Seas Fleet in a tactical situation '. . . not greatly to the disadvantage of the Grand Fleet'. Up to now the Grand Fleet had always reacted when news was received of the High Seas Fleet putting to sea. This policy was dropped (understandably, without any publicity). When Scheer did go to sea again, at about midnight on 18—19 October 1916, the Grand Fleet shortened notice for steam, but did not leave harbour; Tyrwhitt at Harwich was alerted. But after a brush with British submarines Scheer returned to harbour, having accomplished nothing. This was the High Seas Fleet's last sortie until April 1918.

Although as he said he seldom read the papers, as the autumn days shortened into the third winter of the war Jellicoe could hardly have omitted to notice that the Board of Admiralty was once again undergoing one of its periodic bouts of public disapproval and criticism, just as it had at the beginning of the war when the German ships *Goeben* and *Breslau* escaped to Turkey, and had again, earlier that same year of 1916, when there had been complaints of too long a period of inactivity in the North Sea. The latest discontent had several causes. German destroyers had lately raided the English Channel twice – the second time after Balfour had rashly prophesied it could never happen again. The controversy over differences of opinion between the Royal Flying Corps and the Royal Naval Air Service had lately spilled out into public gaze. There were repeated complaints of a lack of offensive spirit, of the staleness of the Admiralty. The Board, it was said, had been too long in office and too long ashore. Lastly, and most importantly, there were the effects of increasing activity by U-boats against shipping. The German Naval Staff's decision to deny Scheer U-boats for scouting had released more for attacks on commerce.

It was the U-boat menace which brought matters to a head. By the closing months of 1916 the Navy had clearly fought off the dangers of a main fleet action and made another Jutland most unlikely, but one peril had been exchanged for another, and greater. In October 1916 Jellicoe could see that the nature of the war at sea had changed. From discussions with his staff, from study of the sinking rates and signals about the progress of the war, Jellicoe came to realize that the true danger to his fleet, the mortal danger to the country, was not a sortie by the High Seas Fleet but slow strangulation from shipping losses caused by U-boats.

On 29 October Jellicoe sent a memorandum addressed to the First Lord, with a copy to the First Sea Lord. It began in sombre vein: 'The very serious and ever increasing menace of the enemy's submarine attack on trade is by far the most pressing question at the present time.' This, Jellicoe went on, would have such a serious effect on food imports and other necessities for the Allies that it might by the early summer of 1917 force the country into accepting peace terms '. . . which the military position on the Continent would not justify and which would fall far short of our desires'. In other words, and not to beat about the bush, Britain would lose the war.

Jellicoe suggested that new ways of tackling the submarine menace should be found. Younger officers should be brought in from the fleet to provide fresh ideas. He himself, making a concession which would have been unthinkable only three months before, would agree to demobilizing one whole battle squadron so as to devote their destroyer screens to the hunt for U-boats. Jellicoe stressed that he was not putting forward 'concrete proposals'. He was only suggesting a committee to formulate proposals for overcoming what he called '. . . the most serious menace with which the Empire has ever been faced'. That was no understatement.

Oddly, Jellicoe made a passing reference to the best solution in this very memorandum. 'The destroyer', he wrote, 'is, of course, very efficient defensively as a screen to individual ships, or to a large number of ships. . . .' Thus Jellicoe brushed against the subject of convoy, which he believed then, and to the end of his life, to be a defensive manoeuvre. Jellicoe could never hoist in the truth that convoy was much more than a means of defence, and that it was in fact by far the best method of offence against U-boats.

Nevertheless, Jellicoe's memorandum was one of the very first glimpses of the mortal danger of submarines to the Allied cause. It also offered an unusually warm welcome to fresh ideas from the young. Although the memorandum had no political motive, it had as great an effect on Balfour as Jellicoe's letter on warship-building had had on McKenna years before. Balfour was profoundly impressed and read the memorandum to Asquith, the Prime Minister, on 31 October. He suggested that Jellicoe be invited to attend a meeting of the War Committee on 2 November; Jackson, Oliver and Lloyd George were also there. Among the subjects discussed was convoy. Lloyd George asked Jellicoe if he had any plan for combating submarines outside coastal waters, and Jellicoe said he had not. There were only armed merchant ships and these could only act when they were themselves attacked; they could not see a dived submarine. Jellicoe suggested floating intelligence centres to direct shipping traffic away from dangerous areas – he had suggested in his memorandum 'a thoroughly organised system of diverting ships with great rapidity from dangerous to safe routes'. Jellicoe said he did not approve of convoys because they would make too big a target. He was thus subscribing to the old fallacy that convoys put all one's eggs in one basket.

Consciously or not, Jellicoe was only reflecting official Admiralty views on convoy when he said that. He was speaking purely as the C-in-C of the Grand Fleet. He had only recently become concerned with submarine attacks on a wider scale, and up to now his whole concentration had been upon defending the Grand Fleet. When first Bonar Law and then Lloyd George suggested that forms of convoy should be tried, using a few warships, Jellicoe said that merchant ships would never be able to keep station together closely enough for a few warships to screen them. Mr Walter Runciman added that convoy was very wasteful from the point of view of tonnage; there was no advantage in speed, in fact quite the reverse; the convoy had to move at the speed of the slowest ship.

However, Jellicoe's suggestion that a special committee or division be formed to find fresh ways of combating submarines was implemented, and a meeting was held on 3 November which Jellicoe attended. Those present discussed existing methods and ways of improving them. They did not discuss convoy. Afterwards Balfour asked Jellicoe if he would be prepared to be chairman of such a committee.

Jellicoe must have considered the idea carefully. The centre of gravity, so to speak, of the naval war had clearly shifted from the Grand Fleet at Scapa Flow. Jellicoe did not believe the Grand Fleet would ever get another chance of engaging the High Seas Fleet. But this question of submarines was vital, and it was now central to the defence of the country at sea. Jellicoe might have served on such a committee, but he talked it over with Jackson and they agreed that it would be difficult and embarrassing for them both if he did. But Jackson did suggest that Jellicoe should become his deputy, and replace him in the near future.

The meetings and the exchanges of ideas had set Balfour thinking that now was as good a time as any to make a change. He felt that Jackson was tired by the strains of the office, and a new man was needed. On 22 November 1916 he sent a telegram marked 'Secret and Personal from First Lord' offering Jellicoe the post of First Sea Lord. It was received on board *Iron Duke* at 2 p.m. and at 3.15 Jellicoe replied: 'I am entirely at your disposal if my services are required. I accept the offer.' Jellicoe discussed the offer with Madden, but his acceptance could never have been in doubt. He was being offered the pinnacle of his profession, and Jellicoe knew he had the knowledge, the experience and the confidence to carry off such a job. He was naturally sorry to leave the Grand Fleet, which he had commanded since the first day of the war, but this new opportunity could not be refused. If all his hopes for the Navy, all his plans and arguments for its future, and his whole previous professional life had any meaning at all, he had to accept.

Jellicoe went to sea on 24 November and arrived at Rosyth two days later; he met Balfour in Edinburgh on the twenty-seventh and discussed future appointments in the fleet. The following day Jellicoe said goodbye to the officers and men of *Iron Duke*. He told them, prophetically, that he fully expected that he would become the target of attacks, just as Jackson had been. He left, he said, with a very sad heart, with feelings of the deepest regret, but he was sure that enemies of their country would meet more than their match in the Grand Fleet, '. . . ship for ship in all classes, and that the result will never be in doubt for one moment'.

Jellicoe carried the speech off very well, although he did not himself believe that the Grand Fleet would ever meet the enemy again. For Rosyth, in November, it was a fine day, with fitful sunshine and patches of blue sky. The ship's company lined the rails and cheered. The marine band played. Jellicoe went down the starboard after gangway for the last time and stepped into his barge. The men stayed on deck to watch it receding towards the shore.

Beatty relieved Jellicoe as C-in-C, with Pakenham in *Australia* in command of the Battle Cruiser Force (the word 'Fleet' was discontinued). Madden hoisted his flag in *Marlborough* as second-in-command, and in command of the 1st Battle Squadron. Burney and Jerram hauled down their flags and came ashore – Burney to be Second Sea Lord, as Jellicoe had asked. Sturdee, doubly passed over by Beatty and Madden, did not ask to be relieved but stayed in command of the 4th Battle Squadron. Halsey went to the Admiralty, as Fourth Sea Lord. So too did Duff, Sturdee's second-in-command, to head the new Anti-Submarine Division of the Naval War Staff, with Dreyer as his assistant. Several other officers went from the Grand Fleet to the Admiralty, giving that transfusion of 'salt' which the newspapers were clamouring for (although most of the newcomers were comparatively ignorant of Whitehall ways and Oliver, as the old hand, had his time much taken up with visits from officers looking for information about their new appointments).

Jellicoe did not take over as First Sea Lord until 5 December 1916, because he was suffering from influenza. So, on his fifty-seventh birthday, still recovering from illness, troubled by bouts of acute deafness, a complaint which had afflicted his mother as she grew older, with occasional pain from his old lung wound, physically spry and ever willing, but mentally weary, John Jellicoe became the professional head of the Service. He had changed one utterly demanding job for another, with no proper interval of rest and refreshment.

Admiral Jackson went to the comparative backwater of Greenwich, as President of the College. Jellicoe wrote to him there a letter of appreciation and thanks. Jackson replied with what Jellicoe called '. . . a very fine letter':

. . . I have as great a confidence in your ability to do the work in the Admiralty as you have done it in the far more onerous post of Commander-in-Chief, and I have no feeling but a sense of relief that it has now fallen into your capable hands, and I feel convinced that your administration will achieve success as far as human foresight and guidance can control such operations.

Jackson's opinion was shared by the whole Service, both serving and retired, with the single exception of Fisher. Having groomed Jellicoe for the post of C-in-C for well over a decade, Fisher saw his move as a betrayal – '. . . absolutely parallel to Nelson coming home to sit on an office stool the week before Trafalgar'. Fisher also had the suspicion that Jellicoe's appointment was intended to keep Asquith's government in office and prevent himself being First Lord. But on 7 December Asquith's administration was replaced by a coalition under Lloyd George, who sent Balfour to the Foreign Office and brought Sir Edward Carson to the Admiralty. Sir Edward did not claim great expertise in naval affairs and was willing to rely on the advice of his Sea Lords, and he and Jellicoe got on together extremely well. Carson's devotion to the Navy, Jellicoe wrote, '. . . was obvious to all, and in him the Navy possessed indeed a true and powerful friend'. He was certainly to be a friend of Jellicoe's at a time when Jellicoe needed friends.

In his first few days at the Admiralty Jellicoe had a curiously wry and revealing meeting with Brownrigg, the Naval Censor. Brownrigg said Jellicoe had had 'a bad press' and

> . . . did he want anything done about it? He said with his quizzical smile, that he knew he had, and no doubt by the time he had told the truth a few times regarding the submarine position he would have a still worse one. So I asked him again if he would not allow me to see what could be done. No, he must allow the Press to form its own judgement, and if it elected to be guided by one set of writers more than any others – well, that was its own business. Anyway, he did not expect to last twelve months, and in any case he had no time to read the papers. So I had no more to say.

Brownrigg had no more success with Jellicoe when he tried to get him to use his influence to have more reporters sent up north, so as to give the fleet more publicity. Jellicoe invariably replied: 'Well, I would not have them up there when *I* was Commander-in-Chief, so how can you expect me to ask Sir David Beatty to do so?' This attitude, though logical in its own way, was not much help to Brownrigg. He began to approach Beatty himself instead – with more success.

Whatever his physical ailments and his reservations about press reception, Jellicoe shrugged them and all other preoccupations aside and plunged into his new tasks with tremendous energy. He attempted, and achieved, a reorganization of the war staff at the Admiralty, removing anomalies which had existed since the era of Churchill in 1912. Before that, of course, there had been no naval war staff; men like Wilson and Fisher had both believed that the less fewer people knew of naval war plans the better. Churchill had established a chief of the naval war staff who had no executive authority. The true chief of staff, in fact if not in name, was the First Sea Lord and Jellicoe assumed this title, absorbing it into the office of First Sea Lord in May 1917. Oliver then became deputy chief of naval staff, with responsibility for operations against enemy surface vessels; Duff became assistant chief, with responsibility for operations against the enemy's submarines and mines. By that time Dreyer had become Director of Naval Ordnance and Captain W.W. Fisher, who had relieved him, took over Duff's place as Director of the Anti-Submarine Division.

Jellicoe had taken office against a darkening background of the U-boat offensive against shipping. It was the frightful weekly losses of shipping which overshadowed the first six months of his tenure, while the various methods and weapons for destroying submarines which Jellicoe introduced had yet to have any effect. Under Jellicoe's direction, Duff and his division instigated a thorough survey of all the means available of catching submarines, both offensively by attacking the U-boats at sea, and defensively by giving the merchant ships themselves more protection.

It was the most determined drive against submarines the Navy had ever known. Special patrolling groups were set up, based on Portsmouth and Plymouth. Air patrols with improved aircraft and airships capable of carrying bombs were flown from various airfields along the south coast. An improved design of depth-charge was set in hand, although it did not appear for many months. The design of hydrophones was also improved, although this too did not bear fruit for some time. Plans were made for British submarines to hunt down their opposite numbers, setting a thief to catch a thief; this was a very sound principle, but again it did not show results for a long time.

The existing programme of arming merchantmen was greatly augmented and improved. Outgoing and incoming merchantmen were routed into 'safe channels' leading to 'safe areas'. The number and variety of 'decoy' Q ships was vastly increased, until it became clear that the enemy had tumbled them. Other anti-submarine projects included extensive mine barrages, smoke-making apparatus, fast coastal motor-boats, improved anti-submarine shells, the fitting of depth-charge throwers, or howitzers.

Everything was tried, in fact, except convoys. Valuable ships such as troopships continued to be escorted, as they had been for some time, but the general view in the Admiralty was still against the general introduction of convoy. Opinions had actually hardened against convoy since Jellicoe took office. The official staff view was published in a pamphlet in January 1917 which made it clear that convoy was not regarded as a sound measure of trade defence:

> Whenever possible, vessels should sail singly, escorted as considered necessary. The system of several ships sailing together in a convoy is not recommended in any area where submarine attack is a possibility. It is evident that the larger the number of ships forming the convoy, the greater is the chance of a submarine being enabled to attack successfully, the greater the difficulty of the escort in preventing such an attack.

A more criminally stupid point of view, a more incredibly erroneous interpretation of naval history, it would be hard to imagine. But such was the official Admiralty view of convoy as late as January 1917. It seems that the writer was expressing the opinions of most of the officers concerned with the defence of trade at that time. Jellicoe, however, did not rule out convoy. Naturally he took note of the view of the majority, but he seems to have withheld judgement on convoy for the time being. It remained something to be borne in mind for the future.

As the New Year of 1917 opened it became brutally clear in the Admiralty that the various methods tried were simply not sinking enough submarines, while the submarines were making terrifying inroads into the nation's capital of merchant ships. In January 1917 368,521 tons of shipping was lost. On 31 January the German government announced that unrestricted submarine warfare would be resumed from midnight. The Germans had made a calculation of British shipping resources and their own submarine force: the British had about 11 million tons of merchant shipping and U-boats were sinking about 350,000 tons a month under restricted conditions. Freed of all restrictions, the U-boats should put the sinking rate up to about 600,000 tons a month, and would also frighten off large numbers of neutral ships. Great Britain would lose some 40 per cent of her shipping in five months. This conclusion was not conjecture – it was supported by cold figures. Britain's defeat was there in the lines of a graph, for all to see, if nothing were done and the present situation allowed to continue.

The Admiralty tried to counter the new submarine offensive by introducing a system of alternative lines of communication in the four main areas of approach to the United Kingdom. The theory was that patrol vessels could be concentrated along these routes, to give added protection, instead of being scattered all over the Western Approaches. In practice the increased number of patrol vessels simply attracted the U-boats' attention, betraying to them the position of the so-called 'safe' routes. Similarly, another system of patrolling lanes near the coast, while certainly keeping down losses due to gunfire (because the U-boats hesitated to surface in the presence of escorts) did nothing to prevent torpedo losses. The figures of shipping losses continued their horrifying climb: 500,500 tons in February 1917, 556,000 in March and a catastrophic 870,000 in April. Defeat for Great Britain was now measured in weeks.

The truth was that the Admiralty had fallen into the seductive trap of believing in an old fallacy. Staff officers talked of 'guarding the sea lanes'. There were plans to '. . . safeguard the sea lanes on which the country's life depended'. It was of course not the sea lanes which needed protection, but the ships which passed along them. During the long hundred years of the Pax Victoriana the old naval art of convoy had been lost; it had been forgotten how many of the most famous naval engagements, from the Armada to the Glorious First of June, had been convoy actions.

On 7 February 1917 a system of convoy was introduced for the ships carrying coal to the northern ports of France, which had been suffering losses. Although the organization of the convoys was quickly impro-vized, and the escorts consisted only of armed trawlers, losses among the colliers had dropped dramatically by the end of March. The figures were so striking that they suggested to Duff that convoy might well be introduced on the Atlantic route. However, it was only a suggestion, not proof; there was some way to go, and many dozens of ships and hundreds of lives yet to be lost, before general convoy was introduced.

Like the fabulous hydra, Admiralty objection to convoy had many heads, and like the hydra's heads, fresh objections grew as soon as one was removed. It was not possible to establish so firm and comprehen-sive a control by the state over merchant shipping. Masters of mer-chantmen, especially tramp steamers which would make up a good proportion of any convoy, could not keep station upon one another. Nor could their quartermasters steer a sufficiently straight course. It was not possible to assemble convoys in neutral ports. There were not nearly enough escorts to introduce convoy for the enormous number of ships which entered and sailed from British ports weekly — some 5,000 per week, it was calculated. Much time would be wasted in assembling a convoy, time in which individual ships could have sailed and carried on earning their living. If many ships arrived in port at once, the unloading capacity of that port would be overloaded, while lying idle at other times when all the ships were at sea in convoy.

Convoys would have to go at the speed of the slowest ship, or even slower, to allow some margin for manoeuvring, thus sacrificing the defence of superior speed which some of the ships would otherwise have had if they had been sailing singly. A convoy would conveniently concentrate all a U-boat's targets into one space, instead of allowing them to disperse.

Apart from the difficulty of assembling convoys in neutral ports, and even that was largely to be removed with the entry of the United States into the war, all these objections were utterly groundless. Moreover, they went in the face of the Navy's own experience in the past. Many times in previous centuries the government had taken over the direction of shipping, when convoy had often been introduced at the outset of hostilities or even earlier. Convoy Acts had been passed, with penalties for failing to join or for leaving prematurely. As for the steering and station-keeping abilities of merchant ships, surely those could be put to the test. It did not require a multitude of escorts to protect a convoy, and in any case the number of weekly entries and departures from British ports had been grossly exaggerated for propaganda purposes. As for delays caused by shipping assembling for convoy, these were nothing compared to the delays already caused by the fear of attacks, and, of course, the delays caused by the lack of ships which were already at the bottom of the sea. Convoy deprived a U-boat captain of the 'soft option' of an unopposed attack. Previous naval history showed that an attack upon a defended convoy was one of the most dangerous undertakings of all. Far from giving a U boat captain the chance of many shots, a convoy reduced him almost always to one. Far from increasing the number of targets, convoy seemed magically to empty the sea of shipping.

But the Admiralty had yet another objection to convoy which lay so deep in the subconscious of the Navy that it approached the irrational. Every new generation believes that its own new weapons make old principles of naval warfare obsolete. Many naval officers were genuinely convinced that the new weapons deployed in the First World War made convoy dangerously out-of-date. Too many senior naval officers had served in a Victorian Navy without convoy for them to adjust mentally to a situation where convoy was a necessity. They simply could not think of convoy as an ancient and successful strategic principle, which had a well-tried and infallible tactical form. They thought of convoy as risky, and very likely to fail.

It was Lloyd George who intuitively detected and defined this secret antipathy to convoy amongst those he called 'the High Admirals' — among whom, of course, he included Jellicoe. But such was Lloyd George's personality that the harder he pressed the Navy, the more fiercely he was resisted. Lloyd George has been criticized for the unduly sarcastic language he employed at the admirals' expense in his accounts of his own part of the way in which convoy was belatedly introduced. He would have replied that when the patient was dying (medical metaphors abound in his text) it was necessary to call a scalpel a scalpel. Lloyd George realized that the official Admiralty pamphlet of January 1917, advising against convoy, was by no means the view of everyone at the Admiralty. There were some officers, especially some of the younger officers, who profoundly disagreed and believed that convoy was not only *one* solution, but the *only* solution, the salvation, in fact. Lloyd George was also aware of papers in the Admiralty written by submarine officers who knew how difficult it was to attack a convoy.

The four cone-shaped approach routes, patrolled by surface craft, down which merchant shipping was directed, Lloyd George described as death-traps. 'In fact, by this egregious plan our ships were in effect often shepherded into the abattoir where the slaughterers lay in wait for them.' In this he was quite right.

With his own inimitable command of polemic, Lloyd George described as 'a paralytic document' an Admiralty memorandum of November 1916 which stated that no conclusive answer had as yet been found to submarine warfare. 'Perhaps no conclusive answer ever will be found. We must for the present be content with palliation.' In other words, '. . . we do not see how the patient's life can be saved, but we can prolong his agony – perhaps ease it a little!'

Lloyd George accused the admirals of not seeing the dangers of submarine attack and then, when they did see it, crouching nervously before its onset. The menace was '. . . not then visible to the fear-dimmed eyes of our Mall Admirals, who had before the War been thinking of naval warfare in terms of gigantic Trafalgars between super-Dreadnoughts. . . .' The difficulties encountered before the introduction of convoy he described as 'amazing and incomprehensible'.

In the first week after unrestricted submarine warfare had been declared, thirty-five vessels, British and foreign, had been sunk in the English Channel or its western approaches. The effect on the Admiralty, Lloyd George wrote, '. . . was to stun and not to stimulate'. Again he called up an extended medical metaphor:

They were like doctors who, whilst they are unable to arrest the ravages of disease which is gradually weakening the resistance of a patient despite all their efforts, are suddenly confronted with a new, unexpected and grave complication. They go about with gloomy mien and despondent hearts. Their reports are full of despair. It is clear that they think the case is now hopeless. All the same, their only advice is to persist in the application of the same treatment.

241

But what, Lloyd George later asked himself, *should* he and the War Cabinet have done? In a question of life and death, as this most certainly was, it was a serious matter for amateurs to interfere and perhaps recklessly over-ride 'the most famous specialists' (again, that medical flavour). There were no other specialists they could call in. Jellicoe stood higher than anyone else in naval councils; Beatty was '. . . a first rate fighting sailor of the dashing species' but nobody would ever claim that his judgement was better than Jellicoe's. Besides, Jellicoe had only recently been appointed precisely because his predecessors had not been grappling quickly or successfully enough with the submarine menace! Jellicoe would have asked to be given a fair trial. 'I decided,' wrote Lloyd George, 'that it was worth spending some time and patience in winning over Jellicoe to the views held by Mr Bonar Law, the Shipping Controller, Sir Maurice Hankey, and myself. We could not take too long over the process, for our ships were being destroyed at an alarming rate.'

Meanwhile, Lloyd George urged Carson to insist on convoy being tried. Carson himself was in favour of convoy but was reluctant to go against his professional Sea Lords. 'The experts', said Lloyd George, 'were unanimously and stubbornly opposed to the experiment.' Lloyd George had the insight to see that it was as much a matter of personal prestige as of naval tactics; experienced and distinguished sailors had publicly staked their reputations on their belief that '. . . convoying was impracticable and dangerous to convoyers and convoyed alike'.

Lloyd George could not ask Carson, a trained lawyer, to cross-examine Jellicoe at the War Cabinet. Carson might well – probably would – defeat Jellicoe in debate and win the case for convoy. But that might also bring about a resignation of the entire Admiralty Board, which would be a Pyrrhic victory indeed. For his part, Jellicoe was also well aware that his training and his background as a naval officer and particularly his recent experiences as commander-in-chief, accustomed to discussion with subordinates, or to considered judgements on prepared papers, made it extremely difficult for him to counter Lloyd George's rapier repartee in the War Cabinet. There, Jellicoe was like a man just beginning to learn a new language; by the time he had thought of a suitable reply to whatever the others were discussing, they had moved on to something else. All Jellicoe's replies, therefore, seemed stilted, strained and too stuffy to impress anyone. Perhaps Lloyd George also realized this. He asked Jellicoe, Carson and Duff to an informal 'working breakfast' at 10 Downing Street on 13 February 1917. He had previously sent them a memorandum prepared by Sir Maurice Hankey which was an admirable exposé of the arguments for and against the convoy system.

242

Duff and Jellicoe admitted that there was a great deal of truth in Hankey's paper. As a statement of strategic position it was faultless, but as a blueprint on which practical action could be taken it had disadvantages. For a start, and in Jellicoe's view damningly, it did not solve the question of how more escort vessels were to be obtained. The breakfast lasted for two hours and broke up with no commitment from Jellicoe except that he did promise to convene a meeting of merchant ship captains to get their opinions on whether they thought the convoy system practical.

The meeting was held on 23 February and according to Captain Bertram H. Smith RN, who attended, it was '. . . fully representative and included captains of every class of ship from the large passenger liner through to smaller passenger ships, the cargo liner and other intermediate types to the ordinary tramp'. It was, he said '. . . a meeting between professionals of the same service, that is—the sea'. Jellicoe put the case 'dispassionately and impartially', explained what was involved in station-keeping and the apparatus used, and asked the assembled captains for their views. They were '. . . unanimously of the opinion, that, as things were, it could not be done'. Lloyd George was unconvinced; he was surprised at the meeting's outcome and commented on it in particularly scathing terms. The meeting's views – the participants were, Lloyd George believed, all captains of passenger liners – was 'simply the arrogant sense of superiority which induces the uniformed chauffeur of a Rolls Royce to look down on the driver of what is contemptuously stigmatised as a "tin Lizzie"'.

Writing many years later in his book *The Submarine Peril*, published in 1933, Jellicoe said he did not recall this breakfast-time discussion '. . . so that it could not have left much impression on my mind'. But there seems no doubt that Jellicoe did accept the consensus view of convoy for a long time. His choice of phrase in that book definitely reveals that to the end of his life he never lost his belief that convoy was defensive. In 1917 he seems to have been curiously neutral: he did not advocate convoy, but neither did he strenuously argue against it. Beatty strongly approved of convoy, and could not understand why the Admiralty were delaying so long before introducing it. But Jellicoe seemed content to wait on events; he was not the dynamic, visionary leader to lay down a new policy and call on everybody to rally and support him and to make it work. Jellicoe was still too much the product of the old Navy.

Fortunately for the country, events were already moving. It is said that there is nothing so irresistible as an idea whose time had arrived. The time for convoy had certainly arrived.

Chapter 15

Perhaps Lloyd George did overstate his already strong case against the Admiralty. Perhaps in later years he did look back with exaggeration over his own part in forcing the introduction of convoy – this volume of his *War Memoirs* was published in September 1934. But his generally withering language about the Admiralty seems justified after what happened in March 1917, when events took an unexpected turn – unexpected, that is, by the Admiralty.

To anyone who paused to think about it, that figure of five thousand shipping movements, entries and clearances in British ports every week must have seemed inherently unlikely. That seemingly enormous total was achieved because it purposely included all the sailings and repeated calls of small coasters and short-journey traders of 300 tons and upwards who could not conceivably be involved in any system of ocean convoy. But their figures had been included by the Admiralty in a laudable effort to confuse the enemy and make him think his U-boat losses had only a pin-prick effect. The enemy knew the true position; and in the event, only the Admiralty was deceived. The origins of this weekly figure became lost in the bureaucratic Admiralty machine and the Sea Lords were properly hoist with their own propaganda petard.

When the figures were checked from a card index – and they were checked and rechecked many, many times, before it was admitted there could be no mistake, and the Admiralty had made an ass of itself – it was discovered that the proper figure of weekly sailings was actually only about 120, or 140 at the most. This, of course, showed how dangerously complacent the Admiralty had been. Against the weekly figure of five thousand sailings the U-boat losses had indeed seemed like a pin-prick; but against a figure of 120, they suddenly leaped into their true and deadly focus.

The new figure also transformed the position as far as the number of escorts required was concerned. It had been estimated that some seventy destroyers would be needed to implement a full convoy system. Now some twenty or thirty of them could be found at once, and, in April, when America entered the war, more destroyers were supplied from across the Atlantic; in fact by July 1917 thirty-four US destroyers were operating in British waters.

It was no wonder that when Lloyd George heard the amended

figures he began to crow in his usual insufferable manner. 'What an amazing miscalculation!' he cried. 'The blunder on which their policy was based was an arithmetical mix-up which would not have been perpetrated by an ordinary clerk in a shipping office. A moment's reflection would have told them that nothing approaching 2,500 deep-sea vessels could be concluding voyages to this country every week.' Jellicoe must bear his share of blame. He was, after all, First Sea Lord and the professional head of the Navy. A man of his experience and intelligence, the Navy's greatest expert on so many aspects of the sea service, should have known at a glance that the figures presented to him were ridiculous. Furthermore, if he read naval history, as Dreyer claimed he did, he should have known that the case for convoy needed no arguing.

However, like some massive log-jam of prejudice, preconceived notions, ill-founded theories and sheer pigheaded ignorance and obstinacy, the objections to convoy were slowly but irresistibly swept away down a broad flowing river of common sense, historical imperative and, finally, apprehensions of imminent disaster. On 3 April, when the French coal trade coastal convoys were already proving their worth, a conference of naval officers was held at Longhope in the Orkneys to consider whether and how convoys could be introduced between the UK and Scandinavia. The conference unanimously decided that convoys could and should be introduced. Beatty welcomed the suggestion at once. He was a supporter of convoy and had been impatient at the Admiralty's tardiness in introducing it. He thought that the patrolling of what he called 'vast spaces of ocean' was simply not practical: there were not nearly enough ships. Here, Beatty was, so to speak, describing a symptom, not the cause of the malady. At the Admiralty Jellicoe endorsed the Longhope recommendations, and ordered them to be put into effect and progress to be reported every fortnight. He also considered applying convoy to the Atlantic trade but decided it was too risky to take escort vessels from patrolling and other duties, thus causing losses elsewhere.

At this distance of time Jellicoe's true attitude towards convoy is curiously difficult to define. He was doubtful about its efficacy, but he never voiced those doubts strongly enough to suggest that he was a real opponent. But if he was not an opponent, he was not an apostle either: he did almost nothing to push it along, to hasten it into effect, yet he never hindered it. Each recommendation was treated on what Jellicoe thought were its merits. He was conservative by nature and by upbringing; he might have been even more unwilling to act if he suspected that he was being shepherded along by others, especially by junior officers whom he thought too hasty and headstrong. Yet if he thought a course of action was in the Navy's best interests, he never hesitated. It would be as wrong to blame him for delaying convoy – which he did – as to praise him for taking the decision to introduce it – which, again he eventually did.

On 6 April 1917 America entered the war and on the ninth Rear-Admiral William S. Sims, another of Jellicoe's old comrades in arms from his China days, arrived in England to act as liaison officer between the US Navy and the Admiralty. Sims had believed, like everybody else, that the Allies were winning the war. Figures published in newspapers in Britain and in the States were not actually false, but they certainly were misleading. Jellicoe took Sims into his fullest confidence and showed him the true figures with the actual tonnage of ships sunk. Jellicoe clearly wished to impress Sims with the urgent need the country had of more escorts from America. At any rate, he did not mince his words but painted the picture in its deepest black.

Sims was appalled – far from winning the war, the Allies were well on the way to losing it, and by the end of the year at that. The figures Jellicoe showed him were three or four times as bad as those published. According to Sims, Jellicoe said that '. . . it is impossible for us to go on with the war if losses like this continue'. When Sims asked what was being done, Jellicoe told him, '. . . everything that we can'. And when Sims said it looked as though the Germans were winning the war, Jellicoe replied that: 'They will win, unless we can stop these losses – and stop them soon.' 'Is there no solution for the problem?' Sims asked. 'Absolutely none that we can see now,' was Jellicoe's quiet answer. Writing of this meeting many years later, Jellicoe's account was not so emphatically gloomy. He said he gave Sims enough information to realize the danger. When Sims asked about a solution, 'What I did say was that the counter measures being devised could not be immediately successful as time was required for their production. I then urged him to do his utmost to obtain fast small craft from the United States.' Whatever was actually said, Sims took the point fairly enough and conveyed the true situation to Washington. The first six US destroyers arrived in Queenstown in Ireland on 4 May.

Neither Sims' account nor Jellicoe's suggests that Jellicoe ever mentioned convoy as a possible solution. In fact by the time their meeting took place, the beginnings of a change in attitude towards convoy had been seen in the Admiralty. The revised shipping movement figures, the prospect of help from the US Navy, and the formation of a Ministry of Shipping to direct shipping, all meant that at least a start could be made.

On 23 April Lloyd George raised the question of convoy again in the War Cabinet. Jellicoe said it was under consideration: Beatty's trial of convoy on the Scandinavian route had not been wholly successful; two ships in separate convoys had been sunk. Lloyd George complained, and with some justification, that this news and indeed all losses, for some time after convoys were generally introduced, were announced to him with a 'We told you so' expression. 'The fact that the [Norwegian] experiment was not a systematic convoy', Lloyd George wrote, 'was imperfectly organised and was therefore not given a fair chance, was not taken into account. It was not a success and the Admirals "had told us so".'

The critical change in attitude at the Admiralty seems to have taken place during the last week of April 1917. On the twenty-third, Jellicoe submitted a memorandum which did not suggest any change. He still believed in the various anti-submarine measures put in train four months before, and he did not contemplate any major change (for example convoy) in the system of trade defence. But it must have been that evening or the next when Duff came into Jellicoe's room at the Admiralty and said that the shipping losses had convinced him that the general system of convoy simply had to be tried. Jellicoe and Duff agreed that Duff should draw up a minute making this recommendation in detail.

On 25 April the War Cabinet again discussed convoy. Lloyd George said he would visit the Admiralty on the thirtieth to investigate all the means – not just convoy – at present being used in anti-submarine warfare. Although the 'threat' of this pending visit did not have quite the electrically galvanizing effect on the Admiralty which Lloyd George later claimed, it obviously did serve to concentrate minds wonderfully. On 26 April Duff produced his minute. It began: 'It seems to me evident that the time has arrived when we must be ready to introduce a comprehensive scheme of convoy at any moment.' Jellicoe approved it but throughout he seems to have played the part of a man willing to authorize convoy without ever really believing it would do any good. On 25 April he was still writing to Jackson that he thought the convoy system on the east coast (that is, the much-discussed Scandinavian convoys) were going to fail for lack of destroyers. Some day, he said, he hoped to carry out convoy in the Western Approaches and arrangements were being prepared. It was not the comment of a man suddenly ablaze with new-found enthusiasm for a particular course of action. While approving Duff's minute, Jellicoe submitted, on 27 April, a memorandum to Carson which only mentioned convoy incidentally and almost as a postscript.

However, that same day a trial system was authorized for a convoy homeward bound from Gibraltar. It left on 10 May, and although the escort had some difficulty in finding the convoy at first before it entered the danger zone for submarines, the convoy did eventually form up in good order and perfect harmony and arrived safely in Plymouth on 20 May.

As a result, when Lloyd George did arrive at the Admiralty as threatened on 30 April, Jellicoe was able to tell him that a system of convoy was under trial. Lloyd George was pleased to hear it, spent a pleasant day at the Admiralty, lunched with the Jellicoes at Mall House, played with the four girls, and had a generally enjoyable time – even, according to Sir Maurice Hankey, the cabinet secretary, '. . . having a great flirtation with a little girl of three', which must have been Prudy.

Even though the decision to try convoy had been made, the Admiralty did not hurry to put it into effect. While the losses at sea continued, like a colossal national haemorrhage, a committee of naval officers, on which the Ministry of Shipping was represented, was appointed by the Admiralty to hammer out the details for bringing in a complete system of convoy. But it did not meet until 17 May, and did not report until 6 June; Jellicoe approved the report on 11 June and passed it to Carson who approved it on the fifteenth.

Convoy in fact was introduced in stages, at first from Hampton Roads in Virginia to run to the UK at four-day intervals. On 22 June convoy was introduced for ships sailing from Canadian ports, on 6 July for ships sailing from New York, on 20 July from Gibraltar, on 31 July for ships crossing the South Atlantic. On 11 August ships sailing from the UK were convoyed; in October outward shipping in the Mediterranean, and in November inward shipping. It was virtually the end of 1917 before convoys were generally introduced and became the rule for almost every kind of ship on almost every ocean route. Most significantly, by the end of October 1917 ninety-nine homeward convoys, with 1,502 ships, had arrived in the United Kingdom. Only ten ships were torpedoed while actually in convoy, and another fourteen after being separated from their convoys by bad weather or an engine breakdown or some other cause. Statistical work after the war showed that ships were thirty-five times more likely to be torpedoed when steaming independently than when in convoy. Convoy did not, of course, win the war at once, or even by the end of 1917. But it did prevent the war being lost in 1917.

The work of reorganizing the naval staff structure in the Admiralty, the long-running saga of convoy, and all the other multitudinous and multifarious cares and preoccupations of the First Sea Lord's office threw a great strain upon Jellicoe. He was, in a way, his own worst enemy. He had never found it easy to delegate; now he tended to become obsessed with detail, ploughing onwards, ever deeper and deeper, into a seemingly bottomless drift of paper.

People found him 'perky' at the beginning of the year, but he suffered a bout of neuritis and his deafness was getting worse. Fisher found him 'deaf as a post' and 'very seedy but indomitable'. After attending dinner, Jellicoe would go back to his Admiralty office and work on papers into the early hours of the morning. The corridors along which he had stepped so briskly and hopefully before the war now seemed endless. The committee meetings at which he was so good, which he had served so cheerfully, where he had made so many valuable contributions, now seemed unnecessary and interminable.

The War Cabinet meetings he found especially irksome. Once, he actually switched his attention away from the business being transacted and wrote a letter to Admiral Hamilton; no doubt the particular subject under discussion did not concern him or the Navy. Nevertheless it seems incredible that the First Sea Lord, attending the country's most powerful committee meetings, at a time of mortal national danger, could divert himself with private correspondence. He vented much of his frustration over War Cabinet meetings in his letters to Beatty. 'War Councils take up hours of my time . . . overwhelmed with work at present . . . no time at all for exercise . . . War Councils waste half my time. . . .' If Jellicoe had had the sense of humour at that time to see it, he would have realized that his correspondence with Beatty was very similar to his exchanges with Jackson, only now the roles were reversed. It was Jellicoe now who constantly tried to remove cruisers or destroyers from the Grand Fleet and Beatty, playing Jellicoe's old part, who protested most strongly.

On the evidence of their correspondence, to each other and elsewhere, Beatty was very much more understanding than Jellicoe had been in his position. Beatty was always making allowances for the strain he knew Jellicoe must be undergoing. It was as though everybody who knew Jellicoe knew that allowances *must* be made for him, because he was so important to the Navy. Just as it had been vital that he succeed as C-in-C of the Grand Fleet, so now it was essential that he should do well as First Sea Lord. Thus, when Jellicoe wrote in somewhat scratchy and suspicious terms, Beatty returned the soft answer.

Beatty and Jellicoe shared their feelings towards politicians. Jellicoe disliked and distrusted politicians, even when he knew little about them, and he came to like and trust them the less the more he came to know them. As that summer of 1917 wore on, this antipathy began to be returned with interest. Jellicoe's habits of work were noted. His behaviour over convoy suggested to some uncharitable souls that he had either been trying to save the Admiralty's face or was not the supreme expert on naval affairs everybody thought him to be. The affair of the misrepresentation of the weekly sailings was particularly damaging.

That strange law of bureaucratic societies, that no sooner has a man been appointed than forces and influences begin to conspire to unseat him, now began to work against Jellicoe. It was odd that a man who was so successful in the Navy, who had always been so clearly marked for the top, who had always been somebody plainly worth getting to know, who had always been so fully in command of men's hearts in his own profession, should appear so peculiarly friendless in Whitehall, where his very popularity in the Navy seemed to weigh against him.

One important ingredient in Jellicoe's discomfiture was the personality of Lloyd George. Jellicoe had never met anybody like him before – somebody who treated senior naval officers so lightly, even flippantly. Jellicoe was used to respect bordering on reverence, and Lloyd George was disrespectful to the point of irreverence. He was always ready to rush in at times when every naval angel would have feared to tread. He was optimistic when Jellicoe was pessimistic, saying, 'We shall get the best of the submarines, never fear,' when Jellicoe was forecasting inevitable doom, with nothing to be done. Lloyd George was sparkling, ebullient, sanguine, quick-witted, and altogether irritating to the 'High Admirals'. The fact that he was also right – at least so far as convoy was concerned – made him intolerable.

Jellicoe was unaware that he was under a bleak, critical scrutiny from another quarter. Douglas Haig met Jellicoe in December 1916 and liked what he saw of him, '. . . though I should not look upon him as a man of great power or decision of character'. The two met again in Paris in May 1917, but this time Haig was not so impressed. 'Indeed,' he wrote in his diary, 'he strikes me as being an old woman!' Haig also recorded the shattering effect of Jellicoe's pessimism at a conference in June 1917. 'Jellicoe said that owing to the great shortage of shipping due to German submarines, it would be impossible for Great Britain to continue the war in 1918.' According to Haig, Jellicoe's words were, 'There is no good discussing plans for next Spring. We cannot go on.' This, Haig said, '. . . was a bombshell for the Cabinet and all present'.

It was not just a bombshell – such a remark was a very serious tactical error. Jellicoe might despise and distrust politicians, but to some extent the office of First Sea Lord, whether Jellicoe liked it or not, did have a political reference. Lloyd George's suspicions and misgivings about Jellicoe had first been aroused at the turn of the year, and each of Jellicoe's gloomy predictions expended just a little more of his remaining store of political capital.

At that first meeting in Paris on 4 May 1917 Jellicoe met Sir Eric Geddes – a name which was to have uncomfortable reverberations in the memory of the Navy for years after the war. Born in India of an Edinburgh family, Geddes was a brisk, blunt, businesslike Scot in his early forties. Circumstances had made him an expert on railways: as a young man he had worked on the Baltimore and Ohio Railroad, and had later managed a light railway in India. In Britain he rose to a high position in the North Eastern Railway, from whose staff he had raised the 17th Battalion, Royal Northumberland Fusiliers, in 1914. As Deputy Director of Munitions in 1915 he had reorganized the supply of munitions to the Western Front and had won the complete confidence and friendship of Lloyd George; in 1916 he became Director General, and later Inspector General of Transportation, with the honorary rank of major-general on Haig's staff. Beaverbrook gives a thumbnail sketch of Geddes: 'Punctuality was his passion, and routine his practice. . . . His way of life conformed to the teachings of the Shorter Catechism. He was looked on as the strong silent man of real power and influence. In his home a telephone was on a pay-box system.'

Geddes was a born organizer, a 'can-do' merchant, who knew little of politics, less of the Navy, and nothing at all of the old, heroic mode of addressing the 'High Admirals'. But he did know, from his experience on the Western Front, the difficulty of a 'civilian' doing anything which had previously been done by Service officers. When Lloyd George asked him to take charge of all warship- and merchant ship-building as Controller of the Navy, he wanted to be reassured of Jellicoe's support before agreeing. Haig had backed him to the hilt, and Jellicoe would need to do the same. Jellicoe readily agreed and assured Geddes of his help in making the rough places plain in the Admiralty. The offices of Controller and Third Sea Lord were separated, Halsey being promoted to become Third Sea Lord.

Jellicoe welcomed Geddes' arrival – the appointment of someone to relieve him of much detailed work had been one of the matters discussed with Lloyd George on 30 April. 'I expect great increase in rapidity of production from the change,' Jellicoe told Beatty. 'Geddes is a superman, an excellent fellow and has the complete whiphand of L.G.' Beatty took a more cautious view, and was sorry that Jellicoe had to introduce a civilian as Controller, but he was glad he had got '. . . such a good one as Geddes'. Beatty assumed it was essential to go outside the Navy 'to deal with the PM and Politicians'; he sincerely hoped '. . . it would be all right'.

John Jellicoe's First Sea Lordship in that summer and autumn of 1917 was a sad spectacle of a dedicated and gifted personality deteriorating, like a finely wrought machine slowing down, through overwork, weariness, exasperation and poor health. Everything seemed to conspire to irritate him. Lloyd George had discovered that none of the Directors of sections working at the Admiralty under Oliver was responsible for forward planning – reorganization of the staff structure was another of the matters discussed on 30 April. There was nobody at the Admiralty specifically charged with the duty to think ahead, to work out contingencies for various events, and to prepare future offensive operations. This was a fair enough criticism, but

Jellicoe found out that Lloyd George had been influenced by Captain Richmond, one of the Navy's 'Young Turks', who had recommended that Jellicoe be replaced by Wemyss. Jellicoe found the Prime Minister's habit of lending his ear to junior officers particularly offensive and distressing. Jellicoe pointed out quite rightly that there was only one authority responsible for planning future operations and that was himself. He had, he said somewhat tartly, '. . . been considering possible offensives ever since the commencement of war'. Junior officers could be left to work out *details*.

Jellicoe was no intriguer, and was comparatively inexperienced in politics. But even he could not fail to become aware of the swelling tide of criticism that summer, directed against the Board of Admiralty and himself. The Admiralty, it was said, were not offensively minded enough, were not taking the war to the enemy, were waiting upon events rather than initiating them. Sir Edward Carson, much more politically sophisticated than Jellicoe, was well aware of the currents running against them, but supported Jellicoe unswervingly in public and in private. He spoke publicly of his disdain for all their critics: 'Let them grumble and growl,' he said, 'and let us get on with our work.'

That was easier said than done, at least where a man of Jellicoe's temperament was concerned. He did feel criticism, but for a man of his temperament such defiant public chest-beating was out of the question, even if the proprieties of the Service had allowed it. The complaints had a most unfortunate effect on Jellicoe: already conscientious, he became even more painstaking; already pessimistic, he ceased even to have occasional periods of lightness among the gloom. Criticism made him work harder, put him under even greater strain, and so made him less efficient and subject to even more criticism. The strains showed on him physically. His attention wandered at meetings, and even his handwriting was much less legible; he had another bout of neuritis and his deafness irritated him more than ever. To his family he still seemed the cheerful and loving father, and nobody would have guessed from his manner with his children that he had a care in the world. He, Gwendoline and the children lived 'above the shop' in Mall House, which was to all intents and purposes part of the Admiralty, so he never really got sufficiently distant from his work. Beatty offered the use of his tennis court at his London house, but Jellicoe rarely had a chance to get to it. Jellicoe's work fell off, by his own high standards, and in August 1917 one of his papers was so lacking in direction and conclusions, so prosily diffuse and confusedly set out, that Geddes wrote on it: 'Better not use this argument.'

Geddes by that time was First Lord of the Admiralty, having taken over from Carson in a cabinet reshuffle which brought Churchill once more back into the government as Minister of Munitions. Churchill lost no time in putting forward his old suggestion for assaults on Heligoland, Borkum and Sylt; Jellicoe blew the dust off his old objections and once again squashed the proposals. Jellicoe was becoming a prickly member of committees, brusquely brushing aside the suggestions of others while himself constantly harping on the gloomy side of naval history.

That paper, on which Geddes had commented so disparagingly, was on the naval air service. This was arguably the failure which had the most important long-term effect on the Navy of anything which happened in Jellicoe's term of office. Jellicoe had an enlightened view, for his time, of aircraft; he was one of the first to see the possibilities for scouting and reconnaissance, although he was much slower to grasp that they could be a potent striking weapon in their own right. The view that aircraft were mere adjuncts to the main fleet, useful to sight and then if possible to slow down the enemy until the guns of the battle fleet could be brought to bear, persisted in the Admiralty until well after the Second World War.

The Navy realized that it was vital to have control of the Naval Air Arm, but the case was not put forcefully or persuasively enough. Geddes defended his brief as well as he could and fought the Admiralty's corner to the best of his ability. But criticism of the Admiralty's lack of aggression, criticism of Jellicoe himself, a general drop in the prestige of the Navy, the long struggle over the introduction of convoy, when anybody who had any knowledge at all of events in Whitehall knew that the Admiralty had not appeared in the best of lights, all turned opinion against Geddes. In short the Navy failed to convince the War Cabinet, and the RAF was eventually set up as a separate entity, with control over Naval Air. Many of the brightest and best 'airborne' naval officers changed over to the new branch and were lost to the Navy. This, compounded by the remaining senior naval officers' inborn mistrust of air matters, contributed to the ignorance, prejudice and parsimony over men, money and aircraft which were all to bedevil the Fleet Air Arm between the wars.

The movement against Jellicoe gathered momentum all that summer, which was a summer only in name — the wettest, coldest and most miserable one anybody could remember. Spring came late, summer went early, the autumn rains began before time and fell seemingly interminably, especially in Flanders. It could well have been that the War Cabinet meeting of 20 June, at which Jellicoe burst his pessimistic 'bombshell' on all present, finally made up Lloyd George's mind against him. Jellicoe urged that the submarine bases at Ostend and Zeebrugge should be captured through a big offensive in Flanders. Lloyd George asked whether naval bombardments could not do the job as well. Jellicoe replied categorically that they could not. All unwittingly, Jellicoe thus played his part in prolonging the British offensives of the autumn and winter of 1917. The hope of ultimately capturing the Flanders U-boat bases was always there, at the back of the staffs' mind, a chimera like the Holy Grail, while whole armies were being swallowed up in the mud of Passchendaele.

After the meeting Haig called on Geddes at the Admiralty and found him, so Haig said later '. . . most anxious about the state of affairs'. Geddes said that Carson was very tired of it all and left everything to his Sea Lords, of whom only Halsey was up to his job. Jellicoe, it was said, was '. . . feeble to a degree and vacillating'.

Jellicoe knew that he had '. . . got himself much disliked by the Prime Minister', as he wrote to Beatty on 30 June. 'I fancy there is a scheme on foot to get rid of me.' He could already see the way the attack would develop. They '. . . say I am too pessimistic.' He expected it to be done '. . . by first discrediting me in the Press'. Jellicoe said that putting aside his duty to the country, he would be delighted to go '. . . and have done with all politicians, but if I am of use here in the opinion of the Navy I certainly should not volunteer to go. I am not conceited, nor ambitious in the least, but I believe I am of use here.' Beatty tried to reassure him and told him not to permit himself '. . . to be worried by what the intriguers set themselves to do'. He must not volunteer to go: 'That would be fatal.'

Jellicoe was all too correct about moves to unseat him. The wheels had already begun to turn. On 25 June Haig saw Lord Curzon and Lloyd George after a cabinet meeting and discussed the 'seriously inefficient state of the Admiralty'. Lloyd George asked Haig and Geddes to one of his working breakfasts the next morning, where again the Admiralty was discussed and again Geddes gave his view of the Sea Lords. This confirmed Lloyd George's suspicions and beliefs; he 'seemed much impressed' and decided that something must be done at once.

Lloyd George also consulted Lord Milner, who recommended that Geddes be made First Lord, and Carson given a seat in the War Cabinet. Milner suggested that the qualities of administration needed at the Admiralty could be imported from outside. Sir Joseph Maclay, the Controller of Shipping, still struggling with the convoy problem and still worried by the Admiralty's dilatoriness in coming to grips with the problem, told Lloyd George that he was '. . . led to believe that confidence in the Admiralty had pretty well gone'.

It is difficult at this distance of time to see whether Lloyd George was allowing himself to be persuaded, or himself subtly orchestrating a great swelling chorus of dissatisfaction with the Admiralty. In July he went to Rosyth to visit the fleet and, in his own inimitable way, sounded out various officers. The wildest rumours flew about, that

Jellicoe was about to be replaced, by somebody, nobody knew who. Beresford later got to hear of some of the rumours and wrote to Jellicoe that he was '. . . afraid there will be a frantic effort to get rid of you owing to the mischievous agitation by political intrigues'. Beresford had heard the suggestion put about that '. . . a former First Sea Lord of German birth would accept the position'.

On 5 July Lloyd George saw Lord Stamfordham, the King's secretary, and told him he was thinking of replacing Carson with Geddes, and perhaps also getting rid of Jellicoe, who was so pessimistic and '. . . apt to get cold feet if things did not go right'. Thus, only thirteen months after he stood on *Iron Duke*'s bridge, deciding which way to deploy the Grand Fleet, and making the right choice, Jellicoe was now being accused of 'cold feet'. On 17 July Lloyd George 'kicked Carson upstairs' and appointed Geddes First Lord. But he dared not, or at any rate he did not, get rid of Jellicoe at the same time. Perhaps he felt Jellicoe was still needed for a little longer; or perhaps he baulked at the storm of outraged opposition he thought might greet such a decision. Geddes had a hard enough task as it was without saddling him with a hostile Board of Admiralty.

It was not long, though, before relations between Geddes and Jellicoe deteriorated. Geddes had been appointed to relieve Jellicoe of some of his workload, but in practice he increased it. Jellicoe took it upon himself to deal with all the problems of settling in new personnel, and overseeing the very large increases in administrative staff, many of whom were civilians who had little experience of the Admiralty or the Navy. Furthermore, Jellicoe began to find Geddes' manner towards him and the other Sea Lords more and more objectionable. Geddes was used to giving orders and having them obeyed, but his methods were not always appropriate. Jellicoe had to point out to him that the organization he had set up as Controller was not producing any more ships, in fact was producing less, than before he arrived. One of the main reasons was that the ship-builders disliked the new organization and could not get on as well with the new men as they had with the old. The armament firms also complained that the new arrangements with the Controller's department delayed matters and were not nearly as satisfactory as the old system, in which they had dealt directly with the Director of Naval Ordnance.

Geddes had begun cautiously in his new office, but as his confidence increased he intervened more directly in the conduct of naval affairs. On 17 November there was a cruiser and destroyer action in the Heligoland Bight which was inconclusive and disappointing. The senior officer, Rear-Admiral Napier, was called upon to explain his actions. Geddes decided that Napier was at fault and that Beatty was protecting him; Jellicoe reminded Geddes that he must wait for

Napier's explanation, which in the event Their Lordships accepted.

The Sea Lords spoke a language incomprehensible to Geddes. In December, when a convoy to Norway was attacked and destroyed in circumstances which appeared unsatisfactory, Geddes leaped to appoint a court of inquiry and nominated its members himself. Jellicoe, who was in bed with a cold, tried to prevent Geddes from misbehaving. But Geddes inexcusably altered the text of a telegram from Jellicoe to Beatty and dispatched it, with another offensive message from himself. When Jellicoe next visited Scapa he had to pacify an insulted Beatty who was fuming with rage; when he returned to the Admiralty Jellicoe told Geddes outright that both messages had been insulting. Geddes, according to Jellicoe, '. . . did not like my frankness'.

Geddes was quite clearly aware of the currents which were running against Jellicoe and did not behave towards him as though he expected to have to work with him for long. He continued to treat Jellicoe and the other Sea Lords as though they were agency staff, hired by the week. When Jellicoe recommended Duff for a KCB in the New Year's Honours, Geddes objected to it because of Duff's manner. Jellicoe had to tell Geddes pointedly that Duff was being commended for his services at sea, not his manner. 'Geddes then said that he did not like his manner to him or the wording of some of his minutes. I then said that I feared he did not realise that the Sea Lords were his colleagues and not his subordinates. . . .'

Although Lloyd George had jibbed at a direct assault on Jellicoe, there were still certain preliminary moves which could be made. There was never anything as definite as a plot to get rid of Jellicoe. Rather, there were just certain contingency moves, a prudent rearrangement of certain personalities. A change of Second Sea Lord was suggested: Burney was Jellicoe's man, through and through. Never a startling performer, Burney had slowed up still further, and his health was intermittently poor. The man chosen to replace him was Admiral Sir Rosslyn Wemyss, who had been just about to take over as C-in-C Mediterranean.

For Lloyd George, Wemyss '. . . although a good sailor, was not a man of outstanding ability'. But he had two qualities which appealed to the Prime Minister, and to Geddes. He was not a 'factionist', in other words '. . . he was neither a Jellicoeite nor a Beattyite'. Secondly, he was '. . . willing to listen to young officers with ideas. He never stared them out of his room.' The implication in Lloyd George's account was that Jellicoe *did* stare junior officers out of his room. A coolness between Jellicoe and Beatty is hardly noticeable in their own exchanges with each other, but it did exist. Undoubtedly Geddes did notice it, and it made his own job harder. Geddes had promised to tell the Prime Minister '. . . without delay if he found that he could not work with or through him [Jellicoe]'. That time was not yet – not quite – but Geddes did think it time to appoint a Deputy First Lord, which was Wemyss. As Wemyss had already been suggested as a successor for Jellicoe, a move for him nearer the fount of power in the Navy suited Lloyd George. But the appointment did not take place without some restructuring of the staff. Wemyss was originally to have been Second Sea Lord, with modified responsibilities, so that he also undertook staff duties. If the First Sea Lord was absent for any reason, the conduct of the war at sea immediately fell upon the Second Sea Lord, who already had enough to do, without also having to keep up to date on naval staff business. Wemyss therefore suggested that it would be better to leave the office of Second Sea Lord as it was, and instead appoint himself in effect Deputy First Sea Lord, with an officer junior to him as Second Sea Lord. This was done: Admiral Heath became Second Sea Lord and Burney went as Flag Officer Rosyth.

Wemyss went to the Admiralty in September 1917 and was at once, he said, quite taken aback by the air of fatalistic gloom which seemed to pervade the whole place under Jellicoe. Rosslyn Wemyss, known to everybody from the King downwards as 'Rosy', could not, of course, have been a greater contrast to Jellicoe in temperament and in outlook. He did not have a great intellect, nor would he have claimed it, nor was he an outstanding naval reformer. But he was a very good organizer, he could get along with people, including Geddes, and he was able to delegate. He was sociable, optimistic, and for a naval officer had an unusually wide acquaintance with society. He was one of King George V's greatest friends; he had been commander of the *Ophir* on the royal visit to the Colonies in 1901. He had served under Beresford, without ever involving himself in the great feud with Fisher – in fact he had strongly deplored it for the disruptive effect it had on the Service. He mistrusted Fisher's methods and personality, although he respected Jellicoe, who was Fisher's protégé.

Wemyss' appointment was intended to give support to Geddes, and to lighten Jellicoe's workload. But once again the attempt to help Jellicoe failed with Wemyss just as it had with Geddes. Jellicoe, as Wemyss himself described it, '. . . could never be brought to see the utility of it. My presence, I am afraid, in no way helped to lessen the burden on his shoulders, simply because he refused to delegate to me any responsibility.'

In December a frustrated Wemyss tackled Jellicoe about the matter. He told Jellicoe he was afraid he was not of as much assistance to him as he had hoped to be: Wemyss pointed out that Jellicoe was not letting him do anything, except give an extra and unnecessary opinion on dockets. Wemyss was in fact the spare wheel on the coach and, naturally, he did not like it. He asked Jellicoe directly, whether he trusted him or not. Jellicoe said that he did trust Wemyss but he could not let Wemyss take over any of the First Sea Lord's responsibilities because it '. . . would not be legal'. Wemyss then said it *would* be legal if the First Sea Lord said so. Jellicoe did not agree and the matter was dropped, leaving Wemyss wondering whether or not he should resign. He hesitated to do that, so soon after being appointed, because he knew the Admiralty was under constant and fierce press criticism and his own resignation would only give the critics more ammunition.

Soon after this meeting, events took a turn which made up Wemyss' mind that he should resign. It seems he never meant to make the affair a resigning issue, but events forced his hand. It happened over Admiral Sir Reginald Bacon, Jellicoe's eventual biographer, but at that time Flag Officer Dover. Wemyss and Roger Keyes, with whom he had served in the Dardanelles and whom he had brought to the Admiralty as Director of Plans Division, had studied the pattern of U-boat movements and sinkings in the English Channel. Both agreed that Bacon, whom Wemyss described as '. . . an extraordinarily clever man of an inventive turn', was spending too much time studying the military situation in France and not enough in stopping U-boats passing through the Straits of Dover.

Intelligence evidence tended to confirm Wemyss' opinion: U-boats were passsing to and fro successfully. Bacon replied that they were not, that his nets and barriers were fully effective, and to prove his case he pointed out that no ship had been torpedoed in his immediate area. Wemyss replied that no sensible U-boat captain would stir up trouble for himself and others in an area which he wished to pass through unmolested when there were easier, fatter, more numerous targets waiting in the Western Approaches. This certainly seemed the correct interpretation. But Bacon thought this contention was, in his word, 'puerile'. Wemyss made up his mind that U-boats ought to be sunk, and since Bacon was not sinking them someone else should be appointed who would sink them. Jellicoe felt that Bacon was the best man for the job and should stay, but Wemyss insisted he should go. The final discussion took place in Geddes' room and Wemyss came away from it feeling '. . . that matters could not go on in this manner'. Wemyss felt sorry for Geddes, who had been in the disagreeable position of finding his two 'principal technical advisers' in direct opposition to each other on a matter which was essentially Jellicoe's final responsibility but on which Wemyss knew Geddes agreed with him. Jellicoe could and should have been more tactful. But Nemesis for him was very near. He had often said he wished to have nothing more to do with politicians, and that wish was about to be granted in the most painful and humiliating manner possible.

Wemyss now decided he must resign and considered how best to do it, tactfully and discreetly, causing the minimum amount of damage to the Admiralty. He and his wife were having dinner at their house in Cumberland Place on 22 December when there was a message from Geddes asking Wemyss to go and see him after dinner. When Wemyss arrived, Geddes told him he had made up his mind to get rid of Jellicoe – possibly that interview about Bacon had been the last straw. Geddes asked if Wemyss was prepared to take Jellicoe's place; Wemyss did not wish to do so and doubted whether he could handle the enormous problems facing a First Sea Lord. But he thought the last three years had given him a good deal of self-confidence and he thought he would bring a 'wider outlook' to the job than before. Wemyss '. . . told him what points I considered were in favour of accepting and what I considered were my disabilities'; Geddes said he had been studying Wemyss for the last three months and thought he was the best man for the job. At this, Wemyss accepted.

Jellicoe was looking forward to Christmas with his family. Mall House was already decorated, there were carol singers in Trafalgar Square, walks in the cold air in St James's Park, strings of lights along the Mall. It would be Christmas in a winter city for the four little girls. Gwendoline was then fourteen, Prudy four – all the perfect age for a family Christmas; Lady Jellicoe was then five months pregnant. Christmas at home would bring relief from the cares of office, and for one day at least the war would recede.

At 6 p.m. on Christmas Eve a special messenger arrived with a blue envelope – what the girls always called afterwards the 'blue letter' – marked 'Personal and strictly private'. Geddes had made up his mind; he himself had wanted to go back to his railways but at a cabinet meeting that day it had been decided that he should stay at the Admiralty. Probably no single person, neither Geddes, nor Lloyd George, nor the continued press campaign of Lord Northcliffe's, was responsible for what was to happen. It was just that the time had come. Geddes wrote:

My Dear Sir John Jellicoe,
    After very careful consideration I have come to the conclusion that a change is desirable in the post of First Sea Lord . . . I have consulted the Prime Minister and with his concurrence I am asking to see the King to make this recommendation to him.

Jellicoe showed this letter to Oliver and to Halsey but made them promise not to say anything of its contents. There was then a flurry of letter-writing. Jellicoe wrote to Geddes: 'You do not assign a reason for your action, but I assume that it is due to a want of confidence in me.' Geddes replied, welcoming Jellicoe's suggestion that he should go on leave. On Christmas Day Geddes went to see the King at Sandringham and wrote to Jellicoe again, offering him a peerage. Jellicoe wrote to Beatty and to the King on Christmas Day, and replied to Geddes on Boxing Day, 'I shall feel it an honour to accept the mark of approval of my services.' He then left the Admiralty forthwith.

Chapter 16

Thus Admiral Sir John Jellicoe, who had served the Royal Navy man and boy for forty-five years and reached the pinnacle of his profession, was acknowledged one of the foremost naval experts of his day, and who commanded the respect, admiration and affection of all ranks and ratings in the Navy, was dismissed from his office on Christmas Eve by an ex-railway manager who had been in the Admiralty since the previous summer – barely half a dog-watch, as the Service saying had it. It was lucky for Geddes there were no newspapers on Christmas Day or Boxing Day. He must certainly have welcomed the respite, although it is most unlikely that he planned it. It is much more likely that the cabinet meeting of 24 December, at which it was decided that Geddes would stay as First Lord; the emotional aftermath of the argument with Wemyss over Bacon; and the slow accumulation of feelings over the previous months, all combined to give the event a momentum of its own which made it come to pass on Christmas Eve.

Stunned and upset though he was, Jellicoe still preserved an almost quaint sense of decorum. He observed the impertinent injuction 'Personal and strictly private' on the envelope, although it had no official sanction whatsoever. (But perhaps a plain envelope without any such cautionary franking might have been even more offensive.) Jellicoe could have roused a furore, summoned the Sea Lords to his assistance, and threatened a damaging dispute which would topple the government. But that was not John Jellicoe's way, and Geddes knew it was not. He accepted the dismissal almost without any demur or consultation, but he did go to see Oliver who, remarkably, was still in his office in the Admiralty at 8 p.m. on Christmas Eve. Oliver had always kept his enthusiasm for Geddes' style of management under tight control: 'We have been upside down here,' he used to say, 'ever since the North-Eastern Railway took over . . . Geddes is mad about statistics and has forty people always making graphs and issuing balance sheets full of percentages. . . . It may be well enough in a Life Assurance business or a railway. . . .' Oliver was appalled and disgusted. It seemed to him extraordinary that Jellicoe should go; if anybody should go, it should have been Geddes. Oliver would have liked to have taken some action but Jellicoe asked him to promise not to tell anyone of the letter's contents. 'I was very unhappy,' Oliver said, 'but could do nothing in view of my promise.'

According to Wemyss, Geddes hated to dismiss Jellicoe, '. . . and did it in a manner which, sudden though it was, he considered the best for him and for all others concerned'. Rosy is too kind. It was a tactless and downright offensive way of dismissing a man who had given such service to the State. Of course, Geddes sincerely believed that Jellicoe was no longer fit for the duty and was no longer the right man for the job, and almost certainly he was right. He very probably did Jellicoe a kindness in the long run, to relieve him of a burden that was crushing him. But it is also quite clear that Geddes screwed himself up to the pitch of dismissing Jellicoe, wrote his mean little letter and sent it round on Christmas Eve before his resolution failed him. After that, well, it *was* Christmas Eve, two days before any newspapers could be published and there could be any public debate or comment.

By dismissing Jellicoe in this manner Geddes united the Board of Admiralty against himself. Ironically he brought about the very situation, of having a unitedly hostile Board, which Lloyd George had tried to avoid for him by not getting rid of Jellicoe earlier. For a time it seemed that the whole Board might resign. A mass resignation, a sort of *Götterdämmerung* of the High Admirals, would have been an attractively dramatic spectacle, but in retrospect it seems that it was never a real probability. Resignation was something a man could think about, something to tell his grandchildren ('I *thought* of resigning. . . . I *wanted* to resign. . . . We *all* wanted to resign . . . but. . . .') But resignation would not have brought Jellicoe back, and in fact he typically and strongly discouraged it, for the good of the Service. The Sea Lords were in any case easily outmanoeuvred by the fast footwork of Geddes, showing the uncommon degree of political agility he had acquired in his short time in Whitehall.

Jellicoe had also showed Geddes' letter to Halsey on Christmas Eve, but asked him to keep the contents to himself. He told Halsey that in the circumstances he could not stay at the Admiralty a moment longer and thought he should go on leave at once. Halsey agreed. On Christmas morning Halsey asked if he might consult the other Sea Lords about their possible courses of action. By that time things had changed. Wemyss, the new First Sea Lord, had given it out that Jellicoe was going on leave and there were rumours flying about that there had been some sort of upheaval in the Admiralty. Jellicoe gave his permission and advised Halsey that the Sea Lords should not resign, as '. . . it would do no good and be bad for the country'.

That evening Heath, Halsey, Duff, Oliver, Tothill (Fourth) and Commodore Paine (Fifth), conferred in Duff's room at the Admiralty and then went in a body to see Wemyss, who shuffled them off to

Geddes who disputed their right to ask him for an explanation of his reasons for dismissing Jellicoe. However, Geddes told Heath he was prepared to tell him 'as man to man' what he was not prepared to tell him as First Lord. The chief explanation, as the admirals understood it, was that the decision was not Geddes' alone. He, Balfour and Carson had had a meeting some time previously with the Prime Minister, at which Balfour and Carson had both declared they did not think Jellicoe the best man to be First Sea Lord.

In the next few days, the Sea Lords tried hard to ascertain the facts of the situation and to decide what their common course of action should be. They failed in both objects and were, in the military phrase, defeated in detail. Geddes agreed to tell the Sea Lords, two at a time, what he had told Heath. He told Halsey and Tothill and then left for Rosyth with Wemyss. Although they were matters of great seriousness at the time, and extremely humiliating for Jellicoe, the Sea Lords' dealings with the First Lord in the next few weeks now have a faintly comic air. While Geddes and Wemyss were away, the admirals met twice, without actually deciding anything. Duff pointed out to them that if Carson and Balfour had, as Geddes said, agreed that Jellicoe was not the best man for the job, that should be that. But when Geddes came back two days later, Duff offered his resignation. Carson meanwhile strenuously denied that he had ever said what Geddes said he had said. Duff did not resign. He was present at a meeting of the admirals at which Oliver drafted a memo, addressed to Geddes, and sent to him next day. In it the Sea Lords threatened that they would all resign unless Geddes could explain how it was that Carson had a different recollection of events.

But with every day that passed the admirals' revolt weakened. People advised them to drop their protest for the good of the country. Geddes said he was amazed at their presumption in interfering with matters that were not their concern. Heath, who should have taken the lead, allowed himself to be first wheedled and then bullied by Geddes. The admirals began to feel that the battleground had been moved without their knowledge from the specific to the general. Their objection was that it had been wrong to dismiss Jellicoe; now they found themselves arguing on whether they had any right to interfere with the dismissal of a First Sea Lord at all. Balfour, who had been ill, was pulled into the argument. He was non-committal. He could not say exactly what had been said. But he did remind Geddes in a most pointed manner that an admission of recalling a certain meeting did not necessarily mean that he approved of a decision taken at that meeting. After more discussions the admirals capitulated. They hastened to make it clear they had never had any intention of misrepresenting what Carson had said. Geddes said he could see there had been an honest misunderstanding and he thought the whole incident was closed.

That was enough for the admirals, but it was not enough for Carson, who carried on a furious exchange of correspondence with Geddes for some time. Geddes did eventually contradict himself when he claimed that Lloyd George had never influenced him and he had made up his mind entirely on his own. If that were so, how could he have argued in mitigation that he had had the agreement of Carson and Lloyd George?

Whatever the feelings of the politicians, the Navy as a whole had no doubts that Jellicoe's dismissal was a disaster. Jellicoe had sent telegrams to the various C-in-Cs telling them that he was relinquishing his post as First Sea Lord, and adding the significant coda: 'For your personal information, I need not assure you that the change is not of my seeking.' He also wrote personally to his friends, who hurried to reply with their own professional *nunc dimittis*. 'I can certainly assure you', the King wrote, 'that you have not failed in your duty and I know that history will agree with me.' Admiral Sir Stanley Colville, Jellicoe's old friend, wrote: 'I knew these damned politicans would do it sooner or later – words fail me old chap to say how disgracefully you have been treated and not even given reasons by 1st Lord in his letter!' Beatty was even more sarcastic: 'The manner of your dismissal was apparently in keeping with the usual way they have at the Admiralty of dispensing with the services of officers who have given their whole lives to the service of the country.' 'God help us!' wrote Burney from Rosyth. 'I think you ought to make it publicly known that the statement made by the Admiralty in the Press is entirely untrue.' Carson thought Jellicoe's departure '. . . little less than a national loss'. Prince Battenberg could '. . . not find words to express my disgust and indignation'. Walter Runciman, President of the Board of Trade, said it was '. . . enough to sadden any Christmas'.

The general opinion of the lower deck was well put in a naval signal from the 10th Submarine Flotilla to Jellicoe, 'c/o GPO'.

We heard with regret of your retirement and would wish to know what was the cause, you know of course that we have implicit trust in you and please do not take it lying down. We want you back. Don't take any notice of armchair critics, what do they know of our wants and desires? Sir, you might ask for a naval election, they can do it in France, why not in the Fleet? You are our Idol and one who we would follow to Death you have shown us the way to possess ourselves in patience you have always been one with us in our sports and you are the Man we want. Don't and we don't think you will let our country our Sacred Island home be led to ruin by a lot of irresponsible Naval Retired Officers who do not know what they are talking about. Come Back is the message from the Lower Deck to you. You quite understand how we are situated and you know that we would not Mutiny because love of England home and beauty comes first. But speak my Lord let us hear your voice in the Grand Fleet for we wish to hear it and when as we hope you will soon be back our Lord and Master then and only then shall we be satisfied.

Some officers took their protest further than the mere writing of letters. Rear Admiral Dudley de Chair, flying his flag in command of the 3rd Battle Squadron in *Dreadnought*, wrote to Jellicoe from Sheerness, and Jellicoe's reply summed up the whole affair and his own feelings:

I should like you to know that I did not resign but was *dismissed* very curtly by the 1st Lord without any reason at all being given. He did not even tell me personally, but wrote me a note. I have had trouble with him, as he wishes to be an autocrat, after the Winstonian lines, and I refused to accept such an attitude. He had treated various Flag Officers badly and I took exception to that. The result you see!!!

De Chair was invited to the Admiralty, where Wemyss began to discuss possible vacancies and invited de Chair to join the Board. De Chair told him: 'I would not and could not take any post at the Admiralty, as I felt so keenly the disgraceful manner in which Jellicoe had been treated. I added that I was surprised that any naval officer on the Board of Admiralty could remain there, as it looked as if they condoned this act of Jellicoe's dismissal.' De Chair 'let himself go', but this 'scene' as he called it, '. . . did no good and had disastrous results'. Shortly afterwards he was relieved of his command and put on half-pay.

Madden had also written to Jellicoe: 'Just received your letter and I am more than ever astounded at not only your dismissal but the manner of it, and I hope you will refuse the Peerage. It is bound to come in time and please don't receive it at Geddes' hand – bad for the Service to feel its most trusted man can be turned out at a moment's notice and squared by a peerage. . . .' But Jellicoe felt that, on the contrary, a peerage would be good for the Service, which did not get all that many honours. He accepted and became Viscount Jellicoe of Scapa on 15 January 1918.

Jellicoe remained as popular as ever in the country at large. At the very time he was dismissed music-hall artistes were singing 'Hats Off to the Stoker' with the refrain:

I'm a stoker
I'm the joker
Who works with a shovel and poker;
The heat and the smell
Is just like – well
No wonder I'm a horrible soaker.
But the Fleet's afloat
And I run the boat
Believe me I'm no croaker,
Ask Jellicoe
He'll say 'What ho!
Hats off to the stoker!!'

So, while his name resounded from the boards, Jellicoe himself was unemployed. He need never again complain of the hours 'wasted' at War Cabinet meetings; the war and the War Cabinet would grind on without him. He need no longer spend his evenings and the early hours of the morning working on papers; he could spend all evening, every evening, with his feet up in front of the fire. The dispatches, the urgent correspondence from all over the globe, bothered him no more. Instead of drafting signals, he could write his memoirs. Jellicoe's idleness evidently reproached Geddes, who seemed to have Jellicoe on his conscience. As the reverberations over Jellicoe's dismissal rumbled on, Geddes may have come to realize that some form of reconciliation was needed, and the best and surest way was to make some use of Jellicoe's great talents and experience. But every move Geddes made was bedevilled by his tactlessness and basic ignorance of how the Navy behaved.

In March 1918 Geddes conceived the idea that Jellicoe should relieve Admiral Sir Alexander Bethell as C-in-C Devonport. Matters were put in train until Jellicoe discovered that Bethell had only served eighteen months in the appointment instead of the customary three years and had not been consulted. There was the strong suspicion that Bethell was being shunted aside into premature retirement to make room for Jellicoe. Bethell himself told Jellicoe that at his age a few more months more or less meant nothing. But premature retirement suggested he might have been incompetent. Bethell would not mind giving up his post for Jellicoe – that would be an honour and nobody could possibly cavil at that. But to give it up for some *other* admiral (Bethell specifically mentioned Bradford) would mean that people would say Bethell could not have been a success in the appointment.

Jellicoe therefore refused the appointment and gave his reasons to Geddes, whose stiff and curt replies show how far apart, temperamentally, the two men still were. Geddes said that he was surprised at the reason Jellicoe gave, and thought Jellicoe had been misinformed. Finally he wrote: 'I have to thank you [Jellicoe] for your letter of the 13th April and note that you do not wish to pursue the matter further.'

On 4 April 1918 Gwendoline gave birth to the long-awaited, joyously received son, christened George Patrick John Rushworth Jellicoe. The christening was performed by Dr Cosmo Lang, the Archbishop of Canterbury, who travelled to the Isle of Wight at the Jellicoes' invitation. He was accompanied by Sir George Callaghan, representing all the admirals whose flags had flown during Jellicoe's command. They had all subscribed to a gold christening cup, which Sir George had insisted he should have the privilege of presenting.

After dinner that evening, Jellicoe said he wanted to show Sir George some papers he had kept which would prove that he had done everything possible to avoid '. . . what he always regarded as the most painful act of his life'. The Archbishop offered to withdraw from what was obviously a very personal and delicate scene:

Jellicoe said he wished me to be present. Accordingly, after dinner we went into his room, then he said with some embarrassment – I think I have a fairly accurate memory of the conversation – 'Look here, old chap, I have long waited to have a chance of showing you some papers to prove that I did everything I could to avoid that painful episode which neither of us can forget. Here they are.' Callaghan at once replied, 'Damn your papers, me dear fellow, I don't want to see them. I have never had any doubt about it.' That was all.

The next suggestion, in May, was that Jellicoe should be Naval Allied C-in-C in the Mediterranean, a sort of admiralissimo in charge of British, French, Italian and Japanese forces. Gwendoline was seriously ill after the birth of her son, and Jellicoe did not want to leave her for at least a month. By that time the matter had settled itself. The French were agreeable to Jellicoe's appointment but the Italians objected, apparently on the grounds that Jellicoe would have the authority to send their ships to sea.

In June Geddes tried again. He wanted Jellicoe to represent the Admiralty on Churchill's committee to consider the reorganization of the Royal Ordnance Factories. This seemed a small-bore task for someone of Jellicoe's calibre but he did consider it, although Geddes with his own brand of ineffable tactlessness wrote that Jellicoe perhaps had not 'fully understood the position' when it was first broached to him. Jellicoe replied that the work '. . . has no real connection with the war and it seems that it may last for some time'. He was anxious to reserve himself for work connected with the war if his services should ever be needed, but the Armistice came before he could contribute anything more.

In one of their famous occasional bouts of callousness towards personal feelings, the Admiralty did not invite, or forgot to invite, Jellicoe to witness the surrender of the German High Seas Fleet on 21 November. He wondered whether to go up north anyway but decided not, fearing that his presence would detract from Beatty's position. So he stayed at home although, as Burney wrote from Rosyth, 'the whole of the work of the Grand Fleet was done and organised by you . . . I was of course very disappointed you did not come up, but I must say I think you were right. . . . There is no honour or justice in the Admiralty. . . .'

In his months of unemployment Jellicoe occupied himself by writing his memoirs, or at least part of them; *The Grand Fleet 1914–1916: Its Creation, Development and Work*, Jellicoe's own account of his stewardship as C-in-C, appeared on 12 February 1919. It was widely, and often hostilely, reviewed, in *The Times*, *Daily News*, *Morning Advertiser*, *Daily Telegraph*, *Morning Post*, *Daily Mirror*, *Daily Graphic*, and *Glasgow Herald*. Generally the press took the view that it was somewhat meretricious of Jellicoe to be as critical as he was of the Navy's state in 1914, when he himself had been one of the very few men in a position to remedy matters. Jellicoe himself, as a pre-war Sea Lord, must bear part of the responsibility for the Fleet's unpreparedness at the outbreak of war.

The *Pall Mall Gazette* headline was 'An Indictment of the Admiralty'; the *Evening Standard* had 'Astonishing Disclosure of Naval Unpreparedness'. Arthur Pollen wrote in the *Weekly Dispatch*, 'If ever a case is made against Lord Jellicoe, it will be Lord Jellicoe himself who proves it.' However, Pollen went on to demonstrate that he had completely misunderstood much of the deployment at Jutland, treating the deployment on the port wing as though it were two *separate* deployments, '. . . the first having failed, and the fleet then deployed again parallel to the German Fleet'. Thus he wrote, '. . . the Grand Fleet was taken out of action altogether'.

The *Daily Mail*'s headline was 'Jellicoe's Strange Disclosures', and under it H.W. Wilson commented upon Beatty's signal asking for the battle fleet to follow his battle cruisers. This Wilson paraphrased as: 'If you follow me sir we can annihilate them.' *The Globe* had 'Old Gang Indicted' and the *Sunday Times* 'Lord Jellicoe's Apologia'. However, Gerard Fiennes in *The Observer* said the book was '. . . neither an indictment nor an apologia'. The *Times Literary Supplement* welcomed it as '. . . a cheering feeling of escape which comes to half-blinded mankind on the lifting of the fog'.

Not many would agree with that; in fact the publication of Jellicoe's book added to the steam and fog that the battle of Jutland was already generating. Some measure of the strong feelings the battle had already aroused is shown in a sharp exchange between admirals in the *Daily Mail*. Admiral E.R. Fremantle wrote on 20 February: 'The plain truth is that Lord Jellicoe, though a good officer, is not a man of action. Even Calder fought in 1805 off Finisterre, though half-heartedly. Lord Jellicoe did not fight at all. His own defence condemns him.' To which Admiral Seymour, Jellicoe's old chief in China, retorted on the twenty-sixth: 'I regret that my old and valued friend felt himself called upon then to criticise a brother officer and it was inopportune that the letter appeared just as Lord Jellicoe left England on duty.'

As Seymour said, Jellicoe had left England by the time this riposte appeared. But in any case Jellicoe never replied to Fremantle or any other of his detractors, in public or in private, then or ever. He had been offered the governor-generalship of Australia but declined it on financial grounds, and also because he had been given reason to hope for the governor-generalship of New Zealand, which he much preferred, when it next became vacant. In the meantime he was offered work of importance to the nation, in the Empire Mission.

After the war naval affairs generally were in a state of strategic upheaval, as they are after all major wars. The Admiralty believed that the best way forward for the navies of the Commonwealth lay in a single unified Imperial Navy, under the central authority of the Admiralty, with each dominion contributing according to its abilities and drawing according to its needs. But at an Imperial War Conference in 1918 the dominions rejected this proposal, and each preferred to have its own navy. But there would still be enormous advantages in the standardization of ships, weapons, equipment, training of personnel, organization of supply, and administration. The governments of Australia and Canada suggested an Empire Tour conducted by a person of great naval authority and reputation – they had Jellicoe in mind from the start and before long they asked for him personally – to examine the needs of the naval dominions, suggest improvements and report. New Zealand and India also agreed. South Africa was considered, but it was decided against it since the Boer War was too recent.

Jellicoe had with him Paymaster Captain Hamnet Share as his secretary, Lieutenant L.V. Morgan as flag lieutenant, and a staff of eleven officers headed by Commodore Dreyer as chief of staff. Lady Jellicoe also went to help with what would be an enormous burden of entertaining. The children, including the infant son and heir George, were left at home in the Isle of Wight with Lady Cayzer. The ship chosen was the battle cruiser *New Zealand*, which had been refitting at Devonport, having some armament removed and extra accommodation fitted. The admiral's accommodation was forward, on the main deck just aft of the forward turret, and extended the whole width of the ship. The wardroom was also forward.

Jellicoe and his staff – with enough documents for a 'miniature Admiralty' – embarked in *New Zealand* at Portsmouth on 19 February 1919, and Jellicoe's flag was formally hoisted next day. The weather was foul, with thick slush lying on the dockyard jetties. *New Zealand* sailed on the afternoon of 21 February, in heavy rain, heading into a rising westerly gale. The dockyard work had barely been completed before sailing – there were rivets missing and numerous leaks; compartments were soaked, and carpets had to be taken up before they floated away. On Sunday it was too rough for church, so standing prayers were read on the midship deck.

Jellicoe's Empire Tour progressed in proconsular fashion, with official courtesies and ceremonial wherever he went. When *New Zealand* secured alongside South Mole in Gibraltar, the governor and the senior naval officer paid official calls. There was a dinner on board, and a garden party at Government House. At Port Said, Jellicoe called on the governor and received a call from the French senior naval officer. Jellicoe's party went on to Cairo and were received by the ADC to HM the Sultan, the military attaché at the residency, the general manager of Egyptian State Railways and the governor of Cairo. They stayed at the Hotel Continental and next day called on the Sultan, had lunch with General Watson, commanding troops in Egypt, and visited the Great Pyramid. The party re-embarked in *New Zealand* at Suez on 5 March.

Jellicoe had asked for the status of commander-in-chief, but for various reasons this had not been approved. However, on passage to India the Admiralty signalled that he had been 'assigned precedence in Class 6 in Warrant of Precedence in India, i.e. after the Army Commander-in Chief and Lieutenant Governors'. *New Zealand* arrived in Bombay on 14 March, when the C-in-C East Indies came on board, and official calls were made and received. Next day Jellicoe and his party went to Delhi by train, a journey of more than thirty hours on the Great Indian Peninsular Railway. India was still in the final heyday of the British Raj and work was still heavily diluted with pleasant sightseeing. There were conferences with Lord Chelmsford, the Viceroy, and sets of tennis; paperwork and documents, and a visit to the incomplete city of New Delhi. They had dinner in the viceregal garden, under a Shamiana canopy, brilliantly lit with Chinese lanterns, and took a moonlight motor drive to the old native fort of Purana Kula, haunted by the ghostly crying of hyenas and jackals. They visited the Taj Mahal, Cawnpore, where Jellicoe was interested in a memorial to 2nd Lieutenant Jellicoe, killed in the Mutiny, and Lucknow, where the

British flag was always flown 'close up', in memory of the heroic defence of the residency.

On 30 March *New Zealand* sailed for Karachi, where Jellicoe met the commissioner in Sind, and received an address of welcome from Karachi Municipality delivered by a Parsee gentleman, Mr Harchandrai Vishindas, who owned the greater part of Karachi and the harbour. They had dinner at the Sind Club and danced at the Gymkhana Club. The only mishap was a fatal accident to Able Seaman Andrew Rennie, who fell from the balcony of the Bedfordshire Regiment's barracks and died of his injuries; Jellicoe and staff went to the funeral that afternoon.

Back in Bombay, Jellicoe and Dreyer carried out a vigorous offensive with big game guns on a target representing a tiger which was suspended over the ship's side. On the evening of 2 April a signal arrived saying that Lord Jellicoe had been promoted Admiral of the Fleet. At 6 a.m. on the morning of 3 April Jellicoe's Union Flag was broken at the main mast.

At Bombay there were rumblings of political discontent. A cricket match at the Willingdon Club was cancelled because of a strike at a cotton mill next door. Demonstrations inspired by Mahatma Gandhi took place on 'Black Sunday', 6 April, and bluejackets and marines were in readiness to land to assist the police.

On 18 April, Jellicoe, Dreyer, the flag commander Bertram Ramsay and the flag lieutenant went by train up to Gwalior for the eagerly awaited tiger shooting, as guests of His Highness the Maharajah. The four days' tiger shoot was an event of curious contrasts. The shooting party dined on the roof of the palace, almost deafened by the howls of hyenas and jackals. They were taken out by Rolls-Royce through an almost totally barren landscape occupied by occasional cattle whose bones protruded painfully through their skins. The tigers were driven by beaters – two companies of the Maharajah's Infantry Regiment, with rifles, bayonets and blank ammunition, two or three hundred villagers armed with gongs and drums and rattles, and a few elephants – through a ravine, where the guns, with .450 Express rifles, waited in 'machans' or shooting butts, made of stone, iron or wood, and raised about twenty feet from the ground. To escape, the tigers had to run past the 'machans'. The tigers, some of whom were reluctant to move and had to be encouraged by blank rounds and hurled bricks, at last came bounding along the ravine, 'roaring blue murder'. Although the guns included such distinguished gunnery officers, the shooting was enthusiastic rather than accurate. However, seven tigers were eventually dispatched in the four days. Jellicoe contributed to several kills and on the last day brought down a tigress cleanly with one shot. Two sepoys were badly mauled and taken to hospital but later recovered.

Jellicoe tipped them 100 rupees each, and the Maharajah made it 400.

Later, when Gwendoline arrived in Gwalior, she was taken to see the Maharajah's two wives and children, whom she found singing 'Scotch songs'. The two little children were named George and Mary, after the King and Queen. They all had breakfast in an enormous, glass-roofed room, with sparrows flying about singing merrily inside, and containing a gigantic red and gold carpet, one of the largest in the world, woven in one piece by prisoners in the local gaol.

It all meant work as well as play for the staff, who in their travels around India had accumulated a vast amount of information which was collated into the Report, printed, and delivered in bound copies to the Viceroy before *New Zealand* left Bombay on 30 April. The Indian government had not asked Jellicoe's advice on any specific point, nor had they put forward any policy suggestions of their own, so Jellicoe made out his own recommendations. The most important was that the old Royal Indian Marine, which had been shown during the war as quite unable to meet the naval requirement of India, should be disbanded and replaced by a Royal Indian Navy, officered partly from the Royal Navy and partly from the Royal Indian Marine. Eventually it should be entirely officered by Indians. Jellicoe suggested quite a large naval force: five light cruisers, six submarines, an aircraft carrier and auxiliary craft, with three sloops for the Persian Gulf, several river gun-boats for the Tigris and Euphrates, and twenty armed convoy escorts.

At Colombo *New Zealand* coaled and they had a cricket match, an official lunch and an exchange of calls with a Japanese cruiser. The ship sailed on 5 May and crossed the Line the next day – Jellicoe was very probably the first Admiral of the Fleet ever to cross the Line flying his flag.

Jellicoe may or may not have wondered about their order of precedence, but from the moment they landed at Albany, Western Australia, on 15 May he and Gwendoline were treated like nothing less than Royalty. They drove through gaily decorated streets to a civic reception in the Town Hall. Crowds gathered by the line to see the special train taking Lord and Lady Jellicoe to Perth; children climbed on fences and waved flags, and more crowds collected to cheer at every station on the way. In Perth Station and on its streets there were yet more crowds, another civic reception, singing of the National Anthem and 'Rule Britannia' and much cheering. They were entertained to dinner at the Royal Perth Yacht Club, with the governor of Western Australia in the chair; they attended a race meeting at Goodwood and divine service in St George's Cathedral; and visited the proposed naval base and the Botanical Gardens. In Adelaide the sailors of *New Zealand* marched through the streets, and then had lunch at the 'Cheer up

Hut', a canteen for returned soldiers and sailors. Once again there were lunches, parties, receptions and a ball at the town hall. Despite a heavy head cold which made him stay in bed for a day on passage Jellicoe was fighting fit for Melbourne, where once again he plunged into a round of official calls and social events. Once more the streets were densely packed with sailors, boy scouts and cheering children. There was an address of welcome by the mayor, and *New Zealand* was open to visitors. The governor of Victoria was ill, so Jellicoe went to see him in bed.

On 31 May Jellicoe received many messages on the anniversary of the battle of Jutland, including one from the captain and officers of *Iron Duke*. On 2 June the ship's company occupied five hundred seats and boxes for a musical at Her Majesty's Theatre. The third was the King's birthday, for which *New Zealand* dressed overall and fired a salute of twenty-one guns. Next day, Jellicoe went by special train to inspect the naval base at Flinders Bay.

But there was a darker side to the Tour: Jellicoe's party was dogged by the epidemic of influenza which was spreading worldwide. At Cawnpore they had seen the River Ganges choked with the corpses of influenza victims. Several members of Jellicoe's staff fell sick: Paymaster Egerton, the padre, the flag lieutenant and, at Melbourne, the governor's private secretary. By 10 June there were several more cases at Government House and Jellicoe returned on board *New Zealand*. This was not the discomforting and annoying but rarely fatal infection of modern times. It was known in Australia as the Black Flu and was frequently a killer. The flag commander, Bertram Ramsay, had contracted influenza in Egypt and had suffered from an extended bout of it for most of the passage to Bombay. He had recovered by the time he reached Melbourne where, on his second day, he met at a dinner party a 'fair pretty nice girl' and within twenty-four hours had fallen seriously in love. The romance prospered and four days later, while sitting out a dance at Government House, Ramsay asked her to marry him. She did not give him her answers there and then and Ramsay hoped he had not spoiled his chances. They played tennis on Sunday, sat next to each other at a dinner party on Monday, and danced together afterwards. That night she contracted the Black Flu and when Ramsay called the next morning to ask after her he was horrified to find two doctors and two nurses fighting to save her life. The girl died the following Sunday.

On passage to Sydney *New Zealand* called at Jervis Bay for Jellicoe to visit the Royal Australian Naval College, which in those days was still isolated by miles of native bush: fresh food was brought up from Sydney once a week in the tender *Franklin*. Jellicoe watched the cadet-midshipmen at work and play, addressed them at divisions on discipline, honour and loyalty, and took the salute as they marched past. On Sunday 22 June *New Zealand*'s chaplain landed to carry out the baptismal service for eleven children, the college having no chaplain; some of them had waited some time and were no longer infants. Gwendoline stood as godmother to three of them. A large party of cadet-midshipmen were to have visited *New Zealand* and have tea on board, but this was cancelled because of an outbreak of influenza.

At midnight *New Zealand* sailed for Sydney where influenza spoiled most of the visit, causing the cancellation of nearly all the official functions and entertainments as well as a planned march by the ship's company through the streets of Sydney. Monday 23 June, when *New Zealand* steamed up harbour from Sydney Heads, was Coronation Day and the Prince of Wales' birthday: the ship dressed overall and fired a twenty-one gun salute at noon; it was a public holiday and enormous crowds gathered to see Jellicoe arrive at a special landing-place on his way to call on the governor of New South Wales.

On the next day the news arrived that Germany had agreed to sign the peace treaty unconditionally. The event was officially celebrated on 30 June. *New Zealand*, the Australian ships *Australia*, *Brisbane* and *Encounter* all dressed ship at 8 a.m. and fired a salute of 101 guns, in conjunction with saluting guns ashore. A thanksgiving service was held on board *New Zealand*, attended by the governor-general: frock-coats and swords, the full ceremonial dress, were worn by officers for the first time since the outbreak of war in 1914. All ships manned the upper decks at noon and gave three cheers for His Majesty King George V, and the bands played the National Anthems of all the Allies. The officers assembled in Jellicoe's cabin afterwards and drank the toast, 'The King', followed by 'The Admiral of the Fleet'. Then, by order of His Majesty, 'Splice the Main Brace' was piped. That evening *New Zealand* was illuminated with coloured lights, and there were displays of fireworks, searchlights and rockets ashore.

In spite of the routine of ceremonial, very tiring for a man in his sixtieth year, the endless handshakes, receptions, dinners, speeches, tours of inspection, waving to crowds, appearing interested in a hundred different personalities and conversations in one forenoon – it *was* a job very much like Royalty's – Jellicoe bore up under the strain extremely well. He was a good public speaker, with an easy manner, authoritative but somehow humble, with a mixture of bluff sailor and bright intellect, and an added twinkle of humour. His health was generally good. His staff might fall by the wayside (Flags was particularly accident-prone; having just recovered from influenza, he fell down a manhole and injured his back while being shown round the magazine and explosive storage at Spectacle Island), but if Jellicoe was unwell he reserved it for the times when *New Zealand* was on passage.

Jellicoe also intended to visit the Northern Territory of Australia and some of the South Sea Islands. For this part of the trip an Australian Steam Navigation Company ship of 2,229 tons, the *Suva*, which had been employed on the Red Sea Patrol during the war, was recommissioned as HMAS *Suva*. Jellicoe's Union Flag was broken out in *Suva* and struck in *New Zealand* on 2 July. *Suva* sailed the same day for Brisbane, where Jellicoe joined her, having travelled up by train.

The ship visited the Solomon Islands, Bougainville, Rabaul, Port Moresby and Thursday Island, and once again crowds gathered to see Jellicoe. At Tulagi, in the Solomons, he was escorted by a giant war canoe, rowed by twenty convicted murderers all yelling their welcome at the tops of their voices, while their paddling easily kept pace with the admiral's barge. Again Jellicoe set a brisk pace, socially and physically: he played tennis at Port Moresby despite the terrific heat; he led the way up a nearly vertical cliff at Sugar Loaf in Duke of York's Island, which left every other member of the expedition lying prostrate and gasping at the top.

Jellicoe left *Suva* at Port Gladstone and returned to Sydney by train, stopping off on the way to inspect the facilities at Newcastle. His tour of Australia was almost over. In spite of the hectic social life the staff had gathered another mountain of documents. Bound copies of the Report were ready on 11 August and a copy was given to the governor-general on the fifteenth. *New Zealand* left Sydney, bound for New Zealand, on the sixteenth.

Jellicoe wrote his report at a time of political vacuum on strategy. The Admiralty had not decided the shape of their post-war policy, and Jellicoe's recommendations as to fleet strengths and numbers of warships could not possibly be fulfilled. But in the basic statements of naval principles, in his warnings of the consequences of unpreparedness, his report was sound, and in some of his comments about Singapore he was prophetic. The main enemy, as Jellicoe saw it, was clearly Japan. He stressed the importance of Colombo, Hong Kong and Singapore as bases. Singapore, he said, was '. . . undoubtedly the naval key to the Far East'. He pointed out how vulnerable Hong Kong and Singapore would be to Japanese attack if not properly armed and defended. His words proved to be almost eerily accurate.

Some of Jellicoe's most pointed remarks were about the officers of the Royal Australian Navy. Amid the social hurly-burly of the mission, the little admiral had been taking shrewd stock of his hosts. Many an RAN officer at a meeting, or at some social function, must have been quite unaware that Jellicoe had been summing him up with his acute judgement of men. He had little to criticize about the Naval College at Jervis Bay, but the standard needed to be maintained. The RN officers who came out to Australia must be first-class – not 'no-hopers' who had opted for a soft life and bright sunshine.

'It is a regrettable fact', Jellicoe reported, 'that quite a proportion of the British naval officers at present working for the Royal Australian Navy are distinctly not of the most efficient type.' In Jellicoe's opinion '. . . some are officers who have failed in the Royal Navy. . . . Others again are RNR officers of a poor type who have taken commissions in the Australian Navy.' Jellicoe paid particular attention to discipline, recognizing that Australians were different from Englishmen and required different handling. But there were certain qualities in an officer which were paramount, always and everywhere: judgement, tact, firmness and broadmindedness; an interest in the welfare of his men; kindness and courtesy, without familiarity; leading by example and not by invective; fairness, restraint and patience in investigating offences and punishing offenders – Jellicoe set out all the lines by which he had guided his own professional life. He deplored political influence in the Australian Navy, by which officers' decisions were often overruled by politicians. He went on to discuss a wide range of topics, including air defence, dry docks and fleet bases. He noted the possibilities of Manus in the Admiralty Islands (the actual base of the British Pacific Fleet in the Second World War) and recommended that the C-in-C of a Far Eastern Fleet should not fly his flag afloat but have his headquarters ashore, and the obvious place was Singapore (the precise decision reached by Admiral Fraser, C-in-C British Pacific Fleet in 1944, although Singapore was not, of course, available to him and he chose Sydney instead).

Jellicoe recommended an Australian fleet strength of the battle cruiser *Australia*, one new battle cruiser, four light cruisers and four in reserve, a flotilla leader and ten destroyers, with two more in reserve, a destroyer depot ship, eight submarines and a small depot ship for them, one sea-going minelayer in reserve, two sloop minesweepers in reserve, two special reserve sloop minesweepers, and, finally, an aircraft carrier and a fleet repair ship. By 1938 Australia actually had four cruisers, five destroyers, a sea-going minelayer, a seaplane carrier, a destroyer depot ship and two minesweepers.

On 20 August *New Zealand* arrived at Wellington, where Jellicoe received the same ecstatic welcome in the streets. It was the antipodean winter and there were occasional downpours of chilling rain, but nothing dampened the spirits of the New Zealanders, in an exotic range of visits and entertainments: a smoking concert or *korero* at the Orphans' Club; a visit to the prison cell once occupied by von Lucknor, captain of the German raider *Seeadler*; a trip by special train to Christchurch through a tunnel '. . . strongly reminiscent in length and odour of the Penge tunnel on the South Eastern and Chatham Railway'; the Lancers danced by sixty debutantes; laying the foundation stone of the Returned Soldiers' Association's new clubhouse; a trotting meeting; inspecting a rally of six hundred Boy Scouts; excellent snooker with the Scotsmen at the Dunedin Club; a Maori *haka* and *poi* dance at Picton; sulphur baths at Rotorua, and a geyser called Googoo eyes; unveiling a memorial to Lieut-Commander William Sanders, who won a posthumous VC as a 'Q' Ship Captain, at his birthplace in Takapuna, Auckland.

New Zealand sailed for the Fiji Islands on 3 October, by which time Jellicoe had attended some forty receptions, fifteen lunches, eight public dinners, a dozen or more balls and many other assorted social occasions. He calculated he had made twenty-five speeches in nine days and a total of 167 speeches since he arrived in India in March. 'I just detest it,' he wrote to Admiral Sims on passage on 6 October. There were more speeches at Suva in the Fijis and a presentation of whale's teeth.

Jellicoe's report on New Zealand was as comprehensive and wide-ranging as that for the Australian government and covered broadly similar topics – in fact some sections, such as those on discipline and the importance of capital ships, were virtually identical. Jellicoe was more impressed by New Zealanders than he was by Australians; as a race he thought them 'markedly in advance' of Australians. He found their attitudes to senior officers, to discipline and obedience to orders, as hard to understand as he had in Australia, but he suggested a much closer relationship between the Royal New Zealand Navy and the Royal Navy than he had for the Royal Australian Navy, even to wearing the White Ensign, with the New Zealand flag as a jack in harbour, and common service and promotion for officers in both navies. As for ships, he recommended that New Zealand should have three cruisers, one small aircraft carrier, six submarines and a small submarine depot ship. Actually by 1938 New Zealand had her three cruisers – one of them small and old, though, and used as a depot ship – but only two sloops and nothing else.

The fact was that many of Jellicoe's recommendations for ship requirements belonged to a more expansive pre-war age and were now financially and politically impossible. His thinking was still governed by the requirements of the old Navy, of large fleets. His reports were admirable statements of naval strategy in general and its applications to the dominions in particular. They showed Jellicoe's old flair for staff work, for drawing conclusions from what he knew of ships, men, ports, and their capabilities, his ability to marshal and collate multitudes of facts and take note of many opinions. But in the naval and political situation of the 1920s they had an archaic ring to them, and there is no evidence that they had much bearing on Admiralty decisions. The mission amounted to a brilliant public relations exercise – though no less valuable for that.

If anything, his reports aroused adverse comment in the Admiralty. By the time Jellicoe left New Zealand in October he had received Admiralty reaction to some of his earlier reports. Wemyss complained that Jellicoe was exceeding his brief, that he had '. . . entered into a sphere never contemplated by the Admiralty and far beyond his terms of reference'. He claimed that Jellicoe was debating questions which the Board themselves had not yet considered properly, although when they did come to consider them they arrived at much the same conclusions as Jellicoe had about the threat of Japan and the means necessary to counter it. But that, of course, did not mean that the ships Jellicoe recommended would ever be provided.

Jellicoe had found it hard work to argue the Admiralty's case for a joint Imperial Navy, especially in Australia. In fact, as he wrote to Walter Long, who had relieved Geddes as First Lord, '. . . any attempt to do so would be not merely beating the air but would seriously weaken any hold that I might obtain on Australian public opinion'. The New Zealanders were a little more amenable and did agree to a New Zealand Division. But Jellicoe had his coolest reception of all in Canada, when *New Zealand* dropped anchor in Esquimault harbour on 8 November.

Canada was on the whole indifferent to sea power. As Jellicoe said, in Canada '. . . the dependence of the Dominion on sea power for its prosperity is not so clearly recognised'. There was no likely enemy to Canada on land, and the majority of the population lived miles from the sea. Fortunately, Jellicoe received the letter from the Admiralty, dropping the idea of an Imperial Navy, which had been forwarded to him from New Zealand; at least he was relieved from this contentious part of his brief. Even so, he was frequently asked in Canada, as in the other dominions, how many and what sort of surplus ships from the Royal Navy would be available for the dominion navies. But he was never able to get a satisfactory reply from the Admiralty. The Admiralty were slow to give guidance on a number of points. Walter Long excused their failure to answer Jellicoe's telegrams on the grounds that '. . . we have been through a really awful time during the last six months'. Jellicoe recognized that the Canadians were in a mood to accept closer co-operation with the Admiralty if only some firm facts could be given. But nobody could or would supply them. Otherwise Jellicoe had to endure the same round of social engagements, but he could see that he was being used for propaganda purposes by the Canadian government and he disliked it intensely. The speeches, too, were getting him down. 'We are all well but I am sick to death of speech-making,' he wrote to Sims, 'and shall be very glad when I can coil up ropes and finish. . . .'

278

That time was not far off. A day after they arrived at Esquimault, they heard that Lady Cayzer had died. Lady Jellicoe went on with the tour and with her entertainment duties, but shortened her stay. They visited Halifax and Quebec and spent Christmas in Ottawa. They were to have visited Admiral Sims at Newport, but Lady Jellicoe had tonsillitis; she eventually sailed for England from New York in the *Adriatic* on 31 December.

Jellicoe continued to Washington. He visited the Navy Yard, and the Capitol, where he was introduced from the floor of the Senate, and went on to the House of Representatives where members gave him a standing ovation in appreciation of his war service. He had tea with Franklin Roosevelt, at that time Assistant Secretary to the Navy, visited Admiral Mayo, and inspected the Navy Academy at Annapolis, where he addressed two thousand midshipmen for ten minutes in the great hall: they gave three cheers for their Navy and three cheers more for Jellicoe.

Jellicoe rejoined *New Zealand* at Key West and sailed for home, although even now his Tour was not quite over. He called at Havana, Port Royal, Jamaica and Port of Spain, Trinidad. There were the final dinners and speeches; somebody gave a demonstration of surfing without a board, which Jellicoe succeeded in doing, and then they made passage for home. *New Zealand* anchored at Spithead on 2 February 1920. Jellicoe had travelled, on land and sea, some fifty-five thousand miles. Lady Jellicoe came on board on the third and they both went ashore the next day, when Jellicoe's flag was struck. His Empire Mission and his active naval career were both over.

The great controversy over Jutland, however, was not over. If anything, it had gathered pace and momentum in Jellicoe's absence.

Chapter 17

Everybody wanted to know what really happened at Jutland. The only proper source of information was the Admiralty, and it was very much in the Navy's interest to dispel rumours and unfair criticism. But the rumours were so critical, so disagreeable and so widespread that it became clear that if the affair were not settled quickly and satisfactorily Jutland and its aftermath would do serious and permanent damage to the Navy's good name. In the end only individuals suffered, although as it happened a most unfortunate combination of events and personalities, assembled as though by some malignant fate, made sure that the publication of the Jutland story took place over a long period and in such a way as to arouse the worst suspicions. There were many who had criticized the Admiralty for not having given the story fully and in its true proportions soon after the event, but by the end there were just as many who blamed the Admiralty for trying to falsify the record, to 'cook the books' afterwards.

The nation had expected another Trafalgar. When it was clear that Jutland was certainly not another Trafalgar, the nation wanted to know why not, and who was to blame. Many naval actions involve only a handful of ships; Jutland was a great fleet action, with an unusual number of ships present and an unusual number of casualties. Every officer and man, and all their relatives, wanted their own squadron, ship, admiral, messmates, to receive their proper credit due, and they resented anything which seemed to diminish the value of their own contribution. Anything less than total victory at sea can always be shuffled round so as to appear almost a defeat. The general public could not be expected to realize the extreme difficulty of operations at sea, how very big even a small stretch of sea really is, how very small even a big fleet appears at sea, how very difficult it is to engage an opponent who is intent on disengaging.

The two main protagonists on the British side appeared in curious contrast. Whatever Beatty may or may not have done at Jutland, he had carried out his main task of bringing the two battle fleets together. But ever afterwards Beatty reacted strongly to the least suggestion that he had handled his ships less than perfectly, that his signalling had been less than crystal clear at all times, and that his gunnery had been other than totally accurate with every salvo.

As for Jellicoe, as the years have passed his achievement at Jutland has emerged ever more clearly, towering up like some massive solid rock from clouds of rumour, false reporting, misapprehension, after-thoughts and sheer wicked sniping. For many years the fog of war at Jutland was easily surpassed in density and extent by the clouds of steam and hot air generated by some of the participants and their partisans. The Admiralty themselves compounded the confusion by dithering over the official account and giving lasting and unjustified offence to some of Jellicoe's supporters. Senior officers who were criticized either openly or by omission had no redress. They had done their best, at Jutland at the time, and as they saw it. They had to suffer the criticisms and some of them found it a great strain.

By the end of the war it was generally known that Jellicoe was using his leisure to write a book on the Grand Fleet's doings. Lesser spirits feared that he might thus get first run and publish his own version of events to the discredit of others; Jellicoe was too big a man to do any such thing, but even Wemyss seems to have succumbed to the fear that he might. On 23 January 1919 Wemyss sent a memo to Walter Long on the necessity of producing a detailed, historically accurate record of the Battle of Jutland.

A small committee was appointed, consisting of Captain J.E.T. Harper, a navigational specialist officer, who had not been at Jutland, and four other officers. Their brief was to examine all the documents and to prepare an official, exhaustive, and authoritative account of the battle, in Harper's own words, '. . . a Record, with plans, showing in chronological order what actually occurred at the Battle'. No comments or criticisms were to be included and no oral evidence was to be accepted. They had the reports of proceedings, the bridge and signal logs, the engine room registers and all the official documentation of the battle, and began work on 6 February 1919.

The first rumblings of the storm to come began as early as March, when there were questions about the production of the Record in the House of Commons. The names of Harper and his assistants were to have been withheld, for the sake of impartiality. But this impartiality was threatened when, in Harper's words, '. . . against all precedent and in spite of my verbal protests', his name was revealed by the First Lord in answer to a question on 26 March. Harper and his assistants worked on through the summer of 1919, checking and rechecking their conclusions, even going so far, in answer to a question in the House by Commander Carlyon Bellairs MP, a keen supporter of Beatty's, as to give the exact position of *Invincible*. Harper's position was shown to be accurate.

Some squadrons and ships kept very scanty records, and Harper had great difficulty in plotting some ships' movements. He referred to this difficulty in his covering notes. He also exceeded his instructions that there were to be no comments or criticisms. He described as 'a disturbing feature of the battle-cruiser action' the fact that five German battle cruisers engaged six British battle cruisers, who were supported after the first twenty minutes by four battleships of the Queen Elizabeth class, and yet were able to sink *Queen Mary* and *Indefatigable*. 'It is true', Harper wrote, 'that the enemy suffered heavily later and that one vessel, the *Lützow* was undoubtedly destroyed, but even so the result cannot be other than unpalatable.'

Harper's comments were correct, and his criticisms were justified, but that did not make them any more palatable and they were to have the most unfortunate effect. The Record was completed in October 1919 and sent to the Board for approval. Wemyss was actually on leave in Paris at the time and the Record was read by Admiral Brock, the Deputy Chief of Naval Staff, who had been in command of the 1st Battle Cruiser Squadron under Beatty at Jutland, and was subsequently Beatty's chief of staff in the Grand Fleet. In Harper's account of what happened,

On 24th October, in my presence, Admiral Brock was on the point of signing his name, signifying Board Approval, when he changed his mind and remarked: 'As Lord Beatty is assuming office as First Sea Lord in a few days it must wait for his approval.' It is of interest to consider that if Admiral Brock had signed his name, on this occasion, and the Record had been published forthwith, there would have been no 'Jutland controversy' in the Press and thousands of pounds of public money would have been saved.

Beatty became First Sea Lord and Chief of Naval Staff on 1 November 1919, with Chatfield, his old flag captain, as Assistant Chief; as somebody said, '. . . the battle-cruiser men took over at the Admiralty'. As First Sea Lord Beatty was responsible for the Record. He read it and, predictably, disliked certain passages in it which referred to the Battle Cruiser Fleet. Beatty had done very well at Jutland, but as time passed his proud spirit came to believe that he had done even better. He became so sensitive on the subject that any tinge of criticism in one part marred his pleasure in the whole.

Beatty sent frequent messages to Harper on various points in the text and called Harper to see him several times. One particular bone of contention was the 360 degree turn by *Lion* at about 7 p.m. on 31 May. Beatty strenuously denied that this had ever happened and insisted that *Lion* had turned to the starboard about sixteen points and then back sixteen points to port. This, as Harper protested, did not square with the facts as represented by other ships' narratives and track charts. Beatty interviewed Harper on 11 February 1920 and gave him orders to carry out several amendments and additions to the text, and to cut out altogether certain passages concerning the Battle Cruiser Fleet's shooting. By coincidence, Harper met Jellicoe that day at the Admiralty, where Jellicoe had come to pay his official call after his return from his Empire Mission. When he first commissioned the Report, Wemyss had intended that neither Jellicoe nor Beatty should read it before publication, and Jellicoe certainly agreed to this stipulation. But from the moment he arrived back in England Jellicoe began to hear rumours that all was not well with the Record. His conversation with Harper that day in the Admiralty must have been one of the first hints of trouble to come.

From the moment of Beatty's intervention controversy was inescapable, and it gathered pace with the publication on that same day, 11 February, of *The Battle of Jutland: The sowing and the reaping*, by Commander Carlyon Bellairs, the same man who had asked questions in the House about *Invincible*'s sinking position. Bellairs was a supporter of Beatty's and a disparager of Jellicoe, as the text of his book soon made clear. His provocative chapter headings ('The Grand Fleet Nibbles But Does Not Bite: I came, I saw, I turned away') and quotations comparing Jellicoe to Dryden's 'faint pilgrim' and to Hamlet 'sicklied o'er with the pale cast of thought' are now the most readable parts of an unreadable and unread book. Bellairs' book libelled Harper, who took legal advice but was prevailed upon by Walter Long, and by the fear that his damages might not cover his expenses, not to sue. Harper '. . . therefore ignored the untruths'.

From February 1920 the picture emerges inescapably of Beatty attempting to impose his own version of events, often only through the medium of his own unaided memory, upon an unwilling and increasingly resentful Harper and an alarmed Walter Long, to the growing uneasiness of Chatfield. There were several meetings that month between Harper and Long, and between Harper and Beatty. At one point Long was concerned enough to suggest that Harper bypass the normal naval chain of command and report direct to him.

Jellicoe, down in the Isle of Wight, had heard that the Admiralty wanted to change the Record but had stayed aloof. On 9 March he avoided becoming personally and directly involved; that day Harper and the Director of Naval Intelligence went down to see him to confer with him about the paraphrases of certain secret wireless signals. Jellicoe agreed to the paraphrases and was then asked if he would like to read the Record and make any criticisms of it. He still said that he preferred not to read it before publication. Two days later, Beatty cancelled his previous instructions to Harper by memo, and it seemed that all would go smoothly at last.

But that was by no means the end of the affair. Copies of the final proofs of the Record were handed to Beatty and to Long on 14 May, with a note to the effect that no alterations had been made since Board approval had been obtained. Almost at once Beatty sent for Harper and the trouble began all over again. Beatty wanted at least one amendment made and it seemed to Harper there would very likely be others. Sure enough, on 26 May Beatty sent Harper a list of alterations to be made, and, as Harper said, 'We were now back to where we were in February.'

Beatty now decided that a copy of the Record should be sent to all the Sea Lords, who would then give Harper their proposals for alterations, additions and deletions. Finally, they should all meet to consider the proposals and Harper's replies to them, and the Record should then be approved by the whole Board. This, as Harper said, was the reverse of the usual Admiralty procedure, whereby proposals were submitted *to* the Sea Lords, not *by* them, and a decision then made. Brock, Chatfield and Admiral Browning (Second Sea Lord) had criticisms to make and certain members did not '. . . like the general tone of the Record'.

On 21 June the First Lord and all the Sea Lords spent an hour and thirty-five minutes discussing the Record. Harper's remarks were invited. Finally, it was proposed to include a foreword, whose first two paragraphs in final form, as proposed by Beatty, were:

> The following narrative of events, amplified by detailed proceedings of each Squadron and Flotilla, shows that the enemy's advanced forces were reinforced by their main Fleet some hours before the British main Fleet was able to reach the scene of action. During this period, therefore, the British were in greatly inferior force.
>
> On learning of the approach of the British main Fleet the Germans avoided further action and returned to the Base.

Beatty was neither a stupid nor an insensitive man, and it is hard to understand how he ever expected two such paragraphs to be included in an official Admiralty record of the battle without causing dissension and discontent. The original drafts may or may not have been unfair to Beatty and the battle cruisers, but this new foreword was quite certainly unfair to Jellicoe and the battleships. To suggest that the Battle Fleet had never been in action at all was quite absurd.

Jellicoe was now drawn into the argument. A copy of the original Record, with the subsequent alterations and additions, and the new foreword, was sent to him. He repeated that he would much rather not read the Record and was quite willing to abide by the first arrangement. But since he had been asked, he had read the Record and naturally he objected to much of the addenda and especially to the foreword, which gave the impression that the Battle Fleet had little or no effect upon the course and result of the action.

On 14 July the Board had another meeting, lasting two hours, to discuss Jellicoe's response. There was an acrimonious discussion about details in the Record, especially such moot points as whether or not *Hercules* was straddled by enemy fire as she turned into line of battle. Beatty insisted there was no need to include it because the enemy were not firing at *Hercules* at the time, although they may have straddled her, and the statement thus had no value. Harper protested that this was one of the only statements in the Record which proved that, at the point of deployment, the British Battle Fleet was within range of the enemy. Just how far the discussion had deteriorated into acrimony and dispute is shown by Harper's account of some of Beatty's remarks. 'If Jellicoe writes books,' he said, 'I do not see that I should not do so.' When Long said that the description of *Hercules* being straddled and her superstructure being deluged with water was of interest to the layman, Beatty said: 'Well I suppose there is no harm in the public knowing that someone in the Battle Fleet got wet, as that is about all they had to do with Jutland.' In such an atmosphere the meeting broke up without any firm decision.

Jellicoe, though still very reluctant to be drawn into any controversy, had read the Record with consternation. He objected strongly to much of the Record and especially to the Foreword, he objected so strongly in fact that he refused to accept the governor-generalship of New Zealand, which he had longed for and had at last been offered, without obtaining Long's assurance that the passages he found so objectionable would be deleted from the Record before it was published.

Meanwhile the Board had further meetings, of nearly two hours on 19 July and two and a half hours the following day, at which the Record was exhaustively discussed. Harper was present some of the time and stuck doggedly to his original brief. He refused to make certain corrections because, as he said, there was no evidence for them. *Lion*'s complete circle of 360 degrees at about 6.52 p.m. on 31 May came up again in discussion. Beatty refused to countenance it, maintaining that *Lion* turned first to starboard and then to port, to resume her original course. Harper pointed out that, if this were the case, then because 'advance and transfer' (the lateral distance any ship is displaced during a turn), *Lion*'s range from the enemy would have been reduced by about two thousand yards. This would have been at variance with the ranges plotted and checked by the Gunnery Division of the Naval Staff. Harper said further that if this correction were to be made for *Lion* then the tracks of every other squadron would have to be replotted, none of the evidence would agree and the result would be chaos.

As a result of Harper's own hints, Walter Long suggested that Harper now be relieved of his task, since his position was being rendered impossible, and the Naval Staff themselves prepare a Record. Harper considered that the Board's meetings were biased. He found, he said, that oral evidence relying largely on memory was permissible if it came from Beatty or any of the Battle Cruiser Fleet staff, but documentary evidence was not admissible if it came from the C-in-C or any of the Battle Fleet staff.

Walter Long had promised Jellicoe he would make the alterations in the Record for which Jellicoe had asked. To a certain extent he was looking after Jellicoe's interests, but it was becoming clear to him that it was impossible to publish the Record so as to satisfy both Jellicoe and Beatty. Beatty was First Sea Lord, ensconced in office in Whitehall, with all the levers of power and patronage in his hand. Jellicoe had retired, and was miles away with his family, on his way out to New Zealand. Nevertheless Jellicoe's presence was still strong in the Admiralty, reinforced by the great respect in which he was held throughout the country. So the problem seemed insoluble and by 22 September, after more meetings, Long was suggesting that all idea of publishing the Record be abandoned.

The Board all agreed, except Beatty, who suggested that the dispatches, charts and signals (as amended at his orders) should be published, but not the text of the Record. When Harper's opinion was asked, he said this would make matters worse. The press were already agitating, and they would agitate still more. 'Either refuse to publish anything or publish everything and hide nothing, as there was nothing to hide.'

There were questions in Parliament about the non-appearance of the Jutland Record. There was renewed gossip and rumour in Service clubs and messes. The Admiralty tried to find another way out of their dilemma by asking the well-known and highly respected naval historian Sir Julian Corbett to write a new preface for the Record, to replace Beatty's. But Corbett was already engaged in writing the official history of the war and his publishers objected; the Admiralty took this as an excuse for doing nothing more about the Record. Evidently, it was hoped that, if nothing more was said, the controversy would go away.

However, the controversy received fresh fuel by the publication in *The Times* of 29 October 1920 of a leading article under the provocative title 'The Jutland Silence', by A Naval Officer. This was the signal for another outburst from Jellicoe critics, among whom Arthur Pollen was again prominent. He had published another of those almost unreadable books about the naval war just after the Armistice two years before. He had no high opinion of Jellicoe's book, or 'confessions', as he called them in his letter to *The Times* of 2 November which, he said '. . . show his dispatch with its accompanying diagrams to have been deliberately designed to deceive the public'. Its 'suppression of vital facts, its misrepresentation of others, its special pleadings, and its diagrams, is no reliable guide'. Pollen's letter received a strongly worded reply from Vice-Admiral Mark Kerr, who recalled that Pollen's fire control device had been turned down by Jellicoe and others before the war. The implication was clear: Pollen was not an unbiased critic of Jellicoe.

'The Jutland Dispatches' was published on 27 December 1920. Invaluable to a naval historian, it was one of the least readable books about the battle and had no appeal to the press or general public: 'a vast mass of undigested facts from which the layman cannot possibly disentangle the true history of this great sea-fight' was one typical and fair newspaper comment.

Harper could see that if the Record were now published with Beatty's amendments included, any naval officer or naval historian with half an eye for the truth would soon spot the discrepancies between the Dispatches and the Record. As Harper had been publicly announced as the author of the Record, these discrepancies would reflect on him. He asked that when the Record was published there should be a statement in it that he, Harper, was not responsible for any corrections in the text which were not in accordance with the documentary evidence. Harper did not get his disclaimer; but then the Record was not published in 1920, or in 1921. It was a strange, anomalous situation. The Admiralty and Beatty permitted publication of the Dispatches, which were presumably accurate and official, but would not pass the Record, which also was ostensibly just as accurate and official. One would have expected publication of the Record to follow that of the Dispatches. But not so.

Jellicoe sailed from England in the liner *Corinthic* on 19 August. He took with him a party of twenty-six, not counting the ADCs and their families. They arrived in New Zealand, via the Panama Canal, in September. During the Empire Mission in 1919 when he was being driven along the coast near Takapuna, near Auckland, Jellicoe had said to the local mayor: 'What a beautiful place! My wish is to come here as Governor-General of your people and end my days in this lovely spot!' He was not to end his days there, but he now had his wish about the governor-generalship, the first sailor governor of New Zealand since Fitzroy of the *Beagle* years before.

Jutland had cast its shadow before him. As one of Jellicoe's staff, Sir Cecil Day, wrote, some of the New Zealanders '. . . had had their minds somewhat poisoned by an ill-informed section of the English press, and the scurrilous attack made on him in connection with his conduct of the Battle of Jutland'. But any awkwardness this involved – and it is probable that Day overstated the position – soon dissolved. John Jellicoe was a tremendous success as governor-general. In just over four years in office, he went out and met more New Zealanders than any of his predecessors and made himself universally popular in the countryside. As Day said, many people, especially from looking at his photographs, had expected

> . . . to see a man stern of expression, staccato of voice and sharp of command, whose will was law, and who would naturally be rather unapproachable. But, when he came amongst them, here was this little man with eyes tired yet kind and wise in expression, to which a twinkle of humour came readily, who was dignified but entirely free from pompousness, who told them good stories, was more approachable than their own democratic neighbours, but seemed to inspire a deep personal attachment, without encouraging familiarity.

Jellicoe and his family lived in the official residence in Wellington from late June until November, then just before Christmas the household moved to Government House in Auckland where they stayed until the following June. Once a week Jellicoe presided at meetings of the Executive Council. He never offered his advice to Mr Massey, the prime minister (a personal friend of Jellicoe's and probably the man who had done most to secure Jellicoe as governor-general), and possibly for that reason his advice was often asked. Massey, leader of the Reform Party, largely representing the farming and countryside interests, had only a small majority over the Liberal and Labour Parties. In spite of falling prices for farm produce, it was a comparatively easy time in New Zealand politics and the main controversy during Jellicoe's term of office was a storm over the use of the Bible in schools.

Jellicoe went literally out of his way to visit the remoter parts of the dominions and meet the people, and broke down a number of barriers of protocol connected with the office of governor-general. He entered into as many aspects of New Zealand life as he could: he fished, golfed, stalked, played tennis, encouraged the sport of sailing by racing in a one-design fourteen-foot dinghy (named *Iron Duke*), and the whole family rode to hounds. He had a royal memory for names and a prince's gift of punctuality. The latter was not shared by Lady Jellicoe: he would wait patiently for her in the hall, saying when she did arrive, 'I used to get the Grand Fleet to sea more quickly than I can get you out of the house'. They had a busy social life, with at least three and sometimes as many as five evening engagements a week.

Above all, Jellicoe was interested in and encouraged the young. They were '. . . the recruits of the future'. He visited boy scouts and girl guides, and with his young family there were always parties of young people at Government House. The two oldest Jellicoe girls went to school in Hawke Bay.

Jellicoe also made special efforts to meet the Maori people and was greatly liked and respected by them. Lady Jellicoe found some of their social niceties disconcerting: she never could accustom herself to the Maori practice of rubbing noses in greeting, and elderly Maoris were always liable to startle her by urging her to '. . . please tell Queen Mary that we no longer eat white babies'.

The weather was Italian, the scenery magnificent. But unfortunately, even in this Eden, there was the persistent serpent of the Jutland controversy. In November 1920, when the matter of Harper's Record seemed to have reached a state of impasse, the Director of Training and Staff Duties, Captain Ellerton, asked Captain A.C. Dewar, a retired naval officer and a naval historian, to prepare an Appreciation of Jutland for use in the staff college. Dewar asked if his younger brother K.G.B. Dewar, who had already crossed Jellicoe's bows in the Admiralty, could assist him with the work.

Using the Harper Record as a basis, and acknowledging the help it was to them, the Dewar brothers prepared an Appreciation which was critical of Jellicoe and of some of the officers in the Battle Fleet. When Walter Long sent a copy out to New Zealand, Jellicoe objected strongly to the Appreciation. Checking the facts with the papers and maps he had – very prudently, as it turned out – taken out with him, Jellicoe went through the Appreciation and found a number of inaccuracies and misrepresentations in text, maps and diagrams.

On 27 November 1922 Jellicoe wrote to the Admiralty setting out his objections and expressing his strong dissent. He asked that if his comments could not be incorporated into the text, they could at least be published in the same volume. In particular he objected to the treatment of Evan-Thomas, who was blamed for the fact that his 5th Battle Squadron was not closer to Beatty's battle cruisers when the enemy was first encountered and was also held responsible for mistakes which brought his battleships under fire unnecessarily. Evan-Thomas was very deeply hurt by the criticism, which may well have hastened his death.

It was ten months before Jellicoe received a list of the amendments the Board was prepared to agree and those they were not. They asked Jellicoe to cable if he was still not satisfied, which Jellicoe certainly was not. He cabled the most important points and offered to send the rest by normal ship mail if the Admiralty would hold up publication. This the Admiralty refused to do, and the 'Narrative' as it was called, appeared in August 1924 as a substitute for the 'Appreciation'.

The Jutland Narrative was one of the least generous publications ever issued, even by the Admiralty. Jellicoe's General Remarks were given in Appendix G with official disclaimers and footnotes which, in their tactlessness amounting to downright rudeness, might have been written by Geddes himself. The first 'It should be noted that this publication is an official Narrative, and not a Staff Appreciation' was hair-splitting over definitions which any intelligent layman would find hard to understand. 'Their Lordships are satisfied. . . .' 'Their Lordships cannot accept that any injustice is done. . . .' 'The facts as stated in the Narrative are correct. . . .' It seems that Beatty, his Board and the civil servants behind them took leave of all the normal rules of courtesy.

Jellicoe had some consolation from Sir Julian Corbett's account of Jutland, published in Volume 3 of his official history. Corbett was not permitted to quote the deciphered German signals which were passed to Jellicoe so belatedly and in such a misleading form, so his account seems to absolve the Admiralty of their share of blame for not keeping Jellicoe properly informed. But his version is much more favourable to Jellicoe – so much so that one admiral reproved it for having been written from the viewpoint of the C-in-C.

Beatty, Chatfield and the 'battle cruiser' faction attacked Corbett's account. Colonel E. Y. Daniel, secretary of the Historical Section of the Committee of Imperial Defence, a long-standing friend of Corbett's, resisted all the pressures put upon him to change his dead colleague's work, and the book was published in 1923 – but with yet another disclaimer from the Board that some of the principles set out in the book were ' . . . directly in conflict with their views'.

Jellicoe himself wrote no articles or letters to the newspapers about Jutland, nor did he give any interviews, nor allow anybody else to write in his name. But he did think about a second edition of *The Grand Fleet*, with an added appendix on Jutland. He sent a revised copy to Alexander Hurd of the *Daily Telegraph*, dealing with some of the criticisms of Evan-Thomas, and comments about Beatty's famous signal: 'Submit van of battleships follow battle cruisers. We can then cut off whole of enemy's battle fleet', showing that the popular view – of Beatty urging strongly, but vainly, for Jellicoe to follow him and thus annihilate the enemy – simply was not possible or feasible. The publishers, Cassell, decided that interest in war books was waning and therefore did not bring out a revised edition.

During the Empire Cruise of 1923 and 1924 the Special Service Squadron visited New Zealand and the battle cruisers *Hood*, (flying the flag of Vice-Admiral Sir Frederick Field), and *Repulse* and the cruiser *Adelaide* arrived at Wellington on 24 April 1924. The next day was Anzac Day: Field took part in a memorial service at the Cenotaph and Jellicoe, who had come specially from Auckland for the occasion, read a message from the King which had been received that morning. The battle cruisers and *Adelaide* sailed on 7 May and Jellicoe was on board for the passage to Auckland. This was one of the last occasions on which Jellicoe's flag as Admiral of the Fleet was flown at sea.

Jellicoe was asked to stay an extra year as governor-general but he and Gwendoline felt that their children should have a European education. So the Jellicoes left Wellington in the RMS *Tahiti* on 26 November 1924, escorted the first part of the way by the New Zealand Squadron, the two ships *Dunedin* and *Veronica*, who steamed ahead of *Tahiti* for a time, while they fired a salute of nineteen guns. Then both turned 180 degrees to port, cheered ship as they passed *Tahiti*, and returned to harbour.

Among all the letters and messages of farewell Jellicoe had one from the Maoris:

Your Excellency, Great is our sorrow that to-morrow you will turn your face from us and from this land. Depart, oh Governor! since it has been decreed that you must leave our land and return to your own far land, from which you came to wear awhile the mantle of our Lord, the King. Depart in honour, having borne that sign of Majesty as befitted a great Chief and a warrior of fame. Farewell. Go then in peace, you who were bred to the mightiest adventures of the great ocean of Kiwa, bearing with you the enduring regard and loving respect of this young Nation. With our *pakeha* brethren we have shared in the honour and good fortune that placed you over our land during the troublous years since the Great War. Farewell. Return then with your wife and your children to your own land, to your own people, there to enjoy yet many years of well-being and happiness. . . .

It was certainly one of the most gracefully worded farewells any public servant ever received. Jellicoe ended his own reply: '*E Noho Ra I to koutou whenua tupuwhenua atahua*! Yours sincerely, Jellicoe.' This was clearly the correct response.

By the time Jellicoe arrived back in England the great Jutland controversy had more or less polarized into two factions. Jellicoe certainly had his own enthusiastic and vociferous (though not encouraged by him) supporters, including Admiral Bacon, his eventual biographer, who published *The Jutland Scandal* in 1925. It was, in its way, as critical of Beatty as the Dewars had been of Jellicoe, and even Jellicoe thought it a bit strong. The Jellicoes had changed ships at Port Said, and embarked on the P & O steamship *China*. '. . . distinctly dirty and of course very old', as Jellicoe called her. On passage home in March 1925 in *China*, Jellicoe wrote to de Chair wondering '. . . if Bacon's book has yet fetched to Australia. It is very clear, but I am sorry that he rubbed it into Beatty so hard. Curiously enough his criticisms follow very closely those that I shewed to you. Of course the criticism is obvious but I think he has overdone it and it is a pity to have done so.'

On 9 December 1924, when Jellicoe was on his way home, the Admiralty sent him official notification of his retirement. After recalling formally Jellicoe's services before and during the war in his various appointments, My Lords concluded that they were '. . . confident that the whole of the Naval Service will join with them in regretting that the time has come for your name to be removed from the list of Flag Officers of HM Fleet'. It was a curious letter and quite inaccurate. As an Admiral of the Fleet, Jellicoe did not retire and of course his name was not removed from the list of Flag Officers of HM Fleet but remained in the Navy List until his death.

Jellicoe was created Earl Jellicoe of Scapa in June 1925, a distinction which to some extent molified Gwendoline. The family story is that earlier, on the Empire Mission, when Gwendoline heard that Beatty was created Earl and granted £100,000, while her husband was made Viscount and granted only £50,000, she had had to be dissuaded from abandoning the Empire trip and going home to complain personally to the King.

Once home, the Jellicoes went to live at St Lawrence Hall, Charles Cayzer's old home near Ventnor, Isle of Wight. There they lived comfortably but very modestly, in every sense of the word, considering that Jellicoe was an Earl and had a towering worldwide reputation as a naval commander, while Gwendoline herself was a very rich woman. With Jellicoe's own fame, and all those daughters, the house was always full of visitors and people coming to stay. Jellicoe made a merry father, always ready to play games with his children and to entertain, and be entertained by them. On very many evenings at home he would play Racing Demon or some other game with the children after dinner, and then, when they were all enjoying themselves, he would disappear into his study to work. He had an enormous correspondence from all over the world and he answered every letter himself in his own handwriting.

Much of Jellicoe's correspondence was for the British Legion, which became one of his special interests. He attended the Legion's Annual Conference in the Queen's Hall at Whitsun 1925, soon after his return home, and made an impromptu speech to the delegates which charmed, captivated and moved everybody present. The thought occurred to everybody that he was a natural man for the Legion. He became first a national vice-president and then in 1928, after the sudden death of the founder and first president, Field-Marshal Earl Haig, Jellicoe became president. He himself felt that the office should be filled by a soldier, but as the King and the Prince of Wales both urged him to take the job, and as everybody had voted unanimously for him, he accepted.

As British Legion president Jellicoe was nothing less than brilliant. He was exactly the man for the post. He refused to employ a secretary at home, so as to save the Legion the expense; similarly when he went up to London, which he did frequently, he always travelled on a third-class ticket. However, all the station masters always insisted on showing Jellicoe into a first-class compartment whatever sort of ticket he had, so it was discreetly arranged with the railway companies that he should travel first on a third-class ticket. Jellicoe's reputation and personal intervention brought employment or cash for many a desperate ex-serviceman or widow. He was quite capable of keeping a great dining-hall full of dignitaries waiting half an hour for their dinner while he listened to the full story of a man's predicament on the steps outside.

Retirement did not mean that Jellicoe gave up the urge to serve. He went to naval conferences in Paris and in Geneva. He was nominated for the committee of the Organization for the Maintenance of Supply during the General Strike of 1926 and served as a special constable, guarding a gasworks. As a County Commissioner for the Boy Scouts he went to jamborees and campfires and rallies at the Albert Hall. As chairman of the National Rifle Association he went to Bisley and was a regular attender, beaming his congratulations when any naval shooting team did well. He captained cricket teams of distinguished admirals at Dartmouth and at Pangbourne. He went skating with Gwendoline at St Moritz, and above all he played golf every day he could.

He wrote forewords for people's books, a popular hazard of life for admirals: Paymaster Captain Ricci ('Bartimeus') wrote many of Jellicoe's forewords and used to say he was in the Grand Fleet, 'borne for foreword-writing duties'. As Jellicoe himself wrote:

I am far busier than I want to be and Lady Jellicoe says I ought to take on *paid* and not *unpaid* work, but you know well how things are forced on me. I am Scout Commissioner in London, Chairman of the National Rifle Association and the Church of England National Settlement Association, on the Council of the Colonial Institute, the

OMS (plenty of work there) all the Sailor Societies, British Legion, Life and Local Institutions.

Unfortunately, even in Jellicoe's latter days, the spectre of Jutland would not lie down. Just as the controversy appeared to have subsided – and papers such as the *Daily Telegraph* were urging that it should be allowed to subside, for the good of the Service – somebody would publish a contentious article or their provocative memoirs. In 1927 it was Winston Churchill, in the third volume of his *World Crisis*. Churchill had evidently used the Dewar brothers' Appreciation as his main source, judging by the similarity of some of the maps and diagrams. He also appeared to agree with many of their numerous conclusions. But what Jellicoe and others found particularly objectionable, and what later historians have found suspicious, was Churchill's seeming unawareness, or disregard, of the fact that the view from a bridge at sea differs greatly from the view from a writer's armchair. Churchill's *World Crisis* was comprehensively answered by a team of respondents, among whom Admiral Bacon represented the Navy, in a *Criticism*. In short, Churchill wrote as though Jellicoe had had all the information laid out in front of him, on the tactical floor, as though he had had in fact the magic mirror the Spaniards credited to Drake, in which he could look and see at once the positions of every ship.

In 1927 the Harper Record, over which so much blood and late-night candle wax had been spilled, finally appeared. It was one of the earlier versions, lacking many of the cuts and amendments which had caused so much grief, and it was greeted with a great roar of uninterest. Harper's own book, *The Truth About Jutland*, took Jellicoe's part and criticized Beatty, but again was not widely read or talked about. Much more excitement was roused by Lloyd George's *War Memoirs*, in which he seemed to claim that when he became prime minister he '. . . found the Navy without an Admiral and the Army without a General', and he had had to supply the place of both. The best riposte to Lloyd George was provided in a newspaper interview by Edward (now Lord) Carson, who showed that in many cases Lloyd George had taken a somewhat overheated view of his own part in affairs. For instance, almost every day, Carson said, Lloyd George '. . . would be demanding that I make a change at the Admiralty. "Sack the lot!" was his favourite expression. "Why don't you get fresh men with sea experience?" One day I said to him "I must be under a strange hallucination, Mr Prime Minister, for I thought that Admiral Jellicoe had just *come* from the sea!".'

Jellicoe ignored most criticism, though he did prepare his own reply to Churchill, whom he considered a worthwhile writer and historian. In his own published writings, however, Jellicoe avoided contentiousness and personalities. In *The Crisis of the Naval War*, his account of his time in office as First Sea Lord, for instance, published in 1920, he refers to his 'departure from the Admiralty' without any other amplifying comment or any criticism, expressed or implied.

But in that book, as in *The Submarine Peril*, published in 1934, Jellicoe showed that his views on convoy had not really changed. He described the immunity of the French coal convoys from submarine attacks as 'extraordinary'. He considered that the transfer of destroyers to convoy duties gave '. . . fewer opportunities for offensive action against submarines', not realizing that convoy escort would give by far the *very best* opportunity for offensive action against submarines. He acknowledged that '. . . convoy sailing was . . . the recognised method of trade protection in the old wars, and this was a strong argument in favour of its adoption in the late war'. It should, however, be clearly understood, he went on, '. . . that the conditions had entirely changed'. But the conditions had not entirely changed; they were the same as they had ever been and the reasons for introducing convoy were as valid in Jellicoe's day as they were 'in the old wars'.

Jellicoe's views on Jutland, however, and his handling of the situation, appeared more apposite, more miraculously correct (considering the information available to him, and the time he was allowed to make his decision) as the years went by. In February 1934 Jellicoe attended a presentation at the Naval Tactical School as a genuine seeker after knowledge. He sat in the front row, truly wishing to know where he had gone wrong and where, given all the information which had by then become available, he could have done better.

The presentation was a triumph for Jellicoe, a vindication at last of his tactics at the crucial moment of the battle. It had taken Madden and the staff hours to examine all the possibilities and to come to the conclusion that deployment to port was not only the best but virtually the *only* correct action – a decision which Jellicoe had made, in battle, in about twenty seconds.

Postscript

In the autumn of 1931 Jellicoe went to Canada to attend a Biennial Conference of the British Empire Service League. It meant missing his usual yearly holiday in Scotland, which he needed, and he knew the trip would be expensive, because he was determined that the Legion should not have to bear the cost. But he was Grand President and he realized that everybody wanted him to be there, so as usual, as a matter of duty, Jellicoe went. Gwendoline was seriously ill on the voyage across and had to have an immediate operation when she reached Canada. Jellicoe had an exhausting programme of official functions, speeches and visits. He carried it all off with his usual skill but he was not properly fit and fell sick when he returned to England and had to stay in bed for many months.

Even in bed Jellicoe was hard at work. His nurse, Miss Bennett, was struck by the size and variety of his correspondence. A large proportion, she said, were from ABS, and from sailors' mothers. 'He was sent recipes and cures innumerable, scriptural texts and much advice, but all had one thing in common a very real love and admiration and intense desire for his recovery, and who shall question the heartening effect of such?'

Although his deafness was worsening, Jellicoe loved to sit up in bed and listen to church services on the wireless, singing hymns along with the congregation. When his deafness was very bad he hung out of bed to listen better. He still adored sardines, which seemed to contrast oddly with hymns. When his eldest daughter Lucy took him up a plate of sardines, she heard him singing and went downstairs again, telling Miss Bennett that '. . . it seemed sacrilegious to offer Daddy sardines when he was singing hymns'. On a diet of hymns and sardines Jellicoe slowly recovered. He went to Madeira to recuperate and, although he had a relapse when he returned, by the end of 1932 he was almost his old self again.

The battle of Jutland was still rumbling on in print. Sir Henry Newbolt was just completing the final volume of the official history which gave, in Jellicoe's opinion, a most unfair version of the circumstances leading up to the introduction of convoy in 1917; Newbolt, Jellicoe thought, gave far too much credit to Lloyd George and not nearly enough to the Admiralty. Pressure had to be brought to bear upon an obviously unwilling Newbolt before he would change the text. It was to give his own version of the same events that Jellicoe published *The Submarine Peril* in 1934; the book's royalties went to the King George's Fund for Sailors.

Jellicoe attended a poppy-planting ceremony on 9 November 1935, where he very probably caught a slight chill. He took no notice and on Armistice Day, two days later, he went to the Foch Memorial in Victoria to place a wreath on behalf of British ex-servicemen, before going straight on to take his customary place at the head of the column for the ex-servicemen's march past the Cenotaph. Next day he was at Euston Station for the official naming ceremony of the London Midland and Scottish Railway locomotive *British Legion*. He was now definitely ill. One lung with the old China bullet in it was slightly affected. He went to bed and died peacefully, at home, on 20 November, in the evening.

John Jellicoe was buried in St Paul's Cathedral on 25 November 1935. It was a raw late autumn day in London, with the air damp and chilly with mist. As Admiral Bacon wrote, Jellicoe '. . . would have been the first to have appreciated, with twinkling eyes, the grim compliment paid him by the presence of his old enemy – the North Sea weather'.

The funeral was an affair of some pomp and ceremony, as a great sailor deserved. The gun carriage was drawn through the London streets by a team of bluejackets, and among the distinguished officers who acted as pall-bearers was Lord Beatty. He was himself a sick man but had got up from his sick bed against his doctor's wishes to pay his last respects to his old Commander-in-Chief. King George V was represented by the Prince of Wales; he and Prince Albert, Duke of York, also a naval officer, walked in the procession. The French were represented by Vice-Admiral Durand-Viel and the Germans by the Kaiser's grandson, Prince Frederick of Prussia. More than five hundred branches of the British Legion were there, their banners dipping as the coffin went by. The band of the Royal Marines played for Jellicoe in death as they had done for him on so many quarterdecks in life. In the cathedral, the congregation sang: 'I vow to thee my country' and 'Oh valiant hearts'. The buglers sounded the Last Post. Outside a vast crowd waited on Ludgate Hill, among them many old sailors and soldiers wearing their medals, and widows and pensioners, for whom Jellicoe had done so much.

There were tributes to Lord Jellicoe in Parliament and press. 'But it is the duty of each generation,' said Stanley Baldwin in the House, 'surely, to pay its tribute to those who, in their view and so far as they are able to judge, may deserve well of the State; and such a one . . . was

Lord Jellicoe.' The obituary in *The Times* of 21 November filled five page-length columns, and there were warm appreciations from old shipmates in *The Naval Review* and other Service periodicals. Letters poured into St Lawrence Hall from all over the world, from high and low, from the Kaiser and from able seamen; extracts from them, though strictly edited down to one or two sentences from each, still occupy two whole pages of Admiral Bacon's biography. The whole nation felt a sense of loss which was typically put by Miss Bennett who had nursed Jellicoe through his nearly fatal illness in 1931:

> It seems almost incredible that the alert quick figure will never be seen again, dashing off to play golf, or shoot with the dog sitting happily beside him in the car, sitting at his desk, writing replies to endless letters or rattling his deaf instruments in church.
>
> That the kindly face and quizzical eyes will be seen no more, nor heard no more the charming voice. Yet he has left such an example of single-hearted service to his King, Country and the Navy, and such a store of memories of personal kindness to so many whom he called his friends, such a wealth of love and gratitude, as is given to rare and choice personalities only to leave as a legacy to those who lived in close personal contact with him.

Bibliography and Sources

Lives

ALTHAM, Captain Edward, CB RN. *Jellicoe*, Blackie & Son Ltd, London and Glasgow, 1938.

APPLIN, Arthur. *Admiral Jellicoe*, C. Arthur Pearson, London, 1915.

BACON, Admiral Sir Reginald, KCB, KCVO, DSO. *The Life of John Rushworth, Earl Jellicoe, CGB OM GCVO Ll.D DCL*, Cassell, London, 1936.

BARNETT, Corelli. *The Swordbearers: Studies in Supreme Command in the First World War. Part II: Sailor with a Flawed Cutlass: Admiral Sir John Jellicoe*, Eyre and Spottiswoode, London, 1963.

CALLENDER, Geoffrey. 'John Rushworth Jellicoe', *Dictionary of National Biography 1931–1940*, ed. L.G. Wickham Legg, Oxford University Press, 1949 (reprinted 1975).

JAMESON, Rear-Admiral Sir William, KBE, CB. *The Fleet that Jack Built: Nine Men who Made a Modern Navy*, Hart Davis, London, 1962.

JELLICOE, Admiral of the Fleet Earl, of Scapa. Autobiography, British Museum Add. MSS.49038.

Obituary of Lord Jellicoe, *The Times*, 21 November 1935.

PATTERSON, A. Temple (ed.). *The Jellicoe Papers*, Volume I, 1893–1916, Volume II, 1916–1935, Navy Records Society, 1966 and 1968.

Jellicoe: A Biography, Macmillan, London, 1969.

'Admiral of the Fleet Earl Jellicoe', *The War Lords*, ed. General Sir Michael Carver, Weidenfeld and Nicolson, 1976.

Chapter 1

Britannia in the 1870s is described in *The Story of the 'Britannia'*, by Commander E.P. Statham RN, Cassell, 1904; *Britannia at Dartmouth*, by Captain S.W.C. Pack CBE RN, Alvin Redman, 1966; and in Admiral Ballard's 'Memoirs, Part I: Burney's and H.M.S. *Britannia*', MM Vol. 61 No. 4, November 1975. Life at Besika Bay and the passage of the Dardanelles are described in *Admiral of the Fleet Sir Geoffrey Phipps Hornby GCB*, by Mrs Fred Egerton, Blackwood, 1896. Ch. XIII; 'Recollections of the passage of the Dardanelles by a British Battle Squadron in the European Crisis of 1878', by Admiral George Ballard, NR Vol. 28, February 1940, also Admiral Ballard's 'Memoirs, Part II:

Midshipman', MM Vol. 62 No. 1, February 1976. Memories of HMS *Cruiser* in the Mediterranean are in *A Naval Scrap-Book 1877–1900*, by Admiral Sir Reginald Bacon KCB KCVO DSO, Hutchinson, 1901, Ch. VII. 'On Naval Education' by A Naval Nobody is from *Macmillan's Magazine*, Vol.37, November 1877–*April 1878*.

Chapter 2
The Operations in Egypt are described in *Report of the British Naval and Military Operations in Egypt 1882*, by Lieut-Commander Caspar F. Goodrich USN, Washington, 1885; *The Sea Is Strong*, by Admiral Sir Dudley de Chair KCB KCMG MVO, Harrap, 1961, Chs. 2–5; *Salt Junk Naval Reminiscences 1881–1906*, by Admiral B.M. Chambers CB, Constable, 1927, Ch. VIII; *The Memoirs of Admiral Lord Charles Beresford, Written by Himself*, Methuen, 1914, Vol. I, Chs. XVIII–XXI; *Life of Admiral of the Fleet Sir Arthur Knyvet Wilson, Bart, VC GCB OM GCVO*, by Admiral Sir Edward E. Bradford, KCB CVO, John Murray, 1923, Ch. IV; *The Royal Navy As I Saw It*, by Paymaster Captain G.H.A. Willis CB RN, John Murray, 1924, Chs. IX and X. The torpedo ram HMS *Polyphemus* is described by C.J. Greene in MM Vol. 39, No.3, August 1953. Whale Island in the 1880s is from *The Inner Life of the Navy*, by Lionel Yexley, Pitman, 1908, and *The House That Jack Built*, by Commander Robert Travers OBE RN, Gale and Polden, 1955. The life-saving incident in *Colossus* is from *Some Recollections*, by Admiral Sir Cyprian Bridge GCB, John Murray, 1918, p.305. The Golden Jubilee Review is described in MM Vol. 62, No. 1, February 1976, 'The Spithead Naval Review of 1887' by Jeffrey L. Lant, *The Times*, 22 July 1887, and *Daily Telegraph*, 18 August 1887.

Chapter 3
The loss of HMS *Victoria* is described in *Minutes of Proceedings at a Court Martial Held on Board Her Majesty's Ship 'Hibernia' at Malta On Monday the Seventeenth Day of July 1893: and, by Adjournment, Every Day Afterwards (Sunday Excepted) to the Twenty-Seventh Day of July 1893 to enquire into the loss of Her Majesty's Ship 'Victoria'*, HMSO, 1893; *Admirals in Collision*, by Richard Hough, Hamish Hamilton, 1959; *Enigmas, Another Book of Unexplained Facts*, by Lieut-Commander Rupert T. Gould RN, Geoffrey Bles, 2nd edition 1946, 'The *Victoria* Tragedy', pp. 106–36; 'The Loss of the *Victoria*', by Commander Hilary Mead RN, MM Vol. 47, No. 1, February 1961; *The Life of Admiral Sir George Tryon KCB*, by Admiral C.C. Penrose, Blackwood, 1897; Admiral de Chair, *op. cit.*, Ch.7; 'The Loss of HMS Victoria', by W.A. Eaton, *Eaton's Popular Songs for Recital*, Simpkin, Marshall, 1893. Eye-witness accounts are in Bradford, *op.cit.* Ch. VI; *Memories of a Bluejacket*, by Patrick Riley, Sampson Low, 1931;

Adventure in the Royal Navy: the Life and Letters of Admiral Sir Arthur Moore, by E. Marjorie Moore, Liverpool University Press, 1966; *The Story of a Naval Life,* by Admiral Sir Hugh Tweedie, Rich and Cowan, 1939. Chambers' comment about promotion in the Mediterranean is from *Salt Junk,* p.282. The anecdote of *Hawke's* burnished anchor davits is from 'Guns and Gunners of Olden Times' by A. Macdermott, MM. Vol. 44, No. 2, May 1958. Percy Scott in *Scylla* is from *Fifty Years in the Royal Navy,* by Admiral Sir Percy Scott Bart, KCB KCVO Hon LI.D. John Murray, 1919, Ch. V.

Chapters 4 and 5
Accounts of the Boxer Rising and Admiral Seymour's Expedition are in Admiral Seymour's Dispatches, *London Gazette,* 5 October, 1900, pp. 6093–6115; *Official Account of the Military Operations in China,* by Major E.W.M. Norie, War Office, 1903, Ch. IV; *The Siege at Peking,* by Peter Fleming, Hart Davis, 1959, Ch. 6; *My Naval Career and Travels,* by Admiral of the Fleet the Rt. Hon. Sir Edward Seymour, Smith Elder, 1911, Chs. XXVII–XXXIII; *Martyred Missionaries of the China Inland Mission,* ed. Marshall Broomhall, Morgan and Scott, 1901; *A Year in China,* by Clive Bigham CMG, MacMillan, 1901, Ch. XIII; *A Picture of Life 1872–1940,* by Viscount Mersey CMG, CBE, John Murray, 1941, Chs X–XII; *The Life and Letters of David, Earl Beatty,* by Rear-Admiral W.S. Chalmers CBE, DSC, Hodder & Stoughton, 1951, Ch. III; *The World's Navies in the Boxer Rebellion,* by Lieut. C.C. Dix RN, Digby Lang, 1905; *Roger Keyes,* by Cecil Aspinall-Oglander, Hogarth Press, 1951, Ch. 6; *HMS Glory,* by A.E. Butterworth RMLI, Log Series, Westminster Press, 1904; *HMS Goliath* by J.B. Brodie and Able Seaman A.F. Ray, Log Series, Westminster Press, 1904; *A China Flagship,* by Engineer Captain Edgar C. Smith OBE RN, *Engineering,* 20 October, 10 November and 24 November 1944; *The Handy Man in China (Barfleur's Contingent),* by Chief Petty Officer H. Harper, Hong Kong, 1902; *The Commission of HMS Terrible 1898–1902,* by C. Crowe, London 1903.

Chapter 6
Biographical details about Sir Charles and the Cayzer family are from *A Victorian Ship Owner,* by Augustus Muir and Mair Davies, published privately by Cayzer-Irvine and Company Ltd, 1978; Lionel Dawson's reminiscences of *Drake* are from *Flotillas: A Hard-Lying Story,* Rich and Cowan, 1933, and *Gone for a Sailor,* Rich and Cowan, 1936; *Donegal's* coaling, and a description of Combined Operations in September 1904, are from *Something About a Sailor,* by Rear-Admiral Sir Thomas J. Spence Lyne KCO CB DSO, Jarrold's, 1940; *Albemarle's* commission is from *A Rough Record,* by Admiral Sir

William Goodenough GCB MVO, Hutchinson, 1943; information about the flat from Mr F.G.P. Budgett, Property Controller, Harrod's Estate Offices.

Chapter 7
Sources for the chapter are the biographies given, with *Winston Churchill, Volume II Young Statesman 1901–1914*, by Randolph Churchill, Heinemann, Chs 14 and 15; *Fear God and Dread Nought, Correspondence of Admiral of the Fleet Lord Fisher of Kilverstone*, selected and edited by Arthur J. Marder, Cape, 1956, Volume II, Part One, II, 'A Navy Scare'; 'The Controller of the Navy,' *Engineering*, 23 December 1910; information about Thornton House from Colonel V.J. Senior MC, of Pinner; and golfing reminiscences from '*J.R.J.' Some Recollections. 1894–1934*, by Paymaster Rear-Admiral Sir H.W.E. Manisty, KCB CMG, NR Vol. 24, February 1936.

Chapter 8
The *Thunderer* v. *Orion* gunnery trials are in Percy Scott, *op. cit.* Ch. XV; *Aim Straight*, by Peter Padfield, Hodder and Stoughton, 1966, Ch.11, and *Guns At Sea*, by Peter Padfield, Hugh Evelyn, 1973, Ch. 33; *A Great Seaman, The Life of Admiral of the Fleet Sir Henry Oliver*, by Admiral Sir William James GCB, H.F. & G. Witherby, 1956, Ch. VI; Altham's account is in his life of Jellicoe, pp. 53–4. An account of the 'Admiral Poore' Incident is in de Chair, *op. cit.* pp. 151–2.

Chapters 9 and 10
A general description of Scapa Flow is in *The Story of Scapa Flow*, by Geoffrey Cousins, Muller, 1965; general reflections on fleet life at Scapa are in *A North Sea Diary 1914–1918*, by Commander Stephen King-Hall, Newnes (in HMS *Southampton*); *Random Naval Recollections 1905–1951*, by Admiral Sir Angus Cunninghame Graham KBE CB JP, Famedram, Dunbartonshire, 1979 (in HMS *Agincourt*) and in various stories in *A Tall Ship* and *The Long Trick*, by 'Bartimeus'. Jellicoe's attitude to press visits is touched on in *Indiscretions of a Naval Censor*, by Rear-Admiral Sir Douglas Brownrigg, Cassell, 1920.

Chapters 11, 12 and 13
Jutland sources: Alexander, Major A.C.B., *Jutland: A Plea for a General Staff*, Hugh Rees, 1923; Aston, Major-General Sir George, KCB, 'Jutland and Mons', *Cornhill Magazine*, June 1920; Bacon, Admiral Sir Reginald, KCB KCVO DSO, *The Jutland Scandal*, Hutchinson, 1925; Bellairs, Commander Carlyon, RN, *The Battle of Jutland: The Sowing and the Reaping*, Hodder and Stoughton, 1920; Bennett, Captain Geoffrey, DSC RN, *The Battle of Jutland*, Batsford, 1964; 'The

Battle of Jutland', *History Today*, Vol.10, 1960; 'The Harper Papers: Fresh Light on the Jutland Controversy', *Quarterly Review*, Vol. 303, No. 643, January 1965; Bingham, Cdr The Hon. Barry, VC RN, *Falklands, Jutland and the Bight*, John Murray, 1919; Buchan, John, *The Battle of Jutland*, Nelson, 1916; Chack, Captain de Fregate, 'The German Submarines during the Battle of Jutland', *The Naval Review*, Vol. XIII, No. 4, November 1925; Copplestone, Bennet, 'Jutland: After the Battle', *Cornhill Magazine*, May 1917, January and February 1918; Corbett, Sir Julian S., 'Naval Operations', *History of the Great War*, Vol. III, Longmans Green, 1923 (and revised edition 1940); Dewar, Vice-Admiral, KGB CBE, 'Battle of Jutland', *The Naval Review*, Vol. XLVII, No.4, October 1959, Vol. XLVIII, Nos 1 and 2, January and April 1960; Dreyer, Admiral Sir Frederic, GBE KCB, *The Sea Heritage*, Museum Press, 1955; Fawcett, Lieut-Commander H.W., and Hooper, Lieutenant G.W.W. (eds), *The Fighting at Jutland*, Macmillan, 1921; 'Fleet Surgeon at Jutland', *Cornhill Magazine*, April 1917; Frost, Commander Holloway H., *The Battle of Jutland*, Stevens and Brown, 1936; Frotheringham, Captain Thomas G., USN, *A True Account of the Battle of Jutland*, Bacon and Brown, Cambridge, Massachusetts, 1922; Gibson, Langhorne, and Harper, Rear Admiral J.E.T., CB MVO, *The Riddle of Jutland*, Cassell, 1934; Harper, Rear-Admiral J.E.T., CB MVO, *The Truth about Jutland*, John Murray, 1927; 'The lessons of Jutland', *Journal of RUSI*, Vol. LXXII, No.486, May 1927; Hase, Commander Georg von, *Kiel and Jutland*, Skeffington, 1934; HMSO, Cmd 1068 (1920), *Battle of Jutland 30th May to 1st June 1916, Official Despatches with Appendices, Narrative of the Battle of Jutland*, 1924, Cmd 2870 (1927), *Reproduction of the Record of the Battle of Jutland*, by Captain J.E.T. Harper and others; Hurd, Sir Archibald, 'The Admiralty, The Fleet and the Battle of Jutland', *Fortnightly Review*, June 1917; 'The truth about the Battle of Jutland', *Fortnightly Review*, April 1919; Irving, Commander John, RN, *The Smoke Screen of Jutland*, Kimber, 1966; 'Jutland, Ten Years After', *Cornhill Magazine*, June 1926; Legg, Stuart, *Jutland*, Hart Davies, 1966; Leslie, Shane, *Jutland: A Fragment of Epic*, Ernest Benn, 1930; MacIntyre, Captain Donald, DSO DSC RN, *Jutland*, Evans Bros, 1957; McLachlan, Donald, 'Intelligence: Britain's Lost Opportunity', *Purnell's History of World War I*, p.1414; Marder, Arthur J., *From the Dreadnought to Scapa Flow, Volume III Jutland and After (May 1916–December 1916)*, Oxford University Press, 2nd edition revised and enlarged, 1978; Mountbatten, Admiral of the Fleet, Earl of Burma, 'The Battle of Jutland: An Appreciation given at the Annual Jutland Dinner in HMS *Warrior* on 25 May 1978,' MM, Vol. 66, No. 2, May 1980; Paschen, Commander SMS *Lützow* at Jutland, *Journal of RUSI*, Vol. LXXII, No. 485, February 1927, Pastfield, Rev. John L.,

New Light on Jutland, Heinemann, 1933; Pollen, A.H., The *Navy in Battle*, Chatto and Windus, 1919; 'Jutland and the Unforeseen', *19th Century*, August 1927; Pollen, Lieut-Commander John H., 'The Jutland Scandal', *English Review*, February 1925; *Purnell's History of the First World War*, Vol. 4, pp. 1377–1432, 'Jutland'; Roskill, Captain Stephen, DSC RN, 'Truth and Criticism in History – and Jutland', *The Naval Review*, Vol. XLV, No. 2, April 1957; Scheer, Admiral Reinhard, *Germany's High Seas Fleet in the World War*, Murray, 1920; Jutland: The German Point of View', *Fortnightly Review*, October 1927 (a reply to Scheer by Lieut-Commander Butt, November 1927); Schoultz, Rear Admiral von, 'The Tenth Anniversary of the Skagerrak', *The Naval Review*, Vol. XV, No. 2, May 1927; Sydenham, Lord, 'The Battle of Horn Reef', *Contemporary Review*, July 1916; 'Battle of Jutland', *English Review*, February 1924; 'Battle of Jutland: An Appeal', *English Review*, January 1928; Terry, C. Sanford, *Dispatches of Admiral Sir John Jellicoe and Vice-Admiral Sir David Beatty*, Oxford University Press, 1916; *The Times*, 29 October 1920, 'The Jutland Silence', by A Naval Officer.

Pamphlets in Naval Library, Ministry of Defence: *London Magazine*, Battle of Jutland Section, September 1916: 'How the *Warrior* fought her last fight', by Sergeant W.E. Shaw RMA; 'The Part the *Fortune* played in the Destroyers' Balaclava', by CPO H. Hammant; 'What *Invincible* Faced in the Battle of Jutland', by E. Dandridge, first range taker; A Pamplet on Jutland, by W.F. Clarke; Battle of Jutland: Memo by W.G. Glover in *Vanguard*; *Impressions of a Gunners Mate at Jutland*. Papers at Public Record Office: Grand Fleet Battle Orders, at time of Jutland, ADM 116/1343; Jutland, ADM 137/1906, 1945, 1946, 1988, 2089, 2134, 2137, 2139, 2141/2, 2151. Papers in National Maritime Museum: Chatfield MSS (papers of Admiral of the Fleet Lord Chatfield); Jerram MSS (papers of Admiral Sir Thomas Jerram); Peachey MSS (papers of Captain A.T.G.C. Peachey RN); Grand Fleet Diaries of Admiral Sir Charles Madden. Papers at Churchill College, Cambridge: Beamish MSS (papers of Rear-Admiral T.P.H. Beamish); Drax MSS (papers of Admiral Sir Reginald Plunkett-Ernle-Ernle Drax); Marsden MSS (papers on *Southampton* at Jutland). National Library of Scotland, Edinburgh: Dickson MSS (papers of Rear-Admiral Robert Dickson); Cunninghame Graham, Notes on Grand Fleet Life, 1914–1916. Imperial War Museum: Diaries of Commander A.H. Ashworth in *Warspite* at Jutland; Brough MSS (papers of Admiral Sir Harold Brough); Milford Haven Collection (on microfilm, restricted access); Pelly MSS (papers of Admiral Sir Henry Pelly). Liddell Hart Centre, Kings College, London: Kennedy MSS (papers of Admiral F.W. Kennedy, *Indomitable* at Jutland). Bodleian Library, Oxford; Commodore Walwyn's narrative of Jutland in *War-*

spite. Royal Marines Museum, Southsea: HMS *New Zealand* at Jutland; *Vanguard* at Jutland. William Salt Library, Stafford: Surgeon Dyott's account of Jutland. Cumbria Record Office, Carlisle: Adam Potts, a Spectator at Jutland. British Museum: Evan-Thomas MSS, Add MSS.52504–52506, correspondence and papers of Admiral Sir Hugh Evan-Thomas; Harper MSS, Add. MSS.54477–54480, correspondence and papers of Vice-Admiral John E.T. Harper; Add. MSS.53738, letters from Jellicoe and Evan-Thomas to Commander Frewen about Jutland.

Jellicoe Papers: *The Grand Fleet 1914–16: Its Creation, Development and Work*, by Admiral Viscount Jellicoe of Scapa, GCB OM GCVO, Cassell, 1919; British Museum Add. MSS.45356. Autograph draft of The Grand Fleet, with notes by Admiral Dreyer; Add. MSS.48989–49057 which include Grand Fleet Battle Orders; German account of Jutland, Jutland dispatches, Record, and Narrative; record of messages bearing on the operation; diagrams of movements of ships at Jutland; records, logs etc. of British and German ships during the battle; three chapters of Appendix for a second edition (never published) of *The Grand Fleet*; replies by Jellicoe to criticisms in printed works; Naval Staff Appreciation of Jutland; account of Jutland by Jellicoe in 1922 printed in *These Eventful Years* by F.H. Hooper; criticisms by Jellicoe of Official History of Great War.

Correspondence and papers of Jellicoe and others about Lord Kitchener and the loss of *Hampshire* are in Add. MSS.49031; an account of Lord Kitchener's death by CPO Telegraphist C.A. Kingswell, of *Iron Duke*, is in the Imperial War Museum; an eye-witness account by a survivor: *The Loss of HMS Hampshire and the Death of Lord Kitchener*, by Chief Shipwright W.C. Phillips, Anglo-Argentine Tramways Co., 1930.

Chapter 14
The introduction of convoy: *The Crisis of the Naval War*, by Admiral of the Fleet Viscount Jellicoe of Scapa, Cassell, 1920; *The Submarine Peril: The Admiralty Policy in 1917*, by Admiral of the Fleet the Rt Hon The Earl Jellicoe of Scapa, Cassell, 1934; 'The System of Convoys for Merchant Shipping', *The Naval Review*, Vol. V, 1917; 'The Introduction of the Convoy System', by Captain Bertram H. Smith CBE RN, *The Naval Review*, Vol. XXIII, May 1935; David Lloyd George, *War Memoirs*, Nicholson and Watson, 6 vols, Chs XL–XLII.

Chapter 15
Jellicoe's dismissal: British Museum Add. MSS.49039, correspondence; Balfour MSS, British Museum Add. MSS.49709, correspondence; 'The Dismissal of Admiral Jellicoe', by S.W. Roskill, *Journal of Contemporary History*, Vol.1, No.4 October 1966; *A Great Seaman*, by

Admiral Sir William James, 1956, pp.160–2; *The Life and Letters of Lord Wester Wemyss*, by Lady Wester Wemyss, Eyre and Spottiswoode, 1935, Ch. XII; *The Sea is Strong*, by Admiral de Chair, Ch. 24, Harrap, London, 1961.

Chapter 16
The Empire Mission: British Museum Add. MSS.49045, correspondence; *Naval Policy Between the Wars I: The Period of Anglo-American Antagonism 1919–1929*, by Captain S. W. Roskill, Cassell, 1968, Ch. VII; *The Cruise of HMS New Zealand*, Vol. I, Simmons, Ottawa, 1919; Lieutenant Vaughan Morgan, Diaries as Flag Lieutenant to Jellicoe, Imperial War Museum.

Postscript
Baldwin's Tribute to Jellicoe from *Service of Our Lives*, Hodder and Stoughton 1937 (speech in the House of Commons, 12 December 1935).

General
ASPINALL-OGLANDER, Cecil. *Roger Keyes*, The Hogarth Press, London, 1951.
BACON, Admiral Sir Reginald, KCB KCVO DSO. *The Dover Patrol 1915–1917*, 2 vols, Hutchinson, London, 1919.
The Life of Lord Fisher of Kilverstone, 2 vols, Hodder and Stoughton, London, 1929.
The World Crisis by Winston Churchill: A Criticism, Chapter V, Hutchinson, London, 1927.
A Naval Scrap-book 1877–1900, Hutchinson, London, 1925.
From 1900 Onward, Hutchinson, London, 1940.
'BARFLEUR' (Admiral Sir Reginald Custance). *Naval Policy: A Plea for the Study of War*, Blackwood, London and Edinburgh, 1907.
BAYLY, Admiral Sir Lewis, KCB KCMG CVO. *Pull Together!*, Harrap, London, 1939.
BEAVERBROOK, Lord. *Men and Power 1917–1918*, Hutchinson, London, 1956.
BENNETT, Captain Geoffrey, DSC RN. *'Charlie B': The Life of Admiral Lord Charles Beresford*, Peter Dawnay, London, 1968.
Beresford, The Memoirs of Admiral Lord Charles, Written By Himself, 2 vols, Methuen, London, 1914.
BLAKE, Robert (ed.). *The Private Papers of Douglas Haig, 1914–1919*, Eyre and Spottiswoode, London, 1952.
BRADFORD, Admiral Sir Edward E., KCB CVO. *Life of Admiral of the Fleet Sir Arthur Knyvet Wilson Bart., VC, CGB, OM, GCVO*, John Murray, London, 1923.
CHALMERS, Rear-Admiral William S., CBE DSC. *The Life and Letters*

of David, Earl Beatty, Hodder and Stoughton, London, 1951.

CHATFIELD, Admiral of the Fleet Lord, PC GCB OM. *The Navy and Defence*, Heinemann, London 1942.

CHURCHILL, Randolph. *Winston S. Churchill, 1874–1965, Vol. II Young Statesman 1901–1914*, Heinemann, London, 1974.

CHURCHILL, Winston S. *The World Crisis*, 4 vols, 1911–1914, 1915, 1916–1918 Parts I and II, *The Aftermath*, Thornton Butterworth, London, 1923–1929.

CLOWES, Sir William Laird. *The Royal Navy: A History*, Vol VII, Sampson Low and Marston, London, 1903.

CORBETT, Sir Julian. *History of the Great War, Naval Operations*, Vols I–III, Longmans Green, London, 1920–3.

CUSTANCE, Admiral Sir Reginald. *The Ship of the Line in Battle*, Blackwood, London, 1912.

DEWAR, Vice-Admiral, KGB CBE. *The Navy From Within*, Gollancz, London, 1939.

FAYLE, C. Ernest. *Seaborne Trade*, 3 vols, John Murray, London, 1922–4.

FISHER, Admiral of the Fleet Lord, of Kilverstone. *Memories*, Hodder and Stoughton, London, 1919.
Records, Hodder and Stoughton, London, 1919.

GEDDES, Lord. *The Forging of a Family*, Faber and Faber, London, 1952.

GIBSON, R.H., and PRENDERGAST, Maurice. *The German Submarine War, 1914–1918*, Constable, London, 1931.

GOODENOUGH, Admiral Sir William, GCB MVO. *A Rough Record*, Hutchinson, London, 1943.

GRETTON, Vice-Admiral Sir Peter, KCB DSO OBE DSC. *Former Naval Person: Winston Churchill and the Royal Navy*, Cassell, London, 1968.

HALPERN, Paul G., (ed.). *The Keyes Papers, Vol. I 1914–1918*, Navy Records Society, 1972.

HANKEY, Lord. *The Supreme Command*, 2 vols, Allen and Unwin, London, 1961.

HOUGH, Richard. *First Sea Lord: An Authorised Biography of Admiral Lord Fisher*, Allen and Unwin, London, 1969.

HURD, Sir Archibald. *History of the Great War, The Merchant Navy*, 3 vols, John Murray, London, 1921–9.

JAMES, Admiral Sir William, GCB. *The Sky Was Always Blue*, Methuen, London, 1951.
The Eyes of the Navy, Methuen, London, 1955.

KENNEDY, P.M. 'The Development of German naval operations plans against England, 1896–1914', *English Historical Review*, Vol. 89, January 1974, pp.48–76.

KENWORTHY, Lieut-Commander the Hon. J.M. *Sailors, Statesmen – And Others*, Rich and Cowan, London, 1933.

KEYES, Admiral of the Fleet Lord. *Naval Memoirs, 2 vols, 1910–1915, 1916–1918*, Thornton Butterworth, 1934–5.

LLOYD GEORGE, David, *War Memoirs*, 6 vols, Nicholson and Watson, London, 1933–6.

MACKAY, Ruddock F. *Fisher of Kilverstone*, Oxford University Press, 1973.

McKENNA, Stephen. *Reginald McKenna 1863–1943*, Eyre and Spottiswoode, London, 1948.

MARCH, Edgar J. *British Destroyers 1892–1953*, Seeley Service, London, 1966.

MARDER, Arthur J. *British Naval Policy, 1880–1905: The Anatomy of British Sea Power*, Putnam, London, 1941.
Portrait of an Admiral, The Life and Papers of Sir Herbert Richmond, Cape, London, 1952.
Fear God and Dread Nought: The Correspondence of Admiral of the Fleet Lord Fisher of Kilverstone, 3 vols, Cape, London, 1952–9.
From the Dreadnought to Scapa Flow: The Royal Navy in the Fisher Era 1904–1919, Oxford University Press, 1961–70.

NEWBOLT, Henry. *History of the Great War, Naval Operations*, vols IV and V, Longmans Green, London, 1928, 1931.

PADFIELD, Peter. *Aim Straight,* Hodder and Stoughton, London, 1966.
Guns at Sea, Hugh Evelyn, London, 1974.

PARKES, Oscar. *British Battleships*, Seeley Service, London, 1966.

RICHMOND, Admiral Sir Herbert W. *Statesmen and Sea Power*, Oxford University Press, 1946.

ROSKILL, Captain Stephen, DSC RN, *Naval Policy between the Wars,* Vol.1 Collins, London, 1968.
(ed.), *Papers relating to the Naval Air Service 1908–1918* Navy Records Society, 1969.

RUTTER, Owen. *Red Ensign: A History of Convoy,* Hale, London, 1942.

SCHEER, Admiral Reinhard. *Germany's High Seas Fleet in the World War*, Cassell, London, 1920.

SCOTT, Admiral Sir Percy, Bart, KCB KCVO. *Fifty Years in the Royal Navy*, John Murray, London, 1919.

SHARE, Paymaster Rear-Admiral Sir Hamnet, KBE CB. *Under the Great Bear and Southern Cross*, Jarrold's, London, 1932.

SIMS, Rear-Admiral William S. *The Victory at Sea*, John Murray, London, 1920.

WALDEYER-HARTZ, Captain Hugo von. *Admiral Von Hipper*, Rich and Cowan, London, 1933.

WATERS, Lieut-Commander David W. 'The Philosophy and Conduct of Maritime War', *Journal of Royal Naval Scientific Service*, May and July 1958 (restricted access).

WILSON, H.W. *The Great War*, Amalgamated Press, London, 13 vols, 1914–19.

YEXLEY, Lionel. *The Inner Life of the Navy,* Pitman, London, 1908.

YOUNG, Filson. *With the Battle Cruisers*, Cassell, London, 1921.

UNPUBLISHED PAPERS

British Museum. Personal and official correspondence of Lord Balfour, with Jackson and Jellicoe, Add. MSS.49714, and with Churchill, Add. MSS.49694; correspondence and papers of Admiral Sir Hugh Evan-Thomas, Add. MSS.52504-52506; correspondence of Vice-Admiral J.E.T. Harper, Add. MSS.54477-54480; correspondence, general papers and books of Earl Jellicoe, Add. MSS.48989-49057.

National Maritime Museum. Correspondence and papers of Vice-Admiral K.G.B. Dewar; of Admiral Sir Alexander Duff; of Admiral Sir Frederick Hamilton; of Admiral Sir Martyn Jerram; of Admiral of the Fleet Sir Henry Oliver; of Admiral Sir Herbert Richmond; and lectures on Jutland by Admiral Sir William Tennant.

Imperial War Museum. Correspondence of Admiral Sir Dudley de Chair.

Public Record Office. Correspondence as First Lord of Sir Eric Geddes, ADM 116/1804–10.

Naval Library, MOD. Lectures on Jutland by Admiral J.H. Godfrey.

Index

311

312

313

Goodenough, William, 105; on Jellicoe, 104, 107; long range test firings, 129; Heligoland Bight (1914), 149, 150; engagement with Hipper (Dec. 1914), 156–7; Dogger Bank action (Jan. 1915), 159; battle of Jutland, 177, 184–7, 196, 197, 200, 201, 206, 211

Gracie, Alexander, 101

Grafton, 59

Grand Fleet, battle of Jutland, 174, 175–218; estrangement from the Admiralty, 230; not to engage south of Dogger Bank, 231–2; centre of naval warfare moved from, 234; Jellicoe removes cruisers and destroyers from, 249

Granville, Charles, 68

Green, John F.E., 87

Grey, Sir Edward, 111

Gun Layers' Tests, 103–4

gunnery development, 54–5, 125–6

Guy, Basil, 85

Haig, Douglas, Earl, 7, 250, 254, 293

Haldane, Lord, 140

Hall, Robert, 9

Halliday, Lewis, 85

Halsey, Lionel, with Jellicoe on *Ramilles*, 53; battle of Jutland, 189, 222; on Jellicoe, 222; becomes Fourth Sea Lord, 235; becomes Third Sea Lord, 251; and Jellicoe's dismissal, 259, 262, 263

Hamburg, 205

Hamilton, Sir Frederick, 116, 137, 144, 249

Hampshire, 175, 187, 220–1, 222

Handy, 37, 60

Hankey, Sir Maurice, 242–3

Hannibal, 153

Hansa, 64

Harper, J.E.T., 281–3, 284–6, 294

Harvey, Major, 183

Hase, Georg von, 182, 183

Hawke, 54

Hawkins-Smith, Thomas, 44, 46–7

Hawksley, Commodore, 202–3, 205–6

Heath, Herbert, 49, 53, 175, 214, 257, 262–3

Hecla, 26

Henderson, Wilfred, 101

Henry, Prince of Prussia, 60, 115, 119, 121

Herbert, 189

Hercules, 113, 121, 124, 125, 129, 131, 200, 285

Hermes, 135

Hermione, 60

Hertha, 80

Hewett, Admiral, 38

Hewitt, Billy, 9

Hewitt, Jimmy, 9

Hext, Captain, 20, 21, 22

Hibernia, 51, 124

High Seas Fleet, Scarborough raid (Dec. 1914), 234; Dogger Bank action (Jan. 1915), 159–60; battle of Jutland, 173–4, 177–218; second attempted bombardment of Sunderland, 226–7; sortie on 1st Oct. 1916, 232; surrender, 268

Hillier, Sir Walter, 87

Hilmers, Lieutenant zur See, 74

Hiltebrandt, Admiral, 83

Hindustan, 9, 10, 124

Hipper, Franz von, 156, 159, 160, 172; battle of Jutland, 173, 174, 177, 178, 184, 187, 194, 202

Hogue, 151

Hohenzollern, 115

Holzendorff, Admiral von, 91

Home Fleet, 102; Jellicoe commands Second Division, 120, 121

Hood, H.L.A., 175, 186, 194

Hood, 290

Hoover, Herbert, 90

Hopkins, Mr, 59

Hopwood, Ronald, 116

Hornby, Sir Geoffrey Phipps, 17, 18, 19, 20–2, 30–1

Hunt, Geoffrey Ward, 12

Hurd, Alexander, 290

Hyacinth, 96

Imperial War Conference, 1918, 269

Impérieuse, 35

Implacable, 116

Indefatigable, 176, 178, 183, 213, 214, 216, 218, 282

India, Jellicoe's Empire Mission visit, 270–2

Indomitable, 106, 107, 159, 175, 211, 213

Inflexible, 29, 38, 44, 45, 154, 175, 213

Ingenohl, Friedrich von, 156, 159

Inglefield, Edward, 53

Invincible, 154, 175, 215, 218, 281

Invincible class, 112

Iphigenia, 59

Iron Duke, 143, 145, 146, 161, 167, 226, 228; last to leave Scapa Flow, 145; Dreyer commands, 147; coaling, 148; leaking condenser tubes, 154; staff of, 164; George V visits, 169, 224; battle of Jutland, 185–215, 225, 273; Kitchener boards, 220, 222; 13 Sept. 1916 Conference, 231; Jellicoe leaves, 235

Jackson, Sir Henry Bradwardine, 221, 226, 247; and design of Dreadnoughts, 101; becomes First Sea Lord, 169; and the battle of Jutland aftermath, 217, 219; disagreement with Jellicoe, 230–1; convoys, 233; Jellicoe replaces, 234, 235–6

Jackson, Thomas, 178

318